DIRECTED BY YASUJIRŌ OZU

The publisher and the University of California Press Foundation gratefully acknowledge the generous support of the Robert and Meryl Selig Endowment Fund in Film Studies, established in memory of Robert W. Selig.

DIRECTED BY YASUJIRŌ OZU

SHIGUÉHIKO HASUMI

Translated from the Japanese by Ryan Cook
Introduction by Aaron Gerow

UNIVERSITY OF CALIFORNIA PRESS

University of California Press
Oakland, California

Originally published in Japanese as *Kantoku Ozu Yasujirō*
First edition: © 1983 Shiguéhiko Hasumi / CTB Inc.
Expanded and complete edition: © 2003 Shiguéhiko Hasumi / CTB Inc.
All rights reserved.
English translation rights arranged through CTB Inc.
English Edition: © 2024 Shiguéhiko Hasumi / CTB Inc.

All stills are from copyrighted Shōchiku Co., Ltd., films unless otherwise noted in the caption, and are reproduced here under fair use.

Cataloging-in-Publication data is on file at the Library of Congress.

ISBN 978-0-520-39671-5 (cloth)
ISBN 978-0-520-39672-2 (pbk.)
ISBN 978-0-520-39673-9 (ebook)

33 32 31 30 29 28 27 26 25 24
10 9 8 7 6 5 4 3 2 1

Contents

List of Illustrations   vii

Translator's Introduction: *Directed by Shiguéhiko Hasumi*   ix
RYAN COOK

Critical Introduction: *Shiguéhiko Hasumi and Viewing Film Studies Anew*   xxi
AARON GEROW

Prologue: The Rules of the Game   1

1. Negating   10
2. Eating   32
3. Changing Clothes   52
4. Inhabiting   75
5. Looking   108
6. Holding Still   149
7. Radiating   181
8. Getting Angry   208

9. Laughing 233
10. Being Surprised 257
   Conclusion: Pleasure and Cruelty 278

   Appendix: *Interview with Yūharu Atsuta* 299
   Index 343
   About the Author 351
   About the Translator and Contributor 353

Illustrations

All stills are from copyrighted Shōchiku Co., Ltd., films and reproduced here under fair use, unless otherwise noted in the caption.

1. "Directed by Yasujirō Ozu"   xxxiv
2. Still from *The Only Son* (1936)   28
3. Still from *Late Autumn* (1960)   29
4. Still from *Early Summer* (1951)   49
5. Still from *That Night's Wife* (1930)   69
6. Still from *That Night's Wife*   69
7. Still from *Late Spring* (1949)   100
8. Still from *An Autumn Afternoon* (1962)   100
9. Still from *An Autumn Afternoon*   106
10. Still from *Late Autumn*   110
11. Still from *Early Summer*   112
12. Still from *There Was a Father* (1942)   139

13. Still from *Late Autumn*   139
14. Still from *The End of Summer* (1961)   142
15. Still from *An Autumn Afternoon*   143
16. Stills from *Early Summer*   147
17. Stills from *Tokyo Story* (1953)   155
18. Still from *Late Autumn*   162
19. Still from *Floating Weeds* (1959)   170
20. Still from *Early Summer*   172
21. Still from *Late Autumn*   179
22. Still from *Tokyo Story*   187
23. Still from *An Autumn Afternoon*   214
24. Still from *Late Autumn*   239
25. Still from *Early Summer*   259
26. Stills from *Late Spring*   290
27. "The End"   297

RYAN COOK

TRANSLATOR'S INTRODUCTION
Directed by Shiguéhiko Hasumi

HOW BETTER TO BEGIN INTRODUCING this translation of Shiguéhiko Hasumi's *Directed by Yasujirō Ozu* than with the title itself? The Japanese title *Kantoku Ozu Yasujirō*, which translates word for word as *Director Yasujirō Ozu*, is deceptively simple. The word *kantoku* names the professional role of Ozu the film director who, we are told, might under other circumstances have become *Tōfuya Ozu Yasujirō*—Ozu the tofu maker. In the context of the Japanese studio system, *kantoku* is also an honorific title: to say "Director Ozu" is akin to saying "Mr. DeMille" or "Dr. Murnau." But *Kantoku Ozu Yasujirō* is also the language that appears in the iconic calligraphic title credits of the films themselves: "Directed by Yasujirō Ozu." And it is this sense that seems especially apt. This book is duly honorific toward Ozu and attentive to his performed humility (as a film director who could as well have been a tofu maker). But more significantly it is a book "directed by Yasujirō Ozu"—that is, a work of ekphrastic criticism.¹ It aspires, in other words, to adapt Ozu's cinematic oeuvre, or at least to relive the experience of it, in the medium of writing. Ryūsuke Hamaguchi, director of the Oscar-winning *Drive My Car* (2021), has said that the book is "virtually an Ozuesque film" in its own right and an "integral part of the Ozuesque experience." Hamaguchi even claimed that the work of translating Hasumi's book into English (among other languages) should be treated with greater urgency than the 4K remastering of the oeuvre.² I make no such claims for the importance of the present translation, but treating Hasumi's book as a part of the oeuvre—as somehow under Ozu's direction—can illuminate certain aspects of his project and also some of the issues it poses for translation.

But first, consider the matter of Hasumi's language. It could be said that Hasumi has invented a kind of "secret code," perhaps akin to the code (*fuchō*) he says the middle-aged men of Ozu's late-period films speak among themselves. The Hasumi lexicon consists of numerous terms that stand out in their novelty, incongruence, or strategic repetition, terms that are in many cases never quite defined. Sometimes these are ordinary words somehow accented or put out of place, and sometimes neologisms or concepts presumably borrowed from elsewhere—*presumably*, because Hasumi tends not to identify such borrowings directly. He also tends to use *kanji* (Chinese character) words instead of the *katakana* syllabary for loan words when translating terms of likely foreign origin, further occulting the source. This results in a game of terminological puzzles—above all for translation. The important term *kōtei*, for example, at times seems to call for a different translation than the first Japanese-English dictionary equivalent *affirmation*, except when one considers that the inspiration for Hasumi's use of this

---

1. Richard Suchenski places Hasumi at least partially in the ekphrastic tradition. See Suchenski, "On Hasumi," *LOLA* 7 (2016).

2. Hamaguchi, "Rencontre et ébranlement," trans. Patrick De Vos, *Ebisu: Études japonaises* 59 (2022). My translation from the French.

term probably lies with Gilles Deleuze (Hasumi had already published several commentaries on Deleuze and an interview with the philosopher in the 1970s). Roland Barthes also undoubtedly lurks behind the repeated use of words like *fukusū* (pluralistic), or the hard-to-translate *hininshōteki* (perhaps "unsubjectivized") and *kōtōmukei* ("absurdity"). These are terms that, as Hasumi uses them, recall the "perte de l'allocutoire" and the "folie du langage," respectively, that Barthes observes in Flaubert.³ The one figure Hasumi does single out for attribution is Flaubert himself, whom Hasumi identifies as the source of his interest in *monkirigata*—cliché or "idées reçues"—as a theme in Ozu.

Hasumi also mingles both kanji word translations and katakana loan words for basic film terminology, sometimes creating playful slippages of meaning, as when the word *gamen* slides between its three senses (screen, shot, and image) alongside intermittent appearances of the loan words *sukurīn*, *shotto*, and *imēji*. This ambiguity is lost in translation. *Setsuwaronteki na jizoku* ("narrational flow") is a rather elaborate kanji neologism, never really defined except in relation to the companion concepts "narrational structure" and "thematic system." *Jizoku*, which translates literally as "duration," is perhaps a translation of the French *durée*, the meaning of which encompasses not only the length but also the quality and sensation of elapsed time. The word *setsuwaronteki* is a terminological invention in itself, a modifier at one remove from *narrative (setsuwateki)*, evidently intended to emphasize the process of narration. (The term *setsuwaronteki na jizoku* is interestingly absent from chapters 8 through 10, which were added twenty years after the first edition of the book.) Then there are the *firumu* (film) terms: *firumu-teki*

---

3. See Hasumi's 1972 interview with Barthes: Shiguéhiko Hasumi, "For the Liberation of a Pluralist Thinking: An Interview with Roland Barthes," trans. Chris Turner, *Cultural Politics* 11, no. 3 (November 2015): 301–14. For another interview in which Barthes discusses Flaubert, see Jean-Jacques Brochier, "Vingt mots-clés pour Roland Barthes," *Magazine littéraire*, no. 108 (February 1975): 28–37.

kansei, firumu-taiken, firumu-hyōsō (cinematic sensitivity, cinematic experience, cinematic surface), which have the aura of theoretical concepts but are not systematically defined. Elsewhere, in more explicitly theoretical texts, Hasumi does offer definitions for some of his recurring terminology, but in the Ozu book, as in much of his film criticism, this language is evocative—a secret code that establishes itself in motivic development through repetition and counterpoint.

There is also the matter of Hasumi's use of Japanese *kagikakko*—punctuation that can function similarly to scare quotes in English—and particularly of his tendency to treat the word "*sakuhin*" this way. *Sakuhin* means "œuvre" or "work" (as in a work of art). In the Ozu context, I translate it as *film*. On several occasions, Hasumi provocatively makes the parallel suggestion that the "films" of Ozu were not really films at all. But in any case, it is probably best to read the scare quotes as signals indicating that "texts" are not to be understood as closed, discrete things.

Hasumi is a Flaubert scholar, and his study of Flaubert—a consummate literary stylist—probably influenced his own experiments with prose style. This style is a hallmark of Hasumi's film criticism, with its vivid, existential language ("groping," "probing," "agitation"—the "living" of film experience), and its long, complex sentences. The long sentence in Hasumi is more a hyperbole of than a deviation from some common features of Japanese prose, like long prenomial modifying clauses, that pose challenges for Japanese-English translation across genres. Masahiko Abe calls his prose deliberately "improvisatory," arguing that his famously "endless" multiclausal sentence (continuing for pages in extreme instances) functions to perform immediacy. The unfolding discourse is sustained through repetition, scare quotes and accents, and especially commas, punctuation that creates a rhythm of "flow and interruption" and an atmosphere of presence and liveness that Abe sees as "anti-melancholic" for the way it continuously pursues new encounters and disrupts fixation and attachment. This immediacy is constructed, of course, and Hasumi walks a fine line between the reality of its effect and the myth of its naturalness.[4]

Hasumi's "longwindedness," to use another of his own terms (*jōzetsu*), clearly negotiates a relationship both to films as aesthetic experience and at the same time also to *writing* itself. The task of writing, for the critic, is to write one's way out of fixity, to preempt sedimentation in pursuit of continuous renewal, to write breathlessly toward aesthetic experience in the immediacy of the unfolding present. *Jōzetsu* (translated here as both "longwinded" and "effusive") is also how Hasumi describes the Ozu he seeks to reveal, in contrast to the "reticence" of the monotone Ozu everyone thinks they know, indicating that Hasumi sees a parallel between what he aims to do in writing and what Ozu has done in cinema. In fact, though Hasumi's career has consisted of basically two parallel paths, of public intellectual work as a film critic and professional academic work as a literary scholar, the distinction between cinema and writing (literature) has been superficial at best, since the two are fundamentally linked by a common concern with representation as a philosophical matter.

Still, in considering matters of translation, it is perhaps worth placing the cinematic Hasumi and the literary Hasumi in direct conversation. To this end, I will briefly introduce a 1977 book by Hasumi that explores many of the same themes as the Ozu text but through specific concerns with language and literature, a book entitled *Han-Nihongoron*, or *Anti-Nihongoron* (untranslated). The *Nihongoron* against which Hasumi announces a polemic is a discourse related to the well-worn *Nihonjinron* theories of the exceptionality of Japanese culture but concerning the Japanese language specifically. In Hasumi's survey of the field, *Nihongoron* is preoccupied with a narrative of decline, with the idea that contemporary Japanese has become corroded and polluted relative to an ideal, pure language that supposedly existed at some

---

4. Masahiko Abe, *Sokkyō bungaku no tsukurikata* (Tokyo: Shōhakusha, 2004), 180–87.

point in the past. Hasumi's critique of this position stages a tension between the abstraction of a system ("pure" Japanese, but also structural grammar) and the vividness of language as the living play of signs in the present—a tension corresponding to the one he describes between the Ozuesque "film" as an abstraction and the vivid reality of the films themselves. Like most of the late-period Ozu films, the book *Anti-Nihongoron* is also a "home drama" in its own right, a series of amusing vignettes portraying Hasumi's bilingual household life with his Belgian wife Chantal and their young son Shigeomi, whose early childhood development into a native speaker of both French and Japanese is a central thread. These vignettes are interwoven with readings of literary texts, and the whole is informed by Hasumi's engagement with Michel Foucault's *The Order of Things* (1966) and Jacques Derrida's *Of Grammatology* (1967)—that is, with what were then relatively contemporary attempts to bring Western thought into a reckoning with its own self-representation in (phonetic) writing. Charming domestic dramas of everyday life conducted in both Japanese and French sketch something like a counter-*Nihongoron,* one in which Japanese forms a productive tension with the French language of Foucault and Derrida.

There are many illustrative episodes in *Anti-Nihongoron,* but one domestic scene in particular bears consideration here. Hasumi recounts the experience of being startled one evening at the dinner table to hear his young son address him with the second-person pronoun *anata* (you): "Anata, mada, gohan taberu?" (Are *you* still eating?). Why was this so startling? The sentence is not grammatically incorrect. But Japanese does not require the pronoun, and it would be more natural to omit it. *Anata* is also not usually what a child calls a parent. Historically, *anata* was a distal pronoun ("over there") that, like other Japanese "personal pronouns" (Hasumi questions whether they can be said to exist), came to be used as a way of indicating an addressee through respectful indirection, by referring not to the person, but to their position relative to the speaker. Today, the word retains a nuance of polite formality, and also of adult intimacy when used by a woman to address a man. But hearing a word of such nuances from the mouth of a child is not what startles Hasumi. What startles him is the way the influence of French reveals itself in the Japanese spoken by his young son, who is still groping his way toward natural command of the family's two languages, and by the way this incongruous pronoun suddenly exposes something dramatic—*systemic*—about language as it orders experience. The pronoun, requisite in French (as *tu*), establishes a startling distance between child and father when it barges unexpectedly into the signifying environment of pronoun-optional Japanese. For Hasumi, this illuminates all at once the theme of what he calls *haijo to senbetsu*, or selection and exclusion. The shock of a pronoun exposes the French language as a "system of exclusion," where pronoun selection turns the pleasant relational atmosphere of the dinner table into a savage landscape of division and difference. Hasumi also complains of his wife and son making him feel excluded by transferring the third-person pronoun *il/lui* from French when the two talk about him in Japanese, referring to him as *kare,* or *"him,"* instead of with something more intimate and relational like *papa*. He reflects on the fact that in French the conjugations and agreements demanded by the grammar even cause pronoun selection to systematically reorder the entire series. His point may be especially relatable to French and English speakers today in light of the contemporary gender politics surrounding our compulsory pronouns and the violence we now understand pronoun selection to be capable of in everyday conversation.

What does this episode have to do with Ozu? For one thing, it relates to what Hasumi says is the widespread tendency to define Ozu as a paragon of minimalism and restraint, a tendency in which the same theme of "selection and exclusion" is at play. In selecting a "pure" Ozu—the Ozu of the low camera position, the static shot, the monotone home drama—commentators have excluded the other impure Ozus that suddenly confront us when we really look at the films. The *anata* spoken by Hasumi's son throws into relief a systemic pattern of selection and exclusion in French and leads Hasumi to reflect on the nature of Japanese itself as a climate characterized by interrelationality before differences of attribute, a climate of comparative *coexistence*. Likewise, the prevailing critical discourse that sees Ozu as having selected certain cinematic means to the exclusion of others leads Hasumi to insist on another theme in Ozu: *kyōzon to heichi,* or coexistence and juxtaposition. This theme goes to the core of the project, which is to see past the Ozu who selected certain details to the exclusion of others and to affirm an Ozu of *abundance,* who preserved all manner of things in a state of coexistence, arrayed on the surface, side by side, and in broad daylight, or around the dinner table.

A further resonance between the *anata* episode and the Ozu book is the word *hininshōteki. Hininshōteki,* which means roughly "lacking grammatical person," names the quality of Japanese that, as Hasumi says, permits the sentence subject to remain unarticulated or peaceably implied. Elsewhere, Hasumi uses this word as a linguistic metaphor related to focalization in literature or point of view in cinema, and I therefore translate it as "unsubjectivized." Similar to Japanese, cinema itself is an "unsubjectivized environment," having no grammar of personal pronouns or agreements. In their closeness to cinema itself, Ozu's films are especially attuned to this climate. "Knowing smiles" and "cheerful exchanges" among the films' disparate details—cinematic civilities that Hasumi invokes throughout the text—signal the solidarity and accord that emerge here, where the particular opposition of *me* and *you* is not systematized, and where "fusion," not isolation, becomes the default. This specific resonance is especially worth considering in relation to Hasumi's writing style, and has implications for translation in turn: the theoretical importance he places on the unarticulated or implied subject in *Anti-Nihongoron* also connects with the strange status of the subject in his prose.

Chris Fujiwara has argued that Hasumi's prose in the Ozu book generally neglects to speculate on, much less make a subject of, any actually existing audience, and is therefore strangely impersonal.⁵ In many instances, subject ambiguity relates to the already mentioned naturalness with which Japanese routinely omits explicit subject articulation, and it is nothing remarkable. But where Hasumi does specify a subject, it tends to be impersonal: "everyone" or "anyone," "people" or "the viewer," "the eye" or "the look." Fujiwara furthermore notes that Hasumi's oddly impersonal subject is at the same time also extraordinarily sensitive, prone to finding things "moving" or "stirring" or "agitating." Just who is the subject of this book, he asks. Responding to Fujiwara, Chika Kinoshita writes of the "degree zero of the spectator" in Hasumi, going so far as to claim that he was perhaps unique among film critics at the end of the seventies in formulating a spectatorial subject at once so impersonal and "carnal."⁶

In other instances, Hasumi deliberately invokes a first-person plural subject: *wareware,* or "we." Does he do so to collectivize his aesthetic judgments? To conscript us as accomplices? Or is this a royal we? Perhaps we should take instruction from Hasumi's own careful parsing in *Anti-Nihongoron* of the mysterious first-person plural pronoun *"nous"* as it appears in the famous first phrase of Flaubert's *Madame Bovary:* "Nous étions à l'étude." Hasumi says this hard-to-attribute plural subject, which is incongruous relative to what follows in the novel (who is *nous?*), functions to signal a separation of narrating from the content of narration, a cleavage of *discours* from *histoire* that announces Flaubert as a "modern" writer.⁷ The "we" of Hasumi's prose is probably best regarded in a similar light, as manifesting the subject itself as a topic and narration as a performance. I have made a general policy of apply-

---

5. See Chris Fujiwara, "The Critical Event of *Director Ozu Yasujiro*," *LOLA* 7 (November 2016), http://www.lolajournal.com/7/hasumi_fujiwara.html.

6. Chika Kinoshita, "Femmes et enfants en lutte. Sur la spectatorialité dans les critiques de cinéma de Hasumi Shiguéhiko," trans. Amira Zegrour, *Ebisu: Études japonaises* 59 (2022), https://doi.org/10.4000/ebisu.7279.

7. Shiguéhiko Hasumi, *Han-Nihongoron* (Tokyo: Chikuma Shobō, 1977), 120–23.

ing "we" in this translation even where the subject is at best implied in the original but disambiguation is necessary. The argument could be made that other grammatical cues indicate a first-person singular voice in places, but Hasumi almost never uses the corresponding personal pronoun, and so I have done the "violence" of generally assigning the "we" throughout.

"Violence" is a word related to language that Hasumi himself uses in describing the annihilation of coexistence through selection and exclusion, but it also resonates with Lawrence Venuti's influential characterization of the relationship between English-language translations and their foreign source texts, wherein Venuti complains of the effects of the Anglophone cultural prejudice for "fluency" and "transparency." A good translation is supposed to "annihilate" itself as a second-order representation, to become "transparent" with the aim of sustaining the illusion of unmediated authorial presence. The violence of this kind of translation does not end with the exclusion of the translator but extends to the domestication of the foreign text itself as it is reconstituted in accordance with English-language values. Venuti calls for translations to acknowledge this violence and looks to historical theories of translation to demonstrate how translators might pursue strategies beyond "equivalence," manifest the cultural other through foreignization, or "stage an alien reading experience."[8] This is practical guidance, and I have been mindful of Venuti's polemic in resisting the culturally programmed instinct to prioritize what reads most "naturally." This translation performs the inevitable violence of disambiguation and syntactic domestication common to Japanese-English translations of all kinds but does not pursue transparency at all costs, and it places emphasis on voicing the motifs and patterns that make Hasumi's writing distinct. It will be a measure of a kind of success if the reading experience feels a little alien.

8. See especially chapter 1, Lawrence Venuti, *The Translator's Invisibility: A History of Translation* (New York: Routledge, 1995).

Venuti's critique also returns us to what it means to say that this book is "directed by Yasujirō Ozu"—as if Hasumi had somehow adapted the oeuvre in words. Hasumi's criticism could be considered a kind of translation, giving voice to Ozu in a new language. His writing performs the ways that this process can only fall short, but departing from a critique of the violence of erasure, the discourse remains resolutely determined to coexist with Yasujirō Ozu. My own contribution is substantially less ambitious, but I hope that this translation similarly merits being called "directed by Shiguéhiko Hasumi."

BUSINESS ITEMS

Because English speakers know the names of many Japanese film personalities in English-style given name–surname order (Yasujirō Ozu, not Ozu Yasujirō as in Japanese), I have followed that convention. I generally observe the rules of Hepburn romanization, including the use of macrons to mark long vowel sounds. One exception is the spelling of Hasumi's first name, as the author prefers the French phonetic spelling: Shiguéhiko. Other English-language sources often use the standard Hepburn romanization (Hasumi Shigehiko).

The translation also preserves Hasumi's characteristic insistence on using only actor names in his discussions of plots—it is not the fictional character Noriko, but the actress Setsuko Hara who "gets married" in *Late Spring*, for example. This conflation of actor and character works to particular effect, such as by emphasizing, through repetition, the recurring presence of certain actors and the resonances they establish across the oeuvre.

Most of the book was written before home video, when the arrival of a film was still a high-stakes event—something to be experienced with heightened sensitivity and committed to memory before it disappeared from the theater. Hasumi claims to have written the book from memory, without reference to the film prints. Considering this, the level and accuracy of detail is impressive indeed. And yet the nature of the "kinetic visual acuity" (*dōtai shiryoku*) at the heart of his method—his near optometric standard for visual attentiveness to bodies in motion—determines that some details will inevitably become distorted. Misremembered details are not all that common here and mostly do little to diminish the argument, but in the interest of accurately presenting the films, this translation either corrects minor slippages or notes them where they occur. Footnotes in the original text are spare if not nonexistent; I have added the footnote commentary that appears in this edition unless otherwise indicated.

Finally, I would like to thank the Suntory Foundation for providing generous financial support for the translation through its Support for Overseas Publication program. Thanks to Aaron Gerow for his minute feedback on the translation, Markus Nornes for very useful input and discussion, and Boyi Wang for helping me puzzle through numerous tricky translation questions along the way. And my fondest appreciation to Michael Tan, without whom this work would have been quite simply impossible.

AARON GEROW

CRITICAL INTRODUCTION
Shiguéhiko Hasumi and Viewing Film Studies Anew

JAPANESE FILM HAS LONG OCCUPIED a central place in thinking and appreciating world cinema. The work of Yasujirō Ozu has garnered the most attention in the last few decades, with the 2012 Sight and Sound Poll placing his *Tokyo Story* (*Tokyo monogatari*, 1953) and *Late Spring* (*Banshun*, 1949) at numbers three and fifteen in the critics' poll, and the former as number one in the filmmakers' poll. There seems to be a never-ceasing flow of writing on Ozu, with several books and numerous articles appearing in English in the last decade. Yet largely absent from this effluence of discourse in English have been the voices emerging from Ozu's own locality, despite the fact that dozens of books have been published in Japanese. While recent years have seen academics from Japan actively publishing in English (as well as American or European scholars writing in Japanese)—a trend that should render national divisions in film studies problematic—the fact that there is yet a fundamental imbalance in flows of film scholarship reminds us that geopolitical divisions still reign. Among the scant English translations of Japanese writings on Ozu, Kijū (Yoshishige) Yoshida's *Ozu's Anti-Cinema* is a miraculous exception.[1] But the fact that Yoshida is a noted New Wave film director is significant, since it has been works of filmmakers that have tended to appear in English in book form.

This tendency reveals that voices from Japan have been listened to mostly to the degree they serve as local informants or provide autobiographical background to Japanese film. Historically, it has more or less been left to the Euro-American scholar to provide the supposedly real analysis and theoretical interrogation of the texts. For too long, the situation has resembled Edward Said's outline of the European Orientalist: "for whom such knowledge of Oriental society as he has is possible only for the European, with a European's self-awareness of society as a collection of rules and practices."[2] This has especially been the case in the more abstract realm of film theory, and not just in relation to Japan. The histories and major anthologies of film theory have long devoted the majority of their pages to European and North American male theorists, offering little space for other regions—or races, genders, or ethnicities. One can understand that Noël Burch's claim that "the very notion of theory is alien to Japan; it is considered a property of Europe and the West" is one strategy for him to construct Japanese culture as resistant to, and thus as a critique of, Western logocentrism and its cinematic equivalent, the classical Hollywood cinema.[3] However, it also replicates the standard, almost ethnographic hierarchy between the Western theorist and the Japanese local informant.

---

1. Kijū Yoshida, *Ozu's Anti-Cinema*, translated by Daisuke Miyao and Kyoko Hirano (Ann Arbor, MI: Center for Japanese Studies, 2003).

2. Edward Said, *Orientalism* (New York: Vintage Books, 1979), 197.

3. Noël Burch, *To the Distant Observer: Form and Meaning in the Japanese Cinema* (Berkeley: University of California Press, 1978): 13.

That is why I believe this publication of an English translation of Shiguéhiko Hasumi's *Directed by Yasujirō Ozu* is so important. Hasumi is not just a film critic/scholar, but also one of the leaders of the intellectual world in Japan since the 1980s. With a PhD from the Sorbonne, he was trained as a scholar of French literature and was central in the introduction of poststructuralist theory to Japan, from Roland Barthes to Michel Foucault. As a thinker, he was central to debates from the eighties on about textuality, signification, interpretation, and narration. As an academic, he eventually became president of the University of Tokyo, itself Japan's most prestigious university. His activities have extended even into literary creation, actually winning the Yukio Mishima Prize at age eighty for one of his novels. The point, however, is not to assert his pedigree, but to underline how profoundly influential Hasumi has been in Japan and, to a degree, outside of Japan as well. This influence is evident first in how he dominated discourse in Japan on cinema in the eighties and nineties, with his book on Ozu in particular both reviving interest in the director and defining how to approach him. As a teacher offering a popular class at Rikkyō University, he also directly taught a generation of filmmakers, from Kiyoshi Kurosawa and Masayuki Suo to Shinji Aoyama and Kunitoshi Manda, who have acknowledged their debt to him in their approach to cinema.[4]

Directed by Yasujirō Ozu is then not just an interpretation of Ozu's oeuvre, but an exploration of what makes cinema cinema. It is a work of film theory, but one that defines itself through its difference from dominant trends in both Ozu studies and film studies/theory. One Japanese film critic this book often quotes is Tadao Satō, who is both the critic most translated into English up until now and the author of a history of Japanese film theory that questions even the definition of

---

4. See, for instance, the roundtable discussion between Kurosawa, Aoyama, Manda, and Hiroya Yabe: "'Eiga Hyōgenron' kara 25-nen," *Shinetikku* 3 (1999): 246–78. One should note that Suo's first film, the pink film *The Abnormal Family* (*Hentai kazoku: Aniki no yomesan*, 1984), is an emulation of Ozu via Hasumi.

theory.⁵ As I have argued elsewhere, Japanese film theory is marked by a "theory complex," in which film theory is often pursued in a self-conscious fashion that interrogates theory itself.⁶ Hasumi is not the first to do this. One can see thinkers ranging from Yasunosuke Gonda to Jun Tosaka and from Midori Osaki to Michitarō Nagae proffering varied critiques of how film is studied and theory is done. Hasumi can be considered the epitome of this, given his own background in the high halls of academia.

Directed by Yasujirō Ozu in many ways defines itself through its difference from other studies, and thus from its context. Film criticism in Japan had long been divided into two camps often defined by politics: if impressionist critics such as Tadashi Iijima and Fuyuhiko Kitagawa used their own cultured sensibilities to elaborate on the effects of a film and its value as cinema—an atomistic and often apolitical approach—ideological critics like Akira Iwasaki and Kazuo Yamada, often aligned with left-wing movements, analyzed films for their political implications and hidden ideologies.⁷ Hasumi's film criticism operated as an intervention against this division. Hasumi himself came to prominence as a film critic in journals such as *Cinema 69*, which was one of three influential but short-lived magazines at the end of the sixties that staked out the then-current divisions in criticism. While *Kikan firumu* (Quarterly of Film), which was centered on Toshio Matsumoto, concentrated on experimental cinema, *Eiga hihyō* (Film Criticism), edited by Masao Matsuda, pursued a committed radical politics that

---

5. Tadao Satō, "Does Film Theory Exist in Japan?," trans. Joanne Bernardi, *Review of Japanese Culture and Society* 22 (2010): 14–23.

6. Aaron Gerow, "Introduction: The Theory Complex," *Review of Japanese Culture and Society* 22 (2010): 1–13.

7. For more on the history of Japanese film criticism, see Kenji Iwamoto, "Film Criticism and the Study of Cinema in Japan," *Iconics* 1 (1987): 129–46; Aaron Gerow, "Critical Reception: Historical Conceptions of Japanese Film Criticism," in *The Oxford Handbook of Japanese Cinema*, ed. Daisuke Miyao (Cambridge: Oxford University Press, 2014): 61–78.

Matsuda himself willingly called "partisan criticism" (goyō hyōron).[8] The *Cinema* journals, which also involved critics such as Sadao Yamane and Tetsurō Hatano, pursued a critique that became the core position of Hasumi and like-minded writers: that cinema must be discussed as cinema, bracketing out issues of politics, society, and economy, in order to understand how the film operates as a film. At the same time, Hasumi also had a role in the academicization of film studies in Japan, carrying on from earlier semioticians like Susumu Okada and Keiji Asanuma (who also studied in France), and helping found Japan's first academic society for the study of the moving image, the Japan Society of Image Arts and Science, although he eventually left it.

Hasumi initially came to fame in the broader intellectual sphere with his conception of "surface criticism" (*hyōsō hihyō*), which was a fundamental attack on many predominant forms of textual interpretation that seek to delve beyond the surface of the text to extract a meaning supposedly hidden underneath. He charged such forms of criticism with essentially ignoring what is visible, denying the text in front of the critic's eyes in order to discover something invisible. Such criticism, Hasumi argues, is less about the text than what is not the text—especially the ideologies on which criticism was founded. It was not uncommon to criticize Hasumi's "surface criticism" for divorcing politics from textual reading, but strictly it was a different politics, one that, stemming in part from a disillusionment with the sixties' radical politics and its claims of authority, critiqued universal abstractions and metanarratives that restricted the inherent creativity of criticism and film viewing.

Directed by Yasujirō Ozu is in many ways "surface criticism" of Ozu. It famously opens with a critique of previous approaches to Ozu, especially those offered by David Bordwell, Donald Richie, or Paul Schrader.

---

8. Masao Matsuda, "Hihyō no rikkyakuten wa nanika," in *Bara to mumeisha* (Tokyo: Haga Shoten, 1970), 188–96.

To Hasumi, not only the effort to locate what is Japanese or what is modern in Ozu, but also the very attempt to describe what is "Ozu-esque" (*Ozuteki*) involves a refusal to truly look at his films. While one may question why it is primarily non-Japanese scholars who bear the brunt of his approbation, Hasumi is not disparaging them for mistaking the Japaneseness of Ozu. We ourselves should not read this book to somehow access the "Japanese" view of Ozu, because Hasumi, rejecting such Orientalism, resolutely refuses such abstractions and avers that Ozu's films show nothing of the Japanese aesthetic values of shadow, nothingness, or the seasons, but rather, through a meteorological brightness likened to that of John Ford's Monument Valley, represent cinema itself (chap. 7).

Hasumi is particularly critical of accounts of Ozu as a minimalist, as a director who subtracted from the full array of cinematic devices—for example, ceasing to move his camera—thereby creating a rhetoric defined by terms of lack and negation: about what Ozu was *not* doing. To Hasumi this creates a false image of Ozu as a maker of films that are defined by stillness, monotone, restraint, or austerity, when to Hasumi they are often overflowing with abundance, motion, variation, even violence—shaped not by negativity but positivity. The rhetoric of negation also, to him, fundamentally misunderstands cinema. When he states that it is impossible to show two sets of eyes looking at each other in cinema, most readers would scratch their heads. Of course we see that in cinema repeatedly. But as Hasumi argues in chapter 6, most filmmakers use either camera movement or editing to make up for the fact that a single shot of two people looking at each other can never fully show where their eyes are looking. Most filmmakers, to Hasumi, attempt to avoid this fundamental limitation by inserting temporal sequencing—showing one looker and *then* another—a fiction that masks their own impotence. To Hasumi, Ozu is the rare filmmaker who, through his famous shot/reverse shot structures with "incorrect" eyelines, exposes the impossibility of the look and thereby takes cinema to its very limits. It is at this point where cinema almost ceases to be cinema that Ozu's films, to Hasumi, shake the audience with a profound and infinitely abundant cinematic experience, one that at times can be shocking—even cruel and violent.

Directed by Yasujirō Ozu includes many close discussions of Ozu's cinematic techniques, but it is not an account of Ozu's film style. As part of his critique of the Ozuesque, Hasumi rejects the notion of style itself, both for its formalism (reducing Ozu to set formal effects) and for its refusal to see that Ozu—as well as cinema itself—can never be reduced to generalized patterns or rules of filmmaking. Ozu is cinematic to the degree that there never could be an "Ozu style." His critique of such accounts of Ozu stems not just from his poststructuralist deconstruction of logocentric epistemology, but also from his understanding of cinema as uniquely resistant to such forms of film study. Due to its motion and temporality—its fundamental presentness—cinema to Hasumi always slips away at the moment one attempts to grasp it. To truly watch cinema is to confront the basic problems of language, time, and meaning. That somewhat terrifying prospect is, to him, one reason film criticism and film studies turns its head away and speaks of something else—Japan, modernism, or politics—rather than facing the film itself.

Hasumi's alternative to this might strike some as odd, if not old fashioned: elaborating the thematic system in Ozu's oeuvre. This poses a challenge to many used to Euro-American film studies of the last few decades, which has long moved beyond interpreting the "themes" of a movie. However, it is imperative when one reads a work from outside one's theoretical tradition, especially from outside the Euro-American sphere, which has been defined so long through an almost imperial dominance enforced by repeated declarations that what others do is not theory, to check one's assumptions at the door and use this as an opportunity to possibly deterritorialize theory.

Hasumi's thematics is actually a complex if not brilliant solution to various problems in film study. When he speaks of themes such as "eating" or "looking," he is not attempting to divulge Ozu's philosophical stance towards those actions. Instead, he notes first that such actions, events, or moments recur throughout Ozu's cinema, though sometimes with more frequency in some periods (thus his tendency to focus on "late-period" Ozu). The author will note where they appear in each film's narrative, in part because their narrative function is one aspect he considers (e.g., the use of laughter to begin a scene in a new location), but the cinematic power of these themes comes from their relationship with other instances at other moments, beyond both the individual narrative and the individual film. Thematic structures, which can and will condense narrative structures, enable Hasumi to see abundance and not lack, and they free film analysis—as well as cinema itself—from both narrative and the ideology of the closed text, if not the rule of time (chaps. 2 and 5). He celebrates conjunctures when multiple moments resonate, crossing the borders of texts and the march of time, to reinforce the continuous present that cinema ultimately is, before foreign things such as stories, language, or meaning are affixed. These also remain on the surface of the film: every theme is clearly visible, without a hidden subtext, even though some themes might require a trained eye. This also avoids the functionalism of purely formal analysis, while maintaining a cinematic focus on the audiovisual. Hasumi is not just looking for sameness in themes but rather tends to focus on certain moments. One example is the appearance of the staircase at the end of *An Autumn Afternoon*—in an oeuvre where, with rare exceptions, it is the invisibility of staircases that fundamentally shapes domestic space (chap. 4)—when difference manifests itself and a theme is twisted. As he repeatedly states, he is interested in both the coexistence *and* juxtaposition of elements in Ozu's work—in resonance and paradox.

Hasumi also uses these juxtapositions of themes to rebuke purveyors of the Ozuesque for not really having watched the films. Those who state that Ozu is a director of quietude who does not move his camera miss how movement—and its dialectical relationship with the act of stopping and holding still—are crucial to the Ozu world (chap. 6). When Hasumi claims that pretty much every declaration about Ozu can be disproven with a contrary example from his films, this does not mean anything goes, but rather that an approach to Ozu—and to cinema as a whole—must show a "sensitivity to difference" (chap. 9). Defining the uniformity of Ozu means that *A Hen in the Wind*, a film often considered "un-Ozu-like" but a crucial film for Hasumi, is ignored and never gets a North American DVD release. Failing to *really* watch Ozu sometimes means others cannot watch him either.

Throughout this book, there is a strong undercurrent of existentialism that makes this study not just an account of Ozu, or even a theory of cinema, but a call for renewed ways of living in the world. The verb *ikiru* (to live) appears repeatedly throughout the work in a way that stresses not only that Ozu's cinema is a matter of living but that our watching is as well. In subtle language, the prologue critiques not simply the intellectual stances of those promoting the Ozuesque but also their approach to existence, as if claiming Ozu is defined by stillness or negative rhetoric were indicative of their own inability to accommodate change and affirmation. First and foremost, Hasumi's call that we actually look at cinema urges us to truly see and engage with the world. While he might object to this, there are affinities between Hasumi and Russian formalism. One could first state that his approach to themes is not dissimilar to Bordwell's formalist poetics, identifying a norm and then its deviation—though while Bordwell's deviations often serve to reinforce the norm, Hasumi invariably questions the very concept of the norm. On the other hand, and more importantly, Hasumi broadly shares the formalist call for art to help us see anew, to break free of conventionalized perception, but he urges that of not just artists but of viewers and scholars as well.

What is also existentialist about this confrontation with a world seen anew is that, to Hasumi, it is fundamentally both terrifying and absurd, defined by nonsense and even, as Ryan Cook emphasizes in his analysis, "stupidity"—which "abandons subjectivity and knowledge and submits to cruel stupidity in order to encounter cinema as change and movement."[9] Hasumi himself had previously written about the impossibility of film criticism: "Words should, before anything else, not take the existence of cinema as a given, but must be released towards the path where cinema might exist, and at the moment they manage to illuminate to a certain degree the shell of that point, they must be prepared for their own death."[10]

That is why this book is often a perilous, but thrilling tightrope walk between extremities. Some readers might protest that after objecting to the Ozuesque in the Prologue, he uses the term in his own analysis throughout. Others might wonder why a translator of Barthes, who was famous for declaring the death of the author, is deeply engaged in a laudatory exegesis of a single auteur—right at the time much of Euro-American film studies was critiquing auteurism. Hasumi is well aware of these problems, but in his mind they did not solve the core dilemmas of the critic. Just as cinema is defined by limits, by impossibilities that cannot be overcome but only recognized in a game of looking into the abyss, writing on Ozu cannot avoid categories like the "Ozuesque" that language necessarily imposes. Just as Derrida playfully declared there is no outside of the text, there is no outside of Ozuesque discourse, which therefore, to Hasumi, enjoins us to position "ourselves within the *gap* between things Ozuesque and the films of Yasujirō Ozu" and play "its continuous movement as a game" (chap. 7). Hasumi is less engaged in an auteurist celebration of Ozu than in finding in Ozu the occasion to critique notions of the auteur, thereby, as he says, "sacrificing auteurist unity" (chap. 3). Against the conception of auteurs as free artists flaunting convention to establish their own personal

9. Ryan Cook, "An Impaired Eye: Hasumi Shigehiko on Cinema as Stupidity," *Review of Japanese Culture as Society* 22 (December 2010): 137.

10. Hasumi Shigehiko, *Eiga no shinwagaku* (Tokyo: Chikuma Shobō, 1996), 51.

styles, Hasumi sees a filmmaker straddling juxtaposition and coexistence, one who is an "open auteur" only through awareness of the limits of cinema, who must engage in difference and contradiction because cinema cannot be controlled. Just as Ozu's cinema is most brilliant when it challenges those limits by exposing them—at the point just before cinema ceases to be cinema—Ozu is an auteur right at the point just before he ceases to be an auteur. This conception of a true auteur as the one who avoids being trapped in auteurist discourse, I should note, was one basis for Hasumi's championing of Kitano Takeshi in the nineties.[11]

Very much a representative of the discourses about postmodernism in the eighties in Japan, Hasumi viewed both Ozu and film criticism as a playful though often serious and frightful game. This is not a detached, intellectual playfulness; one of his primary concerns is explaining how Ozu's films affect us in often raw and vivid ways (e.g., his repeated use of the word *namanamashii*). In some forms, he is engaged in a sort of affect theory of cinema, but one that attempts to explain the affect that occurs only through film. He acknowledges that people express many emotions when watching Ozu films. But rejecting efforts to explain Ozu through what is outside cinema—through notions of *mono no aware,* melodrama, the decline of the Japanese family or of traditional Japan—Hasumi in every chapter attempts to show how we can be moved purely through the play of themes. The fight between the actor and his current partner in *Floating Weeds* is powerful not due to the story but because Ozu is a director of sunny skies shocking us by introducing rain, having the two confront each other in a shot/reverse shot that questions the very possibility that their looks can be represented.

As Cook mentions in his translator's introduction, there is debate over who the subject of this emotional effect is: who are the "persons"

---

11. See Aaron Gerow, *Kitano Takeshi* (London: BFI, 2007).

(*hito*) or the "we" (*wareware*) Hasumi constantly invokes? This is what distinguishes him from the impressionist critics before him, who all clearly defined themselves as the emoting subject. Chris Fujiwara insists on the "impersonality of Hasumi's viewing subject," arguing that the emotion described is less individual than a "cinematic sensibility" that is shared.[12] Yet clearly this is a particular and rather privileged subject: the play of themes can only operate if the viewers have seen all of Ozu's films—albeit through a learning process—such that they can feel moved when a stairway appears. This, and Hasumi's repeated use of the imperative *must* when describing how we *should* feel when viewing Ozu, eventually resulted in what could have been a misreading of Hasumi: a cinephilic culture developing in eighties' Japan that was both cliquish and intolerant of other forms of cinema and other media like television (this despite Hasumi's uncinephilic emphasis on the terror of film). At the same time, younger scholars such as Inuhiko Yomota rose to criticize Hasumi for setting aside crucial issues of politics, race, and gender.

Directed by Yasujirō Ozu has remained influential since its publication in 1983. I would even contend that the aversion to editing, and thus the predominance of the long take in nineties' Japanese film, has much to do with Hasumi's critique of editing and the look in cinema. The book has never gone out of print in Japan, has gone through several editions, and was translated into French in 1998, into Korean in 2001, and into Chinese in 2012. There has been no published translation of the book in English, however. David Bordwell reportedly had a Japanese graduate student do a rough translation so that he could refer to it in his masterful study *Ozu and the Poetics of Cinema*.[13] One excerpt from chapter 7

---

12. Chris Fujiwara, "The Critical Event of *Director Ozu Yasujiro*," *Lola* 7 (2016), http://www.lolajournal.com/7/hasumi_fujiwara.html. Fujiwara's piece is one of several in that issue's valuable tribute to Hasumi.

13. David Bordwell, *Ozu and the Poetics of Cinema* (Princeton, NJ: Princeton University Press, 1988).

was published in English as part of an anthology on *Tokyo Story* edited by David Desser.[14] Other pieces by Hasumi have been translated into multiple languages around the world, with many in English appearing thanks to Adrian Martin and Jonathan Rosenbaum. When Hasumi's agent first contacted me asking me if there was anything from his oeuvre that could be translated, I immediately suggested this book, as well as Ryan Cook who, I can assure you after poring over this translation, has masterfully handled "Hasumi-bushi," as many term his unique discourse.

Fujiwara offers his opinion that it would be "impossible in the context of English-language film studies for the Ozu book to be accepted as an academic work."[15] That might be true, but only under a certain definition of "academic" "film studies." Hasumi's work has certainly been accepted in academic film studies in Japan, in part because Hasumi helped found the field. Yet his academic work has always been based on his critique and rejection of established forms of film study and film theory, precisely for their efforts to contain the undefinability of cinema in set theories and fields. That may be the challenge for those in English-language film studies reading this book. If Hasumi is asking us to see anew, to interrogate how our words and theories blind us to what challenges us in front of our eyes, and to develop a way of living that accepts both juxtaposition and coexistence, can Euro-American film studies see its field anew, interrogate its imperial definitions of theory and film studies centered in the modern "West," and accept *Directed by Yasujirō Ozu* as an academic work? That may be why publishing this translation forty years after its appearance in Japanese is still very much an issue for today.

14. David Desser, ed., *Ozu's Tokyo Story* (Cambridge: Cambridge University Press, 1997).
15. Fujiwara, "Critical Event."

監督 小津安二郎

DIRECTED BY YASUJIRO OZU

PROLOGUE
The Rules of the Game

THINGS OZUESQUE

Everyone knows Yasujirō Ozu. There are certain gestures, certain ways of talking, certain kinds of looks that people encounter and instinctively call "Ozuesque." Casual though such judgments may be, they tend to persuade even those who do not usually give much thought to Ozu. "Indeed! What could be more Ozuesque?" And who would not feel reassured upon seeing the smiles that greet these words, smiles devoid of any trace of antagonism? Perhaps the Ozuesque itself is the culture of such tacitly shared reassurances. In any case, the Ozuesque almost never leads people toward awkward silences or messy disagreements.

In such situations, people always find themselves in between events. No one thinks of Ozu in the heat of the moment when an incident suddenly erupts or when a surprise ending is finally revealed. It is only when we understand that no decisive change is in the offing that we become conscious of things Ozuesque. In this sense, we might think of the Ozuesque as something like a gratuitous lubricant. Ozuesque situations only present themselves when everything is already progressing smoothly, as if to go with the flow:

–You think so? Maybe you're right.

–Yes, I do. I think so. That's how it is.

–Hmm, I guess that's how it is.

Then, just as the circularity of the dialogue in Ozu starts to seem as if it might enclose us in an absurd labyrinth of speech, things Ozuesque quickly retreat. In short, the Ozuesque amounts to something like a game—an entertaining, risk-free diversion that can be stopped at any time. Or call it a form of mischief, but one without sinister intent or any relationship to cruelty. The harmless nature of the Ozuesque is what enables us to believe without question that everyone knows Ozu, even those who do not necessarily give much thought to his films. In fact, it is almost unthinkable that things Ozuesque would cause anyone any undue agitation or intentional confusion. There should therefore be nothing unnatural about thinking that everyone, or at least anyone Japanese, would understand how to enjoy the game.

But is that really the case? If we place Ozu's films alongside what we know as things Ozuesque, the situation starts to look a little different. Most of the films turn out to be rich with details that might in the aggregate be titled *The Rules of the Game* in the Renoirian sense. They depict Japanese social conditions, customs, and sensibilities that were in a state of transformation between the late 1920s and the early 1960s—various features of middle-class life that showed signs of falling apart even as they were in the process of becoming established. Balancing everyday routine and privileged ceremony, the films present all manner of rules, as if compiling examples for emulation: rules about how to graduate, how to find a job, how to get married, how to change jobs, how to raise children, how to prepare for old age, how to mourn the dead. Those who lived during the historical period in which Ozu was making films should recognize events in these successions of episodes that correspond, more or less, to things in their own lives. Japanese viewers of any generation will also almost certainly discover cultural customs and rituals that can still be readily understood by analogy with their direct experience, even where the customs depicted may have faded from contemporary practice. For some, there will be things that lie close to home—details so close that their systems and functions may have escaped awareness—but that come to signify in new ways when viewed in Ozu. These will probably include unpleasant reminders, for some, of social games they voluntarily took part in despite their undeniable misgivings. But it is also a fact that the body ends up learning and remembering such rules. In this sense, things Ozuesque have also involved rules of a game that people could hardly have escaped even if they wanted to. This is why some people in the postwar years, especially from *Late Spring* (*Banshun*, 1949) onward, showed resistance to Ozu simply by ignoring him, even as his films continued to draw large audiences. It is also true that Ozu's late period coincided with a time when the culture of middle-class life in Japan was reaching a stage where these rules alone were no longer sufficient to control the game.

But if the title *The Rules of the Game* aptly characterizes Ozu's films in the aggregate, the reason is not because the people and things the films depict offer faithful reflections of familial coalescence and collapse as experienced by Japan's middle class between the twenties and the sixties. As a reflection of history, it should probably even be said that these rules omit something essential, since the war, which played a central role in such coalescence and collapse, casts only an indirect shadow in the films. In any case, our objective here is not to gather fragments of reality from films—themselves only works of fiction—in order to discover a manual for middle-class living. If that were the aim, what would we do with Ozu's crime pictures, with their abstract mise-en-scène and their men and women dressed in costumes that seem borrowed from a Hollywood production lot? These films hardly even seem to take place in Japan. Just what "rules" could the films *Dragnet Girl* (*Hijōsen no onna*, 1933) and *That Night's Wife* (*Sono yo no tsuma*, 1930) possibly teach us? The titles alone suggest they would get us nowhere in the game known as "things Ozuesque." Any rules we might discover in these films would surely be of a completely different nature than those of the system of rituals that regulated middle-class society in Japan during this period.

Dragnet Girl and *That Night's Wife* showcase Kinuyo Tanaka and Emiko Yagumo brandishing revolvers, but no one would conclude that by watching these films women learned to shoot a gun. What people learn from films is generally not what is represented on the screen, much less the psychology of an auteur presumed to exist beyond the screen. The look is capable of watching the screen, at best. But what do people learn by looking there? For one thing, they learn how difficult it is really to see. Even more importantly, they learn just how much the eye avoids seeing, and how it thus erases the screen in front of it.

The reason everyone thinks they know Ozu and believes they can live Ozuesque situations as if playing a risk-free game is because no one really sees Ozu's films. Things Ozuesque make a game unrelated to the films, one that only becomes possible once the eye has already erased the image from the screen. It is probably utterly impossible for people to indulge in the pleasures of the Ozuesque in the instant of really looking at an Ozu film, since no single Ozu film ever resembles things Ozuesque. The reason it is widely believed that Ozu films are Ozuesque is simply because the eye avoids seeing what is there on screen. If there is a rule of any kind that we can learn in looking at Ozu, it is that Ozu films never correspond to things Ozuesque. The game involves actually giving oneself up to the movement of the *gap* between the two as the distance separating them constantly expands and contracts. This game, which can also be described in terms of the gap between myth and reality, is something very specific to middle-class society. Or perhaps it would be clearer to call it bourgeois. The point, in any case, is that the pleasure we take in playing with myths while at the same time erasing what we are looking at in reality is a thoroughly historical one. As long as we subject the films of Ozu to the interpretive matrix of things Ozuesque, we can remain at ease. Doing so relieves us of any worry that, in looking, our eyes might be subjected to change of some kind. We are dealing, in other words, with a bourgeois virtue—the pleasure of erasure. This virtue preserves things Ozuesque unscathed and causes even the gap that separates them from the films to escape notice. It enables people to believe in a self that remains always protected in a space between events. In this way, change is everywhere avoided. Such techniques for avoiding change do not date to the origins of human civilization. Their cultivation as a virtue is an eminently historical phenomenon dating more or less to the last century. It is among the aims of this book to explore how this virtue relates to Yasujirō Ozu.

TWENTY YEARS

As I write these words, my eyes are not trained on any Ozu film in reality. I will therefore be writing about the films from a position that is, if anything, adjacent to things Ozuesque. Still, I will seek wherever possible to occupy the aforementioned gap. While many have cited the "monotone" nature of Ozu, or his repetitiveness, it remains the case that whenever we really look at the screen, his films come at our eyes with constant incitements toward change. Movement lives here in the raw, as the ever-renewing present, a movement that can be called cruel and that causes us to only ever lose sight of the screen, at each instant, even while always standing in the same position. We might also call this movement in stasis. A shot may appear to be static, but its plurality of elements might at any moment bring stark tensions to life, slicing at the eye or disorienting the look. Things Ozuesque may reassure existence and lead to moments of calm, but Ozu's films constantly subject the eye to strain. To the extent that people actually look at them, there can be no lingering comfortably in space between events. This is because while a film may have a definite beginning and end, images are things that live instant by instant, as a successively renewing present. The game must therefore be played with the utmost seriousness. *Seriousness* here does not mean observing predetermined rules but treating play itself as a process of exposing the rules of the game as it unfolds.

Unfortunately, not all of Ozu's films remain with us. Today we are only able to view thirty-six of the films he made during the period starting in 1929 with *Days of Youth* (*Gakusei romansu: Wakaki hi*) and ending in 1962 with his last film, *An Autumn Afternoon* (*Sanma no aji*). This book is concerned specifically with what we can see on screen, and how it stimulates our cinematic sensitivity. In other words, I would like to attempt to discuss the films only in their capacity to live as real film experience. The immediate subject will consistently be the visible image. I seek to describe how the viewer's being is agitated and enticed toward change in living the images that take shape on the screen only to disappear from one moment to the next. In principle, I will omit biographical narrative about Ozu the auteur. These considerations also explain why this book makes limited reference at best to the films that have survived only in the form of screenplays.

Born in the year that Ozu made his first talkie, *The Only Son* (*Hitori musuko*, 1936), and as a member of the generation that first came to know Ozu's world through *Late Spring*, I am probably not ideally positioned to write a book about Ozu. Some might naturally question how anyone with no direct knowledge of Ozu's debut film *Sword of Penitence* (*Zange no yaiba*, 1927) could justifiably hold forth on this filmmaker. I admit to feeling some discomfort over the fact that I lack any qualification to discuss the nearly twenty films that are no longer extant. But this is not a problem unique to me as the author of this book. It is an affliction for film history as a whole. So poor is the cultural environment in which we live that it is incapable of conveying to future generations nearly half the films made by a director even as exceptionally unique as Ozu. This book is a testament to that poverty. As its author, I can only hope that the day will come when I have to revise this text because somewhere, somehow, the films now thought lost are discovered.

The film I now dream will suddenly be unearthed is *The Sorrow of the Beautiful Woman* (*Bijin aishū*, 1931). I cannot help but resent its loss, if for no other reason than the fact that it had the longest running time of any of Ozu's films. Many who saw it at the time of its release regarded it as a failure, but it is a consistent refrain of this book that such testimonies are not to be trusted. I had the unexpected good fortune of being able to interview Yukiko Inoue, who starred in this film. Words cannot describe my happiness at also having been able to meet Yūharu Atsuta, Ozu's "eye" who shot most of his films after *What Did the Lady Forget?* (*Shukujo wa nani o wasureta ka*, 1937), replacing Hideo Shigehara. If this book has any active significance, it is as a transcription, of a kind, of my conversations with these two figures. I can only hope that my writing in what follows lives up to the excitement I experienced in listening to Inoue and Atsuta's stories.[1]

And yet—I do now also recall something quite personal. It was December of 1963. I had been away from Japan for nearly a year and a half, leading a life of self-imposed austerity and hardly watching any films at all. After going out for a newspaper and strolling through the park, passing a rolling lawn that had not yet browned despite the

---

1. The author's interview with Atsuta is included as an appendix in this volume. His interview with Inoue has unfortunately been omitted due to space restrictions.

winter cold, I came to an iron bench—turned frigid under the grey sky of the fading afternoon—and, following my daily routine, took a seat next to a pond where some ducks were playing. Then, glancing at the paper, a sudden feeling of dread: my eye had fallen on a jumble of text on the back page, words that danced as I tried to make sense of them. Something terribly important had happened. It was confronting me on the page, but the information resisted my comprehension. I had to force myself to take it in. The text started to cohere into a newspaper article, about the death of a Japanese film director—Yasujirō Ozu. The chill rising from the damp ground was making the cold harder to bear. Ozu was dead. A blunt message. Never had these alphabetic letters seemed so clumsy. It was as if they were merely following orders, marching in a phonetic row devoid of sentiment. This can't be true, I said to myself, as I realized with a sense of shame that I did not even know the Japanese title of his last film.

But I have already written about this on a separate occasion. Ozu was taken from me quite unnaturally, by surprise. This book is nothing but an attempt to bring him back. How to assess the nearly twenty years that it took to first realize this attempt, I do not know. But one thing is certain: if not for the Ozu retrospective that took place in Tokyo in January 1981 at what was then the National Film Center, the process of finishing it would have taken even longer.[2] The opportunity to write a short commentary on Ozu for the front page of the catalog that accompanied that retrospective proved quite stimulating and helped bring this book to completion.

During the same period of time that this project was gestating, a number of other books about Ozu were published, each introducing new stimuli as I formed my own thoughts into words. This book is particularly indebted to *Ozu Yasujirō—Hito to shigoto* (Yasujirō Ozu: The

---

2. The National Film Center is now known as the National Film Archive of Japan.

man and his work, 1972).³ Tadao Satō's *Ozu Yasujirō no geijutsu* (The art of Yasujirō Ozu, published in two volumes, the first in 1971 and the second in 1978, untranslated) and Donald Richie's *Ozu: His Life and Films* (1974) were also books I maintained constant awareness of over the course of this writing, even if some of that attention took the form of critique directed at portions of those studies. However, it bears repeating that the focus of the discussion within these pages is on the films of Yasujirō Ozu. The dream of *Directed by Yasujirō Ozu* is that its hopefully many readers will be filled with desire to see the films and rush to the theater before they finish reading, or else will be reduced to trembling with anger wherever Ozu is not being screened and declare the situation unjust and inexcusable.

3. Edited by Kazuo Inoue and published by Ban'yūsha, this volume contains commentary by Ozu himself as well as many reflections on his life and work by cast and crew members, among others who knew him. The book was reissued in revised form by the Ozu Yasujiro Society (Ozu Yasujirō Gakkai) in 2022. At present, there is no complete English translation.

1

NEGATING

ABSENCES AND NEGATIVELY FRAMED RHETORIC

Yasujirō Ozu is often dogged by rhetoric framed in the negative. It is hardly surprising to encounter such rhetoric in the unsympathetic criticism that targeted him during the last years of his career, at a point when he had long been a dominating presence in the Japanese film world. But negatively framed constructions run through even the enthusiastic reevaluations that heaped praise on him in later years. It is as if talking about Ozu in this way were only natural. Critics have gone about cataloging negations of all kinds, seemingly convinced that the essence of Ozu is only to be discovered in what Ozu is *not*. This general situation has remained consistent and unchanged through the past and present of Ozu criticism from East to West. But just what does it mean to validate an artist with litanies of negation?

Anyone will casually observe, for example, that the camera does not move in Ozu. His low camera position never changes, there are basically no traveling shots, and high angles are not employed except on rare occasions. The negations used to narrate such aspects of technique also lend themselves quite naturally to describing the monotone features of the world this technique evokes: in Ozu, there are no passionate struggles, the narration lacks peaks and valleys, settings are limited to the home and do not open onto broader social context. We are all too familiar with how these various observations framed in the negative—and any number of others that we could continue to recite—over time gave shape to the myth of the Ozuesque monotone. Most of the critiques that Ozu endured late in life were directed at the way he supposedly enclosed himself in a world of personal predilections, a world undisturbed by any intrusion of the dark clouds of history. To those of his contemporaries who believed they were living through a time of necessary social upheaval, a process through which postwar Japan inevitably had to pass, such self-enclosure looked like little more than a return to a traditional aesthetic sensibility, one devoid of naturalness and almost abstract. Any number of negatively framed characteristics—the monotone approach to camera technique, the languidness of narrative tempo, the absence of dramatic developments, the tenuousness of social critique—persistently estranged Ozu from the radical sectors of cinematic discourse. It can at least be said that, up to a certain point in time, talking about Ozu was deemed incompatible with those living the present of cinema.

Today, it seems that the situation has changed. Over the past decade, as the world has discovered an overlooked auteur of the highest order in Yasujirō Ozu, the critical reception in Japan has also come around to acknowledging certain validating aspects.[1] But this trend is not necessarily something that merits unreserved celebration, since even now people continue to approach Ozu only through litanies of negation. It is

---

1. Recall that this chapter was first published in 1983.

also true that the rapid momentum behind the contemporary international reevaluation of Ozu reflects a rather conservative inclination—a return to tradition. In fact, it is not entirely unheard of for people to show interest in Ozu while indulging in tendencies like the widespread rediscovery of things oriental. We are not the least bit sympathetic to such tendencies. The aim in placing a deliberate focus on Ozu is to bring him into the cinematic present, and to do so, moreover, by means of the most modest of gestures. For this purpose, it will be necessary to *affirm* him, with claims made in the positive. Such positive affirmation will need to strip away the mythical exceptionalism of the Yasujirō Ozu whom negatively framed rhetoric has exalted as a privileged auteur in defining his films by means of what they lack. It will need to direct attention instead to the structures and limits of the unsubjectivized environment of cinema itself.[2] For this approach, it hardly even matters whether Ozu was a genius as a filmmaker. The task is not to establish consensus about Ozu's relative greatness in film historical perspective. What is important is to train our gaze on the movement of light and shadow across the cinematic surface, and at the point of *film experience*, to feel in the raw what cinema can and at the same time also cannot be.

It is, of course, far from difficult to arrive at a view of Ozu as a stubborn traditionalist. In certain things, he was unmistakably conservative. But this kind of conclusion is also where this negatively framed rhetoric inevitably leads. Ozu did in fact often seek consistency over variation, and if we take at face value his own self-vindication when he famously told a critic not to "ask for *tonkatsu* [fried pork cutlet] from a tofu maker," the conservatism thesis may seem to be strengthened. In fact, it is probably fair to say that Ozu did self-consciously perform the role of the "tofu maker" throughout his career, intentionally cultivating the image of a specialized tradesman lacking any qualifications for things like

---

2. Here and elsewhere, the translator uses "unsubjectivized" for Hasumi's word *hi-ninshōteki*, which literally means "without grammatical person"—a linguistic image probably related to what is otherwise called *focalization* in literature or *point of view* in film.

frying pork. It is therefore perfectly natural that negatively framed rhetoric should dog Ozu and cling to him. He made a conscious choice.

In this regard, it appears that the momentum behind the contemporary reevaluation of Ozu as described above has involved a shift not primarily in the ways that people fundamentally *understand* what conscious choices he made but in people's *attitudes* toward those choices. The recitations of negatively framed rhetoric and of definitions premised on absences that at one time formed the basis for unsympathetic evaluations of Ozu remain unchanged in themselves. They have merely followed the current of the times and drifted in the direction of active affirmation. Things once thought monotone are now celebrated as evidence of authorial consistency, and things once regarded as lacking are now admiringly attributed to rigorous formal unity. If such is the case, it must be our eyes themselves, and not the films, that reveal monotone tendencies as they look at Ozu. Of this we can be certain: the cinematic discourses around Ozu are far more monotone, and the eyes that watch Ozu far more lacking, than Ozu films themselves. This is why the study of Ozu upon which we are embarking must seek to lavish affirmation on the films. But in reality it is no easy task to lavish affirmation on Ozu, since it is indeed possible to find absences everywhere in the films.

CINEMATIC STYLE

Take, for example, the words of Donald Richie, who contributed considerably to the international embrace of Ozu as a great cinematic auteur at a time when he was still thought of as incompatible with Western sensibilities. Richie writes the following in the introduction to his 1974 book *Ozu: His Life and Films*:

> Ozu's pictures, then, are made of very *little*. One theme, several stories, *a few* patterns. The technique, too, as mentioned earlier, is highly *restricted: invariable* camera angle, *no* camera movement, a *restricted* use of cinematic

punctuation. Similarly, the structure of the film . . . is nearly *invariable*. Given the determined limitations of the Ozu style, it is not surprising that his films should all resemble one another. Indeed, there can have been few artists whose *oeuvre* is so completely consistent. In film, Ozu is unique.[3]

What to make of the number of negative constructions that appear in this by no means lengthy quote? "Little," "few," "restricted," "no movement," "invariable," etc.? Richie adopts as-is the kind of vocabulary that we encounter frequently in the unsympathetic critical literature on Ozu, only here the same language yields premises supporting a view of Ozu as a one-of-a-kind filmmaker. Of course, taken individually and as observations of phenomena, these points are not wrong. Anyone who has seen even a single Ozu film will probably easily accept them as fact. Those familiar with the early films will know that these tendencies are not necessarily present from the beginning but become pronounced at a certain point in the oeuvre. The earliest film that we are able to view in its entirety today is *Days of Youth*, Ozu's eighth film, shot in 1929. The seven films before that are lost, including his 1927 directorial debut *Sword of Penitence*. But in *Days of Youth* we find both camera movement and even high-angle shots with pans—in other words, nonobservance of Ozu's characteristic fixed low-position framing. Upon witnessing Tatsuo Saitō chase his runaway ski down a ski slope as if to mimic a chase scene out of Buster Keaton, those who know the films Ozu made later in his career may even reach the conclusion that *Days of Youth* is little more than a common, run-of-the-mill film. Confronted with moments such as this, people tend to start making lists, trying to identify the point in Ozu at which camera movement becomes scarce, or low camera positions systematic, or where pans and fades disappear.

---

3. Donald Richie, *Ozu* (Berkeley: University of California Press, 1974), 9. Later editions of Richie's book bear the title *Ozu: His Life and Films*. Hasumi cites the Japanese edition: Donald Richie, *Ozu Yasujirō no bigaku—Eiga no naka no Nihon*, trans. Kikuo Yamamoto (Tokyo: Firumu Āto Sha, 1978). Emphasis added by the author.

They say that Ozu abandoned various things over the course of his development as a filmmaker, that in pursuing monotone austerity, he succeeded in constructing a rigorous and balanced filmic universe.

In his 1972 book *Transcendental Style in Film: Ozu, Bresson, Dreyer*—a book that attempts to define Ozu's style not by "what he omitted" but by "what was left after his unceasing prunings"—Paul Schrader also raises the topic of Ozuesque austerity.[4] Clearly resonating with Donald Richie, Schrader writes: "It is possible to define Ozu's style by what it is *not*. Ozu is the film-maker who *doesn't do* certain things. This *rarefaction* of technique continued throughout Ozu's lifetime, from his first film to his last."[5] Fair enough. For the author of a book entitled *Transcendental Style in Film*, this position seems appropriate. However, the view that Ozu established himself as Ozu through persistent self-restraint is not a view that we should adopt. This kind of outlook inevitably leads toward schematic oppositions, of the pure versus the impure Ozu, or of the perfected Ozu versus the incomplete Ozu, and ultimately to the selection of only one Ozu as the *true* Yasujirō Ozu. Considering our dream of lavishing affirmation, we can hardly endorse an approach that excludes impurity, selecting only purity as the truth of Ozu. Only an abstraction can result from expelling contradictions and oppositions from our field of view. Arrogance is the ultimate destination of such an approach, one that imagines Ozu in his final years as a finished product and recognizes only secondary value in the films of the early and middle periods, which become transitional stages necessary to Ozu's evolution into something approaching perfection but otherwise not generally worthy of much attention. But is the life work of an author—whether it lives through "film experience" or through the "textual experience" of literary prose—

---

4. Paul Schrader, *Transcendental Style in Film: Ozu, Bresson, Dreyer* (New York: Da Capo Press, 1988), 23. The 1988 edition cited here is an unabridged republication of the edition first published by University of California Press in 1972. In Japanese, Hasumi cites Paul Schrader, *Sei naru eiga—Ozu/Buresson/Doraiyā*, trans. Kikuo Yamamoto (Tokyo: Firumu Āto Sha, 1981).

5. Schrader, *Transcendental Style in Film*, 22. Emphasis added by the author.

really something that can be measured in terms of dualisms like pure versus impure, or rough versus refined? Living itself is an active contradiction, a state of being within the constantly renewing present where no encapsulating instant ever coalesces, and where there is never equilibrium. If Richie and Schrader have trouble acknowledging the ways that multiple disparate elements can play alongside one another without ever integrating, then what they call style ends up becoming little more than a static pattern, nearly abstract in its reductivism. Abstract static patterns do not produce things of the kind that can be experienced in the space of the movie theater. In the cinema of moving pictures, even where those pictures are composed in ways that can basically be called abstract, details that do not readily fall into balance synchronously coexist. In cross-resonating with other details—whether details within the same shot, or details at a distance, in other shots—they stimulate our cinematic sensitivity. To interrupt the possibility of this coexistence—or intermingling—would mean the death of cinema, quite literally. Therefore, to compile negations for the purpose of defining Ozu through what is absent from his films would mean to rob the films of their raw life as moving images. *Productive* signs, signs that live in the constant present, are signs capable of moving our being. They are things in excess and cannot be defined through absence. Ozu did in fact discard many things along the way, but what moves us in his films is decidedly not what is missing from them, nor is it what remains after pruning. This is why the study of Ozu on which we are embarking must be written on a path through excess. It must be written not with rhetoric framed in the negative, but through claims made in the affirmative.

SIGNS AND AFFIRMATION

People often use the word *artifact* when describing things they have prohibited from becoming productive signs. We aim to avoid discussing Ozu this way, as an object of cultivated taste. The word *constraint* should be applied not to Ozu's films, but to much of the cinematic commentary that has surrounded them.

In the interest of avoiding any confusion, it bears stating that neither Richie nor Schrader has any apparent intentions of claiming to be an aficionado of Ozu the artifact, for example. They too are unmistakably inspired by Ozu the productive sign. But their commentary still ends up moving in directions that undermine their own inspiration. This problem is of course not limited to these two authors. Much of what gets written about cinema in general basically ends up cataloging artifacts, a limitation that is exposed especially when people talk about the style of a director, or about cinematic style. Style itself can only be narrated as constant and immutable form. The more it approaches some static, immovable order, the more film style is singled out for praise.

For example: Richie identifies in the constant and immutable order of Ozu's films what he regards as the natural expression of the Japanese life ethic *mono no aware*.⁶ This world of *mono no aware* can be thought of as lacking transformative events, as a world in which characters support each other within a shared "philosophy of acceptance," the product of a kind of resignation. Richie is sensitive enough to highlight that this world characteristically reflects "social problems" in Ozu, and furthermore that human life within it is transient and "susceptible only to change."⁷ And yet he hardly addresses the early-period gangster film *Dragnet Girl* (*Hijōsen no onna*, 1933), a film that takes place in the criminal underworld and is therefore perhaps too incompatible. Perhaps Richie excluded this drama depicting a star-crossed romance between

---

6. *Mono no aware*, commonly translated as "the pathos of things," is a poetic concept, with a history extending to the time of the eleventh-century *Tale of Genji*. It is associated with subtle sensitivity for the fleeting, impermanent nature of things in the world, symbolized by the ephemeral beauty of seasonal cherry blossoms, for example.

7. Richie, *Ozu*, 69. Hasumi does not provide a page number for the citation from Kikuo Yamamoto's Japanese translation. The quoted language from Richie's original English text approximates what Hasumi quotes in Japanese ("'tsune ni genzai no jōkyō' ga han'ei shi, mata, soko ni 'tayō de henka suru ningensei' ga egakiagerareteiru").

a gangster and his mistress because he considered it an anomaly inconsistent with the world of the Ozuesque. And yet *Dragnet Girl*, a film we will later have occasion to address, must surely be counted as one of film history's most beautiful crime melodramas, alongside Howard Hawks's *Scarface* (1932) and Jean Renoir's *Night at the Crossroads* (*La nuit du carrefour*, 1932), to cite two films made during basically the same period, not to mention Fritz Lang's somewhat later film *You Only Live Once* (1937). This is where attempts to define Ozu through litanies of negation end up: rejecting even a masterpiece like *Dragnet Girl*.

Schrader's corresponding neglect of *Dragnet Girl* is likely to be explained by nothing deeper than the fact that he probably had not seen this silent masterpiece when he wrote his book. Admittedly, Schrader's interest lies in Ozu's use of the static shot as a "form which can accept deep, contradictory emotion and transform it into an expression of something unified, permanent, transcendent," which Schrader uses to illustrate his concept of transcendental style in film.[8] He therefore limits his discussion to the postwar films, especially the late-period masterpieces from *Late Spring* onward. Even if he had seen *Dragnet Girl*, the film likely would not have advanced his argument. His premise that "every aspect of Ozu's film-making . . . falls under the tight restriction of the everyday" also reveals, once again, the limitations of a discourse that cannot resist formulating cinematic style as a matter of constant and immutable form.[9] Like Richie, Schrader ultimately cannot avoid descending into a cataloging of artifacts. He writes:

> In Ozu, stylization is near complete. Every shot is from the same height, every composition static, every conversation monotone, every expression bland, every cut forthright and predictable. No action is intended as a comment on another, no event leads inexorably to the next."[10]

---

8. Schrader, *Trancendental Style in Film*, 49–51.
9. Schrader, 42.
10. Schrader, 41.

The reason this quoted passage is comparatively free of negative constructions is that Schrader is describing a pure Ozu film, one that consists only of what remains after the rejection of all sorts of impure elements through constant pruning and restraint. This is therefore not an affirmative affirmation, but clearly a negative affirmation. It would of course be possible to trot out the scene in *A Hen in the Wind* (*Kaze no naka no mendori*, 1948) where Shūji Sano shoves Kinuyo Tanaka down the stairs, for example, to insist that this negative affirmation is rife with contradictions. But we need not dwell on such objections given that Schrader's project is to describe constant and immutable form, something we are well aware requires the exclusion of disparate details. The issue is just that installing an opposition between constant and disparate elements ends up contributing in itself to the calcification of Ozu into an artifact. We would simply like to talk about Ozu in affirming that opposition for what it is, since it is ultimately difficult to conclude that the language Schrader uses to define Ozu deviates all that substantially from the rhetoric of those in Japan who, for a time, criticized him as "monotone." To the extent that everyone involved has observed the same things in Ozu's formal system—from those who up to a certain point saw Ozu as someone run dry of originality to those who later praised his approach as the expression of a unique worldview—the lesson to be drawn must amount to little more than the fact that the times eventually changed. The point, in other words, ends up being only this: that there have been two contrasting evaluations of the world of the Ozuesque, both defined through absences and negative rhetoric; that as the historical period known as the postwar receded vaguely into the distance, a filmmaker who once was an object of criticism was gradually reassessed; and that within this trend of reassessment, non-Japanese critics were able to adopt relatively ahistorical positions, and make admittedly profound contributions, because they belonged to a different cultural context. A "sign," unchanged in itself, came to be read differently. Our aim is not to add to this shift of reading another reading of our own. What we need to do is transform Yasujirō Ozu himself as a sign. To this end, we aim to apprehend the many other elements that also give shape to this sign—to apprehend its plurality of faces, in other words. Changes in reading progress only along the temporal axis, but changes in the faces a sign presents occur synchronically, as play that transcends time. When we acknowledge in a single gesture their plurality of hybrid and coexisting faces, signs become productive in the true sense of the word and move people. If there is some significance to be found in changes of *reading,* it is only in moments when they align with such productive movement.

In their detailed study "Space and Narrative in the Films of Ozu," Kristin Thompson and David Bordwell seem to adopt a position other than that of the critics who dwell on things like formal perfection, at least when they hypothesize that "Ozu films can most productively be read as modernist, innovative works."[11] One can clearly sense, in their perspective that the films enable shifts in *reading* itself, an awareness of the imaginative potential that Ozu opens as an object of analysis. But insofar as modernism and innovation are themselves constructs prefaced on an emphasis of difference, they too offer little promise of yielding a discourse truly framed in the affirmative. Thompson and Bordwell borrow the concepts of "deviation" and "difference" from Russian Formalist theorists in attempting to measure the distance between Ozu and the classical Hollywood paradigm: "Seen against the background of the classical paradigm, the modernity of Ozu's work involves the use of specific spatial devices which challenge the supremacy of narrative causality."[12] Nothing in this quote is worded in the negative. And yet

---

11. Kristin Thompson and David Bordwell, "Space and Narrative in the Films of Ozu," *Screen* 17, no. 2 (Summer 1976): 41. Hasumi cites a Japanese translation: Kristin Thompson and David Bordwell, "Ozu sakuhin ni okeru kūkan to setsuwa," trans. Takehito Deguchi, *Yurīka* (June/August/September 1981). Hasumi wrote this chapter several years before the publication of Bordwell's 1988 monograph *Ozu and the Poetics of Cinema.* Chapters 8 through 10 of this volume were written later and reflect his engagement with Bordwell's study.

12. Thompson and Bordwell, "Space and Narrative," 42.

the very process of foregrounding difference entails a negativity of its own. As it is a key philosophical task of the present moment to critique this kind of negativity, we can hardly endorse the position described here. In fact, it is our mission to liberate Ozu from such gestures—gestures that measure his work negatively, according to its deviation from a paradigm. Of course, it would be meaningless to reject comparison on principle, and Thompson and Bordwell's study does also propose several potentially original contributions within the scope of its aims. But what stimulates us in Ozu is not simply that his films resist neat containment within the systems of cinematic code belonging to a given historical period. More than that, the films stimulate us because they are made in a way that exposes the very limits themselves of cinema as an expressive form. If Ozu is modernist and innovative, it is because he constantly confronts the impossibilities of cinema itself. Signs can only be productive to those living in the raw the moments at which cinema ceases to be cinema. We fixate on Ozu not because his films deviate substantially from the dominant paradigms of his period but precisely because, on occasion, they nearly cease to be films.

AGE AND TASTE

A common limitation of many of the Ozu commentaries that have been written to this point is that they do not attempt to apprehend Ozu's films as sites where a plurality of disparate elements synchronously coexist. This is precisely why the stakes of Ozu criticism often end up being reduced to the dull question of whether to embrace or reject a tofu maker who refrained from frying pork. And yet, at the instant when Ozu himself speaks of those two things, tonkatsu and tofu, does the theme of coexistence and intermingling not already at least begin to arouse our cinematic sensitivity?

It goes without saying that when Ozu invokes tonkatsu and tofu to represent an opposition of tastes, the image is no mere casual metaphor. Anyone who has followed Ozu's work from the early silent films through the late masterpieces will hardly need convincing that taste is a significant thematic detail in itself. The Japanese title of his final film *An Autumn Afternoon* translates directly as "the flavor of mackerel pike" (*Sanma no aji*) and thus echoes the title of *The Flavor of Green Tea over Rice* (*Ochazuke no aji*), a film he had already planned during the war but only completed, if in rather unnatural form, in 1952.[13] The late-period films in particular often have titles that make reference to taste, along with seasonal references like "late spring" or "early summer."[14] It could even be said that, without meal tables, whether in restaurants or households, Ozu's narratives would be incapable of beginning or ending. The next chapter will examine the narrational functions of eating in detail, but for now it bears observing that the opposition of the two terms *tonkatsu* and *tofu* as invoked by the filmmaker himself also plainly reflects some broader oppositions belonging to the culture of the Japanese table, such as between fatty foods and light fare, or between expensive dishes associated with eating out and economical meals prepared at home. As he aged, Ozu's tastes clearly drifted toward the simple and the everyday more than toward the rich and robust or the ceremonial. It could even be said that his claim to be a "tofu man" who made "nothing but tofu," which he made with a hint of boasting shortly before his death, amounted to an announcement of an aesthetic choice, between meat coated in batter and fried in oil on the one hand, and a soft, white plant protein often served uncooked on the other. The significance of opposing tastes, an opposition that might also be reduced to a plant/animal binary, becomes even more persuasive when we recall that Ozu left behind notes for an unwritten script that was to be titled *Radishes and Carrots* (*Daikon to ninjin*).

13. Mackerel pike, or *sanma*, is a fish associated with the fall season in Japan.
14. *Early Summer*'s Japanese title, *Bakushū*, refers to the wheat harvest and is a seasonal word associated with summer in Japanese poetry. Japanese cuisine also tends to feature seasonal ingredients in ways that associate different culinary tastes with different times of year.

But such analogies involving taste might also come across as products of a defensive stance toward the numerous critics Ozu faced in his later years, and therefore as rather abstract. In any case, it would be too naïve to take Ozu at his word when he tells us that his work was really that of a tofu-making tradesman who renounced pork. We should avoid falling for the familiar appeal here to the kind of wizened image that Japanese artists are ideally supposed to attain in their old age. Cinema is not the sort of relaxed expressive genre within which to ascend to the realm of elegant simplicity by devoting oneself to tofu. Above all else, it is a domain of physical action, one where someone eating nothing but tofu would hardly be fit for the role of director. We can also assert, to put it very concretely, that tofu is even unthinkable as a food of preference in the films of Ozu.

There is of course a character in *Late Autumn* (*Akibiyori*, 1960) who observes that with age he has found himself wanting to eat simple foods like *hijiki*, carrots, shiitake mushrooms, dried radish, and tofu, whether fresh or fried.[15] But when his friend teases him, calling his sincerity into question by pointing out his equal appreciation for steak and tonkatsu, he can only laugh at having been exposed. This exchange plays out between Nobuo Nakamura and Ryūji Kita, both admirers since their university days of the now-widowed Setsuko Hara. Hara, who has listened disinterestedly to this conversation, will later go out with her daughter Yōko Tsukasa for a tonkatsu dinner and even break into a satisfied smile as she declares that she has eaten herself full. Such scenes demonstrate that the world of the Ozuesque is by no means an unsophisticated one easily reducible to either/or choices between such binary alternatives as everyday simplicity or ceremonial indulgence. We find whiskey and sake, but also beer bottles on the tables at restaurants where former university or high school classmates meet from one film to the next. Meat-based European-style dishes and vegetable-

---

15. *Hijiki* is a variety of seaweed often served steamed or boiled with other vegetables.

based Japanese dishes are also not mutually excluding, but bountifully coexist. What is characteristic of Ozu, if anything, is precisely such intermingling phenomena, as they might be called. The character who talks about wanting to eat things like *hijiki,* dried radish, or tofu as a reflection of his changing tastes is merely parroting a familiar cliché in attempting to drive home a point: that he has reached an age at which to make marriage arrangements for his daughter. His close friend knows from experience that these lines are a pretext. We should also know from experience that they do not express Ozu's own true sentiments either, since the words *"hijiki"* or "dried radish" or "tofu" do little more here than emphasize a clichéd relationship between aging and taste in food. In this sense, we can think of Ozu characters as creatures destined to speak platitudes, to repeat clichés mechanically and with monotone affect, as if reciting entries from Gustave Flaubert's satirical *Dictionary of Received Ideas.*[16]

Another such exchange of clichéd dialogue occurs in *Early Summer* (*Bakushū,* 1951), for example, a film that begins with a hurried breakfast before the morning commute and a conversation about what kind of food to prepare for an older relative arriving on a visit from the countryside. Addressing Kuniko Miyake as the housewife of this intergenerational home, grandfather Ichirō Sugai says not to bother making anything special, that their visitor really likes simple things like *okara* (soybean pulp).[17] We have here the same commonplace cliché about tastes acquired with age. But then, mid-breakfast, the youngest son of the family, who is not even old enough for elementary school,

---

16. *Dictionnaire des idées reçues* is a compendium of aphorisms, published posthumously in 1913. It is viewed as a companion piece to Flaubert's unfinished comic novel *Bouvard et Pécuchet,* about two Parisian copyists who form a friendship around their enthusiastic yet misguided pursuit of all forms of knowledge. Hasumi is a Flaubert scholar, and the Flaubertian theme of the stereotype or cliché as a particularly bourgeois form of stupidity is discernable throughout this book and appears in his other writings as well.

17. *Okara* is a by-product of the tofu production process commonly used in simple vegetarian side dishes.

suddenly declares that he loves *okara,* instantaneously laying waste to the common received wisdom about the relationship between aging and taste in food. His words get a laugh out of the other family members seated around the table. But the important thing here is not whether *okara* has some deep relationship to tofu, for example. What is at issue is a certain kind of relationship of coexistence or juxtaposition, a relationship revealed through a young child's enthusiasm for a dish assumed to gratify the austere preferences of old age. Details such as a father old enough to marry off his daughter eating both tofu *and* tonkatsu in *Late Autumn* or an old man and a young boy sharing the same taste in food in *Early Summer* demonstrate how laughable it would be to believe, based on Ozu's own assertion, that his films reflect the exclusive craft of a tofu maker. What should not be overlooked here is the way that disparate elements coexist without mutual exclusion. It is through such phenomena that speaking of Ozu in the affirmative becomes possible.

JUXTAPOSITION AND COEXISTENCE

Such Ozuesque phenomena of juxtaposition and coexistence extend beyond the framework of family, lending highly symbolic valences to relationships between teachers and students as well. In Ozu, people who are supposed to occupy generationally distinct domains—domains that should be mutually exclusive from the perspective of social position or mentorship relationships in matters of knowledge or character—very often end up coexisting at the same level.

Take, for example, the country schoolteacher and his pupil who meet by chance in Depression-era Tokyo during the latter half of *Tokyo Chorus* (*Tokyo no kōrasu,* 1931). Former teacher Tatsuo Saitō and his old student Tokihiko Okada are each taken aback to see the other's difficult circumstances in the capital city. We also observe a similar relationship between father Chishū Ryū and son Shūji Sano in *There Was a*

Father (*Chichi ariki*, 1942) and between teacher Chishū Ryū and pupil Shin'ichi Himori in *The Only Son* (*Hitori musuko*, 1936). A rather strange feature of the early salaryman films is that it is not only students pursuing educations and careers who go to Tokyo, but also teachers who for one reason or another often leave behind positions in the provinces and take up new occupations in the city. The first dimension of the Ozuesque theme of juxtaposition and coexistence reveals itself in these character patterns, in the fact that no one stays behind in the countryside to continue teaching, that teachers show up in Tokyo and even change careers, as though following in the footsteps of their students. Reflecting the difficult times, teachers and students alike face daunting obstacles to securing suitable work. Similar characters appear even in Ozu's last film *An Autumn Afternoon*, but in that case there is a clear reversal of social position between the teacher and his students, with the emphasis placed on the way the students—now adults who have all attained a certain level of professional stability—decide to help their former teacher, now fallen on hard times, in recognition of his past service. The circumstances may thus be somewhat different than in *Tokyo Chorus* or *There Was a Father*, but a new aspect of juxtaposition and coexistence reveals itself here as well.

As a theme, the class reunion staged around the figure of a former teacher constitutes a very Ozuesque kind of scene. We also encounter this in *There Was a Father*, but what is characteristic in *An Autumn Afternoon* is the less-than-emphatic depiction of the former pupils' gratitude toward their old mentor. It is not necessarily to pull heartstrings that Ozu deploys the touching student-teacher trope here. The middle-aged men of *An Autumn Afternoon*, having all attained a certain level of social status, are even a little cold toward their old teacher when he reveals that he has never eaten *hamo* (sea eel), a relative delicacy, despite knowing how to write the Chinese character as he demonstrates by drawing it in the air with his finger. Their reaction is not quite cruel, but nearly so in its undisguised pity. It is also interesting that *hamo* is the only fish specifically singled out at a meal in a film with a title that translates literally as "the taste of mackerel pike" (*sanma*). But the important thing to note here is the setting to which the former students deliver their old teacher Eijirō Tōno once he has drunk himself to oblivion: an out-of-the-way ramen shop attached to his home and managed single-handedly by his daughter. In this instant, a pattern is clarified, wherein country teachers who follow their pupils to Tokyo mostly end up running humble lunch counters. In *An Autumn Afternoon*, Eijirō Tōno has become a purveyor of "Chinese soba" (ramen). In *The Only Son*, Chishū Ryū sells tonkatsu. And in *Tokyo Chorus*, Tatsuo Saitō runs a curry rice shop. There is not a tofu maker in sight, but there is a former teacher who makes his living from none other than tonkatsu, and even brazenly advertises "Tonkatsu" with a banner flown over the entrance to his shop—the very pork cutlet that Ozu himself claimed, however figuratively, never to make. In fact, there is no trace whatsoever here of dishes that would fall under the category of simple, light fare of the kind the filmmaker supposedly preferred as a matter of taste. Why then do these former middle school teachers end up running small single-item lunch spots, each specializing in his own dish, as if they had segmented the market by mutual agreement?

Here we can immediately point to the fact that shops serving things like curry rice, tonkatsu, and ramen, as venues offering casual meals to workers on a budget, occupy a space in between the daily routine of home cooking on the one hand and the exceptional, ceremonial quality of dinner parties in restaurants on the other (figs. 2 and 3). As we will have occasion to examine in detail later, the dramatic settings of Ozu's films include both dining rooms in family homes and private rooms at fine restaurants as privileged spaces, and the people who gather in and drift away from these spaces enact quiet conflicts, conflicts that can hardly even be described as dramatic. By comparison, spaces like curry rice shops offering casual lunches for salarymen are little more than sites of momentary passage, not places where people take root. As sites

2. *The Only Son:* Back of a pork cutlet banner in front of a shop run by former middle school teacher Chishū Ryū.

through which people pass without taking root, these lunch spots constitute an environment quite similar to middle schools. This is why those who as teachers once sent pupils off to Tokyo later end up performing the role of satisfying the appetites of young urban salarymen, however momentarily—this time not through knowledge but through simple and affordable cooking. Through the two quite distinct gestures of teaching and feeding, these former teachers repeat the same basic function in relation to young people. In other words, the new occupations that former country middle school teachers choose in the city are fundamentally continuous with their previous work, even if at first glance they may appear to be different. This is where we can observe the most striking expression of the theme of juxtaposition and coexistence in Ozu.

On this point, *Tokyo Chorus* is probably especially representative. Young salaryman Tokihiko Okada stands up to his boss, displaying the

3. *Late Autumn:* People dining at a restaurant in formal kimono and business suits.

kind of moral indignation one might expect of an earnest college student, and ends up losing his job in the process. Without informing his family, he sets out looking for new work and happens to encounter his former teacher Tatsuo Saitō. The teacher conscripts his assistance in the curry rice shop he has recently opened, and eventually helps his former pupil secure a position as a provincial middle school teacher, a position that leads eventually to his departure from Tokyo. Note the parallel here between a middle school and a curry rice lunch spot as sites of passage. The roles performed by the former teacher in both these sites of passage are also similar. The boundary line that separates teacher and pupil at the start of the narrative, when the positions they occupy are distinct, turns gradually ambiguous until their roles ultimately fuse at a lunch spot in the capital. Saitō and Okada, whose respective roles in the beginning were to teach and to be taught, come to support one another, working together to serve casual lunches to lowly salarymen. This shared activity then transforms unemployed Okada into a country teacher in his own right. It thus becomes clear that a lunch spot constitutes a very crucial site of passage for this salaryman.

But the important thing here is not that Saitō performs the same role in relation to young people at both the country middle school and the lunch spot in Tokyo. More significant than this readily observable consistency of roles is that details such as this are permeated by a synthesizing force, which ends up fusing things disparate and opposing, not expelling anything in the process. In other words, the same Yasujirō Ozu who instructed us not to expect tonkatsu from a tofu maker, and who declared that he himself made "nothing but tofu," made films that reveal themselves to possess many more faces than the opposition of tofu and tonkatsu, faces that transcend such simple binary relationships. Or rather, in the interest of avoiding whatever suggestions of a dialectical process the word *transcend* may evoke, call this a dissolving of oppositions, an interpermeation. It is this interpermeation that is distinctive of Ozu. Our aim is to follow the movement of fusion at sites of coexistence, such as where country middle school teachers and proprietors of cheap Tokyo lunch spots are both affirmed, and in so doing to affirm the being of Yasujirō Ozu. An Ozu narrative in the true sense is the movement itself of opposition into fusion. We will call this the *narrational structure* in order not to confuse it with the unique stories that organize the specific sequences of shots in each individual film. And we will call *themes* the significant details through which this structure shifts narratives, as integrated flows, toward different domains. The world of the Ozu film is a space of play intricately woven by the theme of juxtaposition and coexistence. Here, everything is mutually affirming, living a process of abundant fusion. And when this fusion becomes palpable in the form of some concrete event, the narrational flow pulsates with vivid rhythm. At such moments, the films of Ozu are no longer subjugated by static principles but descend upon the viewer's cinematic sensitivity as the pure movement of cinema. These are moments in which cinema quite literally *moves* us. Only those moved by the fertile chatter between narrational structure and thematic system will be able to liberate themselves from the image of Ozu as defined through absences and negative rhetoric. And liberation, precisely, is the mission that any discourse about cinema should embrace.

2

EATING

FOOD AND AUDITORY SIGNS

One effect of that low camera position we are all familiar with is that the contents of the plates and bowls arranged on Ozu's meal tables for the most part never enter our field of vision. It can thus be said that food is visually excluded from Ozu's compositions. Characters maneuver their chopsticks in ways that might even be called abstract, and only on rare occasions are we able to confirm with our eyes what they are eating. The meal table is generally depicted more as a place for conversation than as a place for consuming food. Conversation, in turn, is depicted more as a complex of eyelines than as a process of transmitting and receiving the content of speech, so much so that we find ourselves focusing mainly on apprehending the positional relationships among characters around the table rather than on following what is being said. This applies whether the scene is an everyday meal at home or a more or less ceremonious dinner party at a nice Japanese restaurant. The viewer mostly only understands what Ozuesque characters are eating by means of nonvisual signs—signs like the word *hamo* (sea eel), spoken by the former teacher in *An Autumn Afternoon*. In *Early Summer,* Kuniko Miyake remarks on the "delicious rice" while eating out with her husband Chishū Ryū and her sister-in-law Setsuko Hara. Her words give apt expression to the pleasure this housewife must feel as a restaurant patron liberated from the kitchen, while they also serve to skirt a mealtime debate over the social advancement of women in postwar Japan. But there is no close-up here to emphasize her expression as she savors this delicious rice. The camera remains exiled to the periphery of the man and the two women seated around the table in this private dining room. We know that they are eating tempura, but even that is mostly only communicated through their conversation. We learn from a casual comment that the tempura is *shako* (mantis shrimp), but the *shako* itself is barely pictured on screen. Compared to auditory information, visual information concerning food is exceedingly spare. The same is true of the scene later in the film when Hara comes home too late for dinner and sits alone in the kitchen at the end of the hallway to make a meal of leftovers. Following a long shot picturing her from the hallway, the camera then frames her from the front, showing her raising her chopsticks to her mouth from the plates and bowls arrayed on the table. But even here the information about her meal can hardly be called visual, since what is conveyed to us when she raises the rice bowl to her mouth is mostly only the sound of her slurping down what is probably the remainder of some *ochazuke*—rice and green tea. As a result, her gestures seem quite abstract. The same unrefined slurping sound is also the only thing emphasized when Shin Saburi eats in *The Flavor of Green Tea over Rice*.

Abstract though they may be, meals constitute a very important thematic system in Ozu, extending from the early silent films to the late masterpieces. Call this the theme of "eating," a theme that connects on a deep level with narrational structure in the films of Ozu while also supporting the unfolding of the plots. "Eating," as it forms a major Ozu-esque theme, does not necessarily require that things being eaten appear on screen. When Setsuko Hara acquiesces to marrying the son of Haruko Sugimura in *Early Summer,* for example, her future mother-in-law suddenly breaks into a wide grin and says, "Let's have some bean jam buns!" Spoken in the heat of the moment, the word *anpan* ("bean jam buns") is deeply moving, in part because it so directly communicates Sugimura's feelings as she loses her composure, but even more so because we find ourselves caught off guard by the richness of "eating" in its thematic expansion in Ozu. It may seem odd that the rather childlike image of bean jam buns is what narrates both the elation of Sugimura and the acquiescence of Hara to a marriage destined to uproot her to a place far from her family home, but while the presence of the word *anpan* may seem out of place, we come to realize that it is actually a thematic necessity. It will also become clear that this theme is charged with a narrational function, since this scene in which no bean jam buns are actually eaten will catalyze the transformation of Hara into a woman who defends the validity of her own decisions to both her parents and her older brother. Not that she becomes impudent or insistently self-assertive, but there will be subtle shifts following this episode in how everyone in the family relates to her. Her brother becomes angry, hardly believing that his younger sister would decide this most important of things without first consulting anyone. Her parents can only sigh in despair. Her sister-in-law is at first taken aback but tries somehow to understand her decision. The different attitudes within the family are highlighted, but her close family members are not the only ones bewildered by her determination where this marriage is concerned. We viewers are the first to be surprised when Hara gives her assent to marry Hiroshi Nihon'yanagi, an old friend of her brother who died in the war. The reason for our surprise is nothing so dramatic as an inability to comprehend her decision. We are surprised because its necessity as a matter of psychology has for the most part not been established in the plot. She does of course explain that she has discovered an ordinary but seemingly reliable partner in him, someone who was right there all along, and this explanation, in her own words, impresses us as being very Ozuesque indeed. But when we search for a *psychological* motivation, for just what has stimulated her change of attitude toward this single father who lost his first wife and who happens to be a fellow commuter on her regular train route from Kita Kamakura, we do not arrive at any narrative details that indicate necessity. What does come to mind is Sugimura's rather agitated exclamation of the word *anpan,* along with our surprise at the incongruousness of its effect. Intruding suddenly, as an auditory sign, the never-eaten bean jam buns have disrupted the narrational flow, sending Hara packing for faraway Akita Prefecture where her future husband has been transferred for work, causing her elderly parents Ichirō Sugai and Chieko Higashiyama to retreat from the extended family household to their birthplace in Yamato, and shifting her elder brother Chishū Ryū's career from the university hospital to a path in private practice in Kita Kamakura. The word *anpan* has been decisive to each of these transitions. That is to say, an unexpected intrusion by the theme of eating—which is not the least bit visual here—has transformed the narrational flow.

Some will perhaps protest that what is at stake is not the word *anpan* itself, but the way the situation reflects a particular social reality of postwar Japan: the dissolution of large, intergenerational households and what was then the increasing prevalence of nuclear families. That counterargument would not be invalid, in a sense. The postwar films, especially those made after *Late Spring,* do vividly reflect the fragmentation of the intergenerational household that was taking place in Japanese society at the time. But Ozu's films depict too many incongruous details to be mere symbolic expressions of that reality. If we were to discuss Ozu only from the perspective of how the films reflect social realities, most of those incongruous details would end up excluded, starting with the word *anpan*. And that is not all. The films before *Late*

Spring would also end up relegated to secondary status, as transitional experiments along the path to fully formed accomplishment.

We have already established that we are against such positions. This is not at all to say that we fundamentally reject observation of the ways social reality is reflected in Ozu, but we do oppose such approaches to the extent that they suppress the rich expressive features of the films. There are details that clearly appear extraneous when viewed through the lens of social realities like the dissolution of the household, and it is with the purpose of affirming these details that we have introduced the concept of the *thematic system*. The thematic system may be a concept, but its themes take persistently palpable form within concrete shots, whether as visual or as auditory information. What requires attention in cinema are the traces of these palpable things ingrained on the cinematic surface. We will therefore probe, in the various details of Ozu's films, the fact that the bean jam buns in question are unmistakably a theme.

EATING / NOT EATING

There is a scene in *I Was Born, but . . .* (*Umarete wa mita keredo*, 1932), a masterpiece of the silent period, that involves some mischievous boys playing in an empty field in a newly developed Tokyo suburb. They are engaging in an esoteric game in which pointing two fingers at a victim's chest causes him to drop to the ground, and the camera fluently tracks their movements across the field. Those who notice a sign attached to the back of one boy, warning that he has a weak stomach and should not be fed snacks, will find it hard not to smile at the attentiveness of the mother who has used a piece of cardboard, or maybe a scrap of wood, as a medium for addressing the other housewives of the neighborhood. Anyone who grew up along Tokyo's suburban rail lines in the thirties and forties will be able to testify, with some nostalgia, that this charming scene accurately reflects a particular kind of mother/

child relationship that existed at the time. Communication through the medium of children's afterschool play was an undeniable part of life for housewives in the new communities that formed along private commuter lines as they were extended from the Yamanote loop in central Tokyo to the peripheral parts of the capital, new suburbs without the history of either the city's affluent residential neighborhoods or its working-class areas, where the nuclear family was becoming the rule. Of course, the sign strapped to the boy's back in this scene is also a gag of the kind one expects from a silent movie. But preventing children from visiting their friends' homes and indulging in snacks without permission was undeniably a core focus of the disciplinary work of suburban mothers, and in this sense, this scene can even be regarded as a precious document of Tokyo history.

But what demands our attention here is not only how social reality thus intrudes into the film. This comic detail, which is insignificant from the perspective of the plot, serves a very important narrational function when it comes to the film's structure. Needless to say, this incidental episode, in soliciting a laugh, also introduces the theme of "eating" into the poignant portrait of salaryman life that *I Was Born, but . . .* paints. Eating also figures here as a comic motif related to the subtle shifts of power among the neighborhood boys, shifts that play out around the question of whether or not to eat a small bird egg. This theme, which might more accurately be called "not eating," even legitimizes the narrational necessity of a hunger strike, an otherwise surprising measure taken by the film's two young leads as their dejection upon witnessing their pencil-pushing father toady up to his boss gradually transforms to inconsolable resentment. Here, it is the theme of not eating that first (and quite vividly) crystallizes a common social phenomenon: the abject position of the lowly salaryman reduced to ingratiating himself with clownish behavior in order to obtain a promotion. The scene in which the two brothers stoke their mutual disgruntlement by mimicking each other's gestures, neglecting to apologize for their behavior even when scolded by their father Tatsuo Saitō, descends into a physical tussle that is both poignant and comical as they stubbornly refuse to eat before going to bed in tears. Reconciliation with their father must wait until the following morning, when it will be depicted through the eating of breakfast. The scene of the father and his two sons eating silently as they sit side by side at the edge of the yard is moving, but not merely because this reconciliation between a father and his sons evokes the powerlessness of the abject salaryman. What stirs the viewer's heart here is the way that the theme of eating takes concrete form in images and thus supports the narrative. The narrational flow of this film is clearly articulated around the theme of *eating*, which is also the theme of not eating.

FROM THE INSIDE OUT

I Was Born, but . . . not only persuades us of the importance of the theme of eating but also reminds us that this theme bears a deep relationship to another one: the theme of juxtaposition and coexistence. Eating not only plays an important part in supporting the Ozu film as a narrational structure; it also energizes a special magnetism capable of reconciling distinct details that, even in the thematic system, might otherwise be expected to oppose and exclude one another.

The distinct and opposing elements that concern us specifically are two kinds of space: the exterior and the interior. One characteristic of spatial structure in the Ozuesque "film" is that eating unexpectedly establishes deep connections between exteriors and interiors. Or alternatively, rather than a connecting or a fusing, it might be better to call what happens here a destabilizing of the spatial relationship between the inside and the outside. The films frequently depict situations where events that seem like spontaneous accidents cause meals meant to be eaten indoors to be eaten outside instead. In Ozu, the theme of eating quite often, and often quite abruptly, sends narrational space outdoors.

We are not limited, in illustrating this point, to the aforementioned oddly comical effect of the mother's snack interdiction attached to her son's back. There is also the scene in *I Was Born, but . . .* where, unbeknownst to their parents, the two brothers skip school to avoid a bully and head instead for the fields. Finding a place to sit in the grass, they open their bento boxes against a natural backdrop of trees and foliage and enjoy an alfresco lunch in what turns into a tremendously beautiful scene. And not only beautiful. There is also an incongruous humor here, when the older shop boy from the liquor store happens to pass by and the young brothers conscript him as an alibi in a clumsy attempt to hide the fact that they have played hooky—a humor that, along with a series of other gags, creates an idyllic and carefree atmosphere. This atmosphere bears a close resemblance to the best moments of the films that Jean Renoir or John Ford made in the thirties. At the point where bento lunches meant to be eaten in the classroom are instead eaten in an open field—a location quite apart from the one intended—the film's narrational flow strikes the lightest, most leisured tempo, and its spatial aspect becomes exceedingly delicate. This scene perfectly evokes the sense of freedom of eating outdoors under a clear blue sky, but more than that, it achieves a purely cinematic freedom as a product of the pleasant alignment of narrational flow and thematic system. Unexpectedly—but also as a narrational necessity—the theme of eating inverts the relationship between exterior and interior, rendering their opposition ambiguous. This gives rise to the impossible space and time unique to the Ozuesque film, and arouses our cinematic sensitivity.

Good Morning (*Ohayō*, 1959) is essentially the postwar version of *I Was Born, but . . .* ; while it of course differs on a number of plot points, it is nearly identical to the earlier film where the theme of eating and the spatial structure of inside-outside inversion are concerned. The revised subplot, in which the two brothers revolt against their father because he will not buy them a television set, clearly reflects the historical period, but in spite of any number of other such variations, the postwar film remains fundamentally unchanged when it comes to boys eating a meal outside. A similar episode is also portrayed in *Early Summer,* when two brothers again make a show of their displeasure with their father, storming out of the house as if to run away from home, but in *Good Morning,* eating is especially central. Because they have already initiated a silent protest against their parents, the brothers in this film are reduced to pantomiming when they find themselves faced with the need to communicate that their school lunch fees are due. The message does not succeed, and they decamp, with the kitchen rice tub, to a spot in the grass above the river. The fact that they make off not with a bento box prepared by a parent, but with cooked rice and its kitchen container, takes the impression of incongruity created by food brought outdoors to new levels. When they return home that evening, they find waiting in the living room the very thing that instigated their protest to begin with: a television set. This silly twist of plot is not the least bit moving, of course. What is moving here is not the narrative itself. We are moved, quite simply, by its spatial features. The moment this wooden rice tub native to the kitchen or the dining table is carried into the outdoors, the sky intrudes suddenly into the scene. In much of the film to this point, the sky has hardly been visible, cropped away by the nearly geometrical rows of rhyming houses and by the high river embankment in the background. Because the brothers choose a place near the top of the embankment to sit and eat their rice, Ozu's customary low camera position now has the effect of emphasizing the cloudless expanse overhead. Cars passing on a bridge in the distance also call attention to a kind of composition in depth that until this moment has mostly been missing from the film.[1]

---

1. The top of the embankment has of course already appeared earlier in the film. The boys walk on the embankment on their way to school, and the sky is dominant in these scenes—even during the fart jokes that open the film. But it is generally true that different spatial features apply in these scenes than in the ones that take place in the neighborhood below.

Mischievous boys in salaryman comedies are not the only ones who bring lunch outdoors. In *A Hen in the Wind,* an early postwar film often dismissed as a minor work, it is a prostitute who eats lunch outside, and also by a river, in an empty field. Returned soldier Shūji Sano is there too, having met this prostitute at the brothel where his own wife once sold her body to earn money for their child's hospital fees, while he was away at war. The prostitute brings her lunch to the riverside because she does not like being confined to the brothel all day long. Anyone can see how this scene relates to *I Was Born, but* . . . .. Indeed, Tadao Satō indicates this correspondence in his book *The Art of Yasujirō Ozu (Ozu Yasujirō no geijutsu)*:

> The idea for the scene in which a prostitute takes her lunch and escapes from a brothel to eat in a vacant lot is clearly a variation on the scene in the earlier film *I Was Born, but* . . . in which two elementary school students escape from school to eat their lunch in a field. But the same idea that was earlier used to humorous effect now becomes tragic, inverted into an expression of the wretchedness of a prostitute seeking respite from her daily life at a brothel. The irony that develops between the rustic wholesomeness of eating lunch in an empty field and the fact that the protagonist is a prostitute ashamed of her work probably encapsulates everything Ozu wanted to say here.[2]

It is clear, as Satō correctly indicates, that the situation has been inverted. Here, lunch is brought outdoors not by innocent children, but by a young woman whose innocence has been lost. What we are calling her lunch is also little more than some coarse homemade bread. The scene is all the bleaker because of the dramatic circumstances surrounding the conversation that takes place between the prostitute and the returned soldier: she has been reduced to selling her body in order to provide for her poverty and illness-stricken family, and he is beset

2. Tadao Satō, *Ozu Yasujirō no geijutsu,* vol. 2 (Tokyo: Asahi Shinbun Sha, 1978), 112.

with doubt about his wife's virtue. And yet, as reflections of the social plight of the immediate postwar years, these characters are perfectly unremarkable. Satō interprets the subject of this film as the "loss of spiritual innocence in Japan," and writes that "Ozu probably did not intend anything more than this. . . . With the defeat, Japanese people lost their spiritual innocence. In other words, they became something close to prostitutes. But even as prostitutes, at least they tried to preserve the innocence of eating lunch in the field." Even though he is aware that this kind of thing "really amounts to nothing more than prosaic didacticism," Satō maintains that it "still offers quite a warm-hearted message." He declares his affection for the film despite its prosaic didacticism, which even "borders on the reactionary," and ventures that filmmakers of this period "were able to depict, with pathos, the wretchedness and sorrow surrounding our collective sense of something having been lost."[3]

Like Satō, we have no intention of excluding *A Hen in the Wind* from the world of the Ozuesque over the fact that it differs in tone from the films of the late period that starts with *Late Spring*. On the contrary, we even maintain that it is one of the most important films in Ozu's entire body of work. But this is not because we are sympathetic to Ozu's "prosaic" yet "warm-hearted message" about preserving, in spite of it all, "the innocence of eating lunch in the field." It is not even clear, first of all, that Ozu intended such a message. In any case, we need to resist treating the scenario of eating in a field in isolation from both the narrational flow and the thematic system—reducing it, in other words, to a metaphor that anyone might easily imagine on an abstract level. The significance of *A Hen in the Wind* goes beyond things like the film's reflection of social reality or authorial intent as it tends to be imagined by those who seek to interpret such kinds of social reflection in psychological terms. Its significance lies instead in the fact that its narrational

---

3. Satō, *Ozu Yasujirō no geijutsu*, 2:112–13.

flow and its thematic system forge a certain inevitable relationship. In other words, this scene is moving not because of the misfortune of a prostitute who steals away from her brothel to chew on coarse bread in a field, but precisely because of the way that Ozu, who could only have staged such a situation outdoors, remains faithful to the world of his own films. "Eating" is also not the only theme that presents itself here. This scene also features the theme of sitting side by side, the Ozuesque significance of which will be addressed later. The fact that these themes narratively articulate two scenes staged in interior spaces—the quite uncomfortable preceding scene in a cramped tatami room at the brothel and the later scene of violence at the top of the stairs in Shūji Sano's house—reveals a raw aspect of the Ozuesque "film." It is quite significant that eating brings internal space and external space into forceful intersection. Indeed, despite seeming placated by his conversation with the prostitute chewing bread in the field, Sano ends up shoving his wife Kinuyo Tanaka down the stairs that very evening. The conflicts between exterior and interior spaces that border each other along the sequence of events—conflicts that can even appear violent—present the viewer with a radical opacity that exceeds things like readily understandable authorial intent. Why does Sano have to shove his wife down an unusually claustrophobic staircase—his wife, who only once sold her body to pay their child's medical expenses, and who also voluntarily confessed the fact—despite having just shown kindness to a prostitute? Psychology is not what explains these dramatic circumstances. They should be explained instead through the necessity of the linkages between narrational structure and thematic system in the Ozuesque "film." And this is where the Ozuesque "film" transcends the kinds of didactic lessons that Ozu himself may very well have intended after all. Before it manages to deliver the author's at once "prosaic" and "warmhearted" message, the scene of the prostitute's lunch in a field already opens toward various images from other films, including the vacant lot in *I Was Born, but . . .* and the riverbank in *Good Morning*. In doing so, it gives us a fresh appreciation for the Ozuesque fertility of the theme of eating. Of course, a different kind of cinematic memory is probably at work in *A Hen in the Wind*, where the impact of the staircase scene is concerned. Satō traces the inspiration for this scene to Naoya Shiga's canonical novel *A Dark Night's Passing*, which contains a scene involving a wife pushed from a train leaving the platform.[4] But the idea more likely came from *Gone with the Wind*, which Ozu had seen while stationed in Singapore during the war, and specifically from the moment in that film when Vivien Leigh tumbles down the stairs. In this respect, what is moving here has to do with the way a lavish Hollywood megaproduction made shortly before the Pacific War ends up reflected in the setting of a far-too-poor postwar Japanese household.

FROM THE OUTSIDE IN

The theme of "eating" not only opens interior space toward the outside, but also functions to summon the exterior inside. This is clear from the fact that what is important when it comes to eating is not only eating itself, but also the ways, through *eating*, that distances between people expand or contract, and how this creates turning points in narratives that then enter new stages as a result. We have just seen how this kind of dynamic introduces an element of passion into the narrative of *A Hen in the Wind*. The theme of eating, as fundamentally distinct from the portrayal of appetites or of the routine consumption of meals, can therefore be thought of as something like a narrational rite. This is why when characters eat, their physical gestures are often abstract.

The scene in *I Flunked, but . . .* (*Rakudai wa shita keredo*, 1930) in which some students place an order with a café girl for a nighttime bread

---

4. *A Dark Night's Passing* (*An'ya kōro*) is a canonical Japanese novel, first published in serial form between 1921 and 1937. The novel follows the life of young writer Kensaku who, like Shūji Sano's character in *A Hen in the Wind*, comes to resent his wife over a similarly traumatic incident involving another man.

delivery to their second-floor boardinghouse room gives quite wonderful expression to the theme of eating while performing the function of inviting the outside in. This film was made at a time when telephones and other modern communication conveniences were not yet everywhere at hand, so when the university students on the second floor of the boardinghouse decide to take a break from studying for their exams and summon Kinuyo Tanaka from the bakery across the street, they rely on the sound of a track-and-field pistol. This is a silent film, of course, so something more than an acoustic gag is required to elicit a suitable effect. After firing the pistol, the students use their bodies to spell the word "BREAD" (パン) in shadow letters on the backlit *shōji* screen in their window, sending a visual message to Tanaka at a distance. The combination of these two gags works to very good comic effect, but we will address that point in more detail later. The issue for the moment is the fact that a series of rather ritualistic gestures performed with the aim of eating to satisfy hunger ends up throwing that agenda to the periphery, ultimately becoming little more than a pretense to lure a popular café girl to the second floor of the boardinghouse. When she arrives in the students' room, the cheerful atmosphere she brings is momentarily disturbed by a neighbor's child, who shows up crying for bread, but her energy succeeds nonetheless in introducing an alluring feminine outside into the squalor of this all-male interior space. Tanaka also quietly passes some paper-wrapped sugar cubes to Tatsuo Saitō, the one among the flunkees who has found a special place in her heart, and when she does, the intrusion of the exterior into interior space by means of "eating"—in this case through a series of rather elaborate and gratuitous rites—performs the narrational function of shrinking the distance between two hearts all at once. Eventually, when it becomes official that Saitō has flunked out of college, he will instinctually stuff his face with cakes, one after the other, from his girlfriend's bakery.

But charming situations of this variety are not the only thing the theme of eating narratively introduces when it brings the outside intruding in. Take, for example, the moment in *The Only Son* when Shin'ichi Himori serves noodles bought from a nighttime street vendor to his mother Chōko Iida, who has come to visit him in Tokyo. Iida is unable to disguise her disappointment, having found her son unexpectedly married with a child and eking out a meager living as a teacher at a night school, and the arrival of the noodles decisively distances her heart from Tokyo. *The Only Son* was Ozu's first talkie. He had long avoided sound, and this film was produced using a system developed by "Mohara" (Hideo) Shigehara, the director of photography on almost all of his prior films. This first talkie deals with rather dark subject matter. As if to emphasize the darkness, the sound of a *charumera* [a reed instrument that noodle vendors of the period played to draw customers to their stands] calls out from the nighttime street behind the rental house where the film's young couple live. This is an unusual film in the sense that Shōjirō Sugimoto was in charge of cinematography, while Ozu's regular cinematographer Mohara worked on sound recording, with his later cinematographer Yūharu Atsuta still in an assistant role. Sugimoto's camera follows Himori outside, taking in the nighttime scenery as he buys bowls of ramen on the street. Here again, eating unmistakably summons the outside in, but this time the atmosphere is one of deep disappointment. When her son seeks her approval of the "pretty good noodles," Iida responds with silence. Disappointment is etched on her face. Anyone can see how these bowls of street noodles brought in from the outside have widened the distance between this mother and son. Here, "eating" is a narrational rite that gives shape precisely to disappointment and resignation. Have we ever seen another meal scene in cinema more disconnected from the subject of appetite? The pathos of this moment does not derive from the pitiful spectacle in itself of a son whose empty wallet has reduced the hospitality he is able to show his mother to a bowl of street food. It is less related to whatever mental image of poverty might have summoned forth the scenery of this bleak meal than to the way the thematic system of connections between the inside and the outside forms deep linkages with the narrational structure of spiritual distance. Beckoned by the sound of the *charumera*, Shin'ichi Himori does not even try to persuade his wife to go out for noodles in his place, but ventures himself into the darkness of the outside, calling out to the noodle man. His return with bowls of street ramen amounts to a more or less unconscious confession of having betrayed his mother's expectations. The nighttime scenery itself, of a bleak alley in a neighborhood surrounded by vacant lots that hardly seems part of the city, thematically conveys the dreariness of the rental houses located near late-night food stands that at the time were probably just starting to become popular. The relationship between outside and inside portrayed here may convince the viewer psychologically about the dramatic circumstances surrounding this dreary and uncomfortable meal, but it also lends this scene a narrational necessity that goes beyond such things.

This scene clearly connects with the bread delivery scene in *I Flunked, but . . .* in that food is brought from the outside in. But the takeaway noodle stand also reverses that relationship between inside and outside, strictly speaking, such that this scene also connects with the prostitute's lunch in the field in *A Hen in the Wind*. In both instances, the spatial displacement of food is an unmistakable source of pathos. Our concern lies within the relationship between the inside and the outside, not merely in the pitiful nature of the dramatic circumstances. The fact that something happens when food moves from outside in (or from inside out), and that that something tends to be either tragic or comic, is a narrational hallmark of the films of Yasujirō Ozu. Spatial features themselves are not especially important here. What is important is to recognize something core to the thematic system of the Ozuesque "film": a third kind of eating, distinct from both the habitual routine of the household meal and the ceremonial exception of the restaurant dinner party. We should acknowledge a further consistency in the fact that when food moves outside it is daytime, and when it moves inside it is night, but that consistency does not extend to the question of whether the emotional distance between characters correspondingly expands or contracts. In any case, relationships between people never remain the same after food has moved.

Now that we have established these characteristics, it should be easy to grasp the narrational significance of the overpriced sponge shortcake that Setsuko Hara brings home with her in *Early Summer*. The reactions that this dessert provokes when it arrives inside the house are comical in ways that recall the case of *I Flunked, but*. . . .. Upon reaching the kitchen, the first thing this shortcake does is ruin the appetite of housewife Kuniko Miyake, who is surprised to hear how much it cost. Next comes the appearance of Hiroshi Nihon'yanagai, a colleague of Miyake's husband Chishū Ryū, who announces that a situation has arisen requiring her husband to spend the night at the hospital where the two men work. Seating himself in the living room, he proceeds to set Miyake's share of the shortcake in his sights (fig. 4). Though the children have been put to bed, the eldest son now emerges, passing half asleep through the hallway on his way to the toilet, and the adults fall into an unnatural poker-faced silence, hiding their plates of shortcake under the table. Because we know Ozu's boys are capable of fierce defiance, we viewers also watch with bated breath until he exits without having caught on to the adults' performance. The harmonization of elements in this scene is superb and demonstrates Ozu's mastery as a director of comedy. But the comic effect of the role reversal performed by adults hiding cake from a child is not the only thing that merits highlighting here. Nihon'yanagi's misreading of the situation is also humorous, when he offers to finish Miyake's piece of shortcake for her, unaware that the extravagance has spoiled her appetite in her role as manager of the household finances.

Still, what commands our attention most is the way that the Ozuesque theme of eating food brought in from the outside at night introduces a change into the relationships among the people seated around this table. The shortcake on which Nihon'yanagi innocently fix-

4. *Early Summer:* Adults eating shortcake before a child interrupts.

ates foreshadows at a distance his eventual marriage with Hara. This cake is not a psychological motivation for their affection, of course. But the theme of eating does narrationally foreshadow the relationship between these two, which will in due course lead to their rather sudden plunge into marriage. No one at the table is conscious of this foreshadowing. Something far closer to anticipation in the psychological sense occurs in the scene where Hara and Nihon'yanagi sit together in a café near the Tokyo Holy Resurrection Cathedral and discuss Hara's older brother, who never returned from the war. His absence creates a privileged bond between them, and when the two look simultaneously at a framed painting hanging on the wall, and their conversation trails off, this anticipation even turns into something explicit. But this scene is connected to the theme of "looking." As for the shortcake brought in from outside, the fact that it reels in none other than Nihon'yanagi is clearly something that cannot lack significance in Ozu. In fact, although the dramatic circumstances are completely different, Hara unconsciously performs basically the same role here that café girl Kinuyo Tanaka plays in relation to flunkee Tatsuo Saitō in *I Flunked, but . . .*, while Nihon'yanagi doubles Saitō in turn when he nearly eats two plates of shortcake due to a small misunderstanding, whereas Saitō receives a package of sugar cubes as a special bonus delivery in addition to the bread for the room. These two films, made more than twenty years apart, also share the detail of a child who unexpectedly interrupts a late-night meeting of adults over food. This is not to say that Ozu consciously set out to recreate the nighttime café girl episode from *I Flunked, but . . .* with the shortcake scene in *Early Summer*. One film deals with student life during the economic crisis at the end of the twenties, the other with familial circumstances in the period following the war when Japan was finally beginning its recovery. But despite the different subject matter, we can nonetheless recognize "eating" as a common theme that, in both instances, fundamentally connects the outside and the inside, while at the same time introducing change into human relationships through the accompanying performances of ritualistic gesture. The point of these observations is merely this: to recognize these shared details as facts.

Whether the trajectory is inward or outward, the spatial position of something to be eaten changes in all of these scenes. The circumstances of characters are also reliably changed through the movement of food. Such movements of things and transformations of people imbue the Ozuesque "film" with a richness of aspect and a sensation of dynamism, whether or not the camera actually moves and regardless of how simple the plotting may be. Even as a purely technical matter, the displacement of food quite naturally harmonizes footage shot on location with footage shot on studio sets. These things can also be observed consistently, from the early silent films to the late masterpieces. In these instances, "eating" is both eating itself and at the same time also a narrational event other to eating that imbues the "film" with both movement and change. The reason we have sought to avoid describing Yasujirō Ozu exclusively from the perspective of cinematic style is because things that go by the name of style stand in the way of our ability to feel this movement and change. Attempting to define Ozu through absences and lack steals from us the look that should be attentive to the play between narrational structure and thematic system, making "eating" eating, and nothing more. Eating in itself does not arouse cinematic sensitivity. It is when it simultaneously occurs as something not eating that we find ourselves feeling deeply moved. To watch a film is nothing other than to feel that these two things simultaneously coexist on the same single segment of celluloid. When these two simultaneously coexisting things begin to multiply into three things or four things, a rich magnetic field of signification takes form on the screen. At such moments, thematic system and narrational structure play directionlessly against each other, preventing the shot sequence from reducing to any one single narrative. Otherwise put, eating exchanges knowing smiles with many things that are not eating, giving shape to images where they affirm one another without any mutual exclusion. The beauty of Ozu is to be found precisely in the ways that such plural narratives coexist. A cinematic sensitivity capable of feeling in the raw the play of signification as it directionlessly weaves is not one that will insist on defining what is specific to Ozu through litanies of negative rhetoric. In Ozu, eating is both pathos and humor, and can either open cinematic space toward the outside or contract it inside, joining people together in the process, or else distancing them from one another. As they link with each other, thematic system and narrational structure introduce decisive changes within the sequence of events, but the direction of their movements remains open, never subjugating a cinematic image to any one single meaning. We call films that teem with such kinds of change and movement free. The reason the films of Yasujirō Ozu are beautiful is above all because they are free. This freedom is something to be affirmed.

3

CHANGING CLOTHES

SARTORIAL STORIES

The films of Yasujirō Ozu are a narrational fabric constantly woven together—and as soon unraveled—by a plurality of simultaneously coexisting stories. Plots that seem to replicate in monotone fashion in the late-period films, such as a daughter's marriage, a father's sadness, or the dissolution of a family, are little more than occasions to send stimuli of various kinds rippling through this narrational fabric. The intention in calling these "occasions" is not to argue that Ozu himself did not believe in these stories, even as pretexts. In fact, he was hardly indifferent to them, much less dismissive of them. These stories are also indispensable to the production of thematic resonances, even as they replicate in monotone. But no relationship exists here in which one privileged story might lurk amid the plurality, putting other stories to use to enhance its own development. Stories of all kinds conspire on equal terms in the films, and the relationship among them is one of purely synchronous coexistence. Subjects like a daughter's marriage or a father's sadness transcend the framework of cinematic fiction specific to any given film and give shape to stories capable of appealing to anyone. But what concerns us more than this is that the theme of "eating" only becomes a story internal to the Ozuesque "film" and should therefore be expected to better demonstrate what is cinematically specific about Ozu.

When we consider what other themes, along with eating, support narrational flow in Ozu, the theme of "changing clothes" comes immediately to mind. In the late-period films in particular, we can distinctly observe a phenomenon in which a dynamic tension of costuming articulates the sequence of events: a tension, namely, between moments when men dress in formal morning coats and women ceremonial black kimono on the one hand, and when they wear informal, everyday attire on the other. A typical example is *Late Autumn* (1960), which begins with a memorial service and ends with a wedding. When such ceremonial costume lives in fertile harmony with everyday clothes, mingling intimately and exchanging smiles, a subtle vibration ripples the narrational fabric and Ozu's images take on the most elegant luster. We may groan a little when, yet again, a character suddenly raises the topic of arranging a marriage for someone's daughter. But however monotone the plot, we also start to wonder about the course of events that eventually will lead all involved to get dressed up, and we may even find ourselves anticipating the spectacle of wedding finery with bated breath. In other words, for the audience, the subject of a daughter's marriage will be presented as a story of "changing clothes." Where this happens, the viewer will have to tolerate a time and space that drifts in midair, spreading the suspense created by the interplay of casual wear and ceremonial clothing everywhere in the background behind shots that may seem to present little more than a slow accumulation of everyday gestures. From the moment that the age of a daughter is matter-of-factly introduced as a subject, what we might call an invisible tension between uncommon time (*hare no jikan*) and common time (*ke no jikan*)—or a drama of interpermeation between the two—is steadily, if quietly, woven together by means of clothing. The play that ensues between ceremonial costume and everyday attire brings fertile thematic expansion and complex narrational articulation to Ozu's films, in spite of the pretend monotony of their plotting. The theme of changing clothes also introduces change and movement into the narratives. Ozu's films are therefore sartorial stories in the truest sense. They are consummate costume dramas, but their costumes are not merely useful details constrained to enhance the narration of foreground plots about daughters and marriage. In fact, what is important here are not even the costumes themselves, but the vibrations that the gesture of changing clothes sends rippling through the narrational fabric.

People often cite Ozu's props and mise-en-scène, and in doing so tend to highlight things like his visual economy or the linear geometry of his compositions. But few have mentioned the role that costume plays in Ozu, despite the numerous occasions on which his characters remove or change clothing. In fact, it is hardly even necessary to reexamine the films to understand how dynamic an element clothing introduces into the narratives—an element that cannot be explained merely by invoking Ozu's personal aesthetic sensibility. Clothing is handed from husband to wife, tossed on the floor, folded, and hung from the lintel. It is left with the pawnbroker one moment and retrieved from a drawer the next. It becomes a dynamic stimulus acting upon all kinds of motions and gestures, a fact that should be clear to anyone. Clothing organizes a consistency of composition that lends Ozu narratives their characteristic features from the early through the late period. This consistency is not a matter of an ordered auteurist universe shaped by a set of monotone principles. It exists to send fertile movement, responsive to the environments of the individual films, rippling all around. What comes into view here is a filmmaker of a fundamentally different nature than the Ozu whose privileges have been bestowed through recitations of things lacking or rhetoric framed in the negative—not Yasujirō Ozu the perfectionist, who limited himself in pruning away possibilities of all kinds, but a more open Yasujirō Ozu, who smiles cheerfully while playing with the phenomena of the external world, performing gestures of affirmation more than exclusion, and of liberation more than restriction.

Recall, for example, the wonderfully staged scene from *The End of Summer* (*Kohayagawa-ke no aki,* 1961) in which the grandfather dresses himself to slip away for a visit to his mistress, sneaking around his nagging daughter while at the same time keeping his grandson distracted with a leisurely game. It should instantly be clear that the whole of this scene is performed as a costume drama—the drama of changing from house clothes into street clothes. Clothing clearly performs a dynamic narrational function here: namely, as part of the ritualistic process through which it is necessary to pass in order to leave the house. Relationships also intersect here in complex ways—between father and daughter, grandfather and grandson, and a man and woman. And then there is the strange coexistence of the adult and the child in the figure of the family patriarch who, despite his age, deploys a plan little different from a children's game to act on his desire. But the most important thing is that his changing of clothes is depicted not in a single coherent motion but as an accumulation of gestures, interrupted by his daughter passing occasionally through the hallway in the background as he skillfully evades her sight line. This scene elicits broad smiles. There is no intrusion of lack or negatively framed rhetoric, only cheerful details that yield a swirl of elegant coexistence. And despite the fact that it consists only of static shots taken from consistently low camera positions, with no traveling shots or pans or fades, the close linkage it establishes between narrational flow and thematic system introduces elegant movement into the film.

But there is more to say about this scene than only that: the success of Ganjirō Nakamura's touching efforts to change clothes and slip out of the house will ultimately end up compelling the entire family to change in turn, but into formal morning coats and crested kimono. A narrative unity thus emerges that should not be overlooked. The final scene, of the men and women of the family dressed in mourning attire, passing in slow procession across a bridge, corresponds precisely, within the Ozuesque thematic system, to the playful spectacle of changing clothes performed earlier by the now deceased patriarch. Death visits suddenly in Ozu's films, but the costuming of these characters in morning coats and black crested kimono has been far from sudden. The theme of clothing, together with the forward movement of the narrational flow, has slowly but steadily prepared this occasion for ceremonial attire. This, precisely, is what it means to say that Ozu's narratives are constructed on the interpermeation of common and uncommon time. This is also why it is hard not to feel a certain foreboding in *Tokyo Story* (*Tokyo monogatari*, 1953), for example, when we spot a baseball uniform hanging on a laundry line outside a window at Shirō Ōsaka's boardinghouse apartment, where his elderly parents Chishū Ryū and Chieko Higashiyama have stopped to rest on their way back home to Onomichi. It would be easy to write off this playful piece of clothing as mere stage dressing, something placed in the background to evoke the atmosphere of boardinghouse life. But within Ozu's thematic system, it is clearly also a detail that inevitably draws the viewer toward clothing, and toward the changing of clothes. In fact, it is only a short while later in *Tokyo Story* that we learn the elderly mother has fallen critically ill. No one who sees this film is likely to forget the conversation that ensues between her son and daughter back in Tokyo, when Haruko Sugimura asks her brother Sō Yamamura if he thinks they should pack formal wear for the trip to Onomichi, despite the fact that their mother is as yet still alive. Of course, circumstances do ultimately require the characters to assemble there in mourning costume. Only Shirō Ōsaka, who is still young and single, joins the funeral procession in an ordinary gray suit rather than a formal coat. Needless to say, in reflecting his difference of social position, his suit at the funeral corresponds precisely to the baseball uniform that we have already seen hanging at the eaves at his boardinghouse. The fact that he is the one able to play the exceptional role of slipping out of the funeral ceremony, leaving the temple building during the chanting of the sutra and sitting on a ledge overlooking rows of gravestones, is also an inevitability brought about by Ozu's thematic system of clothing, and it is far from sudden as a narrative development.

Of course, the close association of narrational flow and thematic system around "changing clothes" also comes into play when the clothing is not mourning dress but festive wedding costume. Consider the case of *Late Autumn*, for example. The plot of this film—a humorous scenario involving three middle-aged men who gang up to arrange a marriage for the daughter of a now deceased friend from their college days—revives the widowed father and daughter character pattern from *Late Spring* but this time substitutes a beautiful widowed mother in the parent role. *Late Autumn* is not obviously a remake of *Late Spring* as *Floating Weeds* (*Ukigusa*, 1959) is of *A Story of Floating Weeds* (*Ukigusa monogatari*, 1934), and unlike the long scene of clothes changing in the earlier film, it is not widowed parent Setsuko Hara who disrobes here, but Nobuo Nakamura, one of the middle-aged men. Upon arriving home, Nakamura passes his bag to his wife Kuniko Miyake, then stands in the middle of the living room removing his clothing piece by piece in the manner of an Ozuesque character. As the scene unfolds, he and his wife will discuss the topic of finding a suitable groom for his late friend's daughter. But as in the case of Ganjirō Nakamura in *The End of Summer*, his changing of clothes will become drawn out by a series of interruptions. First, his hungry young son shows up and demands to be fed, introducing another Ozuesque theme quite separate from clothing. Next comes his eldest daughter, who has run home after a fight with her husband and emerges from the bath to test her father's patience. Kuniko Miyake plays the teasing wife, needling her husband over his attentiveness to his late friend's beautiful widow and probing him about his exploits during his college days. Hunched at the edge of the table, Nakamura is thwarted not only from changing into his house clothes, but also from going straight to the bath, since the gas has been left on and the water is too hot. When he retreats into the darkness of the hallway, looking beleaguered in his long underwear, his young son follows him partway to throw a pantomimed knockout punch behind his back.

In this scene as well, it should be clear to anyone that various disparate elements intersect in complex ways, ways that demonstrate the fact that Ozu's narratives are by no means reducible to any one simple principle. The spectacle of Nobuo Nakamura retreating from the family in his underwear contrasts with the exit performed by Ganjirō Nakamura, who eventually does succeed in changing his clothes, but the scene can also be said to elegantly foreshadow the reluctant mentality his late friend's daughter will exhibit when it comes to her marriage arrangements. Various detours and complications persistently delay the moment when all the film's characters will finally put on festive attire and direct their gazes at Tsukasa Yōko dressed in bridal costume. The interrupted changing of clothes thematically indicates this stagnation of narrational flow. It seems to us that the possibility of liberating Ozu from the image of a great auteur of absence—a definition derived from litanies of negation—depends on viewers recognizing, one by one and with their own eyes, things of just this nature. In fact, at moments when someone begins to change clothes, we can sense in our skin just how much ample thematic swelling and just how many intersections of narrational elements give shape to the films of Ozu. Much like eating, changing clothes is also something around which people both come together and drift apart.

What the foregoing considerations make clear is that sartorial stories, as costume dramas, are most elegantly captured in images where they surpass simple dualisms like the opposition of formal versus casual wear. We made a similar observation about the theme of eating: it does not always consist only of either ceremonial dinners in fine restaurants or everyday meals at home but also involves a second modality in between, where food moves through space, as it were, and in so doing orchestrates the richest of play between thematic system and narrational structure. In both *The End of Summer* and *Late Autumn*, the action of changing clothes takes place in full view of others. Neither Ganjirō Nakamura nor Nobuo Nakamura has a space in which to change in private. As a result, a humorous kind of suspense develops in the former instance, while the latter takes on a comical tone that also elicits a degree of empathy. The comedic effect in these scenes clearly derives from the architectural characteristics of Japanese houses and from customs pertaining to household life. But the theme of changing clothes is not in itself an exclusively humorous one. In *Equinox Flower* (*Higanbana*, 1958), we again encounter basically the same clothes-changing scenario as in *Late Autumn*, and not once, but twice: Shin Saburi changes after the wedding ceremony that opens the film and again when he returns home after stopping at the bar where his friend's daughter works. But despite the presence of his wife Kinuyo Tanaka, who assiduously picks up and folds his garments as he tosses them on the floor, his undressing expresses something severe. Saburi is frustrated. In the first instance, he is dissatisfied by his daughter's indifference toward a proposed marriage arrangement. In the second, he is displeased because he suspects her of having a relationship with a boyfriend of her own choosing. In both cases, his frustration agitates the motions with which he changes clothes.

BUSINESS SUITS AND SCHOOL UNIFORMS

It is worth noting that the theme of changing clothes is not something limited to the late-period films and their narratives about efforts to marry off daughters. Clothing already forms an important narrational element of the Ozuesque "film" in the early silent period, except that in the early films, "changing clothes" is not something directly connected to weddings or funerals, but is instead often depicted in the context of job seeking, a ritual undertaken to transform one's social position from student to adult citizen.

In *I Flunked, but . . .*, for example, flunking is not solely a matter of failing to pass the graduation exam. It figures first and foremost as a matter of sartorial difference, separating those who pass the exam from those who do not. When the graduates in this film change into suits and begin their job search, flunkee Tatsuo Saitō stays behind in his second-floor boarding room, still dressed in Japanese house clothes. His friends, who until just the day before wore stiff-collar button-up school uniforms, present a thrilling sight when they show up outfitted in three-piece suits accessorized with fedoras and hunting caps. Saitō slumps into despondency as this difference of costume brutally illustrates the difference in social position that now exists between them and him. But what is interesting here is not merely how these respective costumes emphasize the separation between students and young professionals. In *I Flunked, but . . .*, clothing is already narrated as a story from the opening scenes, where a perfectly ordinary white dress shirt takes on a complex narrational function. The Tatsuo Saitō we encounter here, in the student boardinghouse the night before the exam, is not studiously memorizing information or underlining passages in his textbooks. Instead of studying, he is dutifully writing the answers to exam questions on his shirt. The previously discussed arrival of café girl Kinuyo Tanaka with a bread delivery takes place in the midst of these preparations for cheating. When she gives her favorite flunkee some sugar cubes wrapped in paper, she also promises to give him a necktie as a graduation gift, something she has been knitting for him while already imagining him in a business suit. Along with the theme of eating, the theme of changing clothes has therefore clearly already been introduced in this second-floor student boarding room.

University exams and the tactics deployed by students to pass them are subjects also depicted in the earlier film *Days of Youth* and will appear again in *Where Now Are the Dreams of Youth?* (*Seishun no yume ima izuka?*, 1932), which features an elaborate cheating scene. This is therefore very familiar territory for the early Ozu of the silent period. But in the case of *I Flunked, but . . .*, it bears emphasizing that the cheating involves a piece of clothing—a dress shirt—conscripted for the purpose. It is hard not to laugh at the seriousness of Saitō's expression when he painstakingly runs the tip of his pen over the white fabric, and at how this garment meant to be worn strays comically from its proper use. But the next morning, while he is still asleep, the shirt is sent to the cleaners, to return as a freshly pressed mess of inkblots only after his exam failure is assured. Saitō's failure to "change clothes" thus leads to his failure to graduate and robs from him the chance to wear a business suit, leaving Tanaka's considerately knitted necktie hanging adrift in midair. In an effort to assuage her man's despondency, she proposes that he put on a suit and take her out, leaving him no choice but to change clothes in front of a female gaze. This changing of clothes marks the climax of *I Flunked, but . . .*: Saitō slowly removes his house clothes, puts on his suit, and hangs the tie around his neck, taking his time much as Ganjirō Nakamura, Nobuo Nakamura, and Shin Saburi will do when they change clothes in the late-period masterpieces. Tanaka tears up as she watches. To be truly moved by this, it is probably necessary to understand the customs that surrounded student life and clothing in the late twenties and early thirties. We can no longer directly relate to the sight of this young couple from an era when putting on a suit and tying a necktie functioned in itself as a rite of passage into adult society. And yet this scene does move us deeply. What is moving is not the love story of a flunkee and a café girl, but the way an accompanying sartorial story steadily unfolds, arousing our cinematic sensitivity in the process. The Ozuesque theme of changing clothes, which achieves its culmination when Tanaka ties the necktie she has knitted around her man's neck, thus links elegantly with narrational structure, stirring emotions related to things beyond mere questions of period custom.

Needless to say, the clothing story that supports the narrational flow in *I Flunked, but* . . . exceeds the boundaries of this single film and activates significant resonances with various details in other Ozu films. *Spring Comes from the Ladies* (*Haru wa gofujin kara*, 1932) is now lost, and *I Graduated, but* . . . (*Daigaku wa deta keredo* . . ., 1929) exists only in incomplete form, but we know from the screenplays for these two films that a clothing tailor appeared in both, in an important role in the former and in the opening scene of the latter, where suit measurements are taken at a student boardinghouse in anticipation of graduation. But even putting on a newly tailored suit and interviewing for work does not mean work is immediately to be found. In *I Flunked, but* . . ., even the students who pass the graduation exam and earn the right to change into business suits fail to secure employment. Therefore, the ritual of changing into a suit does not necessarily confer the credentials of adulthood. In this sense, it would not necessarily be incorrect to conclude that these tailored three-piece suits purchased in vain are not components of a uniquely Ozuesque sartorial story so much as details that simply represent period social conditions, like the difficulty of securing work in times of economic crisis. Yet there is another story in the Ozuesque "film" that clearly corresponds to this repeated motif of ordering suits for unemployment, and it becomes clear that, as a pair, the two give shape to a theme.

The motif that corresponds to men changing into suits is the motif of women parting with kimono. As a symbol of difficult household finances, the pawning of a wife's kimono in itself does not constitute a theme unique to Ozu. Nevertheless, anyone who witnesses how women's clothing is converted into money to survive times of crisis in films like *Tokyo Chorus*, *The Only Son*, and *A Hen in the Wind* will immediately understand that, in prewar Ozu, both changing into suits and parting with kimono bear especially deep relationships to financial matters.[1] Clothes are not mere personal accessories; they are privileged objects that can be exchanged for money. This is also demonstrated in both *A Story of Floating Weeds* and its postwar remake *Floating Weeds*, films in which costume naturally plays an important role since they tell the story of a traveling theater troupe. We see this clearly when the members of the troupe disband and a merciless secondhand goods dealer shows up to take possession of their stage costumes.

THE WOMAN WHO CHANGES CLOTHES

But clothing in Ozu is not always a detail that functions simply to accentuate the economic aspects of the story. Even the mere sight of clothing is often enough to arouse cinematic sensitivity. Moments exist in Ozu when just observing what characters are wearing feels like a startling encounter with an unknown cinematic event, even if the clothing worn is nothing especially showy or opulent. These kinds of cinematic events also tend to occur more often in the films that Ozu himself often dismissed as failures.

Take for example the pleasant atmosphere at the beginning of *Where Now Are the Dreams of Youth?*, a film regarded as a failure for the simple reason that it was made to take advantage of an interruption in the production of *Until the Day We Meet Again* (*Mata au hi made*, 1932). Once again, the subject is the period of transition from student to professional life. A wonderful tracking shot passes across rows of students seated on the grass in stiff-collar uniforms and academic square caps before coming to rest on members of the pep squad gesticulating for the crowd in short-sleeve T-shirts. The repetition of mechanical gestures by these young men flapping their arms and legs and exuding

---

1. *A Hen in the Wind* (1948) is a postwar film, but the story concerns wartime circumstances.

camaraderie in light American-collegiate apparel coexists alongside the stiff collars and angular caps of the seated students uniformed in black. This is a silent film without music or sound effects, and this visual juxtaposition alone sends a vivid sensation of movement, and smiling cheer, rippling through the scene. Such bright optimism contrasts with the oppressive gloom that descends later in the film when the students change into business suits upon graduation. Perhaps the lighthearted tap dance performed here by the pep squad forms something like an invisible center, even in relation to Ozu's subsequent films—something like an ideal image that it will never again be possible to recreate.

Or consider *Dragnet Girl*, a film about which Ozu himself wrote in his notebook during production: "I can't find my stride; I am in distress." It would be very unfortunate if this deeply beautiful crime film were to be understood as little more than a piece of juvenilia, a mistake in the career of a great auteur, merely because of the ways it deviates in subject and setting from the rest of the oeuvre. We know, of course, that Ozu made only one other crime film involving police: *That Night's Wife*. Even if we add *Walk Cheerfully* (*Hogaraka ni ayume*, 1930) with its juvenile delinquents, the total number remains only three. It can certainly be said that such subject matter was not Ozu's specialty. Nonetheless, viewed as a sartorial story on the theme of "changing clothes," *Dragnet Girl* can be said to yield some of the most beautiful of Ozu-esque moments.

As already described, *Dragnet Girl* is a romantic melodrama set in the criminal underworld, but when viewed from the perspective of clothing, it turns out to include some surprising ideas. Kinuyo Tanaka works by day as a typist at an office in the Marunouchi district of central Tokyo, but at the close of business she changes from trim professional dress into loud, provocative outfits and heads out into the nightlife. She is the mistress of boxer-turned-bodyguard Jōji Oka and reigns as queen at a dancehall frequented by gangsters. Her role is quite difficult indeed to reconcile with the image of late-period Ozu. As in

That Night's Wife and *Walk Cheerfully*, the legible text in the scenery of *Dragnet Girl* is written in alphabetic letters, not in Japanese script. Moments like when Jōji Oka appears donning a double-breasted suit under the harsh light of naked bulbs in a dim boxing gym would even be at home in an American film of the period. Japanese elements are limited basically to the kimono worn by Sumiko Mizukubo as the record shop girl who attracts Oka's interest, and the academic stiff-collar uniform and square cap worn by Kōji (Hideo) Mitsui in the role of Mizukubo's delinquent college student brother. Without this kimono and typically Japanese student uniform, the mostly abstract staging might have erased all traces of national specificity, but Ozu deliberately preserves a certain distinctiveness in the costumes we see on screen. This does not mean that he was insistent on maintaining at least some element of Japaneseness. What is at issue here is, quite simply, that the world of the films requires the coexistence of disparate elements. And it is upon such imbalances that sartorial stories in Ozu weave their fertile play. The beauty of *Dragnet Girl* itself derives from an imbalance on the level of dramaturgy, wherein Mizukubo, with her big eyes and pronounced features, wears a kimono and acts with quiet restraint, while Tanaka, with her narrow eyes and classically Japanese feminine charm, plays the role of a willful gangster's moll and even ultimately clutches a pistol. In playing a woman who works as a company secretary by day but by night puts on evening attire and goes out into the underworld, Tanaka inhabits a role that perfectly embodies the Ozuesque theme of changing clothes. But just why should this in itself be so affecting? The film's plot—a gangster finds himself taken with a new woman and pulls a final job on her behalf only to enlist the aid of his faithful mistress in attempting an escape when things go awry—is of course nothing moving. What arouses our cinematic sensitivity relates to the way that Tanaka, as the very embodiment of changing clothes, responds with her whole body when Oka tells her to "get over here," talking like a character from a Raoul Walsh gangster picture. If things like the full-on embrace of a gangster and his moll are to be excluded from the discussion surrounding Ozu because of their remoteness from his late-period style and because they undermine the unity of the oeuvre, we gladly elect to sacrifice auteurist unity in the interest of rescuing this embrace. We also gladly affirm the impact of another moment, when Tanaka's evening dress slips off her right shoulder, revealing soft bare skin from the curve of her neck to her breast. But such affect is perfectly natural where sartorial stories accompanied by the theme of changing clothes are concerned. If anything, focusing our attention on moments such as these should better enable us to touch the richness of the Ozuesque "film."

In *Dragnet Girl,* Kinuyo Tanaka moves the viewer by throwing herself, quite literally, into the role of a "woman changing clothes," but this is not the only early film that revolves around the changing of clothing. Changing clothes is also central to the narrative of *The Lady and the Beard* (*Shukujo to hige,* 1931), a film that places emphasis on the comedic aspects. This film shares characteristics with the comedy of manners and even includes some humor at the expense of the imperial family that would be unthinkable today, but its trivial plot is little more than a pretext for a succession of nonsense gags. Compared to *Tokyo Chorus* and *I Was Born, but . . .*, films made only a little later that both placed Ozu at the top of *Kinema junpō* magazine's annual best ten rankings, this light piece of work can hardly be considered a great accomplishment. The silly excuse for a plot revolves around a university kendo (fencing) captain who at first goes around wearing a full beard and grungy Japanese clothing—a pleated masculine kimono and a square cap of the kind worn by students. When it is time to find a job, he shaves his unkempt beard and dapperly sports a three-piece suit, transforming at once into an elegant "modern boy" who captures the hearts of women. But it should be clear to anyone, despite the foolish scenario, that Tokihiko Okada serves the same thematic function, in transforming from a scruffy college student into an unrecognizable ladies' man, as Kinuyo

Tanaka in *Dragnet Girl*. On its own, changing clothes possesses little significance, but in linking with narrational elements of various kinds, the theme gives way to both a crime melodrama like *Dragnet Girl* and a comedy of manners like *The Lady and the Beard*. Changing clothes does indeed articulate narrational flow, but its direction remains unfixed and always open. Herein lies the thematic richness of Ozu, which leaves no room for the intrusion of rhetoric framed in the negative. When changing clothes comes into play, it introduces what we might call a productive disequilibrium into the sequencing of the foreground plots, a disequilibrium rife with stimuli toward narrational movement.

There is nothing the least bit moving about the plot itself in *That Night's Wife* (1930), for example, which concerns an honest salaryman who resorts to robbery in order to obtain money for his sick daughter's medical care. But the film is deeply affecting nonetheless, once again because a sartorial story unmistakably lives within it. As in the case of *Dragnet Girl*, the title alone indicates that this crime drama will be a thoroughly nocturnal film. The setting in the first part of the film is Tokyo's Marunouchi office district, then an apartment at a remove from the city center in what follows. Nighttime exteriors are central to the film's opening scenes, in which Tokihiko Okada commits an armed robbery and flees police in the shadows of tall buildings, while the latter scenes revolve around the interior drama that unfolds back at his apartment after a detective forces his way inside. Most of the furnishings in the interior space suggest a lifestyle indifferent to Japanese custom, to say the least. Only the kimono worn by his wife Emiko Yagumo as she wearily attends to their sick daughter offers any indication of the nationality of these characters. As is often the case in Ozu films of this period, Hollywood movie posters are visible on the wall—probably authentics. Escaping in the middle of the night to this apartment that could be located anywhere, Okada cannot help but confess to his wife that the yen notes he then pulls from his pocket are dirty money. The doctor has informed them that tonight will be a critical time for their daughter, who lies sick in bed. At this point, there is a knock at the door. The wife urges her husband to hide in the shadows, behind the curtain.

The moment when the detective arrives at the apartment rouses us because it features an effect that in theory should be excluded from Ozuesque technique, at least as it is understood today. First, the camera moves rapidly in the direction of the knocking, closing in on the doorknob. A dissolve transitions to a shot taken from the other side of the door: of a hand, shown knocking in close-up. The same dissolve effect repeats before the detective then makes his appearance, to the wife's protests that her husband is not home and that their daughter is seriously ill. The detective, who seems to have borrowed his rugged look from George Bancroft and his stout build from Walter Huston—a name legible on a movie poster hanging in the background—peers hawk-eyed into the room before announcing that he will just wait if her husband is out, pushing his way inside. Okada has left his hat on the table. As if to reproach the wife for her lie, the detective picks it up and places it gently over her hair, which is wrapped into a bun in the back (fig. 5).

This moment in particular is very moving. Emiko Yagumo, wearing the bun and kimono typical of a Japanese housewife, removes the hat with a slow gesture. But before she does, her eyes point toward the floor, as if she has resolved to do something. Or rather, it seems that this fedora has introduced a transformation into the narrative, in covering her hair for only a brief moment and contrasting with her kimono. In fact, when the detective then senses the presence of the husband in the shadows and draws his gun, the wife retrieves the pistol she has been concealing and sticks it in his back. But she does not stop there. Having disarmed him, she strikes a pose with arms akimbo, brandishing both her weapon and his. Ozu also puts a pistol in Kinuyo Tanaka's hand at the end of *Dragnet Girl,* but what is especially beautiful in *That Night's Wife* is the emphasis on the sartorial disequilibrium of Yagumo clutching two handguns while wearing a housewife's kimono (fig. 6). A similar sartorial imbalance has supplied the immedi-

5. *That Night's Wife:* Emiko Yagumo reproached by a detective for hiding her husband.

6. *That Night's Wife:* Wife with guns.

ate impetus for her transformation from a woman attending to a sick daughter into a woman fighting for her husband: the fedora on her housewife's hair bun. Here again, clothing performs an unmistakable narrational function—of productive disequilibrium, charged with momentum toward movement. But struck as we are by the direct, unexpected beauty of Yagumo as this felt fedora covers her hair for a fleeting instant, it is also hard not to be distracted by the more fantastic, perhaps implausible, idea that the Jean-Luc Godard who accessorized Jean Seberg with Belmondo's fedora in *Breathless* (*À bout de souffle*, 1960) might quietly have seen this silent Ozu masterpiece. In any case, we can assert that Yagumo and Tanaka live two of the most beautiful of moments in the sartorial stories of early-period Ozu: the former when she sports a fedora in *That Night's Wife*, and the latter when her dress slips off her shoulder in *Dragnet Girl*. Clothing in these instances clearly performs a narrational role that goes well beyond mere ornamentation.

CLOTHING AND SEPARATION

Kinuyo Tanaka typifies the woman who changes clothes in *Dragnet Girl*, and Tokihiko Okada the man who changes clothes in *The Lady and the Beard*, but nearly all Ozu characters live within a dynamics of clothing in one sense or another. If we understand clothing in terms of things that generally cover the body or conceal the skin, even the tattoos on Kihachi's arm in *Passing Fancy* (*Dekigokoro*, 1933) or Minoru Takada's wrist in *Walk Cheerfully* can be included here. In fact, Takada's small-time hood in the latter example—a character known around town as "Ken the Knife"—can probably be regarded as another "man who changes clothes," since he ends up having his tattoo removed out of affection for respectable girl Hiroko Kawasaki. *Walk Cheerfully* is a crime film, set in a port town recalling early-thirties' Yokohama, that teems with stylish fashions, so much so that it too should probably be called a costume drama. Character gestures lend punctuating accents to the film, starting with the tap dance routine that a group of gangsters use as a greeting card and extending to things like dusting off a hat dropped on the floor or straightening someone's collar—an exercise in costume play filled to the brim with sophisticated fashions. Hats also serve the function of indicating the end of the workday, by disappearing one by one from the hooks where they hang on the wall at the office. Then there is *Tokyo Chorus,* where out-of-work Tokihiko Okada's hat turns into a fish scoop in the hands of his son. One way or another, hats stray into territory foreign to their conventional use as accessories to cover the head. The expressive richness of hats also immediately recalls the wet hand towels that Takeshi Sakamoto drapes over his head in *Passing Fancy* and *A Story of Floating Weeds,* exercising a Japanese custom characteristic of the hot season that Ganjirō Nakamura will also adopt in the postwar film *The End of Summer.* Hats cease to serve very significant narrational functions in the films made after the war, when adult males generally stopped wearing them, and in this sense they can be regarded as a reflection of contemporary fashion, something eventually excluded from the world of the Ozuesque with the changing times. But the theme of changing clothes remains consistent in its narrational functions from the prewar to the postwar films.

As we have already established, in the postwar world of the Ozuesque, the primary subjects become things like the marriages of daughters and the sadness of fathers, and as a result, the clothing dynamics exposed there become grounded in a tension between ceremonial costume and casual wear. We have also already addressed how such oppositions between ceremonial and nonceremonial clothing come to animate the narratives. And yet, both the Takeshi Sakamoto of the so-called Kihachi films of the thirties and Chishū Ryū as the central male figure of the Ozuesque world of the post–*Late Spring* period encounter fundamentally the same comedies and tragedies around changing clothes—situations that derive from the monotone character of male formal wear in Japan, which from the thirties through the sixties was the same, whether Japanese or Western in style, for rituals of both celebration and mourning.

In *Passing Fancy*, Takeshi Sakamoto plays a widowed worker who meets a poor young woman with neither kith nor kin. Despite the fact that he himself is a single father, he decides to look out for this woman, demonstrating a generosity characteristic of the urban working class but inspired also by a smidgeon of unacknowledged erotic interest—vague romantic feelings that ultimately fade away when he learns that her youthful heart has wandered in the direction of his handsome coworker. This film has been called an adaptation of King Vidor's *The Champ* (1931), but the scenario, of a widowed single father who helps a lonely young woman, only to mistake her gratitude for romantic affection, is actually much closer to Raoul Walsh's masterpiece *The Bowery* (1933), made in Hollywood in the same year as Ozu's film. Because Walsh's film was not released in Japan until the following year, we can set the question of influence aside. But Wallace Beery's character in that film, who gussies himself up, despite his age, and takes pleasure in playing the guardian to a young lady, closely parallels the working man played by Sakamoto. Once he has succeeded in finding employment for this girl at a friend's restaurant, Sakamoto skips work at the factory, pretending to be sick, and puts on a formal *haori* jacket, his finest outfit, to visit her at her job. This is a man who ordinarily goes around in a casual cotton *yukata* and flat cap, if not in his long underpants. The spectacle of him tying his kimono at the waist with a sash and even sporting a formal Japanese dress coat is a narrative signal that points to what, for his age, is his rather naive purity of heart. But more importantly, it is a visual detail that convinces us we are dealing here as well with a "man who changes clothes," and viewed this way, it is quite moving. At the same time, his transformation is received quite differently by the residents of his block. Surprised by the uncustomary care their neighbor has taken with his appearance, they wonder in earnest if he is on his way to a funeral.

The same comic irony is repeated with even crueler irony at the end of Ozu's final film *An Autumn Afternoon*. When Chishū Ryū stops at a familiar bar on his way home on the evening following his daughter Shima Iwashita's wedding ceremony, the proprietress looks at the formal coat he still has on and asks: "was it a funeral?" To which Ryū answers, "something like that." We viewers are aware that the main reason he frequents this bar is because this proprietress, Kyōko Kishida, "somehow bears a resemblance" to his late wife, and we therefore understand that her careless question at this moment is thoroughly enmeshed with the theme of clothing in Ozu. In Ozu, changing clothes is a rite of separation. People who change clothes invariably do so on someone else's behalf. No one changes clothes solely for their own benefit. Ozuesque characters change into things other than their everyday wardrobe on behalf of someone else, whether that someone is a close relative or a stranger, and commemorate that person's departure in the process. Whether starting a life with a new spouse or passing on to the world of the dead, *someone* departs. Changing clothes in Ozu means surrendering and accepting distance. In *Passing Fancy,* when Takeshi Sakamoto goes to the effort of dressing himself up for the solitary young woman to whom he has shown too much consideration on the pretext that she somehow resembles his late wife, he thus lays the groundwork for her to pass from his side to that of his close coworker. The frequent concern with the marriages of daughters in the late-period films also ultimately amounts to little more than an elaborate repetition of changing clothes as a rite of separation. It is there, in any case, that the movement of separation enters the narratives. But this movement is not entirely limited to ceremonies like weddings and funerals. It does introduce those narrational elements into the world of the Ozuesque, but it also becomes a stimulus, investing the spatial features of that world with a thematic magnetic force.

Recall, for example, that in the many late-period films involving the marriages of daughters, the setting where fathers unhurriedly change clothes is the living room on the first floor of the family home. This observation should also lead immediately to another: that the site reserved for the ultimate changing ritual performed by these fathers' daughters—the bridal costuming—is located on the second floor. It is of course true that daughters make their appearance only after having already completed their changing, but in any case, the spatial contrast between the site where fathers change and the site where daughters change ushers a new theme into the films. This theme, which emerges in deep association with the theme of changing clothes and establishes rules of narrational structure for the films, is the theme of the *stairs* that connect the first and second floors. The Ozuesque "film" tells stories of eating and stories of changing clothes, but also stories of ascending stairs. It should be said, though, that this theme is somewhat different from the others discussed to this point. This is because stairs hardly ever appear on screen as distinct visual images. But the theme of ascending stairs is significant nonetheless, and we will now examine why in detail.

4

INHABITING

THE PRESENCE OF STAIRS

The second-floor rooms of Japanese houses in *late-period* Ozu films are strange spaces that can only be described as drifting in midair. Whether located in the Azabu neighborhood of central Tokyo, in Kita Kamakura on the Shōnan coast, or, less representatively, in the Nada district of Kobe, wherever the second floor emerges as a significant setting in the Ozuesque "film," it is a space adrift, along with its hallways and tatami rooms, quite literally in midair. The second floor drifts in midair because it seems, through narrational functions fundamentally different from those of the first-floor rooms, to lack any momentum to touch the ground. The second floor is of course very similar to the first floor when it comes to its props and furnishings. Even the layout of the rooms reflects a uniformity of taste. But because the two play completely different roles on the level of narrative, narrational flow experiences a strange stagnation whenever characters appear on the second floor. Second-floor space seems not to rest on the foundation of a ground floor, but to detach ambiguously from its architectural substructure and hold itself aloft. To put it quite simply, in the Ozuesque "film," the second floor is not connected to the first.

And just why does the second floor drift in midair? The reason is simple: because stairs do not exist. The stairs that undeniably exist in early-period films like *Walk Cheerfully* or *That Night's Wife* vanish from late-period Ozu. Stairs do of course exist in the floor plans, and the framing of shots does also elegantly indicate where they must be located within the house. This is communicated whenever people suddenly disappear at the edges of hallways with gestures that clearly imply the climbing of a staircase connected to the second floor.

In *Late Spring,* for example, the stairs *must* be located in front of the kitchen to the left. Turning immediately right after entering through the front door points us toward the rather dark kitchen situated at the end of a hall. On the way to the kitchen, two contiguous Japanese rooms extend perpendicularly to the left, opening onto each other: a living room on the side closest to the front entrance, and the father's study and bedroom to the rear. The camera mostly frames these rooms from the back of the study, facing the garden located next to the front entrance and capturing the movements of characters—both family members and visitors—as they arrive at the house. This is the space where Chishū Ryū changes clothes at the end of the workday or waits alone for his daughter to come home. People returning home and visitors stopping by always enter this contiguous space from screen right. Those headed directly for the kitchen cross the composition from right to left, with the garden behind them. Meetings and separations take place in a leisurely fashion in accordance with this spatial organization.

The camera positions that Ozu selects depict the layout of Chishū Ryū's house with precision. Even those not consciously aware of this when viewing *Late Spring* should have an unambiguous understanding of the spatial arrangement of the house. Such exacting attention to architectural organization is almost always to be found in the late-period Ozuesque "film." In *Early Summer,* for example, the camera delineates character movement in relation to two similarly contiguous first-floor rooms. It is clear from the opening scene in particular, of a hurried breakfast before the morning commutes to work and school, that elderly couple Ichirō Sugai and Chieko Higashiyama lead a second-floor existence alongside their daughter Setsuko Hara. The stairs in this house appear to be located in front of the kitchen at the end of the hall, at screen right. When the camera frames the living room with the garden in the background, the front entrance also seems to be at screen right. This modest living space even starts to seem familiar, like an environment in which anyone might play or walk freely around. Some have declared this an effect of the fastidious set design and camerawork demanded by Ozu's realism. The house might as well be real.

But even this momentary sense of freedom enjoyed by the viewer soon encounters a difficulty: the fact that this house, through which fastidiously assembled shot sequences make it seem we should be able to wander freely, suddenly transforms into a perverse labyrinth the moment that anyone ascends to the second floor. We find no stairs when attempting to follow Setsuko Hara to where she suddenly disappears from view. She does then emerge in her room on the second floor, but Ozu's camera refuses to film the stairs she uses to get there. We see no climbing when she passes into the nook where the stairs must be located. She simply *vanishes,* quite literally, and seems to transport immediately to the second floor, a space adrift in midair with no direct connection whatsoever to the first floor. The same also applies to the elderly grandparents in *Early Summer,* who continually disappear into unseen stairways. It would not be wrong to call this uncanny.

It goes without saying that cinema has adapted any number of techniques for representing presence with absence. People may therefore object that staircases do exist in Ozu, that he simply alludes to them through the device of ellipsis. This would undoubtedly not be wrong, but the sheer consistency, bordering on insistence, with which stairs remain absent from the screen becomes downright menacing as it confronts the viewer directly with absence in itself. Why should Ozu rob stairs of the means to assert themselves as images? Just what is the significance of this persistent absence? Such questions touch on strange matters that bewilder cinematic sensitivity to much the same extent as problems surrounding things like Ozu's low camera position. Why should Ozu set the second floor adrift in midair, rejecting any direct connection to the first? The task for the moment is not so much to resolve any doubts we might have about this question as to confirm, once again, the consistent reality of the details involving the absence of stairs in the Ozuesque "film," and thus to clarify the features of the cinematic period known as *late* Ozu, a period that we might even define by its absent stairs. After all, *late* Yasujirō Ozu is not merely a stage in the career of an auteur. It is nothing less than a time that disorients and unmoors world film history itself, a time literally adrift in midair.

AGE TWENTY-FIVE AND AGE FIFTY-FIVE

As is well known, one of the preferred subjects in *late-period* Ozu is the deep emotion experienced by fathers with daughters approaching marriage. In fact, starting with *Late Spring,* the film considered to have marked Ozu's full recovery from the slump following his return from military service when he made *Record of a Tenement Gentleman* (*Nagaya shinshiroku,* 1947) and *A Hen in the Wind,* the feelings of parents, and particularly of fathers, form a central theme, treated with subtle distance, across the films made over a period of a dozen years until his final film *An Autumn Afternoon.* Of course, fathers are not the sole privileged subjects here. There are also exceptions like *Late Autumn,* a film that focuses on the emotions of a beautiful widow and her soon-to-be-married daughter. It is of course also true, as everyone knows, that *Late*

Autumn is a remake of *Late Spring*, accomplished through a character substitution that exchanges the father role for a mother. *Late Spring* in turn transposes the themes and characters of the wartime film *There Was a Father* to the postwar social context. All three of these films are therefore products of simple variations within the parent-child relationship, from father/son to father/daughter and mother/daughter patterns. Here, Ozu demonstrates a natural talent for imitating and replicating himself with subtle audacity, a proclivity that recalls the Howard Hawks of *Rio Bravo* (1959) and the ensuing western showdown trilogy. Even the Godard of *Made in U.S.A* (1966), who borrowed the Humphrey Bogart role from *The Big Sleep* (1946) but cast his own ex-wife Anna Karina in the part, has nothing on the Ozu who substituted Setsuko Hara's father Chishū Ryū with a mother, played by none other than Hara herself. Still, the Ozu of the postwar years was not entirely committed to this particular variation of formula, as is clear from a film like *Good Morning*, which centers on elementary school brothers and can hardly deploy marriage negotiations to narrational ends. Then there are the films that deal with the spiritual crises of childless couples, like *The Flavor of Green Tea over Rice* or *Early Spring* (*Sōshun*, 1956). There are also domestic dramas about large families whose relationships extend across three generations, from grandparents to grandchildren: films like *Early Summer*, *Tokyo Story*, and *The End of Summer*. But even in these, a daughter's marriage arrangements form an unmistakable theme, whether implicit or explicit. And then there is *Equinox Flower* (1958), which seems to position itself as a symphonic integration of all these themes.

Equinox Flower begins with employees at Tokyo Station remarking on the numerous honeymoon send-off parties crowding the train platform, then proceeds to showcase a wedding reception—a rare spectacle in Ozu. The way this film so clearly announces the theme of marriage from the outset is rather peculiar, *peculiar* because Ozu films only rarely depict wedding ceremonies and receptions, despite their penchant for dwelling on daughters' marriage arrangements. In most cases, banquet scenes are savagely cut as Ozu's attention focuses instead on the morning of the ceremonies or the evening hours that follow. This is why we start to feel unsettled in the first few minutes of *Equinox Flower*, to feel we are bearing witness to some strange event. But Ozu soon demonstrates a marvelous ability to disarm the viewer's unease. The man and woman celebrating their union at the reception in the opening scene turn out to be incidental details, less-than-supporting characters with hardly any active role to play in the film. The narrative will revolve instead around the relationship between wedding guest Shin Saburi, who makes a congratulatory speech, and his daughter Ineko Arima. In due course, the daughter will decide to get married against her father's will and leave Tokyo, and her mother Kinuyo Tanaka will worry about whether Saburi will agree to attend his own daughter's wedding. Of course, when he ultimately does take part, neither that ceremony nor its reception will be depicted on screen.

At the periphery of the marriage story surrounding this daughter and her two parents, there are two other young women, one with a widowed father and the other a widowed mother. All three defy the vague hopes of their parents. Chishū Ryū's daughter Yoshiko Kuga lives with a boyfriend and works in a bar, while Fujiko Yamamoto resists the arrangements her mother Chieko Naniwa busily makes on her behalf, summarily rejecting every proposal she brings. *Equinox Flower* might therefore be summarized as a domestic drama about the quandaries of parents outmaneuvered by daughters. The screenplay indicates that these women are all slightly past prime marrying age, at twenty-three, twenty-four, and twenty-five, respectively, while parents Ryū and Naniwa are both close in age to Saburi, who is fifty-five. Generational age disparities such as this are absolute in the Ozuesque "film." Starting from around the time of the prewar *Tokyo Chorus* and *I Was Born, but . . .*, numerous films portray the lives of young fathers and mothers whose children are of approximately elementary school age. This continues through *Passing Fancy* and *An Inn in Tokyo* (*Tokyo no yado*, 1935). A

Story of Floating Weeds and *A Mother Should Be Loved* (*Haha o kowazu ya*, 1934) are made as these children have reached roughly the age of graduation under the old middle school system, and their parents have reached mid-life.[1] By the time of *The Only Son* and *There Was a Father*, the children are completing college and entering the workforce. It might be said that Ozu raised his own imaginary children—the ones he never had in real life—at least through the films in which parent-child relationships form a theme, and that he made them grow more or less in rhythm with the kinds of trends featured in the contemporary lifestyle magazines of the time, apart from some occasional deviations.

However, in the Ozuesque "film" of the prewar and wartime periods, the parent/child relationship revolves around mothers or fathers and their sons, whereas the focus in the *late-period* films shifts to parents and their daughters. These daughters also stop growing older, remaining consistently around the age of twenty-five. Setsuko Hara in *Late Spring* is twenty-seven, having missed the opportunity to marry at a suitable age, it is explained, due to a lung condition that she contracted under hard circumstances during the war. In *Early Summer* she is twenty-eight, but if we average the age of the daughters in the other films, we arrive basically at the number twenty-five. Films like *Early Summer*, *Tokyo Story*, or *The End of Summer* depict three generations, from grandchild to grandparent. In these large family settings, with the age of the parents now advancing, the youngest daughters are just this age and still unmarried, despite the fact that their older brothers and sisters are already independent and maintaining households of their own. We should therefore probably revise our definition of what until now we have somewhat vaguely called *late-period* Ozu to the following: a period consisting of a series of "films" in which daughters who cease to age at twenty-five serve a major narrational function. In

---

1. The old middle school system for boys, *kyūsei chūgakkō*, involved a five-year curriculum designed to be completed at age sixteen. This system was largely replaced in 1947.

other words, an absolute late-period Ozu exists in a place unrelated to questions of just where the early period ends and the middle period begins. This late period can be defined, quite simply, through the age of daughters.

But it is of course not as a reminder of the basic character patterns in the Ozuesque "film" that we belabor such points as the conversion of sons to daughters on the parent/child relationship axis, or the emergence of age twenty-five as absolute. These points should be obvious to anyone and are hardly remarkable. It has been necessary to dwell on these matters in arguably somewhat gratuitous and long-winded fashion to make visually palpable how this series of conversions and absolutes introduces a certain irreversible transformation within the procedures that shape cinematic desire. What, then, does this irreversible transformation entail? Nothing other than the strange dislocation of the second-floor rooms of Japanese houses. From the moment that the daughters who impart late-period features to the Ozuesque "film" essentially start ceasing to age at twenty-five, space above staircases becomes incapable of any simple interface with the ground and begins to duplex Ozuesque living environments, setting the upper-layer sections adrift in midair. Once Ozu transferred his attention from boys and their childhood development to daughters of marriageable age, the duplexing of this space became routine. Through the movement of selection and exclusion, this duplexed space also came to privilege the second-floor rooms set adrift in midair. It can therefore probably be said that what we have so far provisionally described as late-period Ozu amounts, quite simply, to the limitless replication—by means of reciprocal imitation—of a cinematic environment that bears the burden of holding such privileged space aloft. How then does the Ozuesque "film," as characterized by such privileging and duplexing, enliven the homogeneity of its cinematic environment? What kinds of events or occurrences lend it energy? Or what kind of momentum toward even violent deviation might be harbored within its pretend tranquility?

STAIRS, OR INVISIBLE WALLS

The situation should now be coming into view. What characterizes late-period Ozu is not simply the visual absence of stairs to the second floor or the reliable presence of a daughter of marriageable age as narrational elements. Rather, the features of the Ozuesque "film" are endowed in each instance by the fact that second-floor rooms not linked to anything by the medium of stairs perform a selection and exclusion function, separating characters into two distinct living realms. Absent staircases are more like invisible walls than ascending passageways, and only those able to pass horizontally through them are able to acquire the privilege of finding themselves on the second floor as a space adrift in midair. It goes without saying that those who obtain this privilege are always unmarried women who have stopped aging at twenty-five.

Ozuesque daughters, from Setsuko Hara in *Late Spring* to Shima Iwashita in *An Autumn Afternoon,* easily pass through the invisible walls of stairs not pictured on screen and transport themselves to space detached from the ground. This applies to Ineko Arima in *Equinox Flower,* as well as to Yōko Tsukasa in *The End of Summer,* both of whom slip abruptly into this alien space, with a suddenness that people tend to leave unquestioned. Vanishing from lonely corridors, they show only the slightest upward momentum, never clearly looking up. The places where these absent stairs must be located are at the interior of the scene, at some distance from the camera, and since imaginary staircases intersect at right angles with hallways, the daughters passing through them disappear from the screen quite literally all at once. Then, for a moment, only a deserted hallway remains. Finding poignancy in these deserted hallways that bear no trace of any dramatic exaggeration is probably the first gateway on the path to intimacy with the late-period Ozuesque "film." What is moving in late-period Ozu is not the awkward expressions of affection that fathers direct at daughters who seem to be in danger of letting marriage pass them by (an awkwardness crystallized in Chishū Ryū's familiar line delivery itself), nor the slumped shoulders of widowed fathers who have at last given their daughters away. Viewers are free to be as moved or upset by such things as they please, but it is the power of images at once more abstract and at the same time also more direct than such things that account for the ability of the Ozuesque "film" to agitate cinematic sensitivity—the power, that is, of images that anyone can unmistakably see but that tend to go unnoticed because they cannot easily be reconciled with what is lyrical. Late-period Ozu is rescued from the monotony of the domestic drama thanks precisely to the vividness of film experience, of the play of contrasts among the contours and shadows of things exposed on the surface, which sends unmediated movements rippling all around, beyond whatever psychological nuances sustain the narratives. This is why it is necessary for people to ruminate on absent stairs—stairs that remain unabsorbed into the narrative order—as the continuous present. Above all, the experience of watching a film has to involve accepting as sheer depthlessness the image the look probes intimately as a surface, and being intimidated by its present existence as something always in excess of the narrational order of the plot, or something that comes close to absolute lack.

Incidentally, neither these absent stairs nor the deserted hallways have the slightest bit of symbolic significance. They merely contribute to the smooth progression of the narrational flow, and with an efficiency not weighed down by any metaphoric effusiveness. The Ozuesque "film" may at times display a plasticity bordering on abstraction, but its flow conforms to an utterly ordinary temporality, one unrelated in any way to the kinds of revolts against sequential causality that the disrupters of rhetorical norms known as the "avant-garde" often play at. This is why viewers never jump to the conclusion that daughters who only a moment earlier were in the first-floor living room have simply vanished at the edge of the hallway. In fact, whether played by Setsuko Hara or Shima Iwashita, daughters in the Ozuesque "film" emerge, without fail, in the very next shot, slipping into their rooms on what appears to be the second floor through the patterned sliding doors that are invariably already open for them somewhere toward the back of the scenery. In fact, a fine-tuned *interval* probably does link these first and second floors, as an effect of Ozu's scrupulously calibrated shot lengths and frame counts. As a result, such shot sequences not only do not strike us as strange but can even come across as perfectly normal. In the foreground of these compositions, which is to say by a window overlooking a garden, there is often a desk and a chair, furnishings that these daughters must once have used for studying when they were in school. Occasionally there is also a sofa set arranged on a veranda with a view of the neighbor's roof, visible through a glass door. These second-floor rooms are places where daughters take pauses, collect themselves, or bring the day to a close.

And yet, as strange details, the absent stairs so thoroughly cloaked in invisibility within the Ozuesque "film" do begin to disturb our cinematic sensitivity. And why is this the case? For two reasons. As we have described, it is mostly only daughters of marriageable age who disappear into the shadows of first-floor hallways, and as a result, the systematic selection and exclusion action performed by stairways as invisible walls isolates them from their fathers and brothers, snatching them from the interplay of gazes as they slip into space adrift in midair. This is the first reason, from which the second follows: once settled in this space, these daughters cease to look at anyone and are not looked at by anyone in return. As a result, they all but lose their narrational function. Therefore, though Setsuko Hara and Shima Iwashita possess a privilege in their ability to pass through invisible walls and slip into second-floor rooms, once upstairs, they cease to play a dramatic role of any kind. Otherwise put, these daughters who suddenly vanish at the edges of hallways retreat to their rooms in order to attenuate their own presence, and the narrational function of the second floor itself thus becomes correspondingly ambiguous. Female friend Chikage Awashima is of course admitted to this space in *Early Summer,* and in *The End of Summer,* Yōko Tsukasa's second-floor room does also become the setting for a conversation with her sister-in-law Hara. But parents and members of the opposite sex are clearly excluded. Within the structure of the Ozuesque "film," this correlation of attenuation and ambiguity detaches second-floor space from the ground, setting it adrift in midair. And yet, the second floor does inexorably exist in late-period Ozu. We should regard this as something quite strange.

Why then does the second floor exist? If neither the space of the second floor nor the daughters who inhabit it are entrusted with dramatic functions, why do these young women disappear so suggestively from hallways? Why do these daughters choose to wield the privilege of slipping through secret passageways and distancing themselves from men if doing so only attenuates their presence as characters and sets the second floor as mise-en-scène ambiguously adrift?

BARREN BANTER

It is now clear that the second-floor rooms of the Japanese houses so characteristic of *late-period* Ozu are sanctuaries for young women around the age of twenty-five. And yet, as sanctuaries, these spaces are awfully flat and devoid of mystery. Daughters do not undergo the slightest of transformations here. There is no sudden self-abandonment, nor any act of indecency performed in private. Nor does transport to these spaces adrift in midair involve any occasion for narrative surprises. Despite being a sanctuary, the second floor excludes men, and matters of feminine heterosexuality are therefore not emphasized. Ozu did of course belong to the prewar generation, and remained single to the end, never raising a daughter of his own in reality. Even so, should the room of an unmarried daughter really be portrayed as something so barren? The decor itself contains little more than sofas and a desk for studying.

And yet, it gradually becomes apparent that this sanctuary for daughters, which might aptly be described as plain and simple, is in fact densely furnished with narrational functions of its own. The reason for this is that another similarly barren space also exists in late-period Ozu: namely, the private dining rooms at restaurants where fathers around the age of fifty-five often gather. Chishū Ryū, Nobuo Nakamura, Shin Saburi, and Ryūji Kita return from film to film, playing middle-aged former classmates—products of the prewar unisex middle school and high school systems—who meet in private Japanese-style rooms at restaurants to exchange reminiscences and engage in silly banter, rooms that become sanctuaries for men, as it were. These fathers do not necessarily share the same occupation or even the same social position. They are linked by the sole excuse of having once studied together at the same school. For the most part, they do not use their sanctuary as a place to debate the state of the world or to grumble about serious social problems. The conversations here mainly consist of gossip shared among old friends, and sometimes also their former teachers—childish chitchat, where someone's shortcoming becomes an object of teasing by the group, and nicknames are traded like a secret code.

In *Equinox Flower*, for example, a simple-minded inquiry animates the men's drinking party: the conversation moves from talk about how many children these fathers have among them, and among those how many boys and how many girls, to the vulgar thesis that the relative vigor of the man versus the woman within a couple determines the sex of the child—a thesis they go around the table applying to one another for laughs. Although the restaurant hostess is permitted to move in and out of this sanctuary, she mostly does not follow the content of the men's conversation. When Saburi suddenly poses the question of children to Toyo Takahashi, who frequently plays the hostess in these restaurants, she answers that she has three. Nakamura then sweeps in with the jab, delivered from behind the glint of his rimless glasses: "They must all be boys," he says. "How did you know?" she asks, taken aback but maintaining her polite smile. The fifty-five-year-old men laughingly conclude that it would be unthinkable any other way as they watch their hostess's puzzled expression. She scolds them for their teasing as she turns her heavyset figure and leaves to bring more sake.

This scene is of course not of any great value as an illustration of Ozuesque humor, invoked here by the men at the expense of Takahashi as an actress with a particular kind of physique. Not that such things are irrelevant, but the important point to observe about the code circulating in the men's sanctuary of this private room at a restaurant—more important than the foolishness of what it signifies—is the fact that it functions to exclude the participation of women. Takahashi returns as the hostess in *An Autumn Afternoon*. Ryū and Nakamura have arranged to meet Ryūji Kita in their private dining room, and here again, the friends indulge in a dumb joke that befuddles their hostess. Shaking their heads, they lament the missing Kita's misfortune. If only he had not succumbed to the temptation of remarriage with a younger woman, he would not have overexerted himself and dropped dead. What a pity. Takahashi stands in disbelief, at a loss for words. At this moment, Kita makes his entrance, apologizing for arriving late, and balance is restored at a beat's delay. This timing is distinctive of Ozu and works to quite humorous effect, even if the humor feels somehow grim when we watch this film now, knowing that it would be Ozu's last. The men exclude Takahashi from the circle of their conversation, ignoring the way she reproaches their childish nonsense with her eyes as they seem to nod in agreement that precisely such intentionally vapid banter is what sets their male sanctuary apart. Women are thoroughly excluded from this space. The hostess alone is permitted entry but remains near the doorway and at the mercy of the men's self-indulgent teasing.

Ryūji Kita's young wife does also show her face in this men's sanctuary in *An Autumn Afternoon*, but Kita instantly recognizes the violation of taboo and hurriedly exits with her.[2] Needless to say, his agitated departure supplies the remaining men with material for another simple-minded joke. Mischievous though the carousing of these overgrown boys may be, speech emerges from within it that will come to regulate the subsequent actions of characters and the ensuing complications of plot, gradually giving shape to something like the nucleus of the men's sanctuary. The subject of Kita's remarriage is something the men basically never discuss with any seriousness. On the contrary, it is a constant target of Nakamura's provocative and cynical joking. Ryū only laughs in response to these jokes, but in due course, they will lead him to an out-of-the-way bar where the young hostess somehow resembles his own late wife. While the banter and jokes exchanged in the private dining room at the restaurant may seem like an involved digression unrelated to the main thread of the plot, and may seem to introduce a stagnation of narrational flow, they actually supply the occasion for the introduction of a very serious theme.

TWO SANCTUARIES

The second-floor rooms of the Japanese houses we encounter in late-period Ozu are a detail that corresponds precisely to the private dining rooms at restaurants as sanctuaries for men. This should now be clear to anyone. Just as second-floor rooms are detached from the common areas of the house by their attenuated and ambiguous atmosphere, these sanctuaries for men are severed from the outside world and can almost be called abstract. Furthermore, just as men's sanctuaries come into existence in thoroughly excluding the presence of women, women's sanctuaries also refuse the intrusion of men. Each is a privileged space in which either fifty-five-year-old men or twenty-five-year-old

---

2. It is actually the young wife who is reluctant to enter the space and who coaxes Kita away as the men invite her to sit, but Kita himself shows no reluctance to depart.

women separate from the vertical axis of familial relations and spend unfocused time with friends of the same sex and generation, exchanging signs that function like a kind of secret code. To understand second-floor rooms merely as sitting rooms or bedrooms for Setsuko Hara or Shima Iwashita would mean to remain insensitive to the specific features of the Ozuesque "film." These rooms are designated first and foremost as sites where women chat. In this function, they become thoroughly detached from the first-floor rooms underneath, but not only this. They also come into unmediated contact with the private dining rooms of geographically ambiguous Japanese restaurants. In light of this, the nonpresence of stairs should probably be regarded as a narrational necessity for the Ozuesque "film." Yōji Yamada's *Tora-san* series also features second-floor rooms in the upstairs of the old shop in eastern Tokyo's Shibamata neighborhood that serves as a central setting in the films—rooms that take on a pronounced sense of presence every time the wandering title character shows up at home unannounced.[3] But as a living space, these rooms are simply an extension of the family's first-floor shop and do not possess any thoroughgoing narrational function of the kind we see in late-period Ozu. In the Ozuesque "film," by contrast, we find ourselves perplexed and intimidated as viewers, because details that are highly attenuated and even ambiguous in dramatic effect can unexpectedly form dense associations and enter into intimate mutual play. We should therefore acknowledge that it is precisely where things appear to be flat and monotone, where we seem to encounter little more than banal and diluted reflections of the everyday world, that true Ozuesque film experience vividly pulsates.

---

3. *Otoko wa tsurai yo* ("It's Tough to Be a Man," known in English as *Tora-san, Our Loveable Tramp*), was an iconic, long-running series starring Kiyoshi Atsumi in the title role of Tora-san, a small-time traveling salesman who wanders in and out of his hometown Shibamata from one film to the next. Tora-san's Shibamata is emblematic of popular nostalgia for Tokyo's old working class *"shitamachi"* neighborhoods. The series consists of forty-eight films made between 1969 and 1995, most of them directed by Yōji Yamada.

Still, it bears noting that men's and women's sanctuaries do not correspond in strictly even fashion in each of the films. In some cases, the two do correspond within a given film and support the narrational flow, while in others they exceed the boundaries isolating the closed system of any single film and work to disturb the respective historical backdrops and narrative environments of the different films, knowingly reverberating against one other. The late-period Ozuesque "film" itself is the homogeneous cinematic environment that takes shape in these reverberations across boundaries—a networked fabric of distantly complicit smiles detached from the specific historical temporality behind each of the films and indifferent to the sequential order internal to the individual narratives. This is a world of free horizontal movement, where men's sanctuaries and women's sanctuaries communicate directly with each other within the network despite occupying fundamentally different space.

For example, when the second-floor room in *Late Spring* welcomes daughter Setsuko Hara and her classmate Yumeji Tsukioka, it suddenly exchanges knowing smiles with the private dining room at the Japanese restaurant in *An Autumn Afternoon*. Of course, the restaurant's private dining room differs from the daughter's second-floor room in that one is a site where several friends often gather, whereas there are usually no more than two women in the other. But in both, conversation gradually progresses from trifling small talk toward topics concerning the opposite sex. Of course, to say that conversation "progresses" does not mean any notable points of articulation emerge on the narrative level. In fact, the dialogue even forms a nearly spiraling circularity. "Marriage is all the same." "Maybe it is." "It is. It's the same. Give it a try." Everyone is familiar with this kind of Ozuesque conversational rhythm, of hesitation and repeated affirmation, a rhythm that harmonizes more naturally with the staging in these two sanctuaries than in any other setting. "I couldn't," says Hara without breaking her smile. "Yes, you can, you will, that's what you'll do," affirms Yumeji Tsukioka repetitiously. The friend who has come to visit is decidedly the expressive one of these two young women facing each other in cane chairs in a second-floor room. Hara cheerfully takes part in the conversation, of course, but when it shifts to the essential topic of marriage, she assumes a passive role, responding in a way that neither confirms nor contradicts her friend's assertions but leaves them ambiguously adrift: "Maybe so."[4] Chishū Ryū plays a similar role in the restaurant. Nobuo Nakamura is always the one who makes assertions, sometimes wryly, sometimes self-deprecatingly. Ryū simply looks on, wearing that relentlessly receptive smile directed at the speaker's mere presence itself. "Is that right? I guess so." His replies neither affirm nor contradict his friend's commentary. His conversational manner in the private dining rooms at restaurants, just like Hara's in second-floor space adrift in midair, seems decidedly unequipped for expressing any objection to his friend's tautological arguments, much less for voicing any matters related to his own opinion. Everything progresses in the absence of any other-directed tension, through smiles and parrot-like verbal nods of acknowledgement uttered as if by automatons. The wandering conversations that take place among men and women in their respective sanctuaries never arrive at conclusion-like closure but instead end up suspended ambiguously in midair. It is as if these men and women talk for no other purpose than mutual confirmation of their existence as talking beings. Certain anthropologists and linguists use the term "phatic function" to refer to this kind of communication, which is also characteristic of the speech of talking birds like mynas. The phatic function, in other words, includes both imitative speech that precedes the communication of will and speech that tends toward the ritualistic. Ozu's fondness for the phatic communication that unfolds in these

---

4. Hasumi may have mingled a conversation from later in the film with his memory of the scene in question. The dialogue translated here is from the later scene, which takes place not in Hara's upstairs bedroom, but at the home of divorcée Tsukioka—another women's sanctuary.

spaces probably lurks somewhere in proximity to the baseless neglect and scorn that Ozu had to endure for a time.

And yet, it is precisely in these parrot-like verbal nods and smiles that we find the beauty of Ozu, the obtuse cruelty verging on madness of especially the *late-period* Ozuesque "film." When Chishū Ryū ("Is that right?") or Setsuko Hara ("Maybe so") takes part in conversations amid such attenuated, abstract appearances, the speech that unfolds in their respective sanctuaries attains a new reality fundamentally different in nature from that of either a monologue delivered in isolation or a dialogue held in dialectical exchange: a superficial play of what may resemble speech, mimicking itself as it glides at the surface, but is really more like a play of signs that attenuates an aspect of semantic content—the signified—in the extreme. Or think of this, perhaps, as a performance of speech that borders on the absurd, speech different in kind from anything that might make claims to dramatic validity through the representation of what is supposedly a conversation. The effect, in any case, is a stripping raw of language that goes beyond even nonsense. Even the raucous, audacious physical comedy of the Marx Brothers can be said to demonstrate a far greater commitment to semantic content than such Ozuesque absurdity. Here, speech easily detaches from the domain of signification and floats in midair, so much so that the very notion of language as inherently endowed with significance such as might be misunderstood or distorted begins to seem like an impossible fiction. In the *Tora-san* films, for example, people laugh at the sight of Tora-san, the "loveable tramp," whenever he tries to play it cool after misinterpreting some situation, a pattern that essentially plays on the deviation between language and meaning. This deviation is what makes Tora-san's habitual rashness and the resulting misunderstandings funny. By contrast, the conversations in the men's and women's sanctuaries are not inherently endowed with any significance that can be said to possess *right* or *wrong* interpretations.

ABSURD REPLICATION

However, the deep connection between the second-floor room in *Late Spring* and the private dining room in *An Autumn Afternoon* is not only a product of the absurd play of phatic communication in sanctuaries. These privileged spaces are also linked by intrusions of members of the opposite sex. We have already seen how thoroughly noncommittal hostess Toyo Takahashi's intrusion is when she trespasses in the men's sanctuary. She merely stands there in the doorway, helpless to respond to Nobuo Nakamura and Chishū Ryū's simple-minded joking, before hurrying from the room. The male who enters the second-floor room in *Late Spring* also does so rather sheepishly, with a lack of confidence suggesting a certain confusion at having transgressed the boundary of the women's sanctuary. It goes without saying that the role of intruder here is performed by the father, Ryū. He arrives bearing tea and bread for his daughter and her friend, who has stopped by for a visit. Because it is not preceded by a shot of him vanishing into the nook at the edge of the downstairs hallway, his appearance is somewhat sudden. The flow of speech in the sanctuary is momentarily suspended. Carrying the tray as if embarrassed by his own presence, he seems to find it difficult to approach these young women lounging in cane chairs.

In other words, the situation is thus: like the restaurant hostess, father Chishū Ryū is a being incapable of freely entering a room in his own house. He remains near the patterned sliding door as if intending immediately to retreat. His awkward posture conveys a certain discomfort. The placement of the camera on the opposite side of the young women accentuates precisely this, positioning him in the background of the scene. In *An Autumn Afternoon*, the same kind of composition similarly isolates Toyo Takahashi from the men. Both father and hostess share a common function: that of quickly exiting the scene. They also resemble each other in that they both arrive bearing food. Even the young women's laughter following the departure of the father, who has neglected to put sugar cubes or even spoons on their tea saucers, replicates the conspiratorial laugh that the men share in the restaurant when the hostess makes her own exit.

Thus considered, both *Late Spring* and *An Autumn Afternoon* demonstrate adherence to quite the same spatial structure where women's and men's sanctuaries are concerned. This along with the precise reversal of gender roles between the two films establishes a reciprocal replication that, in the aggregate, lacks any single source of inspiration. Ozu did of course consciously remake *Late Spring* with *Late Autumn;* the latter originates from a reworking of the character relationships in the former. Just as Raoul Walsh based *Colorado Territory* (1949) on his own earlier film *High Sierra* (1941), Ozu and screenwriter Kōgo Noda made *Late Autumn* by repeating the formula of *Late Spring,* only inverted, exchanging a mother for the father. But when it comes to *Late Spring* and *An Autumn Afternoon,* the deep connections that quietly form between the second-floor room in the former and the private dining room in the latter cause the films to play against each other at the surface of time in the present, and to illuminate each other across all their parts, despite the dozen or so years separating the two productions. We might call this phenomenon a replication with no proper original, an absurd doubling. Like the second-floor rooms of late-period Ozu, it becomes a space adrift, detached from any foundation, and like the private dining rooms at Japanese restaurants, it lives in time cut off from the world. The late-period Ozuesque "film" is like an endless series of masks, worn by this cinematic space and time, with no true face anywhere underneath. From the perspective of subject matter, *Late Autumn* is little more than a watered-down replication of *Late Spring,* dealing like the earlier film with the sadness of a widowed parent marrying off an only daughter. In this regard, its value is something to be measured simply by its distance from the original; it can even be considered rather loose as a film, a remake that fails to live up to *Late Spring.* It leaves the same impression even when compared to *There Was a Father,* a film that lurks in the background of *Late Spring*. This is certainly all true. But such value judgments end up excluding from film experience the raw play of details that form unexpected mutual associations beyond the boundaries of the individual films. They reflect a kind of canonizing mentality and a thoroughly passive way of looking. The reason we hold Yasujirō Ozu dear is not because he tossed a few enduring masterpieces in the direction of our cinematic sensitivity. He is limitlessly dear to us because he made it possible, by means of the Ozuesque "film," to play intimately within cinema as an environment with the capacity to produce constant surprises. The late-period Ozuesque "film" is not a monument erected on a solid foundation. It is the perpetual present itself, transforming in the very process of holding itself aloft. This is why the second-floor rooms of those Japanese houses float in midair, never connecting to the first-floor rooms by means of stairs, and thus exclude men, welcoming pairs of women instead, like Kinuyo Tanaka and Ineko Arima in *Equinox Flower*, or Setsuko Hara and Yōko Tsukasa in *The End of Summer*, as settings for momentary conversations.

A second-floor room with no foundation is a spatial absurdity. No one would have envisioned such a thing, and no one has ever set foot in anything of the kind. When we consider that Ozu persistently focused his attention on the features of a world as strange as this one, he starts to seem less like a visionary auteur and more like a creature governed by an animalistic obtuseness. In this sense, film history does not need to pride itself on having produced an Ozu. As an environment that was capable of accommodating the late-period Ozuesque "film," cinema should only perplex, intimidate, and disturb.

EMPTIED SPACE

Where and when does the late-period Ozuesque "film" begin? Or perhaps it should not be said to *begin* so much as to become ambiguously forged? *Late Spring* is certainly more substantial than *Record of a*

Tenement Gentleman or *A Hen in the Wind*. But *Late Spring* is itself less a beginning than a replication of something. A replication of what then? A replication, namely, of the second floor adrift in midair, and of the women's sanctuary. To the extent that *Late Spring* also replicates an original, its source is the earlier film *Brothers and Sisters of the Toda Family* (*Toda-ke no kyōdai*, 1941). As a story of familial dissolution, this wartime film also bears a relationship of reciprocal replication to the postwar *Tokyo Story,* at least where their similarities of narrational structure are concerned. From the perspective of their shared focus on the death of an elderly parent at the center of a large family, these wartime and postwar films also resemble each other in a way that recalls the resemblance between *Late Spring* and *Late Autumn,* since one likewise exchanges the role of a father for a mother. But such corresponding subject matter is not what is important here. The important thing to note is the fact that the second floor as women's sanctuary makes an appearance, however nondistinctly, from as early as *Brothers and Sisters of the Toda Family.* At the time, the narrational function of this room adrift in midair might not have been fully recognizable, but this function becomes reciprocally clarified as associations form with significant details from the later films.

What kind of space then is the second-floor room in *Brothers and Sisters of the Toda Family?* When the matriarch cedes her position at the center of the family and goes with her youngest daughter to live at her son's house following the sudden death of her husband, the room on the second floor is the space given to the women because they are a burden. The eldest son and older daughters have already married and established households of their own, and they do not by any means accept the second-floor presence of their mother and younger sister as natural, believing that balance will be restored to the family once the two women eventually depart. It is therefore with discomfort that mother Fumiko Katsuragi and daughter Mieko Takamine, like the elderly parents in *Tokyo Story,* must inhabit the second floor. Today this earlier film seems so much like something from the postwar that, if we overlooked Shin Saburi's mention of occupied territory on the continent when he returns from China near the end to rebuke his siblings for their selfishness, it would even be difficult to believe that this was a wartime production. In fact, if we were to consider things only from the perspective of the dissolution of the family as a subject, we might even hallucinate that this wartime production was the very source for an entire line of postwar films extending from *Tokyo Story* to Nagisa Ōshima's *The Ceremony* (*Gishiki*, 1971). Even the "reevaluation of the postwar," which some in Japan have pursued with strange insistence—whether in embrace or rejection of things postwar—is something perhaps destined for abstraction to the extent that it does not account for Ozu's *Brothers and Sisters of the Toda Family*. In any case, this ruin of the domestic drama, made in 1941 and released to positive reviews, narrates the tensions and disarray within a family following the death of the patriarch, and it should therefore certainly be possible to discover within it material suitable for elaborating revolutionary fantasies or holding forth on the emperor system.

But the immediate objective here is not to use Yasujirō Ozu as a pretext for entering such kinds of debates. The task is simply to clarify the narrational function performed in late-period Ozu by second-floor space drifting in midair. What *Brothers and Sisters of the Toda Family* makes clear is that this space is nothing other than a temporary living environment for women who lack entitlement to a more permanent residence. Second-floor rooms that function narrationally as women's sanctuaries are placed within the late-period Ozuesque "film" ultimately to exclude their rightful inhabitants and become vacant spaces. In this light, we can view those who inhabit the first floor as going about their lives envisioning the moment when the second floor will be emptied out, whether they do so in good conscience or with traces of ill will. In fact, even the elderly couple in *Early Summer* will obey the dictates of this narrational structure and disappear from the second floor, if with an attitude of sensible resignation. The late-period Ozuesque "film" is little more than a summation of gesture and thought expended for the purpose of hollowing out space adrift in midair. If the decor of second-floor Japanese rooms seems ambiguous and attenuated, the reason is quite simply that it has been charged with this narrational function. Daughters here are only passing through, as it were, performing more or less prolonged stays while awaiting the decisive moment of a departure. This is also why the time that elapses in this space evokes a sense of aimless stagnation. We are dealing with a narrative detail, the sole purpose of which is precisely to resolve to nothingness. Commentators often invoke the topic of Ozuesque "nothingness" (*mu*), but Ozuesque nothingness has nothing to do with religious or metaphysical concepts.[5] It is an architectural, physical image ingrained on the cinematic surface (figs. 7 and 8). The films that Ozu made in the late period are all narratives of the vivid present that progress toward the materialization of this tangible nothingness. They are experiences of the here and now having nothing whatsoever to do with the afterlife or the beyond. Everything is exposed on the surface, nothing hidden. We might provisionally call this a kind of realism, but a realism that cinema has not encountered anywhere outside of Ozu and may never encounter elsewhere. This is something that still does not seem to surprise people as much as it should.

---

5. The character for *mu* is carved on Ozu's own gravestone, a fact that has inspired some to view the films through the lens of Zen Buddhism. Elsewhere Hasumi highlights the fact that the *butsudan* (Buddhist altars) and *kamidana* (Shintō shrines) commonly found in Japanese homes are conspicuously missing from Ozu's cinematic houses, and he argues that the nothingness of empty space created by eliminating these household objects reflects the absence of such kinds of religious or philosophical concepts in the films. Hasumi writes further that, in eliminating household shrines, Ozu also swept the emperor system from the films. Shiguéhiko Hasumi, "'Reigai' no reigaiteki na yōgo: Ozu Yasujirō *Tokyo monogatari*-ron," *Bungaku* 9, no. 2 (March 26, 2008): 178. See Hasumi's June 2022 correspondence with John Rajchman, trans. Ryan Cook, in Michel Foucault, *The Japan Lectures: A Transnational Critical Encounter*, ed. John Rajchman (New York: Routledge, forthcoming).

7. *Late Spring:* Daughter Setsuko Hara's second-floor room after she has left to be married.

8. *An Autumn Afternoon:* The mirror in daughter Shima Iwashita's second-floor room on the night of her wedding.

STAIRWAY SURPRISES

How then to embark on the journey toward surprise? For this, we will need to continue focusing our cinematic sensitivity on absent stairs. The second floor drifts in midair. It is a sanctuary for women. What function do absent stairs then serve as young women around the age of twenty-five approach exclusion from these second floors, of which they have been the privilege-holding inhabitants? If, with this question in mind, we look across all corners of the Ozuesque "film," watching for the ways smiles exchanged among details send ripples through the fabric of its network, it gradually becomes clear that the stairways we imagine *must* connect these spaces adrift in midair to first-floor hallways are in fact not entirely excluded from the cinematic surface after all. Visible stairs do exist in late-period Ozu. They are sometimes even filmed head-on. Is this fact, for one, not deeply surprising? Should such a thing even be permitted?

Moments when invisible stairways materialize give way to rare events in the Ozuesque "film." In such moments, which are themselves few in number, an extraordinary atmosphere enshrouds the image, and our cinematic sensitivity bristles with the presentiment of things inauspicious. In *The Munekata Sisters* (*Munekata kyōdai*, 1950), for example, there is a so-called Western-style house, located in a wealthy neighborhood of Kobe, furnished with a staircase that the camera captures Sanae Takasugi haughtily descending. Narratively, this conspicuous staircase takes on a somewhat different aspect than the staircases of Japanese houses, but when the full form of a woman descending the stairs is ingrained on the cinematic surface, we understand that we are witnessing the prelude to what will become an insidious rivalry between Sanae Takasugi and Hideko Takamine. This rivalry replicates the one already enacted in the earlier *Brothers and Sisters of the Toda Family* by Mieko Takamine and her sister-in-law Kuniko Miyake, who also descends a staircase. In late-period Ozu, looking directly at a staircase is a thoroughly inauspicious experience. In fact, the stairs that fill the frame in *A Hen in the Wind* will even become the scene of a tragedy when Shūji Sano shoves Kinuyo Tanaka down them. The circumstances here are far from ordinary since high- and low-angle shots of the kind Ozu otherwise so consciously eliminated are also clearly on display. In fact, numerous testimonies indicate that Ozu reviewed the footage for this scene repeatedly during the completion of the film.

The story of a mother who resorts to prostitution to provide for her child while awaiting her conscripted husband's return from war is not in itself something that should move people, even those familiar with the economic circumstances of the immediate postwar years. Praiseworthy though Ozu's use of ellipsis by montage may be, his aesthetic sensibility also leads him to scrape away any trace of grime from the mise-en-scène of prostitution, such that the portrayal of Kinuyo Tanaka's character seems quite implausible. Shūji Sano's psychological motivation is also not sufficiently convincing when, upon hearing his wife's confession, he sends her tumbling down the stairs with a shove. Still, the instant the steep incline of a staircase appears on screen, positioned in a hallway and within a mise-en-scène that substantially recalls the boardinghouse atmosphere of prewar Ozu films, we can only gasp at how the Ozuesque "film" speaks to us, its language seizing us with unmediated force. We sense with confusion that such things are not supposed to be permitted, and a presentiment takes root. And when Tanaka tumbles headfirst down this sharp incline, our foreboding is confirmed. Even viewers unconvinced by the narrative are left dumbstruck when confronted with the reality of the way this "film" speaks. At the moment when stairs acquire distinct outline as a concrete image, the screen compels our direct attention. For as long as they have remained an invisible presence, hidden in a nook at the edge of the hallway, it has been necessary to spread our cinematic sensitivity across the entirety of the film. But as soon as stairs become visible, we sense danger and look away. The Ozuesque "film" seems to keep murmuring to this effect, and we have no choice but to trust it. However absurd its speech, it commands our complete recognition.

A narrative is something that permits both belief and disbelief, something in relation to which it is possible to dispassionately measure distance and determine one's own position. A "film," by contrast, does not allow such straightforward choices. It is a raw environment, a continuous present that threatens people's being, drawing them helplessly into the vortex of a game. In Ozu, stairs become cinematic events in themselves. Some may think of Alfred Hitchcock here. Even without *Suspicion* (1941) or *Notorious* (1946), it would be easy to understand what deeply inauspicious spaces staircases are for Hitchcock. His stairs are more than mere symbolic settings for tragedies or psychological conflict. They are inherently sinister in themselves. Displaying stairs made Hitchcock a master of suspense. Ozu also managed to disturb cinema with stairs, but by keeping them hidden from view, only to reveal them at extraordinary moments. Some may object that *Floating Weeds*—a film made in Ozu's last years—demonstrates otherwise. Do we not see a staircase (more than one, in fact) directly propping up the second floor of the inn where the traveling actors stay? Fair enough. These showy staircases are not sinister at all. Rare for Ozu, they almost seem like stage decor for a play as the actors use them to climb up and go down. And yet, in witnessing the busy movement on these stairs, we come to sense that the people who inhabit this space will have no claims to permanent residency. This is only a temporary domicile, a space that permits an exceptional flexibility only because it will have to be vacated.

Those who have understood how intimidating it can be to encounter visible stairs ingrained on the cinematic surface—a place where surprise renews continuously—will therefore be deeply, unavoidably moved upon witnessing the near full shot of a staircase filmed at close range when it creeps into the scene near the end of *An Autumn Afternoon*. They will sense in their bodies that the appearance of this brief shot of a staircase must, in the context of the Ozuesque "film," constitute a decisive event. At this moment, our cinematic sensibility begins to tremble, as if in the face of something that should not be. If this is not moving, cinema must have no room left for anything that is. This is of course not to say that the solitude of a father sitting alone at the table in a dimly lit kitchen on the evening of his youngest daughter's wedding day is not something moving in itself. The last image of *An Autumn Afternoon,* of Chishū Ryū hanging his head and absorbed in his thoughts, is certainly capable of stirring the heart as it brings the narrative to a conclusion. But this scene is also moving at a level beyond that of character psychology and empathy. The flow of the sequence does in fact accentuate the melancholy figure of Ryū in the dimness of night following the conclusion of his daughter's wedding reception, but it also introduces a series of shots depicting the deserted second floor, the long rectangle of a full-length mirror glinting dully at the back of what was the daughter's room, now devoid of any human presence . . . but it does this only after the insertion, if for a very brief moment, of a single almost full shot picturing none other than the staircase connecting the first and second floors—a shot materializing a loneliness that is not merely the private sadness of a father, but the absolute solitude of the late-period Ozuesque "film" itself (fig. 8).

Marrying off a daughter must be a truly poignant experience for a father. But Ryū did not lose his cheer after losing his wife and will probably continue to smile after the marriage of his daughter. If he endures it for a time, his loneliness will become a manageable sentiment. But the shot of the stairs is another matter. It jolts our cinematic sensibility with a decisive shock that exceeds such kinds of emotions, and the realness of this shock is what makes the end of *An Autumn Afternoon* so moving. Before departing for the wedding venue, Ryū dares to tread, with his eldest son Keiji Sada, into the second-floor women's sanctuary to imprint on his memory the sight of his daughter in bridal attire. When he does, he stands hesitantly to the rear of the scene, much like the Chishū Ryū who brings tea to his daughter and her friend in *Late Spring*. Like Sada, who stands with his back nearly pressed against a chest of drawers, as if denying himself entry into the women's sanctuary, Ryū hides his sheepishness behind an ambiguous smile, making no attempt to approach the bride. The daughter's hair is gathered up into a ceremonial Shimada-style bun as she sits in the foreground of the scene—which is to say to the back of the room as shown in the reverse shot from the father's perspective—next to a window opening onto a garden, with Mariko Okada waiting at her side. Even the women at the periphery of the second-floor room, who have helped dress her, blend more naturally into this space as they move freely about than her own father Ryū does. The spatial positioning of the bride and her attendant opposite the father is almost entirely identical to that of Setsuko Hara and Yumeji Tsukioka in *Late Spring*. Ryū neither advances nor retreats. He simply squats, awkwardly, in the middle of the room, as if in the face of something not to be touched. This is clearly very much the same scene as the one on the morning of the wedding ceremony in *Late Spring*. The father is again capable of little more than lightly placing a hand on his daughter dressed in bridal attire as she leaves her sanctuary behind.

Her room now floats empty above her father's head, having become the ruin of a sanctuary. The narrative must draw to a close when this space adrift in midair evicts a twenty-five-year-old daughter, the inhabitant who has held exclusive privileges. A "nothingness" in the form of the deserted second floor has undeniably been produced internal to the Ozuesque "film," a nothingness that even takes material form, as a forceful reality that refuses to give way to sentimentality. The second floor has not been vacated because a daughter was married. The narrational flow of the "film" has lost its momentum to move because space

9. *An Autumn Afternoon:* An exceedingly rare staircase.

adrift in midair has excluded a woman who was passing through. And what makes the production of nothingness undeniably real is a near close-up shot of a deserted staircase, filmed head-on (fig. 9). A lonely staircase, cruelly severed from the rest of the house. A staircase having lost any function, that will never again offer egress to a sanctuary or prohibit trespass. A staircase that has ceased to be an invisible wall, having returned to the form of a simple architectural detail. When stairs that have consistently remained out of view are stripped of the privilege of absence and emerge, as stairs, on the cinematic surface, the near frenzy of their being in that instant completely upsets the foundations of the late-period Ozuesque "film." This is a punishing instant, in which the "film" attempts to touch its limits. A point of cinematic collapse, breaching the narrational flow that sustains late-period Ozu as a homogeneous environment, and abolishing both filming and viewing at once. A point of collapse, but also of eruption. Is there anything anywhere so uncanny and frightening as this absurd image—an image of both excess and lack at once? How could anyone continue to talk about cinema after laying eyes on such a thing? Then again, was late-period Ozu really cinema?

5

LOOKING

HYPERBOLE AND PROVOCATION

Ozu is often unnatural. At times, his shot sequences lack naturalness to the point of provocation. Contrary to what some might simplistically believe, this unnaturalness is not a product of the impoverished obstinance of an auteur striving to preserve his personal cinematic world against the slightest destabilization. It is also unrelated to the kind of detachment from reality that people tend to imagine when they envision Ozu as an inveterate traditionalist, an image that afflicted him in his last years. It is an unnaturalness persistently related to the aberration of nature we call cinema itself. At a time when many mediocre filmmakers were content to go about their work with ambiguous neglect for this unnaturalness, Ozu made a point of demonstrating and exaggerating it.

Ozu's intentionality toward exaggeration grows increasingly apparent in his later years. Take, for example, the scene in *Late Autumn* where young couple Keiji Sada and Yōko Tsukasa eat ramen noodles side by side (fig. 10). They sit at a counter too narrow to call a table—a board, really—attached to a wall that their noses practically scrape as they maneuver their chopsticks. A similar spatial arrangement has already appeared in the ramen shop scene in *The Flavor of Green Tea over Rice,* where a wall closes in on Kōji Tsuruta as he sings the praises of ramen—so "cheap and delicious"—to Keiko Tsushima. But the wall depicted in *Late Autumn* has a much more oppressive atmosphere. Then there is the scene in *The End of Summer* where Yōko Tsukasa sits side by side on a station bench with her future fiancé Akira Takarada as the two talk. The bench they have chosen also faces a wall at close range. Despite the fact that this bench is on a train platform, it positions the two so that their backs are fully turned to the rails. As a result, what we first lay eyes on in both these scenes are the backs of couples in conversation. Characteristically Ozuesque shots do of course follow, of each character, pictured in alternating sequence, facing in the direction of the other and staring. But this does not erase the impression of unnaturalness. Naturalness is lacking here, both in terms of spatial organization and on the level of psychology. Why should these young couples have to sit with their noses awkwardly to the wall, as if turning their backs to the world? Perhaps a lunchtime rush at the ramen shop has left only these two seats free. But there are few other customers visible in the surroundings. Perhaps the couple on the bench have chosen this spot out of a sense of modesty, to avoid attention. But not many other people are visible on the nighttime station platform. Staring at the wall therefore seems like a gratuitous gesture as performed by these young men and women. Such is the unnaturalness of Ozu. But just how are we to explain this lack of naturalness?

In claiming to describe what is unique about Ozu's films, people often invoke language about his restraint and the extreme simplification of style that followed as a result. Donald Richie treads into this territory in his book *Ozu: His Life and Films,* when he cites Ozu's "quality

10. *Late Autumn:* Yōko Tsukasa and Keiji Sada eating ramen at a narrow counter.

of restraint," writing that, "in even a strictly technical sense, Ozu's films are among the most restrained, the most limited, controlled, restricted."¹ For Richie, this aesthetic of restraint defines Ozu's authorial consistency. Paul Schrader anticipates this line of argumentation, claiming that, "most of all, Ozu refined his technique," and concluding that "Ozu is cinema's consummate formalist."² Such appraisals of Ozu as a rigid formalist are not unique to commentators outside of Japan. Japanese critics have also taken this view, which is probably not an

---

1. This English wording, which corresponds to what Hasumi quotes without specific citation in Japanese, appears in a newspaper article written by Donald Richie as an introduction to his book: "The Appeal of Ozu, the Most Japanese of Filmmakers," *New York Times*, September 26, 1982, https://www.nytimes.com/1982/09/26/arts/the-appeal-of-ozu-the-most-japanese-of-filmmakers.html.

2. Paul Schrader, *Transcendental Style in Film: Ozu, Bresson, Dreyer* (New York: Da Capo Press, 1988), 22.

entirely mistaken way of looking at things. Ozu is in fact insistent on form. Still, it is not as though form in Ozu always pursues balance and harmony. The aforementioned shots in which people's noses practically scrape the wall demonstrate how form in Ozu often becomes something unnatural, even in the extreme.

Recall, for example, the opening commute scene in *Early Spring* (*Sōshun*, 1956), which consists of several shots of crowds heading toward the station at rush hour (fig. 11). Columns of men and women advance in mostly the same direction, from the dense residential side streets near the Rokugō embankment toward the platform at Kamata Station. The commuters maintain consistently the same pace within the flow toward the station, and even when standing on the platform, they look consistently in the same direction. The effect is almost eerie. We can probably come around to the idea that this is more or less what the morning commute does in fact look like, but not without first being struck by this scene's exaggerated unnaturalness. Even a single pedestrian might move against the flow, maybe walking a dog, or perhaps someone in the crowd might break step and overtake the people around them.[3] These are office workers, of course, but do all these men and women really have to be so close in age and appearance? Would it not be more natural if they were not? Do they really need to maintain even the same pace with such single-minded determination?

But Ozu does generally make his characters walk at the same pace, and in the same direction, almost as if to do so were a formal necessity. Not that something like this would be unconvincing if the subject were lovers walking side by side. But in the case of the hiking scene in *Late Autumn*, for example, where half a dozen young men and women form a line across the width of a path and advance at the same pace while whistling in unison, the effect can only be called unnatural. Moving through the field, they neither glance down at the flowers nor cast their

---

3. A single person in one shot of this sequence does in fact move against the flow.

11. *Early Summer:* Unidirectional walking during the morning commute.

gazes at the distant mountain scenery, but instead devote their entire attention to synchronizing their gestures with automaton-like precision. If this is what formal necessity looks like, it can only be said that form itself is unnatural.

Ozu's exaggerated unnaturalness is sometimes likened to that of Dreyer or Bresson, but what we have here is really closer to the world of hyperbole in Fellini. Much as the director of 8½ (1963) seems unable to resist outrageous physical hyperbole when it comes to portraying women, Ozu suddenly abandons all naturalness when filming people walk, as if driven by a compulsion to exaggerate mechanical motion. No casual chatter or impulsive behavior is permitted of his characters in these moments. In any case, nothing could be farther from Ozu than the image of a crowd seething in all directions. The number of people who populate his world seems predetermined, and the trajectories of their movements minutely gauged. If this is to be called attention to form, formalism must lead to the exaltation of things artificial and unnatural. This is not to say that Ozu pursues the kind of graphical geometry we find in Fritz Lang's *Metropolis* (1927), or that he displays decorative plasticity like that of Busby Berkeley. The atmosphere of artificiality that his images evoke is more reminiscent of René Clair's *Le Million* (1931) or *À nous la liberté* (1931), where neither people nor things are quite natural. There are also no seductive physical details that set the cinematic surface trembling, as wrists and fingers do in Bresson, nor any studies of the severity of the human face, as in Dreyer, where low-angle close-ups make people's features stand out. Unnaturalness does reveal itself as such in Ozu, but it also harmonizes with the myths of the Ozuesque image, and in doing so practically makes us forget even the impression of unnaturalness. Where Fellini is concerned, his physical exaggeration of women is probably permitted simply because he is Fellini, because it is seen as something uniquely Felliniesque that communicates the unconscious of his world. But nothing could be farther from concepts like harmony and proportion than such unnaturalness. Such details are alien to both the restraint described by Richie and the refinement cited by Schrader. They awkwardly stand out, revealing an Ozu who lets his imagination run free, not by cultivating the virtues of reticence but by embracing effusiveness. Things like walls closing in on lovers or people walking automaton-like in the same direction do not introduce any significant changes into the unfolding plots and can therefore probably be considered superfluous details from the perspective of narrative coherence. Keiji Sada and Yōko Tsukasa would probably still get married in the end even if they had not slurped ramen noodles together with their noses pressed against a wall, and Ryō Ikebe's salaryman in *Early Spring* would probably still betray his wife and end up pleading for her forgiveness in a location far from Tokyo with or without the unidirectionality of eyelines among the people all marching toward the station on their morning commute.

To the extent that things like walls closing in or automaton-like walking are formal necessities, they must be dictated by demands of a different nature from those of the narrational order. We know, of course, that narrational structure in Ozu is premised on the exclusion of dramatic elements. Nowhere do we witness unexpected developments as the result of some extraordinary action. Everything drifts along in accord with that frequently cited rhythm of even calm. Ozu tells stories in monotone, favoring repetitions of like situations over the privileging of isolated episodes distinctly framed by the fade-in and the fade-out. And yet Ozu's films do have stories, however attenuated their dramatic elements may be. In fact, there is no such thing as a film that does not have a story. This is obviously true of fiction films, which recreate what we know in reality or can imagine by analogy, but it applies also to things like so-called experimental films, even the ones that consist of nothing but abstract form unrelatable to human psychology or the conflicts it entails. As long as a film has a duration greater than none at all, it has a story, and where a story is narrated, there is also a corresponding narrational flow. It therefore goes without saying that the films of Ozu also narrate stories, and things we have been describing with words like *restraint* and *refinement* probably do possess a certain legitimacy as things characteristic of narrational structure in Ozu. The fact that Ozu gradually abandoned fades and mostly stopped using camera movement and close-ups is an issue that should be discussed on the level of his narrative technique, which is to say his avoidance of dramatic elements. But in cinema, where stories can only be narrated by means of distinct images, there is also another system, one that at times harmonizes with and at times also defies the narrational structure of a given film. This other system involves things like significant details and the aspects they present as they transcend the succession of shots and intermingle in a realm other than that of the time axis. This is what we have been calling the *thematic system*. Think of the thematic system as the place where filmmakers give free rein to their imaginations. This applies not only to Ozu, but to filmmakers of all kinds, except that in the case of Ozu there is a contrast between narrational structure on the one hand, which takes on a mostly austere aspect as a result of his restraint and refinement, and this thematic system on the other, where Ozu asserts himself wildly, even to the point of running amok, so much so that the balance of the whole threatens to collapse. Here we find excess and deviation. Hyperbole and unnaturalness seem cheerfully permitted. The walls in the ramen shops and by the platform at the train station form a theme that belongs to this system, like the unidirectionality of walking among the men and women who commute or hike. The Ozu we encounter in these instances is decidedly not reticent or inexpressive. On the contrary, he demonstrates an excessive fixation with certain aspects of things living and inanimate. Such thematic effusiveness should not be regarded as mere attention to form or otherwise obscured through excessively blind faith in Ozuesque myths like silence and stillness. The theme of walls and the theme of unidirectional looking transcend the dimensions of things like adherence to form or the free expression of unconscious worlds and involve problems that touch on the fundamental conditions of our film experience. After all, there is no encounter with a film that does not involve the wall of a screen, and the place called a movie theater only comes into being when we arrange ourselves side by side and point our gazes all in the same direction. Cinema is a highly unnatural phenomenon, premised on these two far-from-natural conditions. Of course, there is no way of knowing whether Yasujirō Ozu himself intended such things, but when we focus our attention on the right places in the films, our convictions about his unnaturalness are renewed. This merits some consideration, since any formalist striving for restraint and refinement alone would find it exceedingly difficult to become a film auteur. Film auteurs are unnatural creatures without exception.

It probably goes without saying, but the point here is not to insist that the wall in the ramen shop is a metaphor for the screen, or that hiking men and women represent the audience in a movie theater. The intent is this: to attempt to play with the thematic system in Ozu by means of the various knowing smiles that strikingly unnatural walls can exchange with things not walls, or that the strikingly unnatural eyelines of people walking can exchange with things not the eyelines of people walking, and in this way to grope at fertile cinematic gestures having nothing to do with austerity, even while recognizing consistency where it exists. Then, to feel just how rich Ozu's thematic system is, in spite of the restraint, the refinement of technique, and the poverty of dramatic events in the narrational domain. To do this requires tracing the transformations in themes like walls and unidirectional looking within the Ozuesque "film," and acknowledging the ways those movements clearly sneer at myths like restraint and refinement, since in this regard Ozu is neither a traditionalist nor avant-garde, but a filmmaker who transcends such kinds of conceptual oppositions to intersect in unmediated fashion with cinema itself. It is at moments such as these that the Yasujirō Ozu otherwise buried under so many myths frees himself from the discourse of Ozu and lays himself bare as a film auteur.

UNNATURAL FRESHNESS

As a process of organizing scenes along the time axis, the act of *narrating* is a constraining cinematic experience. A film only emerges through a process of selection and exclusion, whether in the form of the purely technical procedure of editing and the arrangement of shots, or from the perspective of the narrative thread and the linking of scenes. Filmmakers have no alternative but to place shots one after the other, one scene following another, everything in seamless linearity. They do, of course, maintain sovereignty when it comes to decisions about *what* to select or exclude, and at least in that respect can be said to enjoy a modicum of freedom. But such freedom can only be relative in light of the material limitation that all shots must be arranged successively, from beginning to end, without any surplus or gap. Cinematic narrational flow is an absolute system that no refinement of technique or uniqueness of imagination can resist, a system by which even the most ingenious of filmmakers are bound. In other words, there is a syntagmatic order in cinema from which even Ozu does not diverge in the slightest, and both the ramen shop scene in *Late Autumn* and the morning commute scene in *Early Spring* are composed of shot sequences arranged in compliance with this order.

It is true, of course, that the techniques of narration this system permits can lead to restraint and refinement. They do give form to Ozu's distinct rhythm and his rhetoric of ellipsis, and they promote a certain impression of technical austerity. But in cinema, the information that fills a shot is always plural and spatially distributed, and for this reason, the subject of narration often refuses easy reduction into the narrational flow. What people see in the ramen shop scenes is by no means limited to couples maneuvering chopsticks while talking. These scenes also include walls that strangely come closing in. And what meets the eye during the scene of the morning commute is not just a crowd of people, but a conscientious unidirectionality of looking and a common regularity of step. As already stated, it would be a mistake to interpret these things as products of a rigid formalism, and from there to draw conclusions about restraint and refinement. They should in fact be viewed as exposing the liberty of Ozu's cinematic sensitivity, which could not be farther from restraint. Even if these are probably not places where the unconscious runs rampant, a radicalism does reveal itself here, a radicalism of a kind that can only be enjoyed by those already liberated from rigid habits of thought and the will to control through intellectual contemplation. Although narrational structure is constrained to resolve into sequential linearity, cinema does possess another system to defy that linearity. This other system is the zone where exaggeration and deviation become possible, where excess details draw the eye and transcend the shot sequence, exceeding even the boundaries of the films themselves and resonating across the slightest of similarities with details located elsewhere. These visual details with the capacity to create resonances are what we have called themes. The knowing smiles that such details exchange among themselves are liberated from the linearity of the shot sequence and can be said to possess spatial expansion. But we should avoid reaching immediately for the semiotic term "paradigm" to describe this phenomenon. The thematic system is not a latent reserve of details available for selection. It is thoroughly overt and comes to life as the movement of play among groupings of fragments receptive of things plural. In other words, what we have provisionally called "the ramen shop scene" is at the same time also the scene of the wall, the narrow counter, the backs of a couple leaning over round noodle bowls, the faces of people staring and exchanging words, and many other things. All these things can be observed with certainty. Then, when a wall two people seem to scrape with their noses tips out of balance and comes closing in, this strange ramen shop instantaneously forms an intimate association with the nighttime train platform in a different film. In this way, the ramen shop and the station bench begin to cast knowing smiles at each other, by way of what is a mere trivial detail from a narrational perspective: the close presence of a wall. Just as a certain shot in Fellini's *Amarcord* (1973) resonates with another certain shot in *8½* through the presence of a hyperbolic woman, a deep tractional force is also activated between *Late Autumn* and *The End of Summer,* revealing that what the Ozuesque "film" narrates are not only stories about things like parent-child attachments or the dissolution of households but also stories of walls as surfaces. In Ozu, there are also stories of unidirectional looking and stories of uniform walking, and the one that gives form to the scene of the morning commute within the narrational flow of *Early Summer* will intimately encounter the one that becomes the hiking scene in *Late Autumn*. In other words, things that emerge as fragments in mutual isolation within their respective stories can suddenly join together in relationships of complicity. What we are calling the thematic system is a rippling, a tangible movement that the relationships enabling such encounters and such solidarity transmit to the networked fabric of significant details extending above and across the individual films. We should reserve the name thematic system only for sites where fragments overtly circulate in movements of exchange. It does not apply to the latent presence of details that might virtually form connections across their similarities. After all, the privileged experience possible in cinema is not a matter of using the imagination to stage encounters between things hidden and some deep layer of the conscious mind, but of the movements of things unmistakably visible as they play alongside one another on the surface of the visual field.

As addressed in previous chapters, the Ozuesque "film" contains stories about clothing and stories about stairs. We have also noted that such significant details not only rise above the narrational flow of each individual film and join together in relationships of solidarity but conversely also become a source of momentum internal to the individual films, setting into motion, advancing, and bringing to conclusion what are in themselves rather monotone human dramas. Narrational structure is limited to the syntagmatic order of the shot sequence and is not in itself part of the movement of narration, since narrating a story involves shifting the narrational flow to new and different planes, and what directly supplies the momentum for these shifts is the stimulus itself of the interplay among excess details that attempt to deviate from sequential linearity. The narrational flow of *Early Spring* does not begin with the scene of Ryō Ikebe's commute to work following his morning routine. It draws momentum from the themes of unidirectional looking and uniform walking, which establish a sharp divide between the monotone routines of the household and the rather ritualistic features of work at the office. In disappearing into the columns of commuters that so vividly embody these themes, Ikebe decisively removes himself from the domestic space inhabited by his wife Chikage Awashima and ends up committing an indiscretion with fellow commuter Keiko Kishi. The hiking episode, planned by friends who share the same commute, intervenes to occasion this betrayal, plainly illustrating how the themes of synchronized looking and walking, exaggerated to the point of unnaturalness, articulate the narrational flow and perform the dynamic function of guiding the plot toward a new stage. Ikebe's adultery may be what directly causes his departure with his wife from Tokyo to the countryside, but it is not there primarily to narrate a drama of character desire and psychology. Rather, it is something derived from the logic of the thematic system.

I have argued elsewhere as well that Ozu's preoccupation with the scenery of the morning commute, and particularly with passengers waiting on train platforms, relates not to any special interest in social customs but precisely to the unidirectionality of looking these situations entail.[4] Whenever characters in an Ozu film stand side by side facing in the same direction, as Hiroshi Nihon'yanagi and Setsuko Hara do at Kita Kamakura station in *Early Summer*, a narrational transformation of some kind is sure to follow, even where the scene itself portrays little more than ordinary conversation. There will be further opportunities to address this point in detail later on, but suffice it to say for now that whether characters end up parting ways, starting new lives, or departing for faraway destinations, the narrative will cease to progress within the same setting, venturing inexorably toward new situations instead. The narrative changes produced at such moments are so abrupt that family members confront them with surprise, as when Hara resolves to get married in *Early Summer*. They are abrupt and probably also unnatural from the perspective of the psychology of love, but it would not necessarily be fair to cite them as evidence of Ozu's awkwardness in portraying matters of the heart.

---

4. Shiguéhiko Hasumi, *Eiga no shinwagaku* (Tokyo: Tairyū Sha, 1997), 80.

Of course, Ozu bashfully avoids the subject of romantic love, which he depicts exclusively by means of verbal slips or deliberate ellipses. But this does not prove that he was an innocent in such things, much less a traditionalist with antiquated attitudes toward romance. What it does indicate is his firsthand knowledge of just how much unnaturalness has been foisted onto cinema by those attempting to visualize the tremblings of desire and the unconscious disarray that people tend to associate with love, as well as his awareness of just how banal shot composition and sequencing has been rendered by cinematic techniques aimed at creating the illusion that such unnaturalness is, on the contrary, *natural*. Take, for example, the close-up. Ever since it was institutionalized as an indispensable element of the romantic film, this narrational technique for enlarging facial expressions and wordlessly conveying the swelling of emotion has brought about a banalization of cinematic sensitivity, as we are all aware. In manufacturing false emotional highs and lows, the close-up puts the look that should be focused on the screen pleasantly to rest, all the while coercing the viewer into a psychological acquiescence that erases from memory even the unnaturalness of having been coerced. The intention here is not to declare that the close-up always functions as a technique of banalization. Ozu himself belonged to a generation that was awakened to cinema by Griffith and can hardly be said to have summarily rejected its effects. But he also did not share the naïve faith that many others have placed in this institutionalized technique. Rather, he drew attention to its limitations and exposed as illusory the notion that it was part of a general grammar of film, and in doing so elected to draw cinema closer. "I don't think that cinema has a grammar," Ozu famously said.[5] These words should be understood less as a declaration of self-confidence by a great filmmaker fully convinced of the exceptionality of his own

---

5. Ozu Yasujirō Hito to Shigoto Kankōkai, *Ozu Yasujirō hito to shigoto* (Tokyo: Ban'yū Sha, 1972). No page number is cited in the Japanese.

cinematic world than as a pronouncement of irritation by someone who knew firsthand just how much cinema could be dulled by blind faith in institutionalized technique. He is saying, in other words, that in preoccupying themselves only with how story corresponds to narrational structure, people end up letting cinema itself slip away. "There is no formula that says, 'this is how it has to be done.' When you have a great film, it creates its own grammar, so people should make films on their own terms."[6] This quote from Ozu appears to vindicate Richie when he writes that Ozu "certainly implies that a film that creates its own grammar is also a good one."[7] It would also not be entirely unreasonable to surmise here, as Richie does, that Ozu "may have been speaking of his own pictures, which by and large *do* have one form." [8] It is certainly likely that Ozu was at least in part thinking of his own work when he made these comments, but context reveals that the topic was not himself alone but the film world in general, and specifically its decline. In fact, Ozu follows the sentences quoted above by lamenting a general withering of sensibility among assistant directors:

> In the process of doing the bidding of a director over the course of many years, [assistant directors] end up losing whatever individual freshness they may have had. As they absorb the common sense of established technique, they compromise their own vision. They tell themselves, "this is film grammar." And when they become directors in their own right, their way of making films always ends up the same, like what we see everywhere else. This is why Japanese films lack freshness. Sometimes, like with new talent in Mexico or Italy, we see amateurs arrive at the studio out of the blue and shoot things with techniques that feel surprisingly fresh. I haven't seen the picture that Shintarō Ishihara directed, but I think there are probably some pretty interesting things in there.[9]

6. Ozu Yasujirō Hito to Shigoto Kankōkai, *Ozu Yasujirō hito to shigoto*.
7. Donald Richie, *Ozu* (Berkeley: University of California Press, 1974), 189.
8. Richie, *Ozu*, 189.
9. Ozu Yasujirō Hito to Shigoto Kankōkai, *Ozu Yasujirō hito to shigoto*, 631.

It is almost poignant to read Ozu's words when he pins hope for the revitalization of the Japanese film world on Shintarō Ishihara's wretched piece of work *The Young Beast* (*Wakai kemono*, 1958). It would be unfortunate indeed if these words were merely a formalist's justification of his own unique cinematic universe. But we need not adhere to such a reading. Instead, we should read these reflections as an admonishment directed at those desensitized to just how frightening a thing the system we call cinema truly is—an admonishment, moreover, by someone who was perhaps the first practicing Japanese film director to see and sing the praises of Orson Welles's *Citizen Kane*.[10]

What, incidentally, is the "freshness" to which Ozu refers? We do not have a specific image of what he meant by this, of course, but we can look to the Ozuesque "film" itself and describe just how fresh it was even in Ozu's last years, when many regarded him as an obdurate traditionalist. To summarize what has been stated already, what in the end should be considered characteristic of Ozu consists of a disequilibrium, or perhaps an irreparable deviation, between narrational structure and thematic system. In one sense, Ozu is austere indeed, much as we are told by the commentators who attempt to highlight what is specific about his films through litanies of observation about what they are not. But consider this statement by Richie: "When Ozu relinquished, one by one, most of the grammatical elements of cinema, obviously he sacrificed a great deal—most of the means, in fact, through which film directors ordinarily express themselves."[11] This observation can only be justified if we confine ourselves to things on the narrational level in the films. A modest reticence does envelope Ozu's gestures as he recounts episodes, to the point of cloaking them in a calm that approaches silence. However, this alone does not demonstrate that Ozu "sacrificed many of the film director's techniques of self-expression." The instinct

---

10. See Hasumi's interview with Yūharu Atsuta in the appendix for an account of the circumstances under which Ozu screened *Citizen Kane* while stationed in Singapore during the war.
11. Richie, *Ozu*, 113.

to invoke concepts like self-expression is in itself something of which we are quite skeptical, but even if we take "self-expression" at face value, we have to acknowledge that Ozu was more than a little effusive. This was also no mere rhetorical effusiveness, not merely a technique for expressing a lot by very limited means, but a talkative effusiveness, talkative to the point of excess. Even if we agreed to call this "self-expression," there would still be no "sacrifice" of technique here. On the contrary, it can even be said that Ozu attained a realm of exaggeration on the far side of anything natural. In other words, in contrast to the monotone austerity we find on the level of narrational structure, Ozu spread his cinematic sensitivity in all directions across the thematic system, even lavishly installing circuits of solidarity among significant details. This, precisely, is the nature of the irreparable deviation between thematic system and narrational structure in Ozu. As his gestures of narrating become reticent to the point of silence, images that deviate from the story only to intervene in the narration and influence the movement of its flow give form to a radical effusiveness. The freshness of Ozu resides within this dynamic. As with the views of the commute in *Early Spring,* shots in these instances refuse subservience to the narrative, accentuating themes like synchronized looking and walking with a radicality that, in the context of the narrational order, can hardly be described as anything but unnatural exaggeration, and give shape to excess details that can no longer be attributed to the conscious control of the filmmaker. These excess details, in their deviation from narrational structure, invigorate narrational flow and become stimuli for transformations that articulate the plot. The freshness of Ozu lies in the provocative unnaturalness that such gaps visually materialize. This kind of provocation probably also makes the Ozuesque "film" increasingly fresh as it moves from the early period through the middle years and into the late period. But in order to demonstrate just how essential this freshness is to the films, we need to reexamine the functions performed by Ozu's thematic system in the early and middle period work, where it frequently deviates from the narrational flow. To this end, we should recall the ways that the themes of walls closing in and synchronized looking and walking find expression in *Days of Youth*, the earliest of the Ozu films that we are able to view in complete form today.

STUDENTS LEAVING THE LECTURE HALL

The eye that gazes at the image in Ozu often experiences deep agitation of a sort that we might describe as a kind of archaeological ecstasy. This is something that occurs without fail whenever Ozu's camera enters a university campus, such as the ones that appear again and again in the early-period student comedies starting with *Days of Youth*—a film identified by its original Japanese title as "a student romance"—as well as *I Flunked, but . . .* and *Where Now Are the Dreams of Youth?* Of course, nothing of any particular seriousness is ever depicted in these moments. If anything, the situations that captivate the look here are comic in nature, as when students come flowing out of a classroom doorway after custodian Takeshi Sakamoto accidentally rings the bell that signals the end of class. We feel moved when this crowd of students pours into the schoolyard in their stiff-collared uniforms, their faces beaming just as if final exams had ended and the summer holiday were at last about to begin, as if there were nothing left to do but await graduation. It is as if cinema had suddenly been transported back to the time of the Lumière brothers. We feel moved, but not only because this scene so beautifully expresses the sense of liberation that accompanies the end of the school semester. What agitates our cinematic sensitivity is quite simply the movement of a group of students pouring out of a building at more or less the same pace. This moves us for no apparent reason, much in the same way that we are moved by Louis Lumière's first film *Workers Leaving the Factory* (*La sortie de l'usine Lumière à Lyon*, 1895). Or rather, we sense a kind of mythological atmosphere in Ozu's gesture, an atmosphere of primitive origins, so much so that it starts to seem strange that, in the historical moment when films were attempting to invent themselves as cinema, Louis and Auguste never placed their own tripod in front of "students leaving the university." What is traced across the surface of the screen is what we might call an audacious sensitivity that only the mythological gesture can accommodate, an unnatural naturalness of a kind only an archaeological eye might permit.

In *Where Now Are the Dreams of Youth?*, when the campus custodian discovers a coin purse in the empty schoolyard while class is in session and, in his disappointment at finding it empty, unwittingly rings the school bell, the effect is an acoustic gag that, because this is a silent film, amounts to little more than a conceptual novelty and hardly merits a laugh. But we are soon stirred by the sight of students pouring into the schoolyard, blissfully unaware of the mistake. What stirs us is the unidirectionality of their motion. It is as if Ozu introduced the careless custodian and his accident with the school bell with the sole purpose of filming a scene of students in stiff academic collars leaving a campus building through a doorway.

This unscheduled flow of students is ultimately interrupted by three professors who consult their pocket watches and exchange puzzled looks, but we find more thorough execution of a similar situation in *Days of Youth,* where the scene is also depicted without reliance on a comedic setup. In this instance, the unidirectional motion that visualizes the students' liberation from their exams is emphasized with camera movement. The flow of students moves in the same direction, from the lecture hall doorway across the campus grounds, with the windows of the classroom in the background. In *I Flunked, but . . .* the time is the moments right before an exam, but the setting is utterly identical, and the students are depicted with the same lateral camera movement, only this time they are sitting in a row along a path and looking down at their books. The unnaturalness of late Ozu that compels most of his characters to walk in step and in the same direction, or to look in the same direction, is already vividly apparent in these early student comedies. These students have accepted walking in step and unidirectional looking as the basic conditions of their own gestures and movement, much like the columns of commuters in the opening scene of *Early Spring* or the line of young hikers in *Late Autumn*. But perhaps the special nature of the university campus setting, as a space removed from society at large, diminishes the unnaturalness of their collective behavior, emphasizing its somewhat exaggerated comic aspects instead.

Still, there is basically no depiction anywhere in Ozu of formlessly convulsing crowds. The opening shot of *Dragnet Girl,* an overhead shot depicting several people walking in opposite directions, is an exception. As a rule, the eyelines or lines of motion of Ozuesque characters are only either crossed from the front or tracked in parallel. Whenever it seems that a formless throng might appear, Ozu always has to introduce some kind of incident to reassert uniform walking and unidirectional looking. For example, in *Tokyo Chorus*—which belongs not to the school comedies but to the salaryman films—people stroll about, peacefully unaware, as unemployed Tokihiko Okada sits on a park bench to take a rest from his search for work. Suddenly, the people break into a run, all in the same direction and at the same pace. They have learned that a bear (or was it a tiger . . . a beast of prey, in any case) has escaped from its cage at the zoo, which we imagine is located somewhere in the park. The sight of everyone suddenly crossing the screen, all in the same direction and in front of this character whose job search has led nowhere and who has taken a seat just to pass the time, agitates the eye of the viewer. This is a provocative moment, first of all because the movement of the crowd is initiated by a cause completely unrelated to the story in the process of being narrated. Moreover, despite the fact that such behavior clearly lacks any narrational necessity, the viewer does sense that there is an urgency of some kind here. A cinematic event of a different order from that of the narrative seems to be taking place. This is true of the opening of *Walk Cheerfully* as well, which features a spectacular portside chase scene before any major characters have even been introduced. The Ozu of this early period seems to hide the causes of events by introducing them with gags, as with the clumsy custodian's school bell or the predator escaped from its cage at the zoo. When these contrived causes eventually fall away, late-period Ozu is revealed in all its unnaturalness. From our present vantage point, which allows us to view early Ozu and late Ozu from the same distance, we have the privilege of being able to see both the presence and the absence of causes as part of the same cinematic experiment. This is because Ozu's relationship to cinema is made conspicuous whether he takes care to portray unidirectional looking and uniform walking as *natural* or leaves these things to their unnaturalness. In a sense, this specific unnaturalness is taken farthest in early Ozu. Take, for example, the pep squad in the opening scene of *Where Now Are the Days of Youth?* or the unity of gesture among the flunkees when they assume linear formation and look as though they might start to tap dance in *I Flunked, but . . .*, or else the ritual of orchestrated greetings among the gangsters in *Walk Cheerfully*. The use of such unique choreography to stage gestures of mechanical repetition is eclipsed in late-period Ozu, replaced by moments of unnaturalness that stick out within the context of everyday behavior otherwise generally accepted as natural. But these two approaches ultimately amount to the same thing. Whether we find ourselves accepting something unnatural as natural because it takes place within the special space of the university campus, or whether something regarded as natural within the monotone surroundings of everyday life suddenly stands out as unnatural, Ozu is consistently preoccupied with unidirectional looking and with uniform walking.

BOARDINGHOUSE WINDOWS

Consider again the famous gag where students cast shadow figures that spell the word for "bread" on the sliding paper screen in their second-floor boardinghouse window to place a delivery order with the café girl across the street. This scene from Ozu's *I Flunked, but . . .* would surely have delighted Howard Hawks, depicting as it does a novel deployment, through careful preparation and teamwork, of the human body as a prop. In any case, the visual gag is only possible here because the students have first leaned out their window and fired a track-and-field pistol to summon Kinuyo Tanaka's attention, demonstrating that sound plays an important role even in this silent film. When Tanaka comes out to the nighttime street, her cheerful expression is quite moving, above all because of how earnestly she smiles at the flunkees even though their eyes cannot actually be meeting. The reason their eyes cannot be meeting is that the students gathered at the second-floor window are not looking down to where she is standing at the street below, but straight out, as if the distance across the street erased the difference of elevation. Ozu is clearly already indifferent to the eyeline match. In a shot of the window taken from the front, the students look out, casting their gazes parallel to the ground as if they were at street level. Paradoxically, what this disregard for spatial conditions makes clear is a thorough commitment to unidirectional looking. It seems that what is most important for Ozu is not the positional relationship between the eye and its object, or whether eyelines meet, but the mere fact that they extend in the same direction.

In the example from *I Flunked, but . . .*, the flunkees have a purpose for arranging themselves at the window and looking out in the same direction, but the circumstances in *Days of Youth* are somewhat different. Ichirō Yūki and Tatsuo Saitō are student boarders like the ones in *I Flunked, but . . .*, but these two keep their desks by the window for studying. On the two occasions when they look out through the window, they do so without any particular motivation. The first time is when some money they were expecting fails to arrive, and it seems they will be unable to take a planned ski trip after their exams. The second time is after they have succeeded in getting to the slopes but returned in defeat, having vied for the affections of a pretty girl who turned out to be already engaged. On both of these occasions, the two will cast their gazes outside through the window.[12]

What comes into view here are some utterly ordinary smokestacks, a weathervane that would be at home in a Hollywood western, and ventilation pipes probably connected to toilets. The smokestacks appear in both close-up and long shot, but these things are otherwise shown as a series of individual static shots, each corresponding to a change in the direction of the students' eyelines. The eye and its object are paired in a way that seems more or less to reflect the psychological circumstances of a looking subject. The Ozu of the late period will eventually rob the look of psychological subjectivization and transform scenes of this kind into sequences of unique compositions. Recall the lighthouse in *Floating Weeds,* Tokyo Tower in *An Autumn Afternoon,* or the tall neon advertising signs in *The End of Summer.* These static pieces of manmade scenery come at the beginnings of the films, less as objects of any specific point of view than as landmarks to place the action geographically. Importantly, the shots in *Days of Youth* might be considered prototypes for these kinds of compositions but still appear as objects of two gazes extending in the same direction. As when he establishes the clumsy custodian's school bell as a motivation for filming students flowing through the doorway of a university building, Ozu provides careful indication of who is doing the looking here—indication of the source of the look. In late-period Ozu, the school bell as impetus is erased, and empty scenery is left to drift, unsubjectivized, in midair. The university clock tower that appears at the end of *I Failed, but . . .* is clearly also portrayed as an object colored by psychological subjectification. It can therefore be said that between his early period and his late period, Ozu gradually eliminated from his compositions both the narrational consideration of *cause* and the eye as the source of the view. What Western critics have often singled out as his "empty"

---

12. On the second occasion, only one of the students looks out the window.

shots can be thought of as a by-product of this process. Of course, among the visual objects associated with the smokestacks and weathervanes in the 1929 *Days of Youth*—objects we might call "things looming overhead"—we should also include the tall poplar trees that appear near the end of the 1932 *Where Now Are the Dreams of Youth?*, in the scene where Ureo Egawa gives Tatsuo Saitō a beating on the side of the road to compel him into a decision about marrying his fiancée. A shot of two trees appears here, but no one seems to be looking at them. They are pictured at a distance, their leaves rustling in the wind. What is moving about this shot is no longer a matter of character psychology. Hisashi Okajima has observed that a similar shot appears at the end of the 1933 film *Passing Fancy*, a shot that is also strangely moving, precisely because it portrays tall trees and nothing more.[13]

This returns us to the subject of unidirectional looking, where the mere sight of multiple eyelines extending into the distance in parallel is also sufficient to stir cinematic sensitivity, regardless of the aesthetic qualities of the thing being looked at. Unidirectional looking is everywhere to be found in early Ozu—in theaters in *Passing Fancy* and *A Story of Floating Weeds*, for example, or in classrooms in the student comedies and *There Was a Father*. Then there is the movie theater in *The Only Son* and the home movie screening in *I Was Born, but . . . .* Even the famous cheating gag in *I Flunked, but . . .* consists entirely of a drama of eyelines, performed within the space of the examination hall where everyone is *supposed* to look in the same direction and perform the same gestures. The rule of this particular game is to look astray without being seen—probably a thematically necessary development, as it were, given Ozu's general attachment to unidirectional looking. We find a related set piece in *Where Now Are the Dreams of Youth?* when Ozuesque flunkees attempt to cheat even during a company entrance

---

13. Hisashi Okajima, "Ozu Yasujirō: Manazashi no kajō to shintai no kakunin," *Yurīka* 13, no. 7 (June 1981): 122.

exam. But because the company president is one of their own—a former classmate who endorses and orchestrates their effort from the inside—it is probably fair to say that this scene is more a reflection of Ozu's proclivity for mischief than of his preoccupation with visual effect.

Several major themes of the late period derive from this theme of unidirectional looking, themes that Ozu would develop as he moved toward more ritualistic rules of play. Each of these is an elaboration on something clearly present in outline form in early-period Ozu, such as the theme of "standing side by side" as represented by the father and son fishing next to each other in *A Story of Floating Weeds* and *There Was a Father,* or the theme of multiple people "looking at the same thing" as illustrated by the taking of the class photograph in *There Was a Father*. But at this point, it is necessary to take a wider view of the narrational functions that these themes perform and of the significance of the cinematic forms they acquire. It also remains for us to observe precisely how walls closing in energize the films of Ozu.

INTERIOR GARDENS AND WALLS

It probably goes without saying, but in Ozu, walls do not always close in, and cinematic space is not everywhere dominated by stifling claustrophobia. In *Tokyo Story* an elderly couple sit side by side on a seaside embankment at Atami. In *Early Summer* a young woman sits alongside her older brother's wife on a dune at the shore. In *The End of Summer* we again find a young woman and her older brother's wife sitting together, but on a riverbank. They all face open spaces, not walls. The sister-in-law relationship between Kuniko Miyake and Setsuko Hara in *Early Summer* passes to Hara and Yōko Tsukasa in *The End of Summer,* one pair sitting side by side at the Kamakura shore and the other kneeling on the riverbank at Arashiyama, but in both cases the topic of conversation concerns what it means to be happy as a woman. When outside the enclosed space of the home, these sisters-in-law seem especially voluble.

The latter half of *Days of Youth*—the earliest Ozu film that survives in complete form—takes place on the snowy ski slopes at Akakura. It even includes an action sequence in which Tatsuo Saitō chases his runaway ski down the mountain, further demonstrating that Ozu's world is by no means limited to enclosed spaces. The early-period student and salaryman films often feature vacant lots at a remove from the city center, where kids play or mothers sit side by side with their children. The houses in the new suburban developments where the company men of *Tokyo Chorus* and *I Was Born, but* . . . live with their families have verandas that open onto yards, and in the latter film there is even a single-car train that passes back and forth beyond the fence. These families are practically exposed to wide-open space at the far ends of their yards. There are no walls here to come closing in. And yet, things do block the view in Ozu and prohibit sight lines from extending outward. One characteristic of spatial structure in Ozu is that it does not quite adhere to the customary rules of perspective. The impression of depth is consistent, but it is at times abruptly interrupted by planar intrusions and can hardly be described as conforming to the rules of pictorial design as organized around a vanishing point. What creates this effect is what is visible through Ozu's interior windows. The late-period films demonstrate this point most strikingly, but what is generally visible on the far side of windows are walls. Neighboring houses come closing in, and as a result, we mostly do not even glimpse the sky. Even from the wide-open second-floor verandas, what we see in the background are mostly only the walls and rooftops of neighboring houses.

Take, for example, the typically Japanese Kamakura house that three generations of a family share in *Early Summer*. The elderly grandparents and their only daughter share the second floor (though all three will eventually move out), while their eldest son occupies the first floor with his wife and two children. A living room on the first floor provides a gathering space for the family and leads at the rear to a room with a chest of drawers for clothing. This first-floor space consisting of two connecting rooms is set off on either end by corridors, one leading to the kitchen and the other to the bath. The passage to the bath is an *engawa* veranda from which the side of the neighboring house is visible across a wall enclosing a small garden.[14] Our sight line therefore encounters a dead end. Looking toward the garden from the living room, we find the front door on the righthand side. Adults rushing to catch the train to work and children leaving for school exit here. When they return home in the evening, they enter at the same point, as do visitors stopping by. These comings and goings, or at least the motions of opening and closing the door, are depicted by a camera consistently placed at an oblique angle to the doorway. The exterior that exists beyond the door is carefully excluded and remains out of view. This first-floor space is therefore severed from the outside by a series of walls. We do, of course, glimpse the scenery in front of the entryway in a separate shot outdoors, but even here space is far from open since the street in front of the house is narrow and curves in such a way that people coming or going along it are never visible for long. The field of view is limited in every sense.

We have already observed that the situation on the second floor is much the same, except that the second-floor windows face in two separate directions. There are no neighboring rooftops opposite the veranda-side window, which should hypothetically open onto a view. This impression is reinforced when only-daughter Setsuko Hara's former classmate Chikage Awashima remarks how pretty Kamakura is while casting her gaze through the window into the distance. Standing

---

14. The *engawa* in Japanese architecture is a narrow walkway that runs along the edge of a structure such as a house and can be either open or semi-open to the outside (enclosed by sliding doors or glass). It forms a transitional boundary between interior and exterior space. *Engawa* often overlook gardens but can also connect rooms of the house like a hallway.

alongside her, Hara also focuses her attention in the same direction. But we viewers are unable to glimpse the scenery that the two women are supposedly taking in. This is because the camera remains stubbornly to their side and neglects to pan around, as if deliberately ignoring the window. It can generally be said that when filming indoors, Ozu refuses to position his camera at points from which outdoor scenery might enter the field of view. Exteriors and interiors obstinately maintain their respective coordinates, bearing no trace of any underlying connection.

Another characteristic of Ozu is the fact that he generally avoids using technical means to make footage shot on studio sets and on location coexist. There are no attention-guiding props to create natural transitions between shots of different kinds, and we only rarely encounter cut-ins of exterior scenery that appears to be something at which characters are looking. Ozu might have shown the pleasant natural landscape that supposedly extends in front of Hara and Awashima on the far side of the second-floor veranda. The early student and salaryman films do conscientiously show things that friends look at side by side through windows. The smokestacks, weathervane, and ventilation pipes in *Days of Youth* are clearly meant to be things the students see when they look through their window, and the same also applies to café girl Kinuyo Tanaka in *I Flunked, but* . . . .. But the process of Ozu's cinematic development can be understood as a process of separating the look and its object. Nothing illustrates this more vividly than *Early Summer*'s two marriageable young women standing at the second-floor window in Kita Kamakura. Ozu does not even attempt to show what the young women are looking at. In fact, he severs any sight line that reaches toward the distance, and he does so without even sending walls closing in, simply by positioning the camera in a certain way relative to its subject and by sequencing shots to accentuate the nonconnection between interior and exterior—that is, by means of things not visible to the eye.

PLANAR ABSTRACTION

The Ozuesque shot composition in which the walls of neighboring houses come closing in on the far side of verandas is not something exclusive to the postwar films. In *There Was a Father,* what is visible through the window of father Chishū Ryū and son Shūji Sano's window when they stay at a hot spring hotel is another upstairs room, belonging either to a neighboring hotel or to another wing of the same hotel. There is a wet towel drying on the railing outside each of these facing rooms—a prop that suits the setting but also creates the impression that the rooms correspond to each other in mirror image across the narrow courtyard in between. The short trip that the father and son take to the hot spring in *There Was a Father* also corresponds quite precisely to the mother-daughter hot spring trip in the postwar *Late Autumn*. As mentioned previously, *Late Autumn* is often called a remake of *Late Spring,* but with a mother and daughter substituted for the father-daughter relationship in the earlier film. It is certainly not incorrect to highlight this connection, but as far as the basic character relationships are concerned, *Late Autumn* has more in common with *There Was a Father*. The destinations to which parent and child travel are different—Ikaho Hot Springs in one case and Shiobara Hot Springs in the other—but they share the detail of a window opening onto a facing room of basically the same architectural style. Chishū Ryū, who is a hotel guest in *There Was a Father,* even returns in *Late Autumn* as the proprietor of the inn. *Late Autumn* places special emphasis on the singing of a group of girls staying at the hotel on a school trip, the sound of their voices carrying from across the courtyard. The bedtime atmosphere at this inn is livelier, but it is hard to overlook what is otherwise similar in both these settings: the staging of a conversation between a widowed parent and a soon-to-be-married child, with an opened window directly in the background. The father-daughter Kyoto trip in

Late Spring is also basically identical where character relationships are concerned, but it differs somewhat from both *There Was a Father* and *Late Autumn* in spatial structure, taking place as it does in a space enclosed by *shōji* screens. Beyond spatial structure, *There Was a Father* and *Late Autumn* share the further similarity that both son Shūji Sano and daughter Yōko Tsukasa look down at books during exchanges with their respective parents (fig. 12). These similarities demonstrate two facts. The first is that the visual features of Ozu's so-called late period were basically established by the time of the 1941 *Brothers and Sisters of the Toda Family* and the 1942 *There Was a Father,* even before his experiences at the Southern Command in Singapore or during the social upheaval in the aftermath of Japan's defeat. The second is that, where the visualization of space is concerned, the Ozuesque experiment in exaggerating walls, in making them come closing in on the far side of open windows, is something that sets the late period apart from the early period. In fact, when father and son soak side by side in the hotel bath in *There Was a Father,* a large window opens directly behind them onto what we sense is a sun-drenched exterior, but what we actually see through this window is only the encroaching stone wall of a neighboring building. This kind of composition will be repeated, with a number of variations, across the later films.

Ozu's staging arranges people side by side in spaces where windows open onto nothing but walls or rooftops, and it also leaves unshown the things they look at through windows that open in directions other than where the camera is pointed. On the one hand, this staging limits the positioning of the camera in relation to windows and corridors. On the other, it transforms the Japanese house—a space which the simple everyday gesture of sliding open a *shōji* screen should make porous with the outside—into an environment that is somehow spatially abstract, if not quite hermetically sealed. This abstraction takes the form of the planar space we have already described, a space that prohibits sight lines from reaching into the distance. The movement of the eye pursuing depth must at a certain point be interrupted. We might say that the gardens and courtyards presumably there on the far side of verandas even function as traps, luring the gaze outside only to prohibit it from advancing. The low camera position that people cite without fail when speaking of Ozu should probably also be viewed from this perspective. When the camera is brought into Japanese houses, the linear edging characteristic of tatami floor matting generally results in compositions that exaggerate perspectival depth of a kind the everyday sensibilities of domestic life tend to neglect. Ozu's planar abstraction therefore requires the camera to exclude tatami flooring itself as much as possible. If the scene in the hotel room at Ikaho Hot Springs where Setsuko Hara and Yōko Tsukasa sit on futons laid out side by side were instead filmed at an angle allowing tatami lines to enter the field of view, the veranda and rooms of the hotel wing visible across the courtyard would likely seem substantially more distant (fig. 13). In other words, a wall would not come closing in, and the composition would lose its sense of planarity. Ozu's low camera position is therefore a topic that should be considered in its relationship to opened windows.

From here, it is easy to understand just how fully the staging in *The End of Summer* realizes Ozu's spatial system. First, there is the room where Ganjirō Nakamura retreats to change clothes beyond the detection of his daughter Michiyo Aratama. This room faces the garden across a veranda. Because its sliding screens and doors generally remain open, it is quite airy and bright. The garden itself, by contrast, is enclosed by a gray earthen wall that mercilessly cuts our venturing sight line. Events therefore occur only in the space extending to the veranda, with the garden serving basically no narrational function despite its unmistakable presence. When a medical crisis brings the entire family together here and we behold the sudden spectacle of Ganjirō laid out in his bedclothes with a moist towel on his forehead,

12. *There Was a Father:* Son Haruhiko Tsuda in a hotel room with a view of a facing building that anticipates the inn in *Late Autumn*.

13. *Late Autumn:* Mother Setsuko Hara and daughter Yōko Tsukasa sit side by side by the window in their room at an inn.

this veranda is where the tension of the scene relaxes.¹⁵ In Ozu, the drop in narrational magnetism from veranda to garden is startling. Gardens are absent spaces, both narrationally and thematically. They may be visible, but cinematically they are nonexistent. This point is most elegantly demonstrated by the organization of Chieko Naniwa's house, where Ganjirō is a frequent visitor. Ganjirō will die here, in this house belonging to a woman whose child he fathered, with its two Japanese-style rooms that face each other across an interior garden with a veranda much like the rooms at the hot springs hotel in *Late Autumn*. Here again, when our sight line ventures into the scenery, the other room stands in the way at the far side of the garden, like a wall prohibiting depth.

The same circumstances apply in *Floating Weeds*, a film also drawn from the theme of a reunion with an unacknowledged child. There is a small garden in this film as well, once again in the home of Ganjirō's former mistress Haruko Sugimura, where he pays visits, representing himself to their son Hiroshi Kawaguchi only as an avuncular acquaintance. The place where this traveling actor likes to sit while fondly observing his son's growth is at the veranda, beside the teeming red amaranths in the garden. A giant wall flooded with afternoon sunlight rises behind Ganjirō as he drinks up the sake that Sugimura brings him, but no one seems to find the narrowness of the garden it encloses oppressive—a narrowness that strangely accentuates the vibrant colors of the summer flowers. Ozuesque people relieve the tensions of their daily lives in such spaces, as if taking solace in the protection of encroaching walls. The dressing room where the troupe of traveling actors sleep, on the second floor of a small theater, has windows that

---

15. Hasumi often refers to Ganjirō Nakamura by his given name rather than his surname. This does help to distinguish him from Nobuo Nakamura in passages where the two are discussed together, but it also reflects the fact that Ganjirō came to film acting from the kabuki stage, unlike other regulars in the Ozu unit. Names are inherited along with repertoires and performance styles in kabuki families and therefore have special significance. Ganjirō was born Yoshio Hayashi in 1902 and took the stage name Ganjirō Nakamura II in 1947 twelve years after the death of his father, the kabuki actor Ganjirō Nakamura.

also open onto a bright exterior. But our view through these windows is limited to the rows of tiles lining the unusually large roof of the house across the street. Recall also the windows hidden behind horizontal blinds in the Marunouchi office buildings where Shūji Sano or Shin Saburi do business in late-period Ozu films. A similar sense of enclosure prevails there as well, with light entering but the exterior scenery remaining outside the visual field. Occasionally, there are shots that depict the views from these office windows, but strangely, these are mostly taken from windows other than the ones pictured on screen. This is true of the view of the Marunouchi office district in *Late Autumn*, for example, at which Shūji Sano tells Setsuko Hara to "take a good look" as she is about to leave Tokyo.[16] In this sense, the outside does exist in late-period Ozu, but extends at points not visible on screen, much like staircases. Even on occasions when the camera does venture outdoors, our sight line ends up being intercepted by the walls of non-perspectival buildings.

At this point it should be clear that sight line–blocking walls are privileged elements of mise-en-scène in Ozu. Walls that rise on the far side of open windows take two forms: as physically visible walls belonging to neighboring houses, and as interior gardens or courtyards with no narrational function to perform. Both these types of walls sharply interrupt Ozuesque space at the veranda. This is because *nothing is present* on the far side of verandas and windows. Both gardens and the walls and fences of neighboring houses are flat planes, hardly different from painted theatrical backdrops or trompe-l'œil decor (fig. 14). Any impression of depth is only an illusion. Only once have we observed something similar in another film: the trompe-l'œil sets in the theater

---

16. This scene's view of a street in Marunouchi is not obviously shot through a window other than the one Shūji Sano looks through, but it is immediately followed by exterior shots that weaken the impression of point of view. Hasumi is likely thinking here of cinematographer Yūharu Atsuta's account of climbing stairs to find the right elevation when shooting on location in office buildings. See his interview with Atsuta in the appendix.

14. *The End of Summer:* A wall closes in on Yōko Tsukasa and Setsuko Hara through a second-floor window. Still copyright Toho Co., Ltd.

in Alain Resnais's *Last Year at Marienbad* (*L'Année dernière à Marienbad*, 1961). This, precisely, is the nature of things like the planar abstraction of enclosed space.

Take, for example, the reddish-brown brick wall that extends behind the open windows at the crematorium in *The End of Summer,* where the Kohayagawa family sits arrayed at a table in formal mourning dress, or the factory wall and smokestacks billowing smoke in the opening scene of *An Autumn Afternoon,* visible through a window so large that it nearly throws the space where Chishū Ryū does business out of balance (fig. 15). What to call these things if not planar abstractions? Why is it that the typical Japanese houses in films like *Late Spring* or *Tokyo Story* or *Late Autumn,* houses that are not especially distinguished by trompe l'oeil flatness, mostly share the same spatial structure, organized around an interior garden, that we have examined in *Early*

15. *An Autumn Afternoon:* Windows in Chishū Ryū's office.

Summer? Why are the small, geometrically arranged houses in *Good Morning* laid out in a space where the visual field is interrupted by such a thing as a high grassy embankment? Why do people always walk from left to right, or else in the reverse direction, across the top of this embankment beyond which a river undoubtedly flows? Why? Because each of these things prohibits our sight line from venturing into the scenery. This is also true of the ends of hallways in the Marunouchi office buildings that we encounter numerous times in various films. Does this mean that characters in Ozu never fix their gaze on things far in the distance? As Hara and Awashima demonstrate in *Early Summer,* it is not the case that no one ever gazes outside. But much of the time, Ozu neglects to depict what they are looking at on screen. Does this mean that he never shows both the look and its object as consecutive shots?

INTRUSIONS OF THE OUTSIDE

It is characteristic in Ozu, as becomes especially striking entering the late period, that we do not necessarily see the things his characters look at, and that the scenery we do see on screen is not necessarily the object of their gaze. This is nothing unique to Ozu, of course. It is not as though any and every shot in cinema must be taken from a subjectively focalized point of view. Still, it is natural, cinematically, to interpret the shot that follows a shot of someone looking at something as depicting the thing being looked at. The disappearance of the causal relationship between the look and its object should therefore probably be considered distinctive of Ozu. What we often see in Ozu is "looking" itself, while the thing being looked at commonly does not make an appearance. The scene at the kabuki theater in *Early Summer* is one example, where what we see is only the gazes characters direct at the stage. This is what we have been describing as "unidirectional looking." Of course, the withholding of the play from the audience in the scene at the theater is also an example of the rhetorical device of ellipsis, which is hardly uncommon. But it is not merely a matter of rhetorical technique when, in the scene of the commute at the beginning of *Early Spring*, for example, Ozu makes no effort to show the train that everyone standing on the platform must be looking at, despite the fact that they are shown turning their heads all in the same direction. This indifference to establishing causality between the look and its object is something we can observe from very early in Ozu, as in *I Flunked, but . . .* when Kinuyo Tanaka is shown in a position that is spatially difficult to reconcile with where the flunkees have clearly all directed their eyes from their second-floor window.

In spite of this, characters in Ozu do often stare at the same single object, and the act of standing side by side and casting gazes often ends up performing narrational functions richer than any visual symbolism that the object itself might possess. At such moments, walls suddenly disappear, and interiors form deep connections with the outside. Take, for example, the scene in *Early Summer* where Haruko Sugimura visits Ichirō Sugai and Chieko Higashiyama at home, while their children and grandchildren are out. Sugimura's son was a classmate of this couple's own younger son who never returned from the war, and a turn in their conversation brings out a sadness that the two do not ordinarily put into words. The aging mother expresses hope that her son may still be alive and suggests that he might one day unexpectedly return, but she lowers her eyes. For her husband, such thoughts are no longer realistic. He says that he has given up hope and looks off into the distance. Here, his wife raises her eyes and also looks off to some exterior point beyond our field of view, doing so as if to align her gaze with his. The next shot pictures carp streamers, filmed from a little below as they flap in the breeze.[17] This image is deeply disorienting. Until now there has been no indication of a window or veranda located in the direction the couple have looked. The only exterior space we are aware of in this scene is a small interior garden, but Ichirō Sugai and Chieko Higashiyama are seated with their backs to it. What is moving here is the way that outside and inside suddenly connect. No window frames the view of these carp streamers as their little windmills clatter and spin at the top of a pole. In fact, they are filmed at fairly close range and nearly fill the screen. Their fluttering motion does appear to be what this elderly couple have singled out with their gaze. And yet, it remains unclear whether this shot actually depicts what they see. Perhaps it is only there to indicate a temporal ellipsis. But the unidirectionality of looking that has suddenly been achieved here calls forth the memory of a departed loved one while at the same time also driving home the fact of his death. This is a private ritual of bereavement, something that would not have taken place in the presence of the couple's other children. In the films of Ozu, when people who are close cast gazes side by

---

17. Carp streamers (*koinobori*) are colorful windsocks shaped like fish, flown especially to celebrate the spring Children's Day holiday. Carp streamers often represent family members and were traditionally associated with male children.

side in the same direction and at the same object, this invariably introduces a separation, a departure, or a death.

This elderly couple is now sitting in their living room in Yamato, having sent off their only daughter Setsuko Hara to her new married life and returned to their hometown. The only things visible in the background behind them are a hearth and some bundles of firewood stacked on an earthen floor. Suddenly, their eyes acknowledge something on the far side of a veranda not visible to the audience: a bridal procession passing along a path through the fields (figs. 16a and b). Even before the viewer can empathize with what these parents concerned for a daughter of their own must feel here, the impact of this shot is vivid—the impact of a sudden deep connection between interior and exterior, formed across a veranda not pictured on screen. In Ozu, when the look and its object are shown as consecutive shots, and when there is a clear causal relationship between the two, a narrational event is invariably initiated—a separation, a death, or the disintegration of a family. At such moments, space that was abstract and enclosed suddenly transforms into an extravagantly open world. The last shots of *Tokyo Story* are another example, where a view of the sea expands before Chishū Ryū, now alone in his Onomichi home. Like the grandparents filmed in profile while gazing at the carp streamers in Kita Kamakura or the bridal procession in Yamato, the elderly man in Onomichi is not facing any window pictured within the scene, but outward, screen left. Here, the Inland Sea enters his field of view, filled with midsummer sunlight. His wife should be sitting beside him gazing at the same scenery, and it is her absence that is accentuated as we are poignantly reminded that we saw the two sitting side by side in the same room near the beginning of the film. This is also the same view that Chishū Ryū and Setsuko Hara took in side by side from the edge of the garden on the morning of Chieko Higashiyama's funeral.

In Ozu, sitting side by side, looking in the same direction, and groping at the same single object with two gazes gives way to moments of direct, mutually shared feeling among the living, much more so than

16. *Early Summer:* (a) Elderly couple Ichirō Sugai and Chieko Higashiyama look out from inside their house, with (b) the bridal procession they see at a distance in the barley fields.

when people exchange words or look into one another's eyes. The fact that such moments of deep mutual feeling are often performed as rituals preceding a separation is something we will address later. For now, it is enough merely to emphasize the narrational dynamics of moments when the offscreen outdoors suddenly intrudes into the visual field. When, near the end of *Late Autumn,* Hara and Tsukasa sit across from one another at a lakeside café, their eyelines do of course intersect. But at a certain moment, and as if by mutual agreement, they both turn their gazes toward the offscreen outdoor scenery, and their conversation comes to a pause. The next shot pictures the window filled with a view of the lake and a small mountain. This shot is moving because of the way this mountain seems not to respect distance, brazenly filling the window frame to its edges. It comes closing in on the viewer, just like the walls of the neighboring houses that loom on the far side of gardens. Planar abstraction is exposed, just as in *Floating Weeds* when a wall looms beyond the veranda where Ganjirō drinks sake while fanning himself. Here again, this mother and daughter point their eyes in the same direction, both silently touching, with their gaze, an object at a remove. This unidirectionality of looking, along with the sudden deep connection of interior and exterior, brings their short trip to an end. And because this short trip has served to prepare the daughter for marriage, the substantial narrational role that this shot assumes should be clear to anyone. For mother and daughter, this is unmistakably a ritual of separation. Still, in spite of everything, we have to question why even the outside is subject to such pronounced planar abstraction here. This remains one of Yasujirō Ozu's greatest cinematic secrets.

6

HOLDING STILL

STATIC SHOTS AND CONSTRAINT

We aim to approach Yasujirō Ozu not through litanies of negation but with gestures of affirmation, and not by dwelling on lack but by attending to the play of things in excess. But this does not mean that we should remain silent about things Ozu disliked and focus exclusively on his preferences. Films are not reducible to the ways they reflect the personal predilections or the aesthetic sensibilities of an auteur. Cinema is an institutional system and imposes constraints, in the form of its own limits, on filmmakers of all kinds. The Ozu of the late period did of course prefer sequences of static shots to traveling shots and pans, and it can therefore probably be said that he selected static compositions to the exclusion of camera movement. It certainly would not be incorrect to describe what is unique about Ozu in this way. It is an unmistakable fact that he privileged a particular kind of approach and did that by casting off other possibilities in the process. Still, we should not forget that his privileging of the static shot, which was in fact probably little more than a personal choice, was also a completely relative choice made in the face of the absolute constraints that cinema itself imposes on filmmakers. Whatever the film, there can be only four kinds of shots: traveling shots, pans that rotate horizontally, tilts that rotate up and down, and static shots. These possibilities reduce to three if we treat pans and tilts as a single category of axis-rotation shots. In any case, any filmmaker, no matter how talented, has no alternative but to choose from among these limited techniques whenever attempting to capture a visual object on film. Cinema also lacks any absolute means of justification for choices made among these techniques, whether on the basis of the nature of the thing being filmed or from the perspective of subject matter or story. Nor are there any absolute principles of editing to dictate how shots filmed using these respective techniques should be joined together. Therefore, when Ozu says he does not think that cinema has a "grammar," we should interpret his words not as the self-defense of a director who fixated single-mindedly on the low-position static shot, but as an observation that touches a particular cinematic truth. This observation also accords with a consensus later reached within structuralist semiotics: that nothing does or could exist within cinema corresponding to grammar in natural language, as an absolute order governing enunciaton and interpretation. Therefore, while things of all kinds may be possible, such possibility never transcends the limits that make cinema cinema and does not amount to absolute freedom. Any and every film auteur, no matter how talented, must accept constraint as an inescapable condition.

From this it should be clear that the Ozu who fixated single-mindedly on the static shot certainly did not arrive at that point by relinquishing an abundance of cinematic possibilities one by one. Cinema is an environment thoroughly devoid of freedom and has been from the very beginning. There are only three types of camerawork—the traveling shot, the pan or tilt, and the static shot. Any attempt to capture images on celluloid by means of one of these three techniques, and to arrange them into suitable combination as a complete film so as to avoid creating a monotone impression, will amount only to an immersive exercise in constraint—but a constraint that passes for freedom. Therefore, films of all kinds become little more than temporary distractions to divert our eyes from the absolute constraints that cinema endures as a condition of its existence. Almost all films that do not simply bore viewers are products of constraint, filmed as if in adherence with a grammar that does not actually exist. The freest of films are perhaps those that devote themselves to constraint and that in doing so are able to make the limits of cinema itself conspicuous. By this definition, Yasujirō Ozu must be considered among the freest of filmmakers.

In light of this, we cannot concur with Donald Richie's view that "when Ozu relinquished, one by one, most of the grammatical elements of cinema, obviously he sacrificed a great deal—most of the means, in fact, through which film directors ordinarily express themselves."[1] We could counter this previously cited assertion by arguing that, in cinema, there is no such thing as a "grammatical element." But even if Richie intends grammar in a figurative sense to include any expressive system conforming to the syntactic conventions of a given point in time, for example, we can still object that what Ozu "sacrificed" were not means of self-expression, but the constraints themselves that cinema imposes.

Like any filmmaker, Ozu undoubtedly sought to express some kind of personal vision or outlook on humanity. But like speaking, filming is an act that cannot be performed without taking on certain constraints. In fact, any vision capable of being communicated without a commitment to an unnaturalness that calls attention to the limits of language or cinema as systems is probably something not especially worth expressing.

1. Richie, *Ozu*, 113.

The cinema of Ozu is an experiment in precisely such kinds of limit-zone expression. But what does this mean exactly?

In cinema, there are things possible and things impossible. Much as the techniques of the camera relative to its subject are limited to three, filmable subjects themselves are also far from limitless, for the simple reason that the various and sundry phenomena of the external world are not all visible to the eye. Take the wind, for example, an atmospheric current perceptible to anyone with a cheek, but something that cinema is capable of visualizing only as swaying tree branches or swirling dust. Setting aside the ticking of intervals by the hands of a clock, time itself, as the flow of duration, is also something impossible to record on the screen. We could undoubtedly itemize any number of such invisible subjects, but consider the one that cinema is perhaps most deeply entangled with: the look. However effortlessly cinema may capture the eye on film, it is reduced to confessing its utter powerlessness when confronted with the look. This is one of cinema's greatest paradoxes: the fact that it is possible to record the eye itself as a distinct image on the screen while the look remains absolutely beyond the capabilities of the camera to film. Yasujirō Ozu is a filmmaker thoroughly fixated with this paradox, and it is precisely his persistence at this cinematic limit that liberates him from the myth of Ozu the "I-novel"-style chronicler of things everyday and Japanese to become a cinematic auteur in the truest sense.[2]

Ozu confronts the limits of cinema itself. And what happens when he does? What takes place is a cruel schism between the eye and the look. The eye is a visible object, but looking—or the look—is something absolutely beyond the capabilities of film to record. Here, eyelines that give the impression of looking at things must be expunged from the screen. In cinema, "looking" is not a visual object but some-

---

2. The I-novel, or *shishōsetsu*, is one of the major genres of modern Japanese literature. Informed by nineteenth-century literary naturalism, the I-novel developed as a confessional genre often characterized by the narration of quotidian details from the author's own life.

thing of which we need to be persuaded. Because of this, the camera is rendered completely powerless in the face of two people gazing at one another and has no alternative but to convert that reality into a story. In other words, someone shown looking at someone else has to be followed by a shot of the other person, who is both the object of the first person's look and at the same time also a person looking back. It is possible, of course, to indicate that characters are supposed to be looking at one another by adjusting their positioning within the frame, but Ozu insists on depicting this relationship by means of the shot/reverse shot. Whenever he does, a strange space emerges where eyes are countered only by eyes, and in which eyelines seem not to match.

In a certain interview, François Truffaut, for one, describes this strange space as follows:

> I have not seen any Japanese films as strangely enticing as those of Ozu. There is probably nothing more Japanese than an Ozu film, but what is especially intriguing to me is the sense of space. Or maybe it would be better to say the relationship between characters and space. There are constantly scenes of two people facing each other and talking, with a lot of cutting back and forth, but these cuts give an impression of being strangely *off*. There is no camera movement in Ozu films, but these cuts give the impression that if there were, if the camera were to pan back and forth between two people having a conversation, they would turn out not to be sitting in place, but continually changing positions. Ordinarily, when using a shot/reverse shot setup to film a conversation between two people facing each other, you cut back and forth from the same side of the subjects—in other words, if you're on this side, you stay on this side, and if you're on that side, you stay on that side. It's the same as when you pan, in other words. But in Ozu films the camera seems to film one character from this side one minute, for example, and the next minute we cut to the other character filmed from the opposite side. This is not just an impression. It must have been an intentional directorial choice, and it creates the uneasy sensation that, if you were to follow a character's eyeline, there

might not be anyone there on the other end—that every time we have a cut, the other person ceases to be there.[3]

The impression of strangeness recounted by filmmaker François Truffaut is something that many critics have attributed quite naturally to Ozu's disregard of the 180-degree rule and is also something that audiences have understood through direct experience with the films. Eyes appear to look at each other, but eyelines fail to meet as they extend past each other in parallel.

Why should this be the case? First of all, we can point to Ozu's insensitivity toward what is generally thought of as film grammar. Shot/reverse shot cutting consists of joining shots depicting the points of view of two objects of a look looking back at another looking subject. The camera position ordinarily remains on the same side of these intersecting eyelines. If one set of eyes is shown looking slightly to the right of the lens, and in the next shot the other set of eyes is correspondingly adjusted in the left direction, things fall easily into place. But Ozu did not observe this rule, even though his editor Yoshiyasu Hamamura is known to have raised the issue (figs. 17a and b). As Truffaut observed, this was clearly an intentional directorial policy. How then to explain the reasons for this choice? What does it mean that Ozu insisted, through his career, on what in the craft would otherwise be deemed a failed eyeline match, an utterly elementary technical mistake? We should probably avoid confining this strange phenomenon within negatively framed rhetoric about things like deficiencies of technique. How then to proceed?

We first need to mention two fictions. Or perhaps it would be better to call them lies. People—especially Japanese people—do not in their everyday lives go around peering into the eyes of others as often or as intently as happens in Ozu films. We hardly ever stare straight into the

---

3. François Truffaut, "Toryufō soshite eiga," interview by Shiguéhiko Hasumi and Kōichi Yamada, *Hanashi no tokushū* (August 1980): 10. Emphasis in the Japanese.

17. *Tokyo Story:* (a) Elderly couple Chieko Higashiyama and (b) Chishū Ryū at their house in Onomichi on the morning of their departure for Tokyo. Both face into the camera, in contrast to the father/son conversation in *There Was a Father*.

eyes of others, whether those eyes are harmless and unprovocative like Chishū Ryū's, or whether they exude an air of melancholy like Setsuko Hara's. If, on occasion, we do find ourselves drawn to look into certain kinds of eyes, it is probably not when they are looking directly at us, but at instants when they are distracted by something else or turned downward or aside. The look in Ozu is in this sense presumptuous. To go about life surrounded by such kinds of eyes would be impossible. Ozu himself must have been sufficiently aware of this. We should therefore acknowledge that these eyes are a concocted fiction, which is not hard to do, since this kind of unnaturalness is everywhere to be found in Ozu.

A second fiction that requires acknowledging here is one that cinema itself had to concoct because of a cinematic limitation—the limitation that two sets of eyes looking at each other cannot be captured in a single static shot. There are only two ways to show two people looking at one another: by placing a camera at a point between them and panning one hundred eighty degrees, as described above, or by joining two shots in a shot/reverse shot configuration. But in both of these cases, the spatial simultaneity of eyelines intersecting needs to be replaced by a relationship of temporal succession. This is why cinema can only surrender whenever confronted with two sets of eyes looking at each other. The Ozuesque mutual gaze, staged insistently and repeatedly as a fiction exceeding mere habituated routine, exposes through its very fictionality the cinematic limitation that it is impossible to capture a look on film, despite the fact that it is indeed possible to portray a looking eye. It also lays bare that fiction of technique called editing, which, as an expressive means, easily encourages the false impression that two people are looking at each other. To make a film is to take on the burden of various constraints. And where both spectators and fellow filmmakers alike delude themselves into thinking that those constraints are actually freedoms, Ozu confronts them with unnatural and presumptuous eyes, availing himself of the simplest means to dispel such delusions.

Or perhaps Ozu was inspired by a secret pleasure. Perhaps he insisted on these kinds of shots solely to film women facing the camera, and to capture the beauty of their exposed foreheads and hairlines—of Setsuko Hara's in particular. In fact, it is characteristic of the hairstyles of actresses in Ozu that they do not hide the forehead. The bangs worn by Ineko Arima in *Tokyo Twilight* and Keiko Kishi in *Early Spring* are exceptions, but it is surely no mere coincidence that the former commits suicide and the latter plays the role of a seductress. Of course, if such explanations were adequate, theoretical accounts of things like Ozu's indifference to the 180-degree rule would probably fall apart.

Concocted to conceal a constraint, the technique of editing known as the shot/reverse shot has developed and perfected its faculty for fiction along two general trajectories within world film history: that of psychological convergence associated with the romantic melodrama and that of conflict intensification associated with the action film. Otherwise put, it has widely been employed to give expressive form to two psychological states: empathy and opposition. Where empathy and opposition are skillfully balanced, it can also give way to refined humor. But in Ozu, the shot/reverse shot yields no such psychological effects. What the viewer experiences is only that strange spatial impression described by Truffaut, regardless of the nature of the dialogue. It is probably easy to forget this impression—of a *gap*—to the extent that we give ourselves over to the flow of the narrative and abandon really looking at the screen. But where we fix our attention deliberately on the screen, our eyes succumb to uncontrollable agitation. To look at an Ozu film is to maintain the eye in a state of constant and continuously renewing agitation. This is an exceptionally cruel experience for cinema itself, since it causes a decisive moment to come closing in, a point where it seems that with even one step farther, cinema might cease to be cinema. It also introduces incredible tension into the narrational flow of Ozu's plots, even where the atmosphere appears to be one of utter calm. Take, for example, the way that Ganjirō Nakamura and Machiko Kyō stare each other down from under the eaves of facing houses during a downpour in *Floating Weeds*. This scene is dramatically very dense, but this density has less to do with how Ozu's superb direction gives expressive form to a psychological conflict than with the overwhelming tension created by the meeting of glares. We sense that if this exchange were to continue for even a moment longer, cinema might henceforth cease to be cinema. We will examine this point in further detail later when we come to the theme of rain.

SIDE BY SIDE

One characteristic of Ozu is that this phenomenon of narrational compression intimately coexists with what we might call a relaxation phenomenon. Or perhaps it would be more accurate to say that scenes of people confronting one another directly are the exception, that the meeting of eyelines more commonly involves people positioned at a diagonal to one another, conversing with their heads turned slightly to the side. Take, for example, the scene in *Early Summer* where Setsuko Hara chats with three of her former classmates over tea at a hotel on the way back from a wedding ceremony. The women sit facing each other across a table, two to either side. On the unmarried side, Hara and Chikage Awashima so relentlessly tease the two married women opposite them that one of the latter stands up and announces she has had enough and is leaving. Awashima goads her, saying, "go ahead, leave." But instead of leaving, she moves to a seat at the end of the neighboring table and proceeds from there to defend herself. The remaining woman on the married side of the first table then also rises in agitation and joins her friend at the exiles' table. Two pairs of women who started the scene facing each other across a table thus end up positioned on a diagonal, as if through a movement of parallel displacement. This movement takes on a comic rhythm through the mutual teasing of these women—teasing of a kind only possible among those having known each other since youth. Using the humor of the exchange, Ozu introduces a diagonal meeting of eyelines in a way that seems perfectly natural.

But the sudden relaxation of tension in Ozu is especially pronounced at moments when two characters whose eyes have not necessarily been meeting simultaneously turn their gazes in the same direction and fix on some offscreen object. Take, for example, the scene near the end of *Late Autumn* where the mother and daughter sit across from each other eating boiled azuki beans in a lakeside café, then suddenly look out through the window at Mount Haruna. The following shot pictures the plain green mountain filmed head-on. There is nothing lyrical here, nor anything ominous. What is important is simply the motion of two people fixing their eyes on the same single object across a distance. The motion itself evokes a sense of empathy that a cut between two sets of eyes would not convey. A very similar scene also takes place in *Early Summer,* when Hara meets Hiroshi Nihon'yanagi at a café in Tokyo's Ochanomizu neighborhood. The two sit facing one another for what will be a conversation about Hara's older brother who died at war. Nihon'yanagi was a classmate of this brother. As he begins to reflect on his memories of the deceased, he points out a painting framed on the wall in the background, and both turn their attention toward it. Here as well, there is a momentary lull in the conversation as the two are enveloped in silent empathy.

The lyricism of Ozu emerges neither through exchanges of looks nor through any psychological symbolism associated with things looked at; it derives instead from the simple gesture of two people fixing their eyes on the same object at the same time. This is a dynamic lyricism, never contained by the static properties of the image. The balloon that breaks free of its string in *Early Summer* and suddenly interrupts the conversation of the elderly couple who have been sitting side by side and looking at each other in the front garden of the Tokyo National Museum is another example. What moves us here is not whatever symbolic weight this balloon might carry as it disappears into the sky, but simply the simultaneity of Ichirō Sugai and Chieko Higashiyama's motions as they follow it with their eyes as if in choreographed synchrony. A similar observation can be made of the couple's later gesture, after they have returned to the hometown where they will spend their remaining years, when they both look out at a bridal procession winding through the fields. In all of these scenes, a conversation is broken off, and the movement of two people turning from a facing position to look at something else is traced on the screen. The movement of two parallel gazes cast across a distance in mutual acknowledgement of the same single object turns to empathy itself, joining two people together while at the same time lopping off any weight of psychological symbolism that the image might otherwise bear. The boat that glides across the surface of Lake Biwa as Ryō Ikebe and Chishū Ryū look on near the end of *Early Spring*, along with the crematorium smokestacks that the husband and wife gaze up at from the field in the final moments of *The End of Summer*, are things, among others, that appear at points distant from the center of the narrative to release all at once any suffocating tension from the preceding dramas of looking, and to announce the severing of the narrational flow, which is to say the end of the film.

Still, the cinematic figuration of empathy without lyricism in Ozu does not always serve the function of bringing closure to the films; nor does it necessarily require two people to gaze at the same single object. It is enough for two people who share some kind of bond simply to sit side by side and perform the same motions as if repeating one another. These scenes tend to begin with a shot of a man and woman arrayed side by side, taken from behind and at a diagonal, then progress through a series of shots of each of the two turning to face the other in conversation before ultimately closing on another shot like the first. Throughout the famous scene in *Tokyo Story* where Chishū Ryū and Chieko Higashiyama sit side by side in cotton summer kimono on an embankment near their hotel at Atami Hot Springs, the camera consistently neglects to film the elderly couple from the direction of the sea, where they are facing. They do occasionally turn their heads to exchange words, but what speaks most eloquently here are the backs of these two people, filmed from behind and at a diagonal. The fact that their bodies never move, even when they turn their heads, contributes to the impression that their eyelines fail to meet. The same applies to Yōko Tsukasa and Mariko Okada in *Late Autumn*, when they go up to the roof of their office building and stand side by side to watch for the train carrying a friend off on her honeymoon (fig. 18). In Ozu, people who are intimate do not face one another directly. They look out at something instead, casting parallel gazes as the camera films them from behind and at a diagonal. They express their empathy with their backs, their waists, sometimes their legs. Lyricism in Ozu reaches its highest expression through backs that exhibit exceptional eloquence without so much as a hint of movement. This is why bar counters are privileged settings for the portrayal of friendship among men.

These Ozuesque expressions of empathy are probably most beautifully figured in the moments when a father and child appear silently side by side. In *There Was a Father,* the scene where Chishū Ryū and his son stand barefoot at the edge of a river, fishing side by side, has a far more fatherly atmosphere than the scene where he retrieves the boy from his boarding school, treats him to dinner at the inn, and gives him spending money. As their fishing rods drift with the current, they cast the lines mechanically back upstream, repeating this motion any number of times. The gestures of this father and son as they mirror each other even to the point of unnaturalness convey with breathtaking poignancy an empathy that requires no verbal acknowledgement—an empathy that resides in the motion itself. They do of course also turn their heads and exchange words, but what we mostly see are their backs, their waists, and their bare feet.

18. *Late Autumn:* From the roof of their office building, Yōko Tsukasa and Mariko Okada watch the train taking their friend on her honeymoon.

Having two people repeat the same motion with their backs to the camera and even mechanically cast fishing lines back upstream as their rods drift with the current, repeating the same procedure ad infinitum, is something Ozu had already tried in the prewar *A Story of Floating Weeds* and would later reprise—if in somewhat more static fashion and at the seashore—in the postwar remake *Floating Weeds*. Our purpose here is not necessarily to interrogate just why we find these scenes so very moving. It seems enough just to gaze endlessly at the synchronized repetition of a gesture that could not be more monotone, a gesture unnatural to the point of seeming almost mechanical. Here, the river, the fishing rods, the figures of two humans, *everything* turns to movement itself, and the very look that apprehends movement as such falls into alignment with it, fusing with its specific rhythm and ceasing to be a look. The flow of time itself seems to have become sensible, like wind on the surface of our skin. Our eyes are no longer looking. We have become blind beings living movement itself. But we sense that such a thing cannot go on forever. This beautiful scene will have to end for cinema to remain cinema and not fall to pieces, just as these two human figures will at some point suddenly have to interrupt their mirrored motions and break their side-by-side alignment. The oppressive thought introduces tension into what should be the tranquility of this pastoral landscape. The narrational compression that occurs here links with the tension of those strange interior spaces where eyelines mingle without meeting, and a general turmoil—the turmoil of the moment when cinema nearly touches its limits—ripples across the films of Yasujirō Ozu.

OZUESQUE MOVEMENT

What happens when Ozuesque side-by-side *beings* end up in settings that move in their own right, when two aligned human figures are positioned not at the edge of a river but on the interior of some space in motion—a space such as a commuter train? *Late Spring* demonstrates that making the setting move can produce even more exhilarating images than attaching the camera itself to a moving body.

It is well known that Chishū Ryū's house in *Late Spring* is located in Kamakura. The same is true of his house in *Early Summer*. In both films, he uses the Yokosuka line to commute to work in Tokyo, at a university in one and a hospital in the other. Setsuko Hara, who plays his daughter in the former film and his younger sister in the latter, also uses this line on her own commute as a Tokyo office worker. Strangely, neither of the two is ever pictured riding the train alone. When riding the train, they are accompanied, almost as a rule. In *Late Spring* Ryū and Hara ride side by side. In *Early Summer* Ryū commutes shoulder to shoulder with his colleague Seiji Miyaguchi. Neither pair carries on much of a conversation, but they do seem to develop a kind of intimate complicity just by hanging onto the hand straps, or sitting on the passenger bench, side by side and in silence. Following an exterior shot of the advancing train taken from a window in the direction of travel, Ryū and Miyaguchi quietly trade the newspapers they have been reading, as if on cue. The camera simply observes the figures of these reticent middle-aged men seated side by side, framing them from a slight distance and at a diagonal. Momentarily, there will be a long shot of the Yokosuka line passing horizontally through the Kamakura landscape and its backdrop of low mountains. This same landscape is also visible from within the train, passing by outside the window, but is hardly emphasized. Even so, there is something surprising about the sensation of motion the viewer experiences on this commute in *Early Summer:* the train continues its forward rush all the way to the edge of the Tokyo metropolitan area, as if the various stations along the way did not exist.

Late Spring portrays the trip from Kita Kamakura to Tokyo with greater geographic precision, but here as well, what should be the repetitive monotony of the daily commute becomes endowed with a unique sense of movement. Richie is quite correct when he characterizes Ozu's "chronological travel shooting" as deceptively "simple."[4] Many filmmakers fail at evoking the sensation of forward momentum. What is particularly noteworthy in this instance is the way the spatial relationship between the characters changes as the train advances. At first, father and daughter stand side by side. Following an exterior shot of the forward-charging train, we find the daughter standing alone, now facing her father, who has taken an empty seat. More exterior shots ensue, and the pair are suddenly returned to side-by-side alignment. The idea is probably that Hara has been able to take a seat beside Ryū after Yokohama, where many passengers would have gotten off the train. In any case, seeing them seated side by side, with their faces in their reading, convinces us that this arrangement is the one proper to Ozu, and reas-

---

4. Richie, *Ozu*, 166.

sures us. This reassurance turns the forward momentum of the Yokosuka line into something unexpectedly exhilarating. It is also worth noting, as anyone familiar with the Yokosuka line of the pre- and postwar years will recall, that seating was arranged in two patterns: along the windows and facing inward near the doors, and otherwise in facing rows perpendicular to the windows, like the seating on long-distance trains. This minor point is significant because in both *Late Spring* and *Early Summer* Ozu seats pairs of people on the passenger benches next to the doors, arranged side by side with their backs to the window. This positioning places Ryū and Hara in front of a flowing stream, much like the father and son who fish side by side in *A Story of Floating Weeds* or *There Was a Father*. This is the important point. The outdoor scenery streams in the background behind two people seated side by side. If they were standing, it would flow in front of them. The facing benches of long-distance trains are reserved for unaccompanied travelers like Hara when she leaves Onomichi at the end of *Tokyo Story*, or Shin Saburi when he heads for Hiroshima at the end of *Equinox Flower*. Nobuo Nakamura and Isuzu Yamada are a rare exception in *Tokyo Twilight*, but their trip is by night, and when we see them on the train they are still waiting to depart from the station, meaning the impression of movement is effectively nil. The shot of Machiko Kyō and Ganjirō Nakamura at the end of *Floating Weeds* is of basically the same variety.

It is of course in late-period Ozu where phenomena like these become most pronounced. The trains that appear in the early-period silent films, as in *Days of Youth* or *Where Now are the Dreams of Youth?*, do not become the kind of fine-tuned mobile setting that we encounter in *Early Summer*. For this reason, the relationship between trains and the exhilaration of movement remains thin in those films. In fact, when the camera is placed on moving vehicles in the silent films, as on the streetcars in *Days of Youth* or *Tokyo Chorus*, a comical lurching motion is what tends to be accentuated. In *Days of Youth* the camera even rushes alongside a streetcar, matching Tatsuo Saitō's commotion as he panics over having lost his wallet. In *Tokyo Chorus* the parallel movement of the family breadwinner marching down the street hoisting a banner advertising curry rice and of the passing streetcar from which his wife and children spot him through the window creates an impression that strangely mingles both comedy and tragedy. It is not as if the camera is brought onto transport all that often, but we can also point to *The Lady and the Beard* and the rather lurching sensation of a shot filmed from the running board of a luxury car as another example that solicits a smile. The convertible sportscar that races through the fields in *Walk Cheerfully* is exceptional in this respect.

Traveling shots are by no means numerous in Ozu, but where they exist, people often observe that they are used in ways that do not result in significant changes of composition. Taking *Late Spring* as an example, Tadao Satō writes: "it is a general rule, where the traveling shot in Ozu is concerned, that there is basically no change of composition between the beginning and the end of the shot."[5] He does of course note that this rule does not necessarily apply to the early-period silent films, but even with this qualification his observation does not seem entirely correct. Take, for example, the relatively long tracking shots in *Early Summer* and *Tokyo Story*, where the camera moves laterally across the exterior walls of a hospital building and a Buddhist temple, probably in Ueno, advancing over the wood and plaster of one and the stone face of the other as if lapping their surfaces. These shots ultimately come to rest on human figures, transitioning from barren images of walls to portraits, and it must therefore be said that their compositions clearly undergo significant change. In the case of *Early Summer*, the lateral camera movement comes to a stop when the louvered housing of some meteorological instrument enters the frame in the foreground, accompanied in the background by Chishū Ryū, visible at

---

5. Tadao Satō, *Ozu Yasujirō no geijutsu* (Tokyo: Asahi Shinbun Sha, 1978). Hasumi's original citation gives no page number.

his work through a window in the building. The tracking shot in *Tokyo Story* concludes by framing elderly couple Ryū and Chieko Higashiyama at a diagonal and from the rear as they sit on the ground looking weary, having been tactfully displaced from their children's homes. What people see at the beginning and at the conclusion of these lateral camera movements is therefore strikingly different. But this in itself is not an especially important objection to Satō, since he is correct that the composition often does not change when the camera moves inward or outward instead of side to side. The issue here is simply that there will always be a detail to contradict those who attempt to define Ozu according to some specific characteristic. It is also in the encounter with such nonconforming details that truly moving film experience often comes to life, but we will return to this point later. For now, we are concerned only with the Ozuesque character of shots in which the camera itself does not move in the slightest, but a vehicle on which it is positioned does. We have already discussed early-period streetcars and late-period commuter trains in this context, but two particularly unforgettable examples remain.

The first is the gentle forward motion of the sightseeing bus that Chishū Ryū and Chieko Higashiyama ride with their daughter-in-law Setsuko Hara in *Tokyo Story* when she shows them around the city. The sequence consists of not quite ten brief shots and lasts for hardly two minutes, but in the space of this brief interval, the languid gliding movement of the bus introduces a temporality fundamentally alien to the film's narrational flow. The first shot, filmed through a window at the front of the slowly advancing bus, shows scenery of what is clearly the Marunouchi area, even if the surroundings are not yet as flourishing as they are today. This is followed by a shot picturing the interior of the bus, filmed from behind several passengers. Next comes a close-up of Ryū in his hat, viewed from the front at a slight angle, and then the grounds of the Imperial Palace passing by outside a window. Higashiyama and Hara are pictured sitting, one in front of the other, then back to Ryū, then Higashiyama and Hara once again. The interior shot taken from behind several passengers repeats, and then more forward movement on the main avenue in Ginza. These shots are all we see. Meanwhile, there is ongoing commentary from the tour guide, and background music. No dialogue is exchanged among the three characters, each seated on a different bench. But the languid, almost sensual gliding movement in this scene on the bus is disarming. Passengers bounce up and down and look in the same direction with a synchronized precision that seems unreal. We are lured by a desire to linger indefinitely with this fluid gliding motion. How pleasant it would be to surrender to such carefree undulation! But the sequence is over before we know it. It is an undeniable fact that what we identify with here are not the characters or their states of mind, but the *motion* itself that this brief series of shots creates. We are entranced, as if under the influence of genuine magic, and find ourselves wondering how the films of Ozu, consisting largely of static shots and making only limited use of camera movement, are nonetheless able to pull off such a thing as making us envy *motion,* before gasping at the realization that we have been cast adrift of the narrational flow. Who could possibly continue to profess that the films of Ozu lack movement?

It is of course true that Ozu's static shots often evoke an impression of stillness. Those witnessing the opening shot of *Floating Weeds,* for example, may find it hard not to react with dismay. Here we go again! The shot pictures a wharf, devoid of human presence, an empty beer bottle standing to the right in the foreground, and a graphically matched white lighthouse rising at the end of a breakwater that cuts across the screen about one third of the way from the bottom, nearly touching the horizon line of the sea (fig. 19). Whether one regards this composition as elegant or overly schematic is probably a matter of taste. One way or the other, it permits hardly any intrusion of movement. Following a series of similar static compositions, the film's plot begins in a waiting room at the port with a conversation between a port employee and some visitors who remark on the hot weather. None of the film's main characters are present here. For the moment, those characters are still enduring the heat aboard the ferry that the people at the port are anticipating. The next sequence puts us on the ferry, where the members of the troupe of traveling actors are notified that they are pulling into port and begin to prepare for arrival. At this point, the ferry passes in front of the same lighthouse from the opening shots of the film, and a miracle takes place. The camera, now fixed near the bow with no human figure in sight, frames the lighthouse again, in a composition similarly crossed in the foreground, this time by the boat's gunwale. But here, the white tower, filmed at closer range and in front of a blue sky, slowly traverses the screen from right to left. The fluidity of its gliding movement is breathtaking. The lighthouse literally drifts past. The sensation of movement here, experienced by an anonymous, impersonal point of view bearing no trace of subjectivization, unexpectedly recalls, through its perfectly languid rhythm, the motion of the sightseeing bus in *Tokyo Story*. But in the case of *Floating Weeds*, the vivid sensation of movement belongs to the changing composition of a single shot alone. And because of this single shot alone, we find ourselves unable to resist feeling intense envy toward Ozuesque movement. What follows are more monotone static shots, inserted as if to interrupt any sentimental lyricism of the kind that might accompany such envy, and our desire to become one with the sensuous lateral gliding of this lighthouse is left hanging in midair. This shot is indeed an exception, all the more so because it cannot really be called a traveling shot in the strict sense. But to exclude it from our discussion of *Floating Weeds* for this reason alone would surely be a mistake. The sensation of movement created despite the fact that neither the subject in front of the camera nor the camera itself moves, but because the camera is placed on a moving body—whether a commuter train, a streetcar, a sightseeing bus, or a ferry, is something we should recognize as a very important detail for Ozu.

19. *Floating Weeds:* A lighthouse that has already appeared in a series of static compositions glides across the gunwale of a passing ferry. Still copyright Kadokawa Daiei Studio.

STOPPING TO MOVE

We should by now have a renewed awareness of an Ozuesque paradox: that the greatest of cinematic movements can come to life in "holding still." Even in the Ozu often described as monotone and static, moments when everyone on screen stops moving are not all that common. Yet scenes clearly do exist in Ozu where everyone stops and holds perfectly still. They hold still and fall silent, and the camera captures them directly from the front. Such moments are quite exceptional. There are hardly any frontally framed full shots in Ozu in general, but where they do occur, the people within them all stop moving and even look into the camera.

These conditions are all clearly met when people pose for photographs. Here, anyone should immediately recall the scene near the end of *Early Summer* where three generations of a family pose for a group photograph (fig. 20). This scene comes abruptly, after Setsuko Hara has already announced her decision to get married. Everyone is arranged in the familiar first-floor living room of the family home, with grandparents Ichirō Sugai and Chieko Higashiyama at center, surrounded by their two grandchildren, their son and his wife, and their only daughter Hara. On the photographer's instructions, they pose and hold still. This is an utterly moving sight, not only because we know that this family is being broken apart at this very moment, but even more so because Ozu suddenly seems to permit all the kinds of shot compositions he has otherwise so carefully avoided. At the same time, the static shot we behold on screen when the members of this family stop moving in anticipation of the photographer's shutter also presents us with something close to our own reflection, and we find ourselves looking on in quiet solemnity. These things probably explain why this shot is so moving. In just this moment, we are living film experience, holding still and arranged side by side with others, our eyes all fixed on the same point—just like *them* as they pose for a photograph. To watch a film is to share the experience of holding still and looking in the same direction as others, much as they do in posing for the camera. But whereas *we* are enshrouded in a comfortable darkness, *they* are exposed under a cruel light, despite being indoors. The relationship is not unlike the correspondence between negative and positive photographic images. *They* seem to be under threat without knowing it, excluded as they are from the complicit darkness that gives *us* cover. When the light eventually returns, *we* will cease holding still and looking in the same direction as those seated alongside us in rows, bringing this complicity to a conclusion. And is this not the same fate that awaits *them?* Imagining this, it is hard not to feel a sense of agitation. It is as if we had just touched the limits of cinema itself. Are these people, whose faces betray not the slightest sign of provocation, not also in the midst of living their own extraordinary experience?

20. *Early Summer:* The taking of a family photograph.

At this point, an inversion occurs. It is no longer because the members of this family are about to separate and scatter that they are preserving a moment of togetherness in the form of a family photograph. The very fact that they have ended up subjects of a family photograph has now become the reason their household will have to dissolve. Narrational structure in Ozu always deeply links the taking of group photographs with the thematic system of *separation*. Even in examples like *Early Summer,* where the depiction of group photography is unaccompanied by any narrative premise of familial disintegration, it basically always introduces a narrative of separation or death into the circumstances of Ozuesque characters.

Take, for example, the middle school students in *There Was a Father* who pose for a class photograph in front of the Great Buddha statue at Kamakura during a school trip led by their teacher Chishū Ryū. Nothing about this scene suggests an impending crisis. It merely portrays a common ritual of student life. And yet, over the course of the shots that follow, viewers will have to bear witness to the death of one of the students in the photograph, who drowns when his boat capsizes on the lake. Of course, the boat accident itself is portrayed only symbolically, through a montage of several significant details, in a way that recalls the portrayal of prostitution in *A Hen in the Wind*. It hardly needs stating that the taking of a class photograph is not the direct cause of this unforeseen event, which will lead chaperone Ryū to resign from his teaching post. But on a narrational level, this group photograph clearly does introduce the themes of death and separation. For Ryū this will mean a twofold separation, both from a pupil and from his career as a teacher.

Should anyone require further convincing of the relationship between the taking of group photographs and the theme of separation, it will perhaps suffice to recall the opening scene of *Brothers and Sisters of the Toda Family*. Here, the widowed country teacher of *There Was a Father* is replaced by a large, wealthy urban family. Gathered in celebration of the matriarch's sixtieth birthday, the members of the family pose side by side in front of a hired photographer's camera, using chairs brought out to their rambling yard for the purpose. The scene is of a cheerful family ritual. There is no trace of anything inauspicious on the horizon. At first, eldest son Shin Saburi has lingered behind in his room, and his younger sister Mieko Takamine goes to retrieve him. Saburi looks a little inconvenienced, but he takes his place among the rest of the family and the ritual is achieved. The tranquil sunlight shining on the well-maintained yard seems to bless this family gathering. Since the scene is staged outdoors and the family members are also more numerous than in the group photograph in *Early Summer*, it is difficult to discern the individual faces of the people looking directly into the photographer's lens. The narrative has also only just gotten underway, and we do not yet understand their complicated familial relationships. But the spectacle of everyone facing forward, focusing on the same point, and holding still—starting with patriarch Hideo Fujino and his wife Fumiko Katsuragi at center—is no different from the taking of the family photograph depicted in *Early Summer*. And yet, that very evening, the patriarch will suffer a heart attack after returning from dinner, and before his sons and daughters are able to rush to his bedside at the family home, he will breathe his last. Here too, the taking of a group photograph has become an inauspicious ritual of separation.

Shot in 1941, *Brothers and Sisters of the Toda Family* is the earliest film in which the taking of a group photograph functions, on the level of narrational structure, as a theme connected to death and separation. But what captures our attention here is the fact that the family patriarch expires on the very day of his wife's sixtieth birthday celebration, since Yasujirō Ozu would pass on precisely *his* sixtieth birthday. There are a number of things about Ozu's life that he predicted in the films, but it is hard not to be stirred when death comes for Hideo Fujino on this day in particular, since this so clearly portends Ozu's own death. Ozu portrayed the subject of the death of a father any number of times, in films extending from *Where Now Are the Dreams of Youth?* to *The End of Summer*. *A Mother Should Be Loved,* which opens with a father's death, is especially significant in this respect, since Ozu had to face the real death of his own father during that film's production.

Still, the death of the aging patriarch at the beginning of *Brothers and Sisters of the Toda Family* remains privileged among the various predictive details scattered throughout Ozu's films. First, it involves the taking of a family photograph, a ritual of separation characteristic of Ozu. Then there is the number sixty. This is not the age of the deceased himself, but that hardly matters since the relationship between the late industrialist and his wife is, importantly, an interchangeable one. The circumstances of the elderly couple in the postwar *Tokyo Story* are much the same, but in that film, it is the wife who dies. *Who* dies is not what is important. The important thing is that *someone* dies. The sex of the someone who dies is always interchangeable. We have already observed this interchangeability of sex in the relationships between parents and children in *There Was a Father, Late Spring,* and *Late Autumn.* We can add that *The Only Son* and *There Was a Father* also feature basically the same familial structure, except that the latter substitutes an absent mother for an absent father. The father in *Brothers and Sisters of the Toda Family* might as well have died on his own sixtieth birthday. The result, either way, would be basically the same film. Of course, saying "the same film" means deliberately ignoring the subtle nuances in the details and focusing exclusively on narrational structure, but in any case, Ozu was a director who it would not have been the least bit surprising to find making a film in which a patriarch himself died on his sixtieth birthday. In reality, no such film exists, but that nonexistent film does take form as Ozu's own life, which concluded precisely on his sixtieth birthday. In this sense, we can perhaps think of the taking of the family photograph at the beginning of *Brothers and Sisters of the Toda Family* as the negative center of the Ozuesque cinematic system, the point at which fiction and reality, or negative and positive images, perfectly overlap. This also demonstrates that Yasujirō Ozu was perhaps gifted with something beyond mere talent. That same *something* also seems related to the necessity with which the relationship between the thematic system of "separation"—materialized in the taking of a family photograph—and the narrational structure of the film ends up forming an image inverted from reality: in real life the purpose of the group photograph is often to memorialize a parting of ways, but in the world of the Ozuesque, it becomes a theme with the narrational function of *introducing* a separation into the plot.

The portrait photography scene in *Record of a Tenement Gentleman,* which Inuhiko Yomota has analyzed in detail, also clearly functions as a ritual of separation. On their way home from a visit to the zoo, Chōko Iida and war orphan Tomihiro (Hōhi) Aoki *happen* to stop at a photography studio, then find themselves standing side by side in front of a camera, holding still and looking into the lens. The result of this is that they will have to part ways. The unique thing in this instance is that the opening and closing movement of the photographer's shutter is depicted on screen, and we even see the inverted image of the two subjects looking into the lens as the shutter releases. Here, the relationship between reality and fiction is not merely one of negative/positive photographic reversal. This moment has even demanded a vertical spatial inversion.[6]

Where reversals and inversions cause reality and fiction to overlap, the sheer immobility of portraits, of expressions hanging motionless in midair, paradoxically sets narratives into motion. To say that narratives are set into motion here is simply to say that relationships between characters become different from what they were. In late-period Ozu, families that have been holding together in one form or another ultimately dissolve, whether because of a death or through someone's departure for a faraway place. The fact that scenes of group photography become the direct momentum for such separations demonstrates concretely what it means to say that the greatest of cinematic movements come to life in "holding still." In *Brothers and Sisters of the Toda Family*, the taking of the family photograph comes at the beginning and serves to set the narrative into motion. In *Record of a Tenement Gentleman* it comes midway and performs a modulating function. And in *Early Summer* it arrives at the end, to bring the narrative to rest. *Early Summer* is notable for the fact that two photographs are taken, one of the entire family and the other of just the elderly grandparents. While this second portrait is being taken, the children and grandchildren stand around the photographer, watching the two pose. In other words, there is a doubling of immobile looks here. Ichirō Sugai and Chieko Higashiyama stare into the lens. The other members of the family stare at their staring eyes. It may seem odd to call this "staring" since

---

6. Inuhiko Yomota, "Shishatachi no shōkan," *Yurīka* 13, no. 7 (June 1981): 110.

there is no trace of ill will. Their children even smile as they look on. And yet, there is something cruel about this doubling of looks. The family is arriving at an understanding, even if unconsciously, that this elderly couple, already isolated by the photographer's lens, is about to be sent off to a faraway place. This lends exceptional beauty to the portrait shot of Sugai and Higashiyama holding still and looking into a camera that is itself hardly pictured on screen. We have here a ritual within a ritual, performed through a doubling of looks: not merely a ritual of separation initiating the breakup of a family but a funerary rite, performed in advance, for two people selected from among the group. What, in fact, *is* a funeral in itself if not a ceremony in which the members of a family stare at a face staring into a camera? In *Tokyo Story*, the second film Ozu made after *Early Summer*, the entire family will take part in this ceremony when they stare at Higashiyama's memorial portrait on the funeral altar.[7]

The other situation that most resembles the taking of Sugai and Higashiyama's portrait photograph in *Early Summer* is probably the wedding scene in *Late Autumn*. The ceremony itself is not depicted, of course, but the film is noteworthy for having brought the camera closer to a wedding reception than Ozu's others do. Considering that this is not a marriage of mere secondary characters as in *Equinox Flower*, that Setsuko Hara is about to marry off her only daughter Yōko Tsukasa, it is positively exceptional that this anteroom is pictured at all, much less in the moments preceding the start of the ceremony. Upon glimpsing the bride and groom dressed in wedding costume and posing side by side in front of a photographer's camera, we feel a sense of unease, as if having witnessed something we should not have. The photographer poses Keiji Sada and Yōko Tsukasa in their formal wear. A wedding guest with a camera steals a snapshot of the couple. Hara stands in the

---

7. It is customary in Japan to place a photograph of the deceased (*iei*) on the altar during funeral ceremonies, though the portrait of the deceased is not pictured on screen in *Tokyo Story*.

back, apart from her deceased husband's old friends, and smiles to herself. The relationship of eyelines is exactly the same as in *Early Summer*: a doubling of looks. We feel doubly apprehensive, first because this scene of photography is too similar to the funeral rite in *Early Summer*, and second because a wedding reception of the kind Ozu otherwise so insistently avoided is now showing signs of beginning. And at this instant, there is a shot of the bride and groom holding still and staring into the lens—a shot posed and framed just like the thing everyone knows as a wedding photograph. When it has come to an end, we are reassured, if anything, by the abruptness with which the narrative then retreats from this wedding venue.

But was this portrait of a man and woman standing still and stiff in formal costume really a wedding photograph? Until now, this kind of shot has been connected with rites of parting performed to send off someone close—with funeral rites, not ceremonies of celebration. Has it not? Have we not seen it introduce death and separation into the narratives? Should there really be so much resemblance between a ceremony of celebration and a funeral rite? Was this a funeral? "Something like that," says a voice. Not the voice of the film director Yasujirō Ozu, but of a character from another film: Chishū Ryū in *An Autumn Afternoon*. Recall his reply when bar hostess Kyōko Kishida takes a look at his formal attire on the night of his daughter's wedding and asks him, "was it a funeral?" Does he not mumble something vaguely in the affirmative? Just as weddings and funerals become commingled in stories of clothing, these two rituals are things that also fuse neatly through the theme of holding still. And sure enough, when the shutter is released, the bride and groom holding still in front of the camera will be sent off by their staring friends and family, and a new distance will be created internal to the narrative.

Why then is there no such wedding venue portrait photography in *Late Spring* or *An Autumn Afternoon*, films that deal with the same subject matter? The reason is perhaps that *Late Autumn* is a story in which a

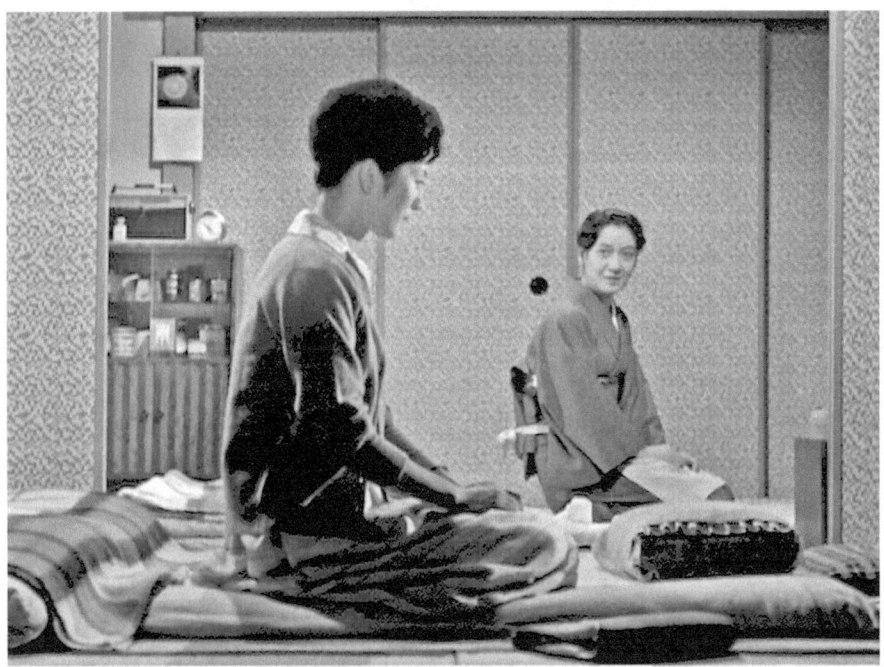

21. *Late Autumn:* Mother Setsuko Hara and daughter Yōko Tsukasa preparing for bed side by side in adjoining rooms of their apartment.

mother gives a daughter away in marriage. Setsuko Hara and Yōko Tsukasa live in an apartment block, not on the second floor of a house. Because the two sleep alongside one another in neighboring bedrooms, the oppositional spatial structure of men's and women's sanctuaries does not take hold as it does when male parent Chishū Ryū parts with Setsuko Hara or Shima Iwashita (fig. 21). In *Late Spring* and *An Autumn Afternoon,* there is no need to stage a scene of wedding photography in the anteroom of the reception hall because the separation ritual has already been performed. It is performed on the morning of the day of the ceremony, at the moment when the father sheepishly sets foot in his daughter's room and lays eyes on the bride dressed in wedding costume. For Ryū, it is enough to climb unseen stairs and enter his daughter's room. That second-floor room will soon be vacated, as we established in chapter 4, on "inhabiting" and spatial structure in late-period Ozu.

It thus becomes clear that the theme of stairs and the theme of taking group photographs are deeply linked in Ozu, and that the two perform basically the same narrational functions. Both stairs and wedding photographs are ordinarily excluded from the world of the Ozuesque and not depicted on screen. *Late Autumn* and *An Autumn Afternoon* are exceptions, but because the parent parting with a daughter is a mother in the former and a father in the latter, the thing displayed in such unusual frontal framing is the wedding photograph in the one and the staircase in the other. One is a product of the magnetic forces that accompany "moving" and "holding still," while the other results from the spatial structure of Japanese houses with first and second floors, but both perform the function of severing the narrational flow and bringing the plot to a close. The Ozuesque "film" is a rich and free cinematic environment in which staircases and wedding photographs—things that bear no resemblance to each other—start unexpectedly to live striking similarities, transcending the framework of individual narratives and exchanging knowing smiles. All things coexist, without negating things that are other.

7

RADIATING

DEATH IN MIDSUMMER

Early in the morning on the day that his wife has passed, Chishū Ryū slips out of the house where members of the family have rushed from Tokyo and Osaka to gather and stands alone at the edge of his garden, looking down across the crowded rooftops of the neighboring houses at a vista of the sea. His daughter-in-law Setsuko Hara scurries toward him and stands at his side. What might Ryū be thinking in this scene near the end of *Tokyo Story*, on the morning of his wife's death? Hara encourages him to come back to the house since everyone is waiting. At this point, he remarks matter-of-factly that this day, on which he will undergo a ritual of separation from his wife, is going to be a hot one. Indeed, we see not a cloud in the sky that extends behind them. What kind of sign should people read within this reference to the weather? Is he trying to say that today will be out of the ordinary, that this is the beginning of what will be an *especially* hot day? Or is he saying that it will be hot again, *as usual?* In any case, the viewer can sense from what is shown on screen that a clear, hot day is almost certainly about to begin. We have here a typical sunny morning in Ozu.

Donald Richie correctly points out that references to the weather are by no means out of the ordinary in Ozu. He writes that the "unusual appreciation of the weather" is striking, even for "weather-conscious Japan," and proposes that such dialogue functions in part to "break a scene of some emotional tension" where it has developed.[1] Fair enough. References to the weather undoubtedly do possess such functions. But they also possess something more than a narrational function, since Ozuesque "beings" are not simply concerned about the weather. Ozu's sky is always clear, whether in *Floating Weeds,* which begins with the line "today's another hot one," spoken by a character who will play no more than a secondary role, or wherever we hear the words "nice weather," which are repeated so often that we forget who said them in which scene of what film. An Ozu film shot on a cloudy day is something almost nonexistent. Even the clouds over a rail crossing along the Yokosuka line that Ichirō Sugai looks up at in *Early Summer* are not the clouds of an overcast sky but accents that emphasize the radiant weather. The sky that fills his field of view is bright, with no indication of dampness. The same is true of the sky that unfurls behind Chieko Higashiyama in the shot that frames her at a slight upward angle when she casually predicts her own death while playing with her grandson on a grassy embankment in *Tokyo Story.*

Of course, when hot weather is mentioned, people do often fan themselves. Men in cotton summer kimono also wear moistened hand towels folded on top of their heads. But this heat is never the damp heat of the rainy season. Heat is consistently an attribute of clear weather.

---

1. Donald Richie, *Ozu* (Berkeley: University of California Press, 1974), 57.

Buildings and people always cast distinct shadows. Ozuesque "beings" breathe the air of a sunny, cloudless day. This is why the whites stand out in the black and white films—white walls, or the whites of women's dresses, or laundry on the line. In the color films, bright blue skies extend in the background. The light in Ozu films is basically the same light of California and its movie town Hollywood, or of Mediterranean Nice and the open-air sets of the Victorine film studio. It is as if Japan were not located in a subtropical climate with a wet season. This is why people in Ozu films are never *worried* about the weather. By saying things like "nice weather" or "today's another hot one," they assure themselves that they are in fact, without a doubt, inhabitants of the world of Ozu. When on rare occasions rainfall or snow flurries do appear, they do so only as inauspicious signs portending some grim narrative development. In Ozu the sky can only be sunny.

Here we see how tremendously misguided it would be to call Yasujirō Ozu a typically Japanese filmmaker. Not only is there no rainy season in his world, but there are not even any intermittent showers. In fact, Ozu is about as far as it gets from the poetic rhetoric of the seasons in traditional haiku. Nowhere does he depict things like budding plum blossoms, falling leaves, blanketing frost, or any other such subtle reflection of seasonal change. He can therefore hardly be said to conform to the image of a filmmaker attuned to nature. Ozu neglects the seasons with a consistency that can almost be called cruel. The films may have titles like *Late Spring, Early Summer, Equinox Flower*, or *An Autumn Afternoon*, but their concern with the seasons ends there. Or maybe it would be better to say that they simply ignore the rainy season, showing little interest in cold or humidity as good weather continues from spring through summer and into fall. Nights are clear and moonlit. The moonbeams that fall on the *shōji* screens at the inn in *Late Spring*, for example, could not be more foreign to the humid nocturnal atmosphere of Kyoto.

In Kenji Mizoguchi fog is an indispensable element of mise-en-scène, and an Akira Kurosawa film without rain would be unimaginable. In

Kurosawa the intense heat of *Stray Dog* (*Nora inu*, 1949) has its polar opposite in the cold of *The Idiot* (*Hakuchi*, 1951), while Mizoguchi excelled at the lyricism of the night. These things are completely alien to Ozu. By the late period, it is even rare for characters to wear overcoats. Men tend to commute to work wearing open-collar shirts. Just when was the last point at which we saw a man or woman wearing a scarf? People do wear coats and sweaters in *Good Morning*. And yet, there is probably no other film in which the words "nice weather" are uttered as often as they are here. In *Tokyo Story* Chishū Ryū does head for Tokyo with his umbrella in tow, and we occasionally glimpse this rainy-day accessory leaning against doorjambs or the wall in the hallway. But there is no depiction of any weather that would necessitate its use.

Nothing could be more un-Japanese than nature without rain or cold. From this perspective, it is exceptionally strange to read comparisons between the Ozuesque "film" and the haiku poem as proposed by Tom Milne, one of the first to introduce Ozu in the United Kingdom.[2] It also feels quite uncomfortable when Paul Schrader trots out aesthetic concepts like *wabi* and *sabi* or talks about *yūgen*,[3] and when Richie enlists *mono no aware*. The light that gives form to shots in Ozu is decidedly not something that should lure people toward such kinds of Japanese aesthetic sensibility. We are not dealing here with glimpses of some profound and elusive world of subtlety. Everything is exposed on the surface, under the radiating sunlight of a clear day. It is hard to imagine

---

2. There is no citation in the original, but Hasumi appears to be referencing Milne's essay "The Flavour of Green Tea over Rice," *Sight and Sound* 32 (Autumn 1963), as cited in Paul Schrader, *Transcendental Style in Film: Ozu, Bresson, Dreyer* (New York: Da Capo Press, 1988), 27.

3. Schrader cites Zen interpreter Alan Watts's 1957 book *The Way of Zen* for definitions of these terms: "Where the mood of the moment is solitary and quiet, it is called *sabi*. When the artist is feeling depressed or sad, and this peculiar emptiness of feeling catches a glimpse of something rather ordinary and unpretentious in its incredible 'suchness,' the mood is called *wabi*. When the moment evokes a more intense, nostalgic sadness connected with autumn and the vanishing away of the world, it is called *aware*. And when the vision is the hinting at an unknown never to be discovered, the mood is called *yugen*." Schrader, *Transcendental Style*, 34.

a ghastlier color than the red of the amaranth flowers that crowd the inner garden at Haruko Sugimura's house in *Floating Weeds,* one of the few films in which rainfall does make an appearance. There is nothing nuanced about it. It is just red. In Ozu nothing is ambiguously evoked in indistinct outline. Ozu is an auteur of broad daylight who insists not on subtle nuance, but on clarity, even to excess. Prohibited any cloudy gradation, his skies are permitted only to radiate sunshine.

This is not to say that Ozu's images lack sensitivity or are insufficiently poetic. Yasujirō Ozu is a filmmaker who understands how to bring out poetry in territory foreign to the kind of Japanese seasonal rhetoric that people too readily take for poetic, and in crueler and more audacious form. His talent is not for filming things already generally considered poetic in some space external to cinema, but for selecting images that only begin to function poetically in the instant they are captured on film. But here, the question of whether to call this poetic already becomes meaningless. "Poetic" is just a provisional way to describe the upheaval of cinematic sensitivity we experience in the instant that cinema is laid bare on the screen. In any case, Ozu consistently avoids moments in which things represented visually on screen are already saturated in their own lyricism. In surfacing the very conditions that make cinema cinema, as he does in the case of the aforementioned family photography scene in *Early Summer,* for example, he bypasses psychology, moving the viewer in unmediated ways. In this sense, Ozu seems correct in having somewhat self-deprecatingly stated that *Tokyo Story* had the "most melodramatic tendencies" of any of his films—the same *Tokyo Story* often hailed as a late-period masterpiece. While this film does move people on many levels, it can also be said to rely more heavily than usual on narrative in order to work on audience emotions. There are no stand-out details that agitate cinematic sensitivity like the family photography session in *Early Summer,* the deserted staircase in *An Autumn Afternoon,* or the quarrel in a downpour in *Floating Weeds.* Even the lyricism of the celebrated sequence on the seawall by the hot spring hotel at Atami can be adequately resolved in psychological terms. The dialogue of the elderly couple here seems almost effusive when compared with the reticence of the looks exchanged by the aging husband and wife who sit in the garden of the National Museum in *Early Summer*. The "melodramatic tendencies" invoked by Ozu refer to the telling of the story in a way that exposes neither the limits of cinema nor the intrinsic features of his own cinematic world.

Still, it must nevertheless be said that *Tokyo Story* is an extraordinarily moving film, moving because of the way it vividly captures on celluloid the crystal-clear sky on the morning after Chieko Higashiyama has taken her last breath and the heat that soon arrives as torrid sun radiates over the surroundings. Once the matriarch's condition has been deemed terminal, the camera suddenly retreats from her sickbed and ventures out into the early morning. What we then lay eyes on is a perfectly ordinary pier at the harbor. The camera is placed low and composes the pier extending in depth into the harbor, the surface of the water and the low mountains drifting in a dull light beyond the silhouette of its backlit poles and awning (fig. 22). An atmosphere of morning hangs over the deserted surroundings. This is only a brief shot, but it creates an impression of surprising clarity, above all because of the absence of any human figure and the unobstructedness of its perspectival organization. The awning of this pier, here shown extending perpendicularly into the scenery, has already appeared at the beginning of the film as a straight parallel line crossing through a shot overlooking the port at Onomichi—a linear accent. And here again, in the shot that follows, we encounter the same composition: the port crossed by the awning as a parallel line. The contrast formed by the juxtaposition of these parallel and perpendicular compositions is deeply moving. Several brief shots ensue, depicting fishing boats and deserted scenery but absent any effulgence of radiating sunlight. What these shots evoke is merely the clear atmosphere of early morning in a

22. *Tokyo Story:* An empty pier early in the morning, representing the death of Chieko Higashiyama.

landscape devoid of people. Still, in their spatiotemporal indeterminacy, they do also convey that we are looking at the start of a hot, cloudless day—the start of a day, and at the same time the last moments of a life. Across only a small number of shots, this brief scenery traces what it is to begin and to end.

Ozu also uses a sequence of brief, elegantly arranged shots in the brothel scene in *A Hen in the Wind*, for example, where the purpose is to represent Kinuyo Tanaka's turn to prostitution by means of metonymy. The technique is probably the same where Chieko Higashiyama's death is the subject. But it is important to note that the sequence in *Tokyo Story* does more than only represent the exceptional event of a transition from life to death. It also flawlessly depicts the routine temporal process of the transition from night to day. This double transition, at once both fateful and universal, is evoked through the texture of the shots themselves, through their dull, dry light—something that sets the early morning imagery in *Tokyo Story* far apart from the rhetorical effusiveness of the brothel scene in *A Hen in the Wind*. The technique is almost no longer even metonymy. It creates a direct connection, internal to the image itself, between the premonition of heat and the impression of life's fragility. "Ahh, it was such a beautiful dawn," Chishū Ryū will murmur momentarily, but there is something about this covered pier extending perpendicularly into the deserted scenery that transcends what we know as "images of dawn." As a metonymic expression of dawn, this shot narrates something in excess while at the same time also giving an impression of lack, of hardly beginning to approach such forms of expression, perhaps because the rows of iron poles extending in perspectival arrangement beneath the silhouetted awning embody something not reducible to the seasonal rhetoric of Japanese poetry. This image reminds the viewer once again of the audacity of Ozu, since he otherwise consistently eliminates this kind of perspectival depth from his compositions. The aesthetic of restraint and reserve that many ascribe to Ozu never selects this kind of image. For us, the sudden appearance of this shot is stunning and leaves us staring. But our surprise barely lasts an instant before Ozu returns us to the room where the family is processing the reality of a death. The poetry of Ozu is to be touched within such moments of audacious sensitivity. His sensitive yet audacious images are never saturated in the lyricism of seasonal rhetoric, and their narrational flow abandons even the cinematic desire to surprise.

AN AUTEUR OF BROAD DAYLIGHT

Most of Ozu's black-and-white films take place under cloudless skies, but among them *Tokyo Story* is especially beautiful for the way it captures the impression of heat. What is moving here is the consistency of its heat. From the perspective of Japanese seasonal sensibility, we should find ourselves wanting to protest that even a single summer shower would be in order, but none of the characters here show any indication of having such thoughts themselves as they patiently submit to the heat and sunshine. When Chishū Ryū says "it's going to be another hot day today" while looking down at the port of Onomichi after having just lost his wife, he almost seems to welcome the heat. Maybe he has sensed that he has not lost sight of the world of the Ozuesque, and he feels suddenly reassured. In any case, it seems that the day of Chieko Higashiyama's death in *Tokyo Story* will be remembered for its radiant heat, much like the day of the funeral service for Setsuko Hara's husband in *Late Autumn,* which gets mentioned on numerous occasions in that film. And despite the fall season, it is a similarly hot day when Ganjirō Nakamura dies in *The End of Summer*. Without exception, the elderly breathe their last on cloudless sunny days. *Tokyo Story* is an especially significant film in this respect, because the clear weather and high temperature are captured in black and white. The later color films lack the dull, dry texture of the images described here.

No other films evoke the glare of sunlight quite so cruelly as this one, despite the fact that it contains not all that many low-angle shots directed at the sky. Looking at *Tokyo Story,* we are struck once again that Ozu was not a filmmaker who dwelled in the shadows but one resolutely committed to the clarity of broad daylight. This is not to say, of course, that the night is nowhere depicted in Ozu. In the early crime films, darkness comes vividly to life. Nevertheless, Ozu is an auteur of broad daylight, and we should be moved by his crystal-clear skies, from which hardly a drop of rain ever falls. Precisely because Ozu is an auteur of broad daylight, it is also moving when rain showers or the cold and dampness of night do unexpectedly intrude.

It hardly matters what, if anything, is going through Chishū Ryū's head as he stands above the port looking down at the water after having just lost his wife, since characters in the Ozuesque "film," starting with him, generally lack anything like psychology. He simply finds himself remarking, almost mechanically, on the sunny sky and the heat in his surroundings, just as anyone might do. There is no deep significance to this moment. It merely reflects the phatic communication so characteristic of conversations in Ozu, performed here with ceremonial reserve. And yet, this inconsequential exchange between Chishū Ryū and Setsuko Hara as they stand in a corner of the garden moves us perhaps more than the rather substantial dialogue about life that the two will later share once the rest of the family have returned to Tokyo, following the conclusion of the funeral services. Nothing could be further from melodrama than the moments when Ozu characters mention the weather. We have already noted that such moments often serve the substantial narrational function of initiating sequences or bringing them to a close, despite the fact that no one says anything of any significance. These moments are not the slightest bit dramatic, but they do transform the narrational flow, performing a role like punctuation at transitions between scenes—a phatic function, quite literally. To put it one way, the films move on their momentum.

As we have just seen, the words that Chishū Ryū says to Setsuko Hara on this morning in the garden are very brief and without any deep substance. They are mechanical, if anything, constituting little more than a monotone utterance, ritualized through repetition. Most Ozuesque "beings" speak much the same kinds of lines in all sorts of circumstances. But here, the repetition has necessity. Positioned in between the scene staged around Chieko Higashiyama's already unconscious body and the subsequent scene of the funeral service, and anticipated by the deserted scenery of the port at dawn, this shot of the two can be said to have the function of demarcating the boundary between life and death. It should also be noted that the family members gathered around the mother's deathbed—including, of course, father Ryū—are all still wearing their regular clothes. When Hara goes to retrieve Ryū from the garden, she is dressed in an ordinary white blouse with short sleeves. From the perspective of clothing dynamics, this death still belongs to everyday time. Ceremonial time begins only after the two return to the house from the garden. Because of the momentum they create, mourning attire will now have to be worn—the same mourning attire that eldest son Sō Yamamura and eldest daughter Haruko Sugimura had debated whether to pack upon receiving the telegram summoning them to Onomichi from Tokyo. A conversation about having to rent mourning costume from a clothing service has also just taken place. It is therefore clear that the transition from the sunny outdoors to interior space has induced a conversion of everyday time into ceremonial time.

The ritualism here is of course emphasized by the mourning attire, but ritualism in the true sense does not reside in such things. When the members of the family kneel side by side at the funeral service, all holding the same posture and facing in the same direction, it is the shot itself that is truly ritualistic, underscoring as it does their formal arrangement. The theme of being side by side is taken further here than in what we have already seen, as is the theme of unidirectional looking. The family members sit in a row across from the Buddhist altar, all lowering their eyes, more or less, amid the droning of the sutra chanting and the sound of the *mokugyo* wooden temple drum keeping the tempo. Unlike in scenes portraying the taking of group photographs, the camera here does not film its subjects directly from the front but at a diagonal. There is, of course, no establishing shot to clarify the totality of spatial relationships among the mourners making up this ritual of parting called a funeral. The arrangement of the characters is indicated through a series of fragmentary shots, much the same as in the depiction of the Buddhist memorial service at the beginning of *Late Autumn*. Outside, the sky is consistently clear, as on the day of the funeral in *The End of Summer*. As if to convince us of this, Ozu has youngest son Shirō Ōsaka leave the funeral service and sit by himself on the veranda. In *Late Autumn* during the Buddhist memorial service for the sixth anniversary of the late husband's passing, sunlight reflecting off what seems to be a pond on the temple grounds plays on the surfaces of the sliding panels and screens inside the building. But in *Tokyo Story*, the sky itself appears, cloudlessly confronting Ōsaka's gaze from beyond some gravestones. Its heat and sunshine intervene as essential elements in this ritual of parting. In *Late Autumn* characters mention on several occasions that the day of their late friend's funeral was also hot—so hot, in fact, that they still remember the weather six years later. Ozuesque "beings" all share the fate of having to die on hot and sunny midsummer days. Funerals and memorial services also require them to wear mourning attire in summer.

RAIN AND EYELINES

Should we claim here that the lack of seasonal sensibility in Ozu reflects a consistency of preference in matters of weather? There is no rain in Ozu films. The temperature also never drops below freezing. It is always sunny outside. Characters mention the heat in place of greetings. Perhaps we should conclude, in light of all this, that Ozu selected sunny skies to the thorough exclusion of rain and cold. But if we did, would we not end up defining the Ozuesque "film" by means of yet another negation?

It certainly fair to say that rain only rarely saturates the scene in Ozu, auteur of clear skies and broad daylight. In fact, we are tempted to declare with the same conviction of those who claim Ozu's camera never moves that no, it does not rain in Ozu. Even Yūharu Atsuta, who for many years was Ozu's "eye" in his role as director of photography, claimed not to remember ever shooting a scene in the rain.[4] Nevertheless, just as it would be incorrect to say that the films of Ozu consist of nothing but static shots, it would not be quite accurate to claim that there is no rain anywhere in Ozu. Anyone intimate with Ozu's films

---

4. See Hasumi's interview with Atsuta in the appendix.

will recall, for example, that there is a scene in *Floating Weeds* that takes place in a downpour—an extended summer deluge that drenches the red amaranths crowding the inner garden at Haruko Sugimura's house. Ganjirō Nakamura has been paying visits to this house, pretending to the other actors in his traveling theater troupe that Sugimura is a mere acquaintance. In reality, he once fathered a child with this woman, and it is to take in the sight of this young man that he spends time fanning himself at the edge of her garden or playing chess on the second floor of her house. The rain introduces a tension to these shots, and with a suddenness that seems determined to disturb his rather self-indulgent peace. This disturbance coincides with the unexpected arrival at the front door of Ganjirō's current feminine companion Machiko Kyō, who has caught on to the situation. What ensues is the famous argument between Ganjirō and Kyō as the two face off from either side of the narrow street in front of the house. The cinematographer who shot this showdown in a downpour was not Shōchiku's Yūharu Atsuta, but Kazuo Miyagawa from the Daiei Motion Picture Company. The season is midsummer, and the man and woman are both dressed in light cotton kimono. Machiko Kyō has set her red oil-paper umbrella opened on the ground, but Ganjirō swings his own folded umbrella at his side as the two argue for what is an unusually long time in Ozu. They face each other and glare, though each seems to look slightly below the other's eyes. Neither attempts to advance even a single step in the direction of the other due to the heavy rain falling in the street between them. As they move side to side under the narrow eaves, only their words and eyelines meet in cruel intersection.

Just why is this scene of an argument in the rain so moving? For one, seeing rain is agitating in itself, since rainfall is so exceptional in Ozu. How could we not be moved by the sudden change of weather in this film, which Ozu made not at his regular studio Shōchiku, but at Daiei? In other words, we are moved to sense the release Ozu himself must have felt while working apart from his accustomed cast and crew. We are also seized by a sense of unease, a sense that such heavy rainfall should not be permitted—much like the staircase that makes a startling appearance at the end of *An Autumn Afternoon* after having otherwise been so thoroughly excluded from the screen. Of course, rain also falls in the prewar *A Story of Floating Weeds,* of which *Floating Weeds* is a remake, even to the point of interrupting a performance by the traveling actors when their makeshift stage starts to leak, as well as under the same circumstances as in the later film. In *An Inn in Tokyo* there is a scene where a sudden downpour makes it impossible to sleep outdoors, and it also rains in *I Graduated, but* . . . (a film that today exists in only incomplete form), while the protagonist searches for work in the midst of a recession. The screenplay for the lost film *The Sorrow of the Beautiful Woman* indicates that it too included a scene with rain. These instances do not move us the way the rain in *Floating Weeds* does as it beats down on the low eaves and drenches the narrow street, but they do demonstrate that rain is not completely unheard of in Ozu's films, even if it is the exception. In fact, a sudden rainfall even seems to precipitate the death of Sō Yamamura in *The Munekata Sisters,* another film Ozu made on leave from Shōchiku, at Shin Tōhō.

Of course, nothing compels us to explain the agitation of cinematic sensitivity the viewer experiences here. It is also not as if it would be impossible to account for the impact of this rain scene in psychological terms. It just seems that this man and woman arguing with one another in a downpour somehow stand out, as if having fallen out of equilibrium with the whole, much like the photography session in *Early Summer.* There is something in excess here that cannot be resolved simply by understanding the significance of this scene within the context of the narrative, something that seems to lure us beyond the boundaries of the Ozuesque "film," toward cinema and its limits. To capture things like a woman's resentment over her aging companion's furtive visits to an unacknowledged son, or her feelings of jealousy toward the child's mother, is something that should have been possible even without any rain. But psychological motivation alone does not cause Machiko Kyō to stand beneath these narrow eaves, and what has Ganjirō so upset here is also not only her rude and unexpected intrusion. If the point were merely to vent resentment and contempt, it should have been enough for Kyō to slap her man's face, as Ineko Arima does in *Tokyo Twilight* (*Tokyo boshoku*, 1957). But despite their impassioned complaints, neither takes a single step toward the other during this exchange of verbal abuse. This in itself is moving. They seem convinced that the rain-drenched space of the narrow street is off limits as they maintain their distance, casting hostile looks. They do change their relative positions, but their motions remain lateral and parallel, neither reducing nor increasing the distance between them. Their gestures here suggest careful mimicry more than an argument. Each performs motions similar to the other's, almost as if they were facing their own reflections in a mirror. Watching the repetitive mimicry of their gestures, we cannot help but recall (if somewhat out of the blue) the celebrated mirror gag from *Duck Soup* (dir. Leo McCarey, 1933). It is as if these two people have faced off with the sole motivation of imitating each other's every motion, despite their obvious differences of clothing, age, and sex.

Imitation and repetition are far from rare occurrences in Ozu, as our discussion of the theme of sitting side by side has demonstrated. Imitation can even take the form of physical comedy, as in the films where brothers mimic one another's gestures while staging rebellions against their parents, beginning with *I Was Born, but . . .* . We find something similar even in *Tokyo Story,* when Chishū Ryū and his old friend Eijirō Tōno show up at Ryū's daughter's house wobbling drunk and stagger precariously through the downstairs beauty parlor before falling into neighboring salon chairs, slumping side by side in front of a mirror and starting to snore as if in synchronization with one another. The staging of this scene works to very good comedic effect, especially when daughter Haruko Sugimura attempts to rouse the two men with an exasperated "hello!" Other such instances of mirrored gesture are too numerous to inventory, but while the Ozuesque theme of imitation and repetition does quite often invite us to smile, the situation is clearly very different when it rains in *Floating Weeds*. We now realize that such kinds of mirrored gestures have never been performed by characters positioned face to face. The desperate spectacle of a man and woman quarreling in the rain is also not something we would have expected to encounter in Ozu. We are not unaccustomed to things like parents scolding mischievous children, but the sight of a grown man and woman airing complaints from their love life in an exchange of foul-mouthed abuse is something downright exceptional. The Setsuko Hara of *Tokyo Twilight*, who cannot contain her resentment toward Isuzu Yamada for abandoning her as a child, does also confront her mother face to face in delivering her devastating rebuke, but the relationship of those two women is far from evenly matched the way it is in *Floating Weeds,* and there is also no repetitive mimicry in their gestures. Dressed in a black mourning kimono and consumed with thoughts of her younger sister, whose resentment for their mother has accompanied her to her grave, Hara glares sharply at Yamada, leaving her dumbfounded in the face of such severity from her own daughter. Much like Kinuyo Tanaka in *A Hen in the Wind,* who silently endures the violent behavior of a husband incapable of forgiveness and ultimately has to tumble down the stairs, this mother, with her sinful past, has no resource but utter passivity with which to meet her daughter's display of emotion. The argument between the aging actor and his girlfriend in *Floating Weeds* is quite unique by comparison. The two assail each other with more or less the same level of hostility. Even their lines are equitably divided, as are the corresponding shots in which each speaks into the camera. The fight is evenly matched, something quite rare in Ozu.

But this is not necessarily what is important here. As we watch this man and woman glare at each other and exchange foul-mouthed abuse through the falling rain, we find ourselves succumbing to the hallucination that what we are witnessing is not merely the scene of an argument, that what we are gazing at is cinema itself. This is the important point. Or perhaps it would be better to say the *limits* of cinema. In following the severe expressions of these two people pictured in alternating succession and with a consideration for parity that is nothing short of conscientious, we come to the realization, whether we like it or not, that these dueling stares are not contained by the shots depicting them in back-and-forth sequence, but exist independently, in consistent duration of their own. We sense once again how utterly powerless cinema is when confronted with the simultaneous phenomenon of two sets of eyes looking at each other, since the technique of editing that divides shots into evenly alternating succession is ultimately nothing other than a method for demonstrating the defeat of the camera in the face of intersecting eyelines, as we have already described.

Here we arrive at a new understanding of just what kind of impact this scene of an argument in the rain has had on us. The sheer monotone repetition of the Ozuesque shot/reverse shot may have escaped our attention while it reproduced itself within a climate of harmony and unity—a climate utterly foreign to that of an argument—but here it reaches the heights of cruelty, and exposes a reality: that for cinema, people looking at each other is something impossible. What it is possible to see in cinema is only the eye. The look is something the camera will never capture on the cinematic surface. When two looks intersect, the camera becomes completely powerless. The scene of the evening downpour in *Floating Weeds* demonstrates this almost painfully. This is why the rainfall here is not merely a matter of coincidence. When the weather changes in dramatic and generally unpermitted ways, the films of Yasujirō Ozu converge precisely with the limit points beyond which cinema might cease being cinema. What we witness there is at once the climax of a film and also the climax of cinema itself. In this sense, the rain in *Floating Weeds* seems even more dangerous than the staircase that sets the stage for tragedy in *A Hen in the Wind*. It is for reasons such as this that rain is not permitted to fall at random in the films of Ozu.

DEATH IN MIDWINTER

In Ozu the sky must remain persistently clear, and the climate must be hot. This is because Ozu is an auteur of radiant weather and broad daylight. Of course, this is not to say that there are no night scenes in Ozu's films. When we consider that more than a couple of the films even end with shots of night trains receding into darkness, it should immediately be clear that Ozu did not make a principle of avoiding the night. To say that Ozu was a cinéaste of broad daylight is only to say that he required the heat of sunny days as a narrational detail. This tendency became pronounced in postwar Ozu, and during his last years in particular. A white short-sleeve blouse is the costume of young women approaching marriage. The cold is mostly not spoken of in the films. Does this mean that Ozu selected only heat to the exclusion of cold?

In fact, much as *Floating Weeds* stands out for its exceptional downpour, there is also a film that stands out for the exceptionally cold weather that defines its general atmosphere: namely, *Tokyo Twilight,* a film that opens with the rare spectacle of Chishū Ryū wearing an overcoat, and even a scarf. He has stopped for dinner at a small restaurant, and the greetings he proceeds to exchange with the hostess include a reference to the frigid conditions outside. Back at his house, we find a *kotatsu* table in the living room, fitted with a quilt for winter use.[5] His daughter Setsuko Hara will later appear in a winter coat of her own, her face half hidden behind a large white mask. *Tokyo Twilight* is at least memorable for the unusual fact that Setsuko Hara never wears a white short-sleeve blouse and even hides behind a face mask despite not having a cold. The Setsuko Hara in this film is not a daughter of marriageable age, but effectively a divorcée, having left her cynical husband and returned with her child to her father's house, and it should therefore probably be said that her face mask reveals her to be a "woman who changes clothes."

---

5. A *kotatsu* is a low table with a heating element that, in winter, is used with a quilt to warm the legs.

When detective Seiji Miyaguchi shows up at a late-night café—a set that somehow recalls the nightclubs of 1920s German cinema—he too sports a long overcoat and a large face mask, evoking an aura of grotesque caricature, like a character from a Fritz Lang crime film. And then, snow, of all things, begins to fall outside.

Of course, this is not the first time that snow has appeared in an Ozu film. The latter half of *Days of Youth* takes place on snowy ski slopes, as already discussed, and early in *A Mother Should Be Loved* we see two young brothers walking up a snow-covered road, shouldering their school backpacks. *The Sorrow of the Beautiful Woman* also seems to have been set in snow country based on what is indicated in the screenplay. But we are hard pressed to identify another film in which the cold is emphasized as intentionally as it is in *Tokyo Twilight*. The cold, the damp night air, and the gloomy darkness all play important roles in this film. *Tokyo Twilight* also portrays a death in midwinter, which corresponds to the midsummer death in *Tokyo Story*. These are events that should fluster people to much the same degree as the evening downpour does in *Floating Weeds*. This death in midwinter is also not the death of an elderly father or mother, but of a young woman of marriageable age. *Tokyo Twilight* was not very well received at the time of its release due to its gloomy tone, but it should nonetheless be considered a very significant film within the system of Ozu's body of work. It is significant precisely as a demonstration of the fact that any attempt to define some characteristic aspect of Ozu negatively, by means of what is absent from the oeuvre, will always come up against a film that disrupts such kinds of conclusions, that something almost violent in Ozu entices us not toward procedures of exclusion and selection but toward the predominance of the phenomena of juxtaposition and coexistence. Indeed, people think that by claiming it never rains in Ozu they can master the features of his cinematic world, but then it does rain in *Floating Weeds,* and with a force that erodes such confidence at the root. *A Hen in the Wind* and *An Autumn Afternoon* fly in the face of the negative postulate that stairs are not depicted in Ozu, and both with an impact bordering on violence. *Tokyo Twilight* similarly demolishes the notion that it is always sunny in Ozu, that winter is never depicted. Films undeniably exist that center things Ozu is often thought to have meticulously avoided and excluded. We do not view these as elements exceptional to the Ozuesque "film"; rather, they are to be affirmed as necessary details without which the whole of this cinematic world would come tumbling down.

Like *Early Spring,* which preceded it, *Tokyo Twilight* has been regarded as a failure, a film reflecting an interest unbecoming someone of Ozu's generation in the behavior of reckless young people immersed in the social mores of postwar Japan. The subject matter is exceptional indeed for postwar Ozu: an aging bank employee whose wife abandoned the family years earlier while he was away from Tokyo on assignment in the colonies can now do little more than look on as his daughter runs around with a deadbeat boyfriend, gets pregnant, and has an abortion, then ultimately commits suicide. The tragedy of this jilted daughter played by Ineko Arima is certainly not material belonging to what we might call the forte of postwar Ozu, but when unreliable boyfriend Masami Taura shows up outfitted in a trench coat and academic square cap, we find ourselves hallucinating that the Kōji Mitsui of *Dragnet Girl* has walked directly into the scene. In fact, the near abstraction of the set design in the aforementioned late-night café or on the interior of the police station, for example, also recalls the prewar *Dragnet Girl* and its less-than-realistic mise-en-scène. When Setsuko Hara presents herself at the police station to retrieve her younger sister from the authorities, the coat she wears over her kimono suggests the return of *Dragnet Girl*'s Sumiko Mizukubo as well, sending us into a state of consternation. This film—the last one Ozu would make in black and white—becomes a re-creation, in certain aspects, of Ozu's own cinematic world at a particular point in time before the war. The question to ask here is not about whether or to what extent Ozu himself had such intentions.

We know, of course, that Ozu and screenwriter Kōgo Noda experienced some disagreements surrounding this film. But what concerns us here is only the strange emotion we feel upon encountering Ozu at play in a damp climate of the night and cold that we had lost sight of. How could we not be surprised at Sumiko Mizukubo and Setsuko Hara appearing as one and the same "being" within the Ozuesque "film," despite the twenty-odd years separating their performances and the fact that there is not even an especially strong physical resemblance between them?

Still, what is most moving about *Tokyo Twilight* is not the fact that it connects in such ways to a film from the prewar years. The father's powerlessness in the face of a particularly postwar form of reckless and dissolute living also subtly overlaps with a theme in the prewar film *A Mother Should Be Loved*, as does the absence of the mother. It is not as if the latter theme comes out of nowhere to derange the sisters in *Tokyo Twilight*; we have already encountered a similar situation involving the older brother in *A Mother Should Be Loved*, a film in which a father's sudden death leaves a mother to raise two sons as a single parent. The older of the two sons, Den Obinata, sinks momentarily into debauchery upon learning that he is not his mother's biological child, delivering an utterly cheerless performance that Ineko Arima will quite faithfully recreate in *Tokyo Twilight*. In the earlier film, it is the younger sibling Kōji Mitsui who rebukes his older brother for his wild living, but the relationship between these brothers clearly mirrors the one between older and younger sisters Setsuko Hara and Ineko Arima. Of course, *Tokyo Twilight* is not a remake of *A Mother Should Be Loved* in the same sense that *Floating Weeds* is a remake of *A Story of Floating Weeds*, or *Late Autumn* of *Late Spring*. But when we see how the two films exchange and substitute character relationships, it emerges that they share basically the same thematic system and narrational structure. As far as visual similarities are concerned, the scenery at the brothel where Den Obinata spends a night in *A Mother Should Be Loved* probably has more in common with the seaside love hotel in *Early Spring* where Ryō Ikebe betrays his wife with Keiko Kishi than with anything in *Tokyo Twilight*. But the internal struggle that drives Obinata toward the pleasures of the flesh is unmistakably of the same nature as what causes Ineko Arima's distress. No matter how much care and concern their single parents demonstrate, both children sense something unnatural in this paternal affection and find themselves living in a constant state of insecurity and imbalance.

But these two films are linked by something more than just the psychological similarity of characters. They also share a privileged detail, which is of key importance for our purposes: namely, the exceptional appearance of snow. Of course, this is hardly the snow of blizzard conditions. In *A Mother Should Be Loved,* it is little more than a blanket of whiteness covering the ground. It appears in only a handful of shots, in a scene where two young brothers who have just lost their father walk to school. And yet, the scenery of this winter morning, composed with a boxy black car in the foreground, has a breathtaking beauty that will likely linger in the memory of anyone who views it. Compared to the light-hearted atmosphere of the gentle ski slopes of *Days of Youth,* an atmosphere appropriate to a college comedy, the snow on the path that these boys follow into the distance in their black caps and school uniforms creates an impression of something exceptional to Ozu having suddenly intruded, and it agitates the viewer, precisely because it introduces a momentary detail with no narrational function to play. The filmmakers did not intend to introduce snow here. The snow was a fortuitous accident of location shooting on a tight schedule in winter, but it stands out nevertheless. And in resonating at a distance with the appearance of snow in *Tokyo Twilight,* a film that emphasizes the cold from the very first line of dialogue, it demonstrates that Yasujirō Ozu was neither a monotone filmmaker nor an evangelist for a consistent aesthetic worldview, but a multifaceted cinéaste who was hardly resistant to change.

Despite the fact that it snows in *Tokyo Twilight*, there is no depiction anywhere in this film of snow-covered scenery. Snow appears on screen only as a white dusting visible through the glass panels in the sliding *shōji* screens at the background of the study belonging to Kinzō Shin in the role of Setsuko Hara's husband. It is artificial, of course, falling inside a studio set. When it does drift down, it is during a visit from Chishū Ryū, whose daughter has returned home with her child, having tired of married life with her self-absorbed spouse. Concerned for her well-being, the father has come to have a talk with his son-in-law—an unpromising lecturer at a second-rate university—but their wandering conversation shows little indication of yielding any progress. Instead, the falling motion of what have become rather large snowflakes visible in the dusk beyond the glass begins to envelop the exchange in an uncomfortable temporal flow such as we rarely encounter in Ozu and draws the viewer into a feeling of unease. If this husband's personality were gloomier, his character would not be unlike the husband played by Sō Yamamura in *The Munekata Sisters,* but in contrast to that one's reticent distance, which is often conveyed with shots filmed from behind, Kinzō Shin portrays his own unfortunate character as a very voluble person, pouring whiskey for his father-in-law while chatting away in a manner that is at once somewhat self-deprecating and also a little defensive. The falling snow visible through the small glass apertures in the background almost seems to be urging him to stop talking.

It is within this cold, damp climate that younger daughter Ineko Arima's life comes to an end, basically by her own doing. We have here a death in midwinter, quite literally, a death that snatches her from whatever intervention might have been possible through communication with family or friends. At the end of *A Mother Should Be Loved,* there is a reconciliation between son and stepmother, but nothing of the kind takes place here. Upon learning of the death of her younger daughter, mother Isuzu Yamada is capable only of leaving Tokyo, which she does on the night train with her male companion Nobuo Nakamura. She watches the platform through the window of the passenger car, anticipating that her elder daughter Setsuko Hara might at least come to see her off. But the cold air outside causes the glass to fog over, severing any connection between the platform and the interior of the train. There is also a fogged train window in *Days of Youth,* on which the flunkees, returning from the ski slopes, use a fingertip to draw their dismal exam scores. Having lost its transparency, the opaque glass is like a wall that severs sight lines—a fitting final curtain on a "death" in midwinter.

This dark, damp world is located at the opposite pole from the death in midsummer depicted in *Tokyo Story*. We might find ourselves tempted to reject this film as a mistake, the result of a filmmaker trying his hand at material to which he was not well suited. The film did not, in fact, enjoy an especially warm reception at the time of its release, and it has not received a great deal of attention since. But to see Yasujirō Ozu is to affirm both death in midsummer *and* death in midwinter. *Tokyo Twilight* is not the blunder of an auteur of broad daylight who stumbled in the evening fog, but a film that renews our appreciation for the radiant allure of the sun and the heat in Ozu, while at the same time also deepening our awareness of the fact that such things alone do not determine the horizon of his world. If we dismissed *Tokyo Twilight* as a minor, misguided effort, and in so doing expelled its snow from view, the Ozuesque "film" itself might just collapse. In fact, despite the departure from his usual role as the good-natured father, even Chishū Ryū does not give the slightest impression of having been miscast as a stubborn bank employee, a man whose wife left him and who will even lose his daughter while remaining obtusely committed to his good intentions, behind the glint of his reading glasses. This Chishū Ryū is undeniably also Ozu's Chishū Ryū. The intention, once again, is not to insist that coming into contact with unusual films such as this brings the world of Yasujirō Ozu more clearly into view. The point is this: that what is needed is a cinematic sensitivity capable of fresh surprise at the fact that, in filming the tragedy on the staircase in *A Hen in the Wind*, the verbal abuse exchanged in an evening downpour in *Floating Weeds*, and the midwinter death in the dark, damp atmosphere of *Tokyo Twilight*, Ozu continually thematized absent stairs and absent rain and absent cold. The Ozuesque "film" is not a world that can be defined negatively, by exclusively citing absence or lack. The Ozuesque "film" is a world in which presence and excess can be discussed abundantly and in equal measure with absence and lack. This is why Yasujirō Ozu is decidedly not a monotone "auteur." He is also not an obstinate "auteur" who insists single-mindedly on a personal aesthetic. He is an open "auteur" in the truest sense, one capable of making rich and abundant details play on the cinematic surface, where uniformity and diversity coexist with the same entitlements. An open "auteur" is not a filmmaker who goes about filming things freely, according to personal tastes, and under the protection of the environment called cinema. Open "auteurs" are cinéastes who, in the process of filming, maintain constant awareness of the limits of things that sustain cinema as a system. The Yasujirō Ozu who pushed the shot/reverse shot to its limits with the scene of a downpour in *Floating Weeds* and thus exposed the utter powerlessness of the camera in the face of the look was by no means a conservative filmmaker mired in tradition. He can hardly even be called a "Japanese" filmmaker given his savage disregard for seasonal sensibility. He is something exceedingly rare among movie people in our nation Japan: an unmistakable citizen of the Republic of Cinema. When it comes to seasonal sensibility and nature imagery, Akira Kurosawa and Kenji Mizoguchi are the more Japanese filmmakers by far. In spite of the rain and snow of *Floating Weeds* and *Tokyo Twilight*, do Ozu's sunny skies not have far more in common with the blue sky of California? The sky Jean Renoir also chose when he retired in Beverly Hills? Or the one over John Ford's Monument Valley? The sunny skies of Yasujirō Ozu, auteur of broad daylight, can only be persistently clear, like on the American West Coast, where cinema was born, developed, and matured. Ozu excluded the season poetically named *tsuyu,* or "plum rains," and with it the wet climate characteristic of Japan, to make a selection that would bring him ever closer to cinema.[6] Perhaps this reflects what we might call an archaeological desire in relation to cinema, a desire shared by many filmmakers of Ozu's generation. Of course, the allure of night and darkness in cinema was also something developed under the California sky. In this sense, the near reckless Ozuesque desire to recreate in Japan the sunshine of California and its movie city Hollywood is far more significant than any influence of Hollywood as demonstrated by Ozu's early enthusiasm for American comedies and his clever attempts during the silent period to transplant several of them to a Japanese climate. But we need not belabor the point that descriptions of Yasujirō Ozu as a "typically Japanese" filmmaker are based on misunderstandings of his cinematic world. Ozu selected ceaselessly to approach cinema and its limits rather than to immerse himself in that ambiguous adjective "Japanese." He chose to release people and things that were by custom unmistakably Japanese from the ambiguity of shadows and dampness and indistinct outline, and to place them instead under the radiating sunshine of a dry climate. We insist on affirming these selections. Of course, this probably needs to be a pluralistic gesture, one simultaneously also capable of affirming both Kurosawan rain and Mizoguchian fog. Here we simply observe how strange it is that the easy complicity of those content to erase the image from the screen should end up labeling Ozu a "typically Japanese" filmmaker—Yasujirō Ozu, who remained an auteur of broad daylight even when immersed in rain and dampness or surrounded by snow and cold.

Of course, it would be foolish to claim that Yasujirō Ozu was an *anti-*Japanese filmmaker. In avoiding the world of shadows and ambiguity, and in continuously seeking the radiating sunshine of midsummer,

---

6. The wet season is probably so named in Japanese because it corresponds to the season in which plums ripen on the branch.

Ozu did in many respects position himself at odds with what is thought of as typically Japanese aesthetic sensibility. And yet he remains an unmistakably Japanese filmmaker—a filmmaker of Japan. Here, having positioned ourselves within the *gap* between things Ozuesque and the films of Yasujirō Ozu, and having played its continuous movement as a game, we now find ourselves enticed to relive the *gap* between things Japanese and Japan itself. Much as Yasujirō Ozu never corresponds with things Ozuesque, Japan also never corresponds with things Japanese. Erasing the films of Yasujirō Ozu with things Ozuesque must be avoided at all costs.

8

GETTING ANGRY

A TOWEL AROUND THE NECK

In a corner of the living room in *An Autumn Afternoon,* which we have had occasion to visit several times already, Shima Iwashita is now ironing intently. Her expression is unusually serious as she goes about her work without so much as humming a tune. We see a small lamp hanging from the ceiling, though the ceiling itself is out of view. The bulb glowing behind its frosted glass shade keeps the darkness closing in from the veranda at bay while also casting shadows around the room, staging the nighttime setting. There is no indication that other family members are present in the surrounding space as this young woman diligently applies herself to the ironing with both knees pressed together against the floor beneath her body, a striped towel hanging around her neck. She exudes virtue: a daughter assuming the role of housewife in a household lacking a mother figure, devoting herself to chores while waiting for her father and younger brother to come home on their respective schedules.

This scene depicting her evening chores in the living room provokes a strange unrest in the viewer, lacking as it does the usual impression of what we might call "Ozuesque balance." Despite having witnessed the activities of any number of young, unmarried daughters across the films, we have seen no other comparable actress display so casual an appearance as Shima Iwashita does in tending to housework with a towel thrown around her neck, at least not from *Late Spring* onward. There is nothing especially unnatural about Chikage Awashima when she sets about her work in the kitchen with a towel hanging around her neck in *Early Spring*, but this is because she plays a low-wage salaryman's wife weary of the life she is living. We find no other example of Ozu placing an unmarried young woman in the same situation. Some may protest that in cinema there is nothing unusual about the sight of a young woman ironing with a towel draped over her shoulder, that a detail such as this should even make the scene read more naturally. But such skeptics might as well sign a confession proclaiming their ignorance of Ozu. Something very special is taking place at this precise moment in Ozu, something announced by a striped towel casually covering the back of Shima Iwashita's neck.

Mieko Takamine does of course wear a cloth over her hair while helping restuff futons in the prewar *Brothers and Sisters of the Toda Family*, but the way she dresses for chores in that film—in a kimono and hair covering—reflects little more than a particular protocol imparted from mother to unmarried daughter. If anything, her appearance can even be said to reflect a conformity to proper etiquette. Among Ozu's postwar daughters, Setsuko Hara in *Late Spring* and *Early Summer*, Hideko Takamine in *The Munekata Sisters*, Ineko Arima in *Equinox Flower*, and Yōko Tsukasa in *Late Autumn* and *The End of Summer* all stop at aprons when it comes to dressing for housework. There is not a single instance in which any one of these daughters appears with a towel around her neck. In fact, whether they wear blouses or sweaters, the light tends to set the napes of their necks aglow for the camera, which meticulously captures these smooth contours on film. Except in the case of *Tokyo Twilight,* a film that quite uncharacteristically takes place in the cold season, it is only on rare occasions that Ozu's leading ladies obstruct the neckline, even with scarves.

Of course, the striped towel we have here is not a completely unfamiliar prop. At different moments in *An Autumn Afternoon,* the same towel hangs from a bamboo laundry pole under the eaves in the garden, and it also appears draped over the back of a chair. In *Late Autumn* a towel with much the same pattern hangs over the window railing in the room facing the courtyard at the Ikaho Hot Springs hotel. This towel probably belongs to Yōko Tsukasa, whose marriage is approaching. In the color films, a red-and-blue-striped towel seems to become a prop vaguely associated with young women. But there is not another occasion when such a towel covers the neck of an unmarried woman. In *An Autumn Afternoon* bar hostess Kyōko Kishida does of course make an appearance with a cloth wrapped around her hair upon returning from the baths. Looking like she just walked out of a foreign film, she catches the eye of widower Chishū Ryū. Nobuo Nakamura's daughter in *Late Autumn* also wears a bath turban on her head after showing up at home following a fight with her husband. To the lament of her father, she explains from beneath this accessory that she intends to stay home awhile this time to teach the husband a lesson. But these women are all secondary characters, not daughters living with their fathers before marriage.

Towels and handcloths are props that we generally expect to be associated with men in Ozu. In the prewar films, male students from the countryside wear handcloths hanging from their belts. A white towel also hangs at aging father Eijirō Yanagi's hip when he weeds in the garden in the postwar film *The Flavor of Green Tea Over Rice.* In *Equinox Flower* Shin Saburi even sports a hip towel while playing golf. Takeshi Sakamoto, in the prewar "Kihachi films,"[1] and Ganjirō Nakamura, in the postwar *Floating Weeds* and *The End of Summer,* both exude postbath relaxation as they chat up old female acquaintances with damp hand towels folded on top of their heads. In *Late Autumn* when Nobuo Nakamura returns home to pestering from his family and retreats to the bath in his long underwear, we glimpse a white towel slung defiantly over his shoulder.[2] Many will also recall the playful gag inserted at the beginning of *Early Summer* in which a young boy wets a towel but does not wash his face. Towels in Ozu are props mainly consigned to male characters, whether young boys or old men. This is why it must be acknowledged that the sight of Shima Iwashita ironing with a towel around her neck is something highly unusual.

Does this mean that the towel around the neck of this young unmarried daughter in the last film Ozu would make before his death somehow subjects her to a quiet masculinization? Quite the contrary. Her gestures are exceedingly feminine as she handles this fabric prop in front of her father. The moment is even seductive, and it is probably fair to say that anyone who overlooks it has not really seen the film *An Autumn Afternoon*.

SWEEPING ASIDE

We now hear the sound of someone opening the front door. The daughter surmises that her father has come home and, without interrupting her work, shouts to leave the door unlocked since her younger brother is still out. Her face, pictured in profile, bears no trace of anything like resentment toward her father or brother, both of whom seem to think it only natural that she should tend to them as she does. As he passes

---

[1]. This is a series of films made by Ozu in which Takeshi Sakamoto stars as characters all named Kihachi: *Passing Fancy* (1933), *A Story of Floating Weeds* (1934), and *An Inn in Tokyo* (1935).

[2]. On close inspection, the towel in this scene seems to be the collar of the outer shirt Nakamura removes on his way to the bath.

through the dimness of the hallway into the living room and crosses in front of her, her father does not even try to hide the fact that he is a little unsteady on his feet after what has almost certainly been an evening of heavier than usual drinking. Ordinarily he would change into house clothes upon returning home, but tonight Chishū Ryū remains in his business suit, sitting cross-legged on the floor and leaning against the low dining table as he looks at his daughter with a strangely stiff expression.

Anyone who has followed the film's course of events to this point should immediately understand what this drunken father wants to say. Having witnessed the sight of his widowed former middle school teacher running a ramen shop with a never-married daughter well past her prime, he has started to think it is about time to see to his own daughter's marriage arrangements. On this point, the Chishū Ryū of *An Autumn Afternoon* seems to be dutifully executing the role of the father as it exists in Ozu films of the period extending from *Late Spring* onward. Still, he does seem to have taken rather seriously the needling of a close friend who has warned him he could end up in the same boat if he is not careful. In fact, the spectacle their old teacher Eijirō Tōno creates when he drinks himself senseless and brings his aging daughter Haruko Sugimura to tears is downright ghastly. Ryū seems intent on sweeping this dismal image aside as he suddenly broaches the subject of marriage in front of his own young daughter bent over her ironing. But she does not indulge him for a moment, meeting his abrupt proposition with a curt refusal. He repeats several times that he means what he says, but he makes no effort to explore the fact that she apparently has some interest in one of his son's work colleagues. He merely insists that she get married.

Despite his typically Ozuesque tone of voice, this father is unusually serious when he tells his tirelessly ironing daughter to "come here a minute." The sincerity with which he nods and admits to "having had a few" when she chastises him for drinking again is probably something only Chishū Ryū could pull off. But however much he may have her best interests at heart, his behavior on this evening is quite awkward. It would not be strange in the slightest if this daughter, at her age, were experiencing some private attraction to some particular member of the opposite sex, but he just keeps repeating the word "marriage," demonstrating what can only be described as an absence of the kind of consideration that should be expected from a male parent in this situation. In fact, we feel some irritation of our own as viewers, a sense that it would be better to approach this matter differently. This is not to say, of course, that we feel this father should proceed more strategically, like the widower in *Late Spring* who pretends that he plans to remarry in order to convince his daughter to take a husband. But if this were the Chishū Ryū of *Equinox Flower*, who also plays a widower living together with a daughter, we would expect him to know to move more indirectly, to take his worries to Shin Saburi instead, a close friend worried about his own unmarried daughter who has left home to live with a boyfriend. The Chishū Ryū of *An Autumn Afternoon* shows no such consideration, bluntly broaching this sensitive topic and intruding unself-consciously into the hidden folds of his daughter's emotional life. In this regard, he probably bears a resemblance to the obstinate widower in *Tokyo Twilight*, a man who treats his daughter with blind severity, unaware that she has secretly had an abortion. In that film, he ends up driving his daughter toward her death.

The daughter in *An Autumn Afternoon* responds in a chilly fashion when her drunken father tells her to get married. In fact, when she begrudgingly interrupts her ironing to stand and approach him, then kneels in front of the low tea table where he sits slouched, her expression seems close to rage. As he often does when his characters stand up or sit down in Japanese rooms where depth is limited, Ozu begins the ensuing uncomfortable exchange with two shots taken from different distances. In the first, Shima Iwashita is shown full figure as she wraps up her ironing and stands, gathering the laundry, then silently approaches the low table. The moment she kneels, the camera reframes her at a shorter

23. *An Autumn Afternoon:* Enraged Shima Iwashita sweeps a towel from around her neck.

distance, picturing her in a medium shot taken from the waist up as she glares icily at her father. In this second shot, she tilts her head and removes the striped towel from her neck, quickly sweeping it aside while maintaining her eyes fixed provocatively on her father (fig. 23). This instantaneous gesture exposes a feminine charm that startles the viewer, but that her own drunken father lacks the sensitivity to perceive.

Over the course of the next several shots, Ozu's characteristically low-placed camera captures the towel through the legs of the table as the daughter plays with it in her lap before gripping it firmly. Even without recalling the moment in *Late Spring* when Setsuko Hara picks up a piece of string and winds it taut, or in *Late Autumn* when Yōko Tsukasa tightly clutches at a cloth, each quietly attempting to suppress an intense rage, it is clear from Shima Iwashita's feigned composure that she has surrendered here to unprecedented indignation. The use of match-on-action cutting conveys this very clearly. The uncomfortable discussion between these two thus begins in a way that emphasizes the awkwardness of the father—who probably does not see the towel at his daughter's knees given their relative positions to each other—and comes to an end without any understanding having been reached. Iwashita simply stands and departs with the ironing, rebuking her father for being so inconsiderate. Needless to say, the striped towel remains gripped in her hand as she leaves her father sitting silently with a look of dejection on his face. All he can do is mutter to her younger brother, who returns home at just this moment expecting a late dinner from his sister, to go make himself something in the kitchen. Glum-faced, brother Shin'ichirō Mikami reluctantly obeys his father's words without understanding what has taken place.

This is where the significance of Shima Iwashita having draped a striped towel around her collar becomes clear. Vigorously sweeping the towel from her neck is her way of unleashing her indignation on her father, and Ozu has methodically set the stage, from the beginning of this scene of ironing in the living room, for the movement of a towel in a moment of barely controlled anger. His staging visualizes this movement of a perfectly ordinary prop, from neck to knees, with the greatest of care.

REMOVING SCARVES

Witnessing Shima Iwashita clutch this striped towel at her knees in a gesture of anger, we cannot help also recalling what Setsuko Hara does near the famous last scene of *Tokyo Story* when newly widowed Chishū Ryū—here her father-in-law—tells her that she is "truly a good person" as she folds clothes before returning to Tokyo following his wife's funeral. "Not at all," she replies, in a tone approaching hostility, gripping the laundry she has been folding in her lap as if on the verge of tearing it to shreds. This goes unnoticed by her father-in-law, and it is also hardly the case that people in general have adequately appreciated the significance of her sudden seriousness. She is seriously angry at her father-in-law's inability to understand. Needless to say, this situation casts a shadow on the father-daughter confrontation in *An Autumn Afternoon*.

A rectangle of cloth hiding the neckline of a young woman slides from her collar, changing position from her neck to her lap. If we overlook this instantaneous—and because instantaneous also decisive—movement, we are likely to read what this scene narrates entirely from the perspective of the father. But it is the daughter's agency that controls the sliding motion of this towel, and the significance of its movement should be analyzed accordingly. After all, daughters in late-period Ozu films are not puppetlike creatures who fulfill their roles in following their fathers' wishes and docilely becoming brides. It is true that their interior upheavals are not easily glimpsed. Ozu does demonstrate a preference for aposiopesis, in most cases going so far as to omit any spectacle of a wedding. This preference generally results in a kind of narration that declines to make the anger of young women explicit, even as it sketches this anger again and again. This is why the viewer must keep an eye on each and every gesture these daughters perform, however latent such gestures may be. Then, it becomes immediately clear that *An Autumn Afternoon*'s Shima Iwashita is far from the only young actress in an Ozu film who performs a motion like sweeping a towel from around the neck. In *Early Spring*, Chikage Awashima wears a towel around her neck as she goes about the housework in her role as the wife of a low-wage salaryman. When her husband Ryō Ikebe returns home one morning following an indiscretion with his female colleague Keiko Kishi, and she infers what has happened, she brusquely pulls the towel from her collar, then stands by the front door gripping it in her hands. But the camera in this instance is not positioned quite as close to its subject as in *An Autumn Afternoon*, and the sliding motion of the towel does not match what is captured in that vivid medium shot. Closer to Shima Iwashita's gesture is the moment in *Tokyo Twilight* when a troubled-looking Ineko Arima removes her scarf, suddenly exposing the bare skin of the nape of her neck, a moment anyone should remember. Just what are the circumstances that lead a scarf to change position here?

Having begun to suspect that she is not her father's biological child, *Tokyo Twilight*'s Ineko Arima pays an unexpected visit to her estranged mother Isuzu Yamada at her dim mahjong parlor and tries to learn the truth. The place is busy with customers, but the daughter enters undeterred and stands silently in front of her mother. Having no knowledge of the trouble in her daughter's heart, Yamada welcomes her smilingly and offers her a cushion to sit on. The daughter kneels and looks straight ahead at her mother, then tilts her head slightly, for only an instant, to whisk her scarf from over her coat collar with a single pull. Upon witnessing this, no one will expect that she is about to take off her winter jacket and settle in. In fact, it is hard to react with anything but alarm to this stark scene. Her momentary gesture is charged with a cold determination announcing from the start that this will not be a conversation.

The daughter goes straight to the point: "I want to know who my father is." Taken aback, yet containing her dismay, Isuzu Yamada protests that she never had an affair, that it is horrible her daughter would even suspect such a thing. But her words cannot pacify Ineko Arima's troubled expression. The daughter says she will never have a child of her own, rebuking the mother who abandoned her, then departs in an inconsolable state. That very night, she will breathe her last breath following an accident that is effectively a suicide. The gesture she performs when she vigorously pulls her scarf from over her collar poignantly recalls the motion of the towel Shima Iwashita sweeps from around her neck in *An Autumn Afternoon*, as if the two were superimposed on each other. Here, the gesture, which is one of parting with a mother, also decisively estranges a father from his daughter's personal tragedy, despite the fact that he is not there to witness it.

It is clear that Shima Iwashita in *An Autumn Afternoon* occupies a position not all that distant from the lonely misfortune of Ineko Arima in

Tokyo Twilight. We can easily qualify this, of course, by pointing to the fact that one daughter confronts a widowed father and the other a mother who abandoned the family. We can also readily observe that the father is the one who initiates the conversation in the former instance, while in the latter it is the daughter. Iwashita is also not destined to meet a tragic end like Arima and her apparent suicide in *Tokyo Twilight*. Nonetheless, it is a matter of the gravest significance that the gesture performed by Iwashita in this color film, the last film Ozu made before his death, precisely reproduces that of Arima in the last of Ozu's black-and-white films. In Ozu it is often the trivial gestures that narrate the situation most eloquently, far more so than the dialogue tends to do.

In light of this, the gesture of the daughter who sweeps the towel from around her neck in *An Autumn Afternoon*, much like that of the daughter who whisks away her neck scarf with a single pull in *Tokyo Twilight*, should perhaps be understood as a demonstration of cold rejection more than of anger. Maybe the two gestures are even something close to Chikage Awashima's display of mistrust in her husband in *Early Spring*. In any case, from this moment in *An Autumn Afternoon*, Shima Iwashita will approach her wedding day without ever recovering any deep sense of trust in her father. The situation is similar in *Late Spring* as well, though the daughter in that film is an only child who maintains her attachment to her father until the end. In *An Autumn Afternoon* the daughter is obliged to take care of her father, not because she has no siblings, but because those siblings are brothers. But both these daughters should be seen as shaping the features of the films, if within their own differing circumstances.

THROWING SUITS

At this point it bears addressing the fact that the Chishū Ryū of the aging father roles in late-period Ozu is a creature who, in one way or another, has been deprived of a wife. From the prewar *There Was a Father* onward, this actor so indispensable to the films of Ozu is prohibited, with strange consistency, from having a wife. He generally has been married, of course, and has children, but as in *The Munekata Sisters* or *Late Spring*, he has usually already lost his wife by the start of the film. There are exceptions, as in *Tokyo Story* where he and his wife travel together to the capital to see their grown children, seeking to take pleasure in this privilege of aging, but as if predetermined by fate, he will have to face the sudden death of his spouse upon returning home. There are also films like *Early Summer* and *Good Morning* where we find Chishū Ryū still married to Kuniko Miyake and with two sons, but even here this actor seems to suffer from an existential privation: the fact that, when married to Kuniko Miyake in Ozu, he cannot be a father of girls. His role in five of the late-period films—*The Munekata Sisters, Late Spring, Tokyo Twilight, Equinox Flower,* and *An Autumn Afternoon*—is otherwise as a widowed father who does not know quite how to deal with the behavior of a daughter who seems at risk of letting marriage pass her by. How should we interpret the fact that Ryū acquires a rather inscrutable aura whenever he lacks a wife, including at the end of *Tokyo Story*? What was Ozu seeking from this actor in depriving him of a spouse and making him play mostly widowed fathers living with daughters?

It should be noted that the composition of families in Ozu is often incomplete, with or without the presence of Chishū Ryū. The "Kihachi films" in the prewar period often deal with widowers, starting with *Passing Fancy*, while *A Mother Should Be Loved, Walk Cheerfully, The Only Son,* and *There Was a Father* are all stories about single-mother or single-father households. In the postwar period, the secret love child theme of the prewar *A Story of Floating Weeds* returns unmodified in its remake *Floating Weeds*. Even as figures like the traveling actor or the country schoolteacher disappear from the films, and as the households depicted become comparatively secure in social class, such kinds of family circumstances continue to be the rule. *Late Spring, Early Summer,* and *Tokyo Story* all feature parents whose inner lives have been irreparably hollowed out by the loss of a son who never returned from the war. When absent spouses are added to missing children, the image of the widowed father living together with a daughter emerges on the horizon of the incomplete family, and with it a role for which Ryū was destined.

In *Late Spring* it is not explained when the father lost his wife. He lives together with his daughter, having also lost a son during the war. At the inn in Kyoto, he does describe how he and his wife went through some troubles early in their marriage, but the daughter does not mention any memory of her own involving her mother. The silent-period film *A Mother Should Be Loved* is an exception here, but in late-period Ozu, we rarely encounter fond recollections of decisively departed wives or mothers. In fact, with the minor exception of the watch given to Setsuko Hara in *Tokyo Story* as a keepsake of her mother-in-law Chieko Higashiyama, we mostly do not lay eyes on anything in Chishū Ryū's surroundings, such as a photograph, that might be taken as a remembrance of a late wife. With the exception of observances for Ganjirō Nakamura's late wife in *The End of Summer,* Ozu films mostly do not depict Buddhist memorial services for the death anniversaries of wives. As a result, even imagining the married life that Chishū Ryū may have shared with any of his wives becomes nearly impossible. It is as if Ozu's Chishū Ryū were born to be widowed, so natural is his apparent acceptance of the absence of a spouse.

In *Tokyo Twilight* we learn that his wife ran off with one of his coworkers while he was away on assignment in the colonies, and we therefore understand that his "widowed" life began before the end of the war. When he hears that his former spouse is now earning a meager living running a mahjong parlor, he shows little reaction and seems resigned quietly to endure the fate of growing old alone as an abandoned husband. When he rotates to a supporting role in *Equinox Flower* as Shin Saburi's friend, it is not entirely clear that he plays the widower we have come to expect. But based on the helplessness he displays in attempting to deal with a daughter who has left home to live with a boyfriend and is working in a bar, it does seem that his wife is no longer in the picture. There is something austere about him that makes this kind of conjecture seem quite natural. The Chishū Ryū of *An Autumn Afternoon* is probably of a somewhat different character type than the rest of these self-denying widowers, given the uncustomary innocence with which he talks about his attachment to his late spouse, as when he happily announces to his children that a friend took him to a bar where the hostess bears a striking resemblance to their mother. And yet, because he is so insensitive to the discomfort this confession causes his daughter, he too comes across as a lonely figure, isolated within his role as a widower. Masao Mishima in *Late Spring* and Ryūji Kita in *An Autumn Afternoon* both remarry, but this is something generally not permitted of Chishū Ryū, a creature denied even the suggestion of sexual desire. His self-denial evokes not the placidity of someone having attained a state of contented simplicity but the prudish insecurity of a man of little experience.

The task here is not to account for why wives so often have to die early in Ozu. It is also not to trace the ways Chishū Ryū's male confidence is shaken from one film to the next as he is deprived of a spouse under various different circumstances. What demands our attention is the fact that the first-floor living room, where his daughter goes about her ironing in *An Autumn Afternoon,* seems not to be a room in which Ryū feels very at ease, unlike other Ozuesque husbands. This is something that becomes apparent when he returns home at the end of the day and finds no wife waiting in the living room to help him change into his house clothes—that is, when the absence of a spouse is made evident. Recall, for example, how self-indulgently Nobuo Nakamura behaves in front of his wife Kuniko Miyake in *Late Autumn*. It is true, as we have already seen in the chapter on "changing clothes," that Nakamura endures pestering from his daughter and son upon his return home, and that his wife sees through his pretend indifference to the charms of his late friend's widow. Nevertheless, as soon as he walks through the front door, he begins to remove the clothes he has been wearing and tosses them uninhibitedly on the floor, starting with his suit jacket and outer shirt, and then even a white handkerchief, which he removes from his pocket and drops on the tatami as if for emphasis. The one who nimbly stoops and retrieves these items from the floor is of course Miyake, an action she also performs as Sō Yamamura's wife in *Tokyo Story*. In fact, there is perhaps no other actress in film history who has so nonchalantly picked things up off the floor and put them away.

Scenes of Ozuesque husbands casually changing clothes occur repeatedly, regardless of the individual features of the films, to the extent that they seem to become almost formalized into ritual. After removing wallets and glasses cases from their pockets and setting them conscientiously on the table, the husbands, who in many cases are returning home from drinking with friends, seem innocently at a loss for what to do with their suit jackets, and what they have been wearing gets tossed carelessly aside. The role of wives in these moments is reduced to methodically picking up the business clothes their husbands so casually discard. When Nobuo Nakamura tosses his crumpled handkerchief in *Late Autumn*, his gesture repeats quite precisely the one Shin Saburi performs in front of his wife Kinuyo Tanaka in *Equinox Flower*. In late-period Ozu, the living rooms of Japanese houses are spaces in which wives conscientiously retrieve and carry clothing that Chishū Ryū's former university or middle school classmates toss almost mechanically to the floor. It would not be altogether incorrect to observe in this spousal relationship of tossing and picking up an unconscious tyranny on the part of men and a self-aware submission among women, and to critique, accordingly, the conservative character of the family in Ozu. But things are actually not quite so simple.

For one, Ozu prohibits Chishū Ryū from performing the same gestures as these other men. This eternal widower denied a carefree changing of clothes is clearly differently conceived as a character than his former classmates played by Shin Saburi and Nobuo Nakamura. If the living room in which Shima Iwashita irons in *An Autumn Afternoon* feels somehow different from those in other houses, its difference emerges through the fact that Ryū seems compelled to refrain from the kinds of self-indulgent gestures with which his married peers change clothes. Perhaps what this reflects is a father's earnest effort to show consideration toward a daughter of marriageable age. His attitude is clearly different from that of widower Ganjirō Nakamura in *The End of Summer*, for example, who does not demonstrate the slightest such consideration toward his own already married daughter Michiyo Aratama.

It also bears noting here that this formalized ritual is not always strictly observed even in the living rooms of married men's homes. In fact, there are moments when Ozu depicts wives behaving even in plain disregard of this ritual. Take, for example, what Kinuyo Tanaka does in *Equinox Flower* when Shin Saburi returns home looking displeased late one evening and proceeds to announce that he still does not accept their daughter's engagement and does not even intend to take part in her wedding. His wife has been holding his suit jacket, but her patience with him runs thin, and she suddenly drops it on the floor. If the wife's role is to walk around carrying discarded clothes picked up off the floor, Tanaka clearly abandons it here, performing precisely the role prescribed for the husband instead, but more audaciously. The woman of the house also throws clothes in front of the patriarch in *The End of Summer*, of course, if under somewhat different circumstances. That scene depicts a daughter's irrepressible anger, provoked by the self-centered behavior of her widowed father. Daughter Michiyo Aratama does not hide her displeasure at the fact that Ganjirō Nakamura has rekindled a relationship with a former mistress despite his already advanced age. Ignoring her husband Keiju Kobayashi's attempts to mediate, she tells her father that if he wants to see this woman so badly, he should just go see her right now, and then pulls his street clothes out of a chest of drawers and throws them on the floor. The surprisingly defiant gestures that women direct at men in Ozu, whether as wives, as in *Equinox Flower,* or as daughters, as in *The End of Summer,* are not to be overlooked.

When we find ourselves unexpectedly stirred by the bold behavior of Kinuyo Tanaka or Michiyo Aratama, we are reminded that the ritualistic repetition of various kinds of gestures in Ozu can at times produce striking exceptions—exceptions that nevertheless conform to consistency as a system. At the same time, we also cannot help feeling that Tanaka's unwifely gesture bristles with an assertiveness no less impressive than that of Shima Iwashita or Chikage Awashima when they pull towels from around their necks, or of Ineko Arima when she whisks a scarf from over her collar. These women are also quietly indignant. We will not dwell on the consequences of their barely contained anger. We note only that Ozu's consistently surly husbands remain completely unaware of the angry gestures their supposedly submissive wives perform in the open.

COMING TO BLOWS

Getting angry is generally not considered to be something very Ozuesque. Even the elderly couple in *Tokyo Story* do not appear to get very upset when tactfully displaced from their children's homes in the capital. The same is more or less true of the mother and daughter in *Brothers and Sisters of the Toda Family,* who are shown a similar lack of consideration by family members following the death of the patriarch. Most characters accept change with resignation, as if to refrain from causing any unexpected disturbances or deviations in the narrative. Their conduct seems guided not so much by a sense of right and wrong as by the goal of maintaining harmony at all costs.

In light of this, it should not seem strange in the slightest to think of anger, especially the anger of women in the home, as something alien to Ozu. This is why stories of widowed men in late-period Ozu all tend to be interpreted as portraying the sadness of fathers letting go of their dutifully raised daughters, to the neglect of the complex feelings of the daughters themselves in the face of their transitions to married life. In fact, the widower Chishū Ryū is not the only one who reflects on the sadness of giving up a daughter. Many married men do so, starting with Nobuo Nakamura. Even Ozu himself said that the main point of *Tokyo Twilight* was to depict the solitude of a man abandoned by his wife. But if this characterization actually described the film, Ineko Arima's captivating gesture when she whisks off her scarf would be little more than a trivial aside. Is the anger of Shima Iwashita, when she deliberately hangs a towel with eye-catching stripes around her neck only to sweep it aside in front of her father, merely a minor, soon-to-be contained defiance? And when Kinuyo Tanaka, looking unusually stern, thrusts her husband's business suit to the floor in *Equinox Flower,* is her gesture really just an exception?

It is not the case, of course, that characters who surrender to intense emotional excitement are completely banished from the films of Ozu. In fact, there are not a few characters who sometimes even resort to violence. We witness Ogawa Ureo striking his older sister Yoshiko Okada in *Woman of Tokyo* (*Tokyo no onna,* 1933), for example. In *Tokyo Twilight,* Ineko Arima also slaps her unreliable boyfriend Masami Taura in an empty restaurant by the train tracks, then runs out into the dampness of the night. And it is not only in films considered by Ozu himself to have been failures that such kinds of scenes take place. As everyone knows, in the silent-period films, children still too young to respond with resignation to the status quo are often depicted cursing and abusing their fathers over some minor disagreement, only to be restrained and spanked. In fact, the irrepressible anger of children is something that only intensifies with time, from the brothers who come to question their father's social position in *I Was Born, but . . .* to the boys who refuse to tolerate their father's failure to fulfill a promise in *Early*

Summer or *Good Morning*. Brothers who once took on their father despite not standing a chance—the older one desperately assailing his leg, the younger one lending pantomimed support from a safe distance—will eventually go so far as to run away from home.[3] We have subjected the significance of this and other scenes of flight to detailed analysis in the chapter on "eating." Here, it is enough to observe that each is the result of the irritation of children unable to accept the financial position of their family, unleashed on a father deemed powerless. We do feel deep sympathy in *I Was Born, but . . .* upon witnessing Mitsuko Yoshikawa tearfully ask her husband Tatsuo Saitō if he might not handle the children a little more gently, but the choreography when he valiantly puts down the boys' futile rebellion also invites us to smile. In any case, little disturbances of this kind never decisively upset family harmony. On the contrary, they even strengthen familial bonds. They also never modulate the progress of the narrative in any meaningful way.

More serious, of course, are the passions to which grown men succumb. Ureo Egawa in *Woman of Tokyo* even commits suicide after learning that his older sister has engaged in some indecent work. But what bears noting here is that characters who show unreserved anger, as if to demonstrate their independence from the supposedly Ozuesque qualities of acceptance and resignation, are often "outsiders," people who have for a time been separated from the familial home. Shūji Sano, who succumbs to violent emotion and shoves Kinuyo Tanaka down the stairs in *A Hen in the Wind*, is a returned soldier who was absent during the immediate postwar disorder at home in Japan. Shin Saburi in *Brothers and Sisters of the Toda Family* is likewise newly returned from the Chinese mainland when, indignant with the improper treatment that his mother and younger sister have received from the family in his absence, he expels his older brother and sister, together with their

---

3. While the younger brother does mimic his older brother at other points during this scene, he should be duly credited for joining directly in the fight here, with a kick to his father's leg.

spouses, from the banquet following the Buddhist memorial service for the deceased patriarch. The same is more or less true of the head of the traveling kabuki troupe in both *A Story of Floating Weeds* and *Floating Weeds*, who has returned, after a long absence, to the village where his publicly unacknowledged child still lives. His visits to the home of his former mistress, where he goes to see this son, will lead him to unleash ferocious verbal abuse on the actress who is his current companion and even to strike her. But the rage of this itinerant performer lacks any substantial power to persuade his girlfriend, giving way instead to an argument in which both man and woman participate on equal footing, a showdown that can therefore probably be said to exhibit aspects of the lover's quarrel often found in the *ninjōbanashi* narratives of the *rakugo* storytelling repertoire.[4] By contrast, the returned son and soldier are characters who represent the incompleteness of the Ozuesque family, and the violent emotions to which they temporarily succumb seem like rituals of reentry from the "outside," something quite distinct from any assertion of paternal authority. "Getting angry" in Ozu is a thing of privilege permitted only to those positioned outside the family.

GETTING ANGRY

Now we understand the significance of Mariko Okada's sudden anger in *Late Autumn*. Her role in this film is merely that of a work colleague to Yōko Tsukasa, who has resisted getting married. She is neither a family relation of the beautiful widow Setsuko Hara nor a daughter of one of Hara's late husband's former classmates, much less a mistress. In other words, she is a complete outsider in relation to the meddling men and their marriage plots for the widow and her daughter. When this

---

4. *Ninjōbanashi* is a generally dramatic and sentimental genre of *rakugo*, a form of storytelling that is otherwise often comic.

peripheral character suddenly begins to play a central role, the film becomes interesting beyond our expectations. Since what motivates this shift is irrepressible anger stemming from her concern for a close coworker, this young woman is probably the ideal character to embody the theme of getting angry as we have been examining it in the Ozuesque "film."

Having *apparently* shown up unannounced at the campus office of the university professor among Yōko Tsukasa's late father's friends and extracted from him the identities of his partners in crime, and having then *apparently* used him to take a second culprit hostage—this one a business executive—before then intruding with the two in tow at the offices of the company where the third friend works as a section chief, Mariko Okada subsequently has this remaining accomplice summoned to the reception room, interrupting his business, and proceeds to conduct herself like a hardened prosecutor. This is *apparently* what has happened because Ozu does not depict the course of events that enables this young woman to behave so defiantly on first encounter toward these three men old enough to be her father, a course of events merely indicated in brief when the professor Ryūji Kita, having been dispatched to retrieve section chief Shin Saburi from his office, timidly announces that "things have taken a strange turn." When Saburi asks what he means, Kita replies evasively: "She's an odd one." "What?" "Just come and meet her." "Who?" Saburi rises from his desk, not comprehending anything.

From the announcement that an "odd one" has shown up unannounced and that things have taken a "strange turn," we can anticipate that the men are about to be confronted with a difficult situation. And in fact, what we will witness in the reception room is an impassioned oral argument by a young woman of surprising self-possession, and the rather bewildered self-defense of three middle-aged men from whom we might have expected a little more composure. No one having followed the course of events in this film to this point would have anticipated a meeting in the same space between this trio of aging former classmates and Mariko Okada, whose role has otherwise been limited to that of Yōko Tsukasa's coworker. Her surprise attack is as startling to the viewer as it is to the characters. She is quite literally an intruder from the "outside," having barely introduced herself before launching into a critique of these father figures and their irresponsible behavior, assailing them for their obliviousness to the harm they have caused her friend by involving her widowed mother in a remarriage plot. In this sense, she can probably be said to resemble the brother returned from the continent in *Brothers and Sisters of the Toda Family,* who admonishes his older siblings and their spouses during a ceremonial dinner. There is probably also something about her that resonates with Ineko Arima silently standing before her mother in her overcoat and looking tormented in *Tokyo Twilight*.

But the sudden anger Mariko Okada unleashes in *Late Autumn* is also different from what we see in either *Brothers and Sisters of the Toda Family* or *Tokyo Twilight*. It makes the sequence tremble with unanticipated momentum but also unexpectedly makes us smile. Due to the spatial layout of the room, the characters are not framed together in the same shot. The scene unfolds in a series of rigidly composed shots that place Okada, standing and glaring severely, in opposition to the men, seated at random and looking on in disbelief. Ozu's sensibility as a comedic director comes to life through the freewheeling interplay of parts. Of course, Ozu could hardly have been indifferent to the arrival at Shōchiku of his late friend Tokihiko Okada's daughter Mariko. Perhaps he even conceived this scene for her with the deliberate aim of drawing out what he must have seen as her comedic potential.

Thoroughly indignant at the behavior of these men who should know better than to behave with such disregard for the sensitivity of a young woman, Okada pays no attention when they invite her to "have a seat," demanding instead to know just what they find so "amusing" about all of this. Like a true company manager, Shin Saburi has taken note of her name during her brief self-introduction and now renders it as the familiarizing "Yuri-chan" in an attempt to steer the conversation. "Call me Yuriko," she retorts before interrupting Nobuo Nakamura ("I'm not talking to you") when he starts to interject that he has already tried explaining the situation to her. We feel compelled to applaud her brashness. Despite her anger, she does not allow herself to be swept away by emotion. She counters the tired tactics of the aging gentlemen with vigor and resolutely admonishes their faults without ever losing her composure, leaving them no choice but to accept that their usual joking will not defuse the situation. These former classmates, products of the prewar educational system who make repeated appearances in late-period Ozu, are not supposed to shrink so apparently when confronted with the anger of a mere young woman. The fact that they do is a clear indication that something exceptional is taking place. Indeed, despite facing off against such regular performers as Shin Saburi, Nobuo Nakamura, and Ryūji Kita, Mariko Okada, in her first appearance in an Ozu film, quite literally "steals the scene." What exactly is it that makes this possible?

In postwar Ozu films, the role of the close female friend to the heroine can be said to form a lineage that includes Yumeji Tsukioka in *Late Spring* and Chikage Awashima in *Early Summer*. But because Mariko Okada is made to embody the theme, exceptional in Ozu, of "getting angry," and because of the element of effortless humor that her straightforward delivery elicits, her presence as an intruder permeates this scene with a uniquely refreshing sensibility.

What should we make of this refreshing impression? How should we position this strikingly vivid image of young womanhood within the Ozuesque "film"? In throwing the men's faults into such scolding relief, it introduces an element of incongruous humor but at the same time also genuinely strips the men of authority. A certain kind of person will undoubtedly understand this situation as little more than an unexpected occurrence, a "strange turn of events" precipitated by an "odd" young woman. But it seems also to function as a forceful critique of the inadequacy of such vocabulary, which is all these aging men are able to summon in response to their female prosecutor, and of the status-quo attitude—the resistance to change—that this vocabulary by chance reveals. One of the men does of course later say, "sometimes that kind of thing is good." But does Ozu really introduce the vigorous anger of this woman, a woman who neither accepts things with resignation nor sacrifices herself for the sake of preserving order at all costs, only as something "sometimes good"? Only as a little delicacy to cleanse the palate?

Anyone having traced the theme of getting angry this far should immediately understand that the reason this scene is refreshing is not because of some exceptional value introduced by something "sometimes good" but because a dutifully repeated sketch of a gesture has unexpectedly become an action taken in reality. In fact, it *should* be only women who are able to surrender themselves to the emotional disturbance of getting angry in Ozu. But in front of a father or mother, or else a husband, the anger of women ends in sketches of gestures, never acting on its target in reality. When Shima Iwashita sweeps the towel away from her neck in *An Autumn Afternoon,* or when Ineko Arima undoes her scarf and slides it from over her collar in *Tokyo Twilight,* or when Chikage Awashima pulls the towel from her neck and grips it at her waist in *Early Spring,* or else when Kinuyo Tanaka drops the suit she has been holding in *Equinox Flower* or Michiyo Aratama pulls her father's street clothes out of the drawer and throws them on the floor in *The End of Summer,* no one in the family appreciates the meaning that these sketches of gestures are ultimately supposed to impart, however unmistakably they may trace the outlines of anger. And yet, these sketches of gestures are steadily ingrained on the surface of the Ozuesque "film," where only outsiders are able to follow their tracings and make conspicuous what had remained latent.

As a woman from "outside," Mariko Okada does precisely this in *Late Autumn:* she is able to give conspicuous form to sketched gestures of anger. The reason her scene feels refreshing relates to the ceremoniousness with which she makes overt any number of sketched gestures that she herself has not even witnessed. Only those who have learned to see films as "films" and not just consume them as stories will be able to grasp in the aggregate the significance of the multiple actions woven together by traces of sketched gestures. But to see does not require procedures of any real complexity. It should be enough to remain constantly sensitive to the various movements that develop on the screen. To be surprised by the movement of the striped towel that changes position from Shima Iwashita's neck to her lap is a right equally available to anyone. It is by exercising that right that we come undeniably to live the *gap* between things Ozuesque and the Ozuesque "film."

9

LAUGHING

AFTER THE CEREMONY

For some reason, laughter in Ozu is a group phenomenon. Solitary laughter is carefully excluded from Ozu's world, almost as if to laugh alone were an impossible contradiction in terms. It is of course true that characters of all kinds are filmed smiling, looking out at us with not the slightest hint of provocation. But it is probably fair to say that Ozu's camera almost never captures them directly in the act of laughing. In most cases, when people join one another in a spontaneous outburst of laughter, they do so not in response to any especially humorous topic of conversation but simply because they happen to be together in the same time and place, partaking in the sheer carefree pleasure of coexistence with others. What happens here is also not people laughing but *hearing* people laugh. Only on rare occasions do the sound of laughter and images of laughing align. Ozu routinely introduces the sound of laughter before picturing the people doing the laughing, as if to demonstrate that to see laughing and to hear laughter are two essentially different experiences.

When, at a beat's delay, already laughing people do appear on screen, they are among friends, serenely unaware that their voices have carried to third parties in adjoining rooms as they enjoy one another's company. This kind of laughter in Ozu is something close to an unconscious mechanical reflex, a group behavior devoid of any distinct individual subjective agency, and it even tends to produce an atmosphere of unaccountability, of palpably (if unintentionally) cliquish comradery. What then should we make of the slight deviations between sound and image in Ozuesque laughter, and of this unconscious cliquishness, which even seems anonymizing?

First of all, it is clear that Ozuesque laughter is an audible sign charged with functions that are more narrational than descriptive. This is clear from the fact that, on the occasion of a transition to a different narrative setting, the people who find themselves within the new scenery often burst into laughter, as if to accentuate the change of locale. While a tone of unconscious cliquishness does accompany such outbursts, if we isolate the sound of the laughter itself, we can understand it as functioning to announce the start of a new sequence. Laughter in Ozu is something almost abstract, a sign bearing no relation to the will of laughing subjects. In fact, it often signals the beginning or the end of an interval of time associated with things ceremonial, things at a remove from the everyday of household routine.

Take for example the two moments in *Late Autumn* when we hear men anonymously laughing. Unreserved laughter of more or less the same kind erupts after both the memorial service that opens the film and the wedding ceremony near its end, and in both cases the laughing subjects themselves are excluded from the screen, just as we have already described. In the first instance, we see only a waitress passing with a tray, and then the deserted hallway after she exits. The men's laughter echoes in the background of this brief shot, its sound carrying from one of the restaurant's private dining rooms.

A reflection of what looks like moonlight on water shimmers on a wall at the end of the hallway, indicating that this restaurant is probably located beside a river. From the preceding shot of a large bridge pictured dimly in the dusk through a window framed by sliding *shōji* screens, those who recall the landscape of Tokyo in the late 1950s will quite naturally understand that this location must be along the Sumida River. The men in the next room have just observed religious rites at a temple in the nearby Shiba Park area, and the laughter we hear probably represents that they are enjoying a feeling of release. In any event, it is collective, and it belongs to a space different from that of the home. The camera has just captured the interior of the temple complex, picturing it in a series of shots taken from different angles while pulling back from the memorial service in the main building with the ceremonial chanting of the sutra still underway, before then framing the silhouette of the bridge and the deserted hallway at the restaurant. Over the course of this sequence, the soft sutra chanting and the percussive striking of the wooden temple drum have given way to the droning sound of a steamboat engine on the river, which has ceded in turn to the outburst of male laughter. In *late-period* Ozu, where there are never any fades or dissolves, sound montage of this kind establishes a rhythm that comes to typify transitions to settings located at a remove from everyday space. In such instances, we basically never witness characters changing trains or taking cars en route to some new location. They have always *already* settled in within their new surroundings, and the narrative only catches up with them once cued by their laughter carrying from an offscreen room.

Of course, in the case of *Late Autumn,* the very next shot does make clear whose laughter has drowned out the sound of the steamboat engine. Shin Saburi, Nobuo Nakamura, and Ryūji Kita are seated at a table in a private Japanese dining room, with Setsuko Hara and Yōko Tsukasa facing them, kneeling and smiling in crested black mourning kimono. The Buddhist rites depicted in the preceding scene at the temple were for the man who was respectively husband and father to these two women—rites performed on the occasion of his sixth death anniversary, in accordance with custom—and it seems natural that the mood has now turned comparatively lighthearted. The sound of laughter is not out of place. The men are close friends and former classmates of Setsuko Hara's late husband, and they joke about how the sutra chanting at his service went on for too long. Judging from their talk about having known the widow years ago when her family operated a pharmacy out of their home near the university neighborhood of Hongō Sanchōme, we can surmise that the three are graduates of what was then Tokyo Imperial University. But establishing their shared academic credentials is not what is important here. We are more concerned with what these three middle-aged men now talk about in the private dining room where they have just burst into laughter.

The men's conversation in the restaurant is limited to basically two topics. Their attention gravitates first to their deceased friend's beautiful only daughter Yōko Tsukasa and the matter of her marriage prospects. Fathers preoccupied with daughters nearing marriage are central to late-period Ozu, but in *Late Autumn* the father is already deceased. As a result, the responsibility of finding his daughter a groom falls to his old friends, who all seem to occupy positions of responsibility in their professional lives but will nevertheless apply themselves busily to the task. Whether they are adequate to this undertaking is rather questionable since each has a daughter of his own who is also either of marriageable age or has only recently been married off, but the ongoing affections the men harbor for the beautiful widow of the deceased do supply a marginally plausible pretext, more than whatever sense of responsibility they express toward the late husband himself. It therefore seems quite natural when their attention next turns to the beauty of Setsuko Hara in her youth, the second topic of conversation. Mother and daughter have already left the dinner party at this point, and the discussion now reveals that Shin Saburi and Nobuo Nakamura share a bittersweet history with this widow whose charms still have not faded, something they reflect upon with more than a little feeling. Both once had her in their sights when she was the beautiful star attraction of the pharmacy, and they used to visit her regularly until their late friend came and stole her away. These reminiscences give way to a dubious hypothesis of the kind that tends to accompany the flowing of alcohol: that men who marry beautiful women are bound to die young. Laughter ensues as this premise develops into an inside joke involving the full-figured waitress who serves their sake—her husband must be "very healthy" indeed! But we will return later to the function of this laughter at the expense of actress Toyo Takahashi in the role of the unsuspecting hostess.

Widower Ryūji Kita lets slip that he finds the daughter more appealing than her mother, but in an ironic twist, when the men eventually float the idea of remarriage for Hara, he is the one they propose as the groom. He ends up taking to this prospect with unexpected enthusiasm, but Nakamura's less-than-disinterested dithering in the role of key mediator leads to nothing but confusion, and we need not concern ourselves with those details. For now, it is enough to note that the narrative of *Late Autumn* revolves around a series of advances and setbacks in the marriage or remarriage prospects of two women of different generations as well as the restless meddling of the middle-aged men who monitor the unfolding of these situations. In short, the narrational structure is basically that of *Late Spring*, with two simultaneously developing marriage plots, one involving a daughter and the other her widowed parent, only distinguished by the mere variation of the parent's sex. A dinner conversation initiated by carefree laughter sketches the basic outline of this structure, demonstrating that these restaurant scenes do take on rich narrational functions despite their lighthearted appearances. It should therefore be unsurprising that when a second outburst of laughter echoes the first at the end of *Late Autumn,* it plays a similar role.

The second outburst occurs on the evening following Yōko Tsukasa's wedding, after the joyous occasion has at last been celebrated and the meddling middle-aged men have returned once again to the same restaurant on the bank of the Sumida River for some lighthearted post-reception conversation. Neither the bride nor her mother makes an appearance this time, clearly distinguishing this scene on the level of character composition from the dinner party following the Buddhist memorial service at the beginning of the film. And yet, the same shot of the deserted hallway begins this sequence as well, the light off the nearby river again shimmering on the wall. Right before this, the familiar shot of the bridge in silhouette has also repeated. Anyone witnessing this will sense a renewed appreciation for how conscientiously beginnings and endings are balanced in Ozu. And here again, the laughter of unseen men functions to signal an immediate transition, from the wedding hall where the bride and groom have just had their wedding picture taken to a private dining room at a restaurant. Though introduced by a shot picturing Shin Saburi mid-laughter, glimpsed in profile and at a distance through the gap of a partially opened sliding door, the subsequent sequence mostly follows the same pattern as after the Buddhist memorial service (fig. 24). Inside the "men's sanctuary" of the restaurant, the middle-aged friends raise their glasses to the lovely mother and daughter no longer in their presence, then proceed once again to trade foolish inside jokes and laugh amongst themselves. But the sound of their laughter is less vigorous now and less distinct as a sign than the laughter we overheard in the deserted hallway at the beginning of the film. The reason for this is that there is no longer any remaining narrational function for these middle-aged men except to recede. The next sequence pictures Setsuko Hara instead as she prepares for bed in her cotton house kimono, having returned from the

24. *Late Autumn:* Shin Saburi seen through a doorway, laughing.

wedding ceremony alone. Framed in partial profile, she gazes quietly downward, and the film comes to a close. The silent expression with which she confronts her solitude is of course not something that she would reveal in front of any man.

THE ABSENCE OF NUANCE

The scenes of reunions among former classmates that are often depicted in late-period Ozu are always introduced with laughter such as we have just observed, with slight deviations between laughter heard and laughing seen. The class reunion in Ozu's final film *An Autumn Afternoon* is no exception. A profile shot of Nobuo Nakamura silently reviewing paperwork at his office is followed suddenly by a nighttime city view to the accompaniment of swelling music, and then two shots of a hallway, composed in depth, at the end of which a large paper lantern advertising a restaurant is visible through a window. At this moment, we hear a burst of male laughter. Thus begins a sequence depicting what we learn is a reunion of middle school classmates forty years after graduation, the transition music giving way to the sound of their laughter in the deserted hallway just as before. Shots of deserted hallways into which laughter carries from off screen seem almost systematized in late-period Ozu, but the impression they create is hardly monotone. On the other hand, they tend not to become conspicuous objects for analysis.

These shot compositions and sound montages indicate that we are dealing with a filmmaker who strictly refrains from handling space and time by means of privileged symbolic details or effects of compression. Ozu intentionally avoids editing to create the impression of time elapsing smoothly or unconsciously or scenery changing inconspicuously. In *Ozu and the Poetics of Cinema,* David Bordwell correctly observes that by around 1933 Ozu was "using synecdoches to establish every locale: typewriters for an office, rings for a gym, saxophones for a nightclub."[1] But compared to such handling of space and time in the films of the silent period, where there are even still title cards to place the action, the use of synecdoche is clearly diminished in the sound films of late-period Ozu. It cannot really be said that images of deserted hallways stand in for restaurants in part-for-whole relationship since these hallways can also belong to private residences or can be ambiguous enough to resist immediate spatial identification, as we will see later. In any case, in late-period Ozu, where we find no privileged significant details or compression effects, both temporal shifts and spatial displacements become direct to the point of brusqueness, and nuances of the kind that tend generally to accompany transitions are eliminated. Or else think of this

---

1. David Bordwell, *Ozu and the Poetics of Cinema* (Princeton: Princeton University Press, 1988), 245. Hasumi cites the Japanese translation: David Bordwell, *Ozu Yasujirō—Eiga no shigaku,* trans. Teruo Sugiyama (Tokyo: Seidosha, 1992), 408.

as Ozu leaving everything exposed on the surface, with no gradation. It seems strange indeed that the many critics who readily invoke absences in Ozu mostly neglect to mention his methodical exclusion of nuance and gradation.

As we have already seen, Ozu does not attempt to depict time or space that is in the course of transitioning. In fact, it is safe to say that his films almost never show characters traveling from one place to another. In *The End of Summer* the camera does *seem* to track Ganjirō Nakamura's every movement when he sneaks off to Kyoto to visit his mistress Chieko Naniwa without his family's knowledge, and it even shows him turning down a narrow alley. However, it quickly becomes clear that what we are following is not the route to his mistress's home but a diversion the old man has created in order to mislead and corner an employee from the family company who has been sent to tail him. Even where Ozu does film characters riding moving vehicles—as in the last scene of *Fighting Friends—Japanese Style* (*Wasei kenka tomodachi*, 1929), when the fighting friends drive their truck alongside the train carrying their shared love interest off to her new life without them, or in *The Flavor of Green Tea over Rice,* when Ozu pays gratuitous attention to the motion of the express train carrying Michiyo Kogure away from her husband in Tokyo, or else in *Early Summer*'s depiction of the daily commute on the Yokosuka Line—the point is not primarily to portray characters in the process of traveling to some new setting but to thematize vehicular movement in itself. *Tokyo Story* is another clear example: a film that entirely omits the round-trip journey of the elderly couple between Onomichi and Tokyo, never depicting the interior of the train. Chishū Ryū and Chieko Higashiyama appear suddenly, along with their luggage, at their eldest son Sō Yamamura's doorstep, just as if there were no such thing as the in-between space of characters in motion in Ozu. Ozuesque people always place themselves in new surroundings without any intermediary movement, and therein lies the *directness* of Ozu, a directness verging on cruelty. This kind of directness forms a conspicuous contrast with the way Mikio Naruse depicts the same Yokosuka line commute from Kamakura to Tokyo in *Sound of the Mountain* (*Yama no oto*, 1954) where he shows the passing external landscape through the train window. Starting from around the time of his silent-era film *Apart from You* (*Kimi to wakarete*, 1933), Naruse often invested his images with what we might call a lyricism of in-between space, something Ozu was compelled strictly to reject. The point is of course not to determine which approach was superior but only to highlight that these two filmmakers, who both came to disdain camera movement with age, adopted completely different approaches to filming landscapes passing by behind characters.

A second example of Ozu's self-restraint toward what are often thought of as especially cinematic approaches for handling space and time is his exclusion of the gesture of approaching. Even when the setting is an exclusive restaurant in some removed locale, Ozu declines to use long shots to depict the exterior, thus preempting the establishment of any far-to-near or outside-to-inside perspective, whether visual or psychological. Instead, he places his camera suddenly within hallways—a world in the wings of the new scenery of dining rooms—and then fills this deserted space with the sound of laughter. This too demonstrates a *directness* verging on cruelty in its exclusion of intermediary steps. Ozu does approach people's faces from the front, but little else. When it comes to architecture, any attempts to approach happen from the side or from behind, even in the case of important settings where multiple characters are gathered together.

The restaurant in *An Autumn Afternoon* seems less formal than the one in *Late Autumn*, but the pattern is no different: carefree laughter carries from a nearby room into a hallway deserted but for the brief presence of a hostess who crosses the screen carrying food. When the camera takes its cue to enter the room, a dinner party is already in full swing, with former teacher Eijirō Tōno, whom everyone calls "The Gourd," as the apparent guest of honor. Here too, the viewer encounters the ongoing proceedings at a delay, reinforcing the impression that whenever possible Ozu avoids depicting the moments at which things begin and end. Both the funeral that closes *Tokyo Story* and the wedding reception that opens *Equinox Flower*, for example, have already begun by the time we lay eyes on them.

Things take on an even more radical appearance in the case of *An Autumn Afternoon*, which in true Ozu fashion concludes without any depiction of the wedding reception itself. The separation enacted by Chishū Ryū and his daughter Shima Iwashita, dressed for her wedding in her second-floor "sanctuary," recreates almost identically the separation scene performed by Ryū and Setsuko Hara in *Late Spring*, and once again, it is followed by several shots depicting the daughter's now vacated room from different angles as the music swells. But this time, the camera suddenly finds itself not in the daughter's room by morning, but inside a different house, in a deserted hallway, which it composes in depth and in lighting designed to indicate that the time is now evening. At this moment, a burst of male laughter drowns out the music and we join Ryū and Ryūji Kita inside a room in Nobuo Nakamura's home where the men are cheerfully drinking whiskey and ginger ale, the two guests having already removed their formal jackets and made themselves comfortable. It hardly needs stating that the slight deviation between the sound of laughter and the image of these men laughing announces the end of what for Ryū has been a long and exceptional day—the day of his daughter's wedding. The audacious transition has transplanted us directly from morning to night, and from Ryū's house to the home of his friend Nakamura, having omitted the entire spectacle of the wedding ceremony. It is also clear that some time has elapsed since the characters' arrival in this new space, since host Nakamura has changed into house clothes, and his wife Kuniko Miyake has also already traded the black crested kimono she must have worn to the reception for casual wear. Ozu represents this leap and transition with a single outburst of laughter.

Ozu makes no attempt to depict movement through intermediary space and refrains from using long shots to establish exteriors even of important settings, instead sliding in through the background of the action, at a slight delay and from the side. What he initiates with the sound of laughter is therefore the sequence itself, and whether the episode being narrated is a reunion of former classmates or a gathering of old friends at the Nakamura home, he seems quite unconcerned by the fact that it is already underway. In *An Autumn Afternoon* the sound of laughter carrying to a deserted hallway initiates nothing less than the sequence portraying the first night Chishū Ryū will spend alone after parting with his daughter. Despite the warm company of his friends, he takes leave of them at an unexpectedly early hour, then stops by the bar where the hostess bears a resemblance to his late wife, before returning home to find his eldest son and daughter-in-law waiting up for him. After they have left, he isolates himself in the kitchen, ignoring his younger son urging him to turn in, and soon will stagger in front of the stairs that lead to the second floor and to the room that used to be his daughter's. Of course, from a narrational perspective, there is not necessarily anything unique about the deviation between a scene and a sequence that we observe here. Filmmakers of all kinds adopt similar approaches and are even obliged to do so. But because of the way Ozu exaggerates this, calling attention to it through a slight deviation between laughter heard and laughing seen, he reinforces our conviction that he is unique as a director. What then happens if, in seeking to grasp this uniqueness as a cinematic reality, we listen even more closely to the sound of laughter as it precedes images of people laughing?

HALLWAYS AND VERANDAS

In *The End of Summer* we again twice encounter the sound of laughter in the absence of people pictured laughing. As in *Late Autumn,* both these bursts of laughter follow the conclusion of ceremonies that have commemorated exceptional occasions. The first instance occurs, once again, at a fine restaurant located beside a river. We know from dialogue earlier in the film that plans have been made to eat in the Arashiyama district of Kyoto following a ceremonial visit to the family graves for the death anniversary of Ganjirō Nakamura's late wife, and we can therefore surmise that the restaurant where we find the members of the Kohayagawa family gathered around a table is probably on the bank of the Hozu River. We can only surmise this because the sequence has been initiated by a spatiotemporal transition of the aforementioned *direct* variety: we witness neither the process by which the family has traveled to Kyoto from their home in what is probably the Nada area of Kobe nor their arrival at the restaurant, much less the spectacle of the meal they have shared in a private dining room. Group laughter, which now includes both men and women, is an audible sign representing the conclusion of this meal—a scene unto itself having already unfolded. Here, the sound of laughter carries not through a deserted hallway but out to the restaurant's veranda, where Setsuko Hara and her sister-in-law Yōko Tsukasa are kneeling side by side at the ledge watching the flow of the offscreen river. The abrupt outburst of laughter turns their heads, and then, as if responding to a cue, they stand and remove themselves from its vicinity. Only after Hara and Tsukasa have exited the veranda does Ozu's camera picture the people laughing.

Once again, laughter heard has preceded laughing seen. When, at a beat's delay, the men and women of the family appear seated around patriarch Ganjirō Nakamura enjoying the postmeal atmosphere, the topic of conversation turns quite naturally to the subject of marriage prospects for daughter Tsukasa, who is of marriageable age. People who conclude meals in front of Ozu's camera reliably take up the topic of daughters and marriage, as we see both at the restaurant on the bank of the Sumida River on an evening following a Buddhist memorial service in *Late Autumn* and at the restaurant beside the Hozu River on an afternoon following a visit to family graves in *The End of Summer*. At least in this sense, these two films are strikingly similar, in spite of some differences of staging and in the relationships among the characters. The similarity extends even to the presence of Tsukasa and Hara, whose marriage and remarriage are once again the focus of postmeal discussion, except that this time the two are sisters-in-law instead of daughter and mother. Note again that bursts of laughter are what accentuates these structural similarities between the narratives, laughter such as we have already encountered at various other points.

A further similarity between these films is that neither of their screenplays contains any direction about the laughter we hear in hallways or on verandas, which was likely added on the spot, after the writing stage. In any case, there is at least one respect in which the meal following the Buddhist memorial service in *Late Autumn* and the one after the visit to the family graves in *The End of Summer* do substantially differ: namely, the fact that the laughter we hear at the veranda overlooking the Hozu River in the latter instance clearly takes on a function of exclusion. All of the family members who have remained inside the private dining room are coupled, including widower Ganjirō Nakamura, whose late wife's death anniversary has supplied the occasion for a family meal at Arashiyama at his own suggestion, but whom we have already witnessed running off to visit a mistress on more than one occasion. The reason Hara and Tsukasa quietly retreat from the veranda while looking in the direction of this sudden burst of offscreen laughter is because they share concerns different from those of the people who have remained inside around the meal table. When the group inside turns to the topic of marriage planning, discussing with almost businesslike detachment what arrangements should be made for the two single women of the family, older sister Michiyo Aratama becomes annoyed and remarks that no one is really sincerely concerned for their happiness, in spite of all the enthusiasm for matchmaking. She then makes indirect reference to her father's trysts, looking rather provocative as she stands and leaves the room for the veranda. Here, there is a cutaway to a high-angle shot picturing Hara and Tsukasa side by side, now on the riverbank below.

This beautiful scene has already come up in the chapter on "looking," and we will not dwell on it further here except to call attention to how laughter, as an audible sign, has performed a function of exclusion and announced the end of a meal while at the same time also having the narrational function of initiating the new sequence by the river where these two sisters-in-law now kneel side by side looking at one another. Having taken the laughter as a cue to distance themselves from the private dining room, these single women—one a beautiful widow who tends to preface every statement with qualifications about her age, and the other a never-married young daughter—now talk about men and relationships on the bank of the Hozu River, exchanging things almost tacitly, beyond the perception of the rest of the family. They are quite exceptional within the Kohayagawa household, to which they belong but not as full stakeholders, as the laughter of the family members in the private dining room has demonstrated in excluding them. As in *Early Summer* when Setsuko Hara and Kuniko Miyake talk on the beach in Kamakura, Ozu shows a distinct fixation here on a relationship between sisters-in-law, a preoccupation that seems far stronger than his interest in the relationship between biological sisters Kinuyo Tanaka and Hideko Takamine in *The Munekata Sisters*, for example. Perhaps this fixation has more to do with the actresses playing these characters than the characters themselves. It does seem clear that the Ozu of *The End of Summer* has set out to cast a very particular kind of gaze at these actresses, the same ones he earlier cast as mother and daughter in *Late Autumn*.

The second time we hear the sound of people laughing in this film is that very evening. When, under a clear blue sky on the bank of the Hozu River, Setsuko Hara remarks as if to herself how very nice the weather is, another leap through space and time transplants us instantaneously to new surroundings, again with Ozuesque directness. The camera suddenly finds itself in the Kohayagawa home at the deserted veranda, which it frames in a depth composition accented by a hanging lantern indicating the season of the Bon Festival. Needless to say, a burst of laughter then carries from a nearby room, and here, at a beat's delay, the members of the family are pictured sitting on the tatami and reflecting cheerfully on their day trip to Arashiyama. It should once again be clear that this slight deviation between laughter heard and laughing seen intervenes in the film as a sign marking the conclusion of an interval of time outside that of the everyday. Here, that interval was a day spent visiting family graves and sharing a meal at a restaurant. At the same time, it also takes on the narrational function of signaling the start of a new event. Ganjirō Nakamura, who until now has been the picture of health, will undergo a sudden change of condition in what follows, demonstrating that when we fail to notice the sound of group laughter in an Ozu film, we may also fail to grasp the logical thread of the narrative. To the extent that we overlook the density of narrational functions performed by images of deserted hallways, details not necessarily even included in the screenplays, Ozu's films probably do end up looking like monotone repetitions of uneventful everyday episodes. But decisive events do occur, in liminal zones like the hallways or verandas that extend in the wings of living rooms and dining rooms, and to the accompaniment of perfectly ordinary sounds. This is why it is essential that we not neglect the sound of laughter unaligned with images of people laughing.

CLIQUISHNESS

There is no one who does not know what a hallway is, nor should anyone need to ask the definition of laughter. And yet, no one anywhere could have known what would happen when the hallways and laughter we all know so well became one. Unanticipated by anyone, Yasujirō

Ozu presented hallways and laughter together as an experiment at a particular kind of audiovisual sign—hallway laughter, of which people were not even aware they were unaware. The reason it is difficult to really see Ozu's films, composed though they may be of details that should be familiar to everyone, is because experiments of this kind are scattered casually in all directions. This is why it is necessary to spread both our visual and aural faculties everywhere across the films.

Because these slight deviations between laughter heard and laughing seen involve synchronous sound as a natural precondition, we might assume that this technique would not apply in the Ozu of the silent period. And in fact, this approach to transitions *is* unique to the Ozu of the late period, starting from the point where gatherings of old classmates and family meals at restaurants become frequent subjects. Still, it is important to note that the anonymizing group atmosphere and the cliquishness associated with these outbursts of laughter are things to which Ozu was already drawn even before his first talkies. We do not hear the sound of laughter in the silent films, of course, but images of people laughing are made to take its place through editing. Anyone who recalls the home movie screening that the two young brothers endure at the luxurious home of their father Tatsuo Saitō's boss in *I Was Born, but . . .*, for example, should understand this immediately.

By the point in the film where he rallies his subordinates to take part in a home movie screening at his house one evening, company executive Takeshi Sakamoto has already been portrayed as a fad chaser, swinging a tennis racket and going around shooting footage with a Pathé Baby 9.5 mm Cine Camera. The screening venue is an impressive parlor appointed with several sofas. The boss's young son has invited his classmates, including Tatsuo Saitō's two sons, who now sink into one of the sofas in anticipation of the show. The boys joke when a lion makes an appearance on the screen, then debate the nonsensical question of whether the stripes of a zebra are white on black or black on white. Saitō intervenes to shush his sons, but his own screen debut comes next. Children and adults alike burst into innocent laughter at his clownish performance for the camera, which has captured his exertions to toady up to his boss by making funny faces. The boss's son tells the two brothers sitting next to him on the sofa that he thinks their father is funny, and their classmates laugh in unison. Seeing this, the father ventures a timid laugh of his own, but his sons are unable to share in the humor and fall silent with humiliation at his hitherto unimagined sycophancy. Feeling isolated in the darkness of this parlor filled with inaudible laughter, they quietly remove themselves from the proceedings and head home, consumed with inconsolable anger at what they have just witnessed—a thing not to be seen.

David Bordwell uses the term "tendency film" (*keikō eiga*) in connection with *I Was Born, but . . .*,[2] observing that it concentrates on "a grim lesson about power" in social relations and is more distinctly didactic than Ozu's other films of the period.[3] It is true that the film thematizes the inevitable emasculation of a salaryman low in the ranks of the company culture that was taking shape at the time, along with the feelings of powerlessness that affect his entire household, and in this sense it is not wrong to underline its social lesson. There is no ambiguity about what kind of lesson to take from the scene of the screening party in the boss's parlor, where the home movie itself exposes relationships of social hierarchy and power. But whether or not we insist on the word

---

2. Bordwell, *Ozu and the Poetics*, 174. Tendency film, or *keikō eiga*, was the name for a genre of socially conscious "protest" films produced within Japan's commercial studios during the 1920s and 1930s.

3. Bordwell, 56. Bordwell's classification of *I Was Born, but . . .* is actually somewhat more nuanced than this. He cites studio head Shirō Kido as the source of the idea that Ozu "steered a course between Shochiku's humane optimism and the 'tendency film' of social protest," and sees *I Was Born, but . . .* not as a tendency film per se but as a film exemplifying Ozu's own tendency of "'polysemous' appropriation," noting that its merging of genres divided period viewers as to whether it was on balance a "melancholy" or a "cheerful" film (174). He also cites the film as an example of split-structure narration in Ozu, noting its division into a comedic section and a more serious reflection on social hierarchy (56). The text quoted by Hasumi is from the already cited Japanese translation of Bordwell's book (Bordwell, *Ozu Yasujirō*, 379).

power, we should not overlook the fact that this scene sketches softer, more everyday kinds of interpersonal dynamics as well—dynamics unrelated to the hierarchical relationship between boss and employee—and with these the subtle outline of an Ozuesque theme.

One such dynamic, and a detail that Bordwell strangely neglects to mention, is what is revealed of the boss's marital relationship when stray footage of him flirting with two geisha on a city street corner treats his wife to a glimpse of how her husband behaves behind her back—a projection glitch that seems to guarantee her the upper hand in the household, as if in preview of the marital dynamic we will later encounter in *What Did the Lady Forget?* Anyone can see that from this day forward Takeshi Sakamoto will be obliged to grovel before his wife. But the more important thing is to recognize how this moment exposes another dynamic, that between a very Ozuesque kind of laughter that occurs in spaces to which formal social power is foreign and the effect of exclusion that this laughter produces. Confronting the hitherto unimagined social inferiority of their father is not the only thing that enrages Tatsuo Saitō's boys. In fact, what they seem most unable to accept is their isolation within the laughter his clownish behavior has provoked—a kind of isolation they are experiencing here for the first time. We need not analyze the embarrassment of these brothers excluded by a sudden outburst of group laughter; their unusually brooding expressions alone are sufficient to trace a cruel sketch of the theme of laughing in Ozu in all its unconscious cliquishness. What moves the hearts of viewers in this scene is not the lesson it probably does contain but the unanticipated encounter with the rawness of expression that crosses the faces of these young boys as they fall into an uncomfortable silence, unable to join in the visible laughter of the people surrounding them. In the end, all they can do is remove themselves from the parlor, much the same way that Setsuko Hara and Yōko Tsukasa quietly remove themselves from the vicinity of the laughter at the restaurant in *The End of Summer*.

More such unconsciously cliquish parlor laughter presents itself in *The Lady and the Beard*—another film from the silent period—when bearded Tokihiko Okada crashes a party thrown by his friend's younger sister and provokes an outburst from her girlfriends, who dislike his scruffy uncouthness. The young women taunt their unwelcome guest with an unreasonable request to dance, whereupon the unkempt kendo master lands on the idea of performing a solo sword dance and exits the room to make his preparations. In his brief absence, the women gleefully descend on the party table, consuming the cakes and drinks without him before excluding him with their collective gaze when he then reappears. We encounter a similarly cliquish effect at both the country middle school in *Tokyo Chorus* and the urban university in *What Did the Lady Forget?* when students collectively laugh at a classmate whom a teacher or professor has reprimanded. Such laughter has set the stage for the appearance, after a period of time in the talkie years, of the slight deviation between laughter heard and laughing seen as a late-period theme.

RITUALS OF PARTING

Even in late-period Ozu, laughter heard does not *always* precede laughing seen. Exceptional though they may be, moments do unquestionably exist in which the camera films laughing characters directly. This happens in *The End of Summer*, for example, when Setsuko Hara and Yōko Tsukasa kneel side by side as if recreating their pose on the bank of the Hozu River but this time on the veranda of the family home, a space introduced with the familiar depth framing. These sisters-in-law have mostly gone about their business apart from the other family members since fleeing the laughter at the restaurant in Arashiyama, but with Ganjirō Nakamura finally showing signs of recovery from the heart attack he has suffered in the interim, they now make an appearance on the veranda. This very veranda is where an outburst of laughter from inside the house earlier signaled the end of a day spent visiting family graves, but the lantern that was previously hanging from the eaves is now gone, its absence representing the passage of time. The next shot frames the two women more or less from the front as they watch what seems to be something funny and react with reflexive laughter. We understand quite naturally from the sequence as it unfolds that their laughter has been triggered by the sight of the convalescent grandfather, looking quite vigorous in his summer house kimono and long underwear as he plays catch in the street with his grandson—a peaceful scene that makes the viewer smile as well. It seems that anyone would readily welcome the laughter of these women as an expression of genuine relief at the recovery of the family patriarch.

And yet, having maintained such sensitivity to the deviation between laughter heard and laughing seen, we cannot help but sense something inauspicious in this alignment of sound and image. We know better than to think that an exception like this will be unconditional in Ozu. In fact, the words these two next exchange with the patriarch when he sits at the veranda perspiring from exertion will turn out to be their last with him. No one stops Ganjirō Nakamura as he tricks his grandson during a game of hide-and-seek, slyly changing into his street clothes and slipping out of the house to visit his mistress Chieko Naniwa, at whose home he will suddenly drop dead. Should we therefore conclude that the laughter of these sisters-in-law has also taken on an unintended exclusion function, despite bearing not the slightest trace of hostility? Or perhaps, in laughing, they have unconsciously bidden their father farewell.

It is hard not to smile at the comical seriousness with which Ganjirō moves through the open rooms of this house with no space in which to hide from view, skillfully deceiving his inquisitive daughter and his innocent grandson as he changes into his street clothes and scurries off to see his mistress. Watching this scene is strangely pleasurable, even after multiple viewings of the film and with full awareness of how brief his remaining time will be. Why? Much like this character, who manages to evade observation in spite of the open plan of the family home, Ozu himself sketches something invisible here despite the fact that his direction deliberately displays each and every detail in plain view, hiding nothing from sight. And like his character, Ozu also gets away with it. This something invisible is not merely a new garnish on the Ozuesque theme of "the dissolution of male authority" represented by an "old man who behaves like a carefree child," as Bordwell puts it.[4] As demonstrated in chapter 3 on "changing clothes," changing is a ritual of leave-taking in Ozu and is therefore to be performed with the utmost solemnity. And yet, like Takeshi Sakamoto and many other characters from the silent period, Ganjirō is incapable of solemnity. Has anyone witnessed another film in which a character deploys such strategy or expends so much time and effort, in spite of such handicaps, just to succeed at changing clothes? The gestures he performs here, which are at once desperate and gratuitously exacting, go far beyond the terrain of mere childish joking while also exceeding the initial aim of sneaking away from the house under the noses of his daughter and grandson. What entices us as viewers extends to the performance of Ozu himself as director, which makes this all possible and can almost be called absurdist. It is hard to think of another moment in film history that rivals the absurdism of staging we find here. Perhaps only the monkey-catching contraption that Red Buttons designs and deploys in Howard Hawks's *Hatari!* (1962) comes close. There as well, absurdism hovers around Hawks's performance as director and the conscientiousness with which he records the sequence of events on film, from the childish concept that inspires the plan through its implementation in a monkey-capturing operation executed with gestures that are also as desperate as they are gratuitously exacting. Indeed, no one would expect anyone to have seen another film in which such strategy is

---

4. Bordwell, *Ozu and the Poetics*, 367.

deployed, or so much time and effort expended, in spite of such handicaps, just to succeed at rounding up a cartload of monkeys.

We therefore hardly need ponder the question of why Ozu fixates so much here on "changing clothes." As a director who was involved in writing the screenplays for his own films, Ozu would have been more than sufficiently conscious of the fact that the changing of clothes at this moment represents nothing less than the preparatory ritual for an old man's journey into the beyond, however childishly playful it may appear. It is likely that the staging of this entire scene was conceived precisely to anticipate death's visit that very night, starting from the moment when Setsuko Hara and Yōko Tsukasa let out a reflexive laugh while watching him play catch. The something invisible that Ozu sketches here is nothing other than the premonition of this fate, a premonition not at all conveyed by the exactingly edited sequence of changing clothes in itself. Precisely this is what defines the direction of Ozu: displaying everything in plain view while also sketching the outlines of things invisible. We have to fixate on the image, but to keep from missing the film of things that we cannot see just by staring as they develop on screen, we also have to cultivate ways of looking that are adequate to Ozu.

Ways of looking that are adequate to Ozu have nothing to do with locating directorial intentions hidden deep within the image. Nothing is hidden and everything is exposed on the surface. But things hardly perceptible are also sketched in subtle outline. We can only begin to grasp these outlines by using our eyes to recognize the kinds of configurations created, from one film to the next, by things we could not possibly have expected would constitute such significant details before we really looked at Ozu—things like "changing clothes" as it forms a consistent theme. We should be similarly attuned to the occurrence of slight deviations between laughter heard and laughing seen—a uniquely Ozuesque phenomenon of a different order from that of the general human truth that everyone laughs—and should meet this misalignment between sound and image as an event, taking account of it as we touch its function and its significance in each of the films. What is required for this is nothing more than a perfectly ordinary sensitivity to difference. In fact, all it really takes is the ability to recognize that in some films laugher heard and laughing seen do not align, while in others they do. But it is also true that our world suffers from a nearly universal affliction: that in watching a film, it is not considered essential to remain sensitive to shots of deserted hallways framed in depth, shots that may seem to have been included only casually at best. The films of Yasujirō Ozu are nothing other than a cinematic joy created to upset this widely shared affliction.

In fact, at this very moment, unknown people are bursting into laughter somewhere nearby. But of course, the figures to whom this laughter belongs are nowhere to be seen on screen. Seeing Ozu begins with understanding this not as lack, but as abundance—an abundance of joy.

10

BEING SURPRISED

SUSPENSE IN THE LIVING ROOM

Having at last been released from her daily duties, with her two children in bed and her parents and husband retired to their respective rooms, the woman responsible for the running of the household has settled down with a book. We find her reading at the same table in the living room where, in the opening scene of *Early Summer,* we earlier witnessed the family's busy breakfast routine. It now seems to be well past dinner, though it is probably still not terribly late. The room is somewhat darker than what we have seen in other interior shots to this point in the film, and a pronounced shadow spreads across the *fusuma* wall panels behind Kuniko Miyake as she reads. The title of the book on the table in front of her is not visible, but we might surmise that she is reading a volume from Roger Martin du Gard's novel cycle *Les Thibault,* which has been mentioned earlier in a conversation between her sister-in-law Setsuko Hara and an old friend of her brother, in a scene on the train platform during the morning commute. Miyake is framed from the elbows up, at fairly close range, as she follows the lines of text across the page with her eyes, a strangely captivating glow radiating softly from her forehead. Presently, we hear the sound of someone opening the front door. Turning her head in the direction of the sound, Miyake calls out to confirm that the person at the offscreen door is her sister-in-law, who has been out at a friend's wedding. Hara answers in the affirmative and asks in turn if she should lock the door for the night, then enters the living room carrying a bouquet of flowers from the wedding reception and a wrapped box containing a sponge shortcake that she says she bought in Ginza. During the ensuing conversation, she will offer this shortcake to housewife Miyake as the latter questions her still single sister-in-law about a bachelor who has been introduced to her by a manager at her work and about her intentions regarding marriage. "Maybe I'll get married too," Hara says, laughing bashfully. "Yes, you should, do it," says her sister-in-law as she transfers a piece of the cake to her plate with a fork. Hara stands and exits. A shot taken at somewhat greater distance now pictures the whole living room with Miyake in her house kimono slowly raising the fork to her mouth under low lighting appropriate to the nighttime setting. This moment will indirectly lead to the shortcake incident discussed in the earlier chapter on "eating," but eating is not the theme that concerns us at present.

At this point, a patterned *fusuma* panel crossed at the top by a dark shadow suddenly slides open in the background and Chishū Ryū appears in the gap, dressed in his bedclothes and lurching from the adjoining room. Startled by his intrusion, Miyake leaps backward (fig. 25). She might as well have seen a ghost. While lasting only a moment, there is something seductive about her frightened reaction, and her slightly coquettish reproach, all the more so because they are not quite plausible as a response to her husband's admittedly boorish entrance. Are wives in Ozu's home dramas really supposed to lose their poise in the middle

25. *Early Summer:* Chishū Ryū startles his wife Kuniko Miyake in the living room at night.

of the night the way Miyake does here? As she starts to express some embarrassment over the fact that he has been awake listening all this time, he motions for her to be quiet, indifferent to her surprise. He is focused on the marriage talk concerning his younger sister and the bachelor introduced at her work, a topic he now pursues in a hushed tone of voice. Regaining her composure, his wife confidently tells him not to worry, that she will find a way to ask for more details. He urges her on but senses his sister returning and hurriedly ducks back into the other room. Hara enters the living room once more and unsuspectingly slides the opened partition shut as her sister-in-law remains seated at the table, smiling.[1] The timing of the staging that so matter-of-factly depicts Hara's elegant entrances and exits and Ryū's own tactless appearances

---

1. Hasumi writes that Hara sits a second time next to her sister, but he appears to misremember this detail.

and retreats is something that would be at home in a comedy. In fact, while we may hesitate somewhat over the slight exaggeration of Miyake's gesture when she loses her composure at the sight of her lurching husband, it is generally hard not to smile at this sequence of a wife's evening reading interrupted by relentless character entrances and exits.

Chishū Ryū and Kuniko Miyake's hushed exchange continues after Setsuko Hara retires to her room for the night, but we will set the details of that conversation aside. What requires our attention is the way this scene and its choreography of people coming and going so clearly differs in tone from the other parts of *Early Summer*. Or perhaps it differs from other Ozu films in general. It is true that, from the perspective of narrative subject matter, what we find here can hardly be said to deviate significantly from the rest of the film. There is nothing unfamiliar about the focus on Hara as the unmarried adult woman of the household, or the preoccupation with questions of when, with whom, and in what way she will be coupled. But the same cannot be said of her older brother Ryū and his narrow-minded and unpleasant attitude, which is unromantic to say the least. There is no trace in his unrelenting seriousness of the caring consideration a brother might be expected to extend to a younger sister.

In his book *Ozu's Anti-Cinema*, Kijū Yoshida reads *Early Summer* as a film conceived of as the "anti–*Late Spring*." He observes that the same actor who in *Late Spring* "hopes for his daughter's marriage" while simultaneously regretting that he will have to part with her also appears in *Early Summer*, only this time as an older brother, "depicted as a worldly-minded person" demonstrating only the most ordinary of concern for his younger sister's marriage prospects. Yoshida sees in this shift a determined effort by Ozu to establish distance in *Early Summer* from the innuendo of *Late Spring*, where he toyed with "something dangerous that could easily be mistaken for incest."[2] He makes the

---

2. Kijū Yoshida, *Ozu's Anti-Cinema*, trans. Daisuke Miyao and Kyoko Hirano (Ann Arbor: University of Michigan Center for Japanese Studies, 2003), 124. Hasumi cites the original Japanese text: Kijū Yoshida, *Ozu Yasujirō no han'eiga* (Tokyo: Iwanami Shoten, 2011), 249–50.

excellent observation that Ozu almost seems to have wanted to "punish" the actor who played the father in the earlier film, and that casting him in the role of the "banal," all too "worldly-minded" brother in *Early Summer* was perhaps a way of degrading him. We seem to behold "punishment" itself in the Chishū Ryū who so tactlessly frightens Kuniko Miyake by sliding open the *fusuma* in the living room, showing insensitivity even to the surprise he has caused her as he prattles in a hushed voice, and with gestures almost like those of an automaton, about his younger sister's marriage prospects. This actor seems to have accepted punishment, having been reduced to a caricature of mediocrity and vulgarity. Precisely this is *Early Summer*'s "anti–*Late Spring*" moment.

But it seems that there is something more to this scene of a partition being furtively slid open than only an "anti–*Late Spring*" impulse—something almost anti-Ozuesque. Ozu hardly staged any frights or scares over the course of his career, but here he devotes himself to an attempt at visualizing surprise, albeit with an actress in a supporting role, and with the light-hearted touch of someone who seems to be playing a game. In Ozu's films, there are almost never any characters who clearly react to things with fright or surprise, which is another way of saying that the films themselves basically never conform to the kind of narrative framework in which events unfold in ways that might betray expectations. And because unexpected events hardly ever occur, things like pretexts for surprise are also generally missing. The absence of astonishment is even defining of the world of the Ozuesque.

There is, of course, an unanticipated meeting between Setsuko Hara and Masao Mishima in *Late Spring,* and similar kinds of unexpected encounters occur several times in *An Autumn Afternoon,* including when Chishū Ryū has a chance reunion with Daisuke Katō, a former petty officer from his ship during the war. But even at moments such as these, no Ozuesque character ever expresses anything like profound surprise. Even if some development were to deviate dramatically from expectations, it would be unimaginable for anyone to become agitated or unduly confused. In *An Autumn Afternoon,* for example, when Nobuo Nakamura improvises a wild joke about a funeral wake for their friend Ryūji Kita, Chishū Ryū just ambiguously plays along. It certainly seems that there is no one anywhere else who suddenly recoils or openly loses composure the way that Kuniko Miyake does here.

Why then did Ozu make her react with such surprise? Was it to emphasize the sensitivity of this housewife engrossed in her reading, a side of her not ordinarily on public display? Or was he less well-intentioned, seeking to exaggerate the vulgarity of her husband instead? No one can know the answers to these questions. What we can say for certain is that the director of *Early Summer* unmistakably possessed a formidable talent for staging that would have been more than adequate to the task even of making a suspense film. In fact, both the relationship of things animate and inanimate as evoked by the sliding of the patterned *fusuma* panel and the emergence of an expressionless man from the shadows beyond are things that would be at home in a horror film. Since Ozu mostly refrained from the kind of staging we encounter in this moment, its sudden deployment here, in the living room at night, and cued by a conversation about a young woman's marriage prospects, is clearly something that should elicit an incongruous laugh. How terribly mistaken it would be to think that Ozuesque time and space are permeated only by monotone reserve.

THE ABSENCE OF ASTONISHMENT

The world of the Ozuesque may be defined by absent astonishment, but as we have already established, this does not mean that chance encounters are entirely excluded. Still, what unanticipated encounters do occur mostly do not provoke any reactions of profound surprise. In fact, moments undeniably exist in Ozu when the sheer inexpressiveness of men and women who happen upon one another in unexpected places turns the absence of astonishment into an event in its own right. One such moment is the encounter between Takeshi Sakamoto and Yoshiko Okada in *An Inn in Tokyo*.

Made in 1935, *An Inn in Tokyo* is the last of the so-called "Kihachi films," following *Passing Fancy*, *A Story of Floating Weeds*, and *An Innocent Maid* (*Hakoiri musume*, 1935). It was also basically Ozu's last silent film. He had already shot the documentary talkie *Kagamijishi* (also known as *Kikugorō no kagamijishi* and *The Lion Dance*, 1936) in the same year, and would make his first dramatic talkie *The Only Son* the year after. In a sense, *An Inn in Tokyo* can therefore be called a turning point for Ozu, an achievement attained through eight years of cinematic trial-and-error beginning with his debut film *Sword of Penitence*. Ozu was known for student and salaryman comedies by the early thirties, but with the "Kihachi films" the focus shifts to the world of laborers and itinerant actors, people who cannot even be said to belong to the masses, living day to day and without proper households of their own, even when they are fathers or mothers. There is a strange dissonance worth noting here between the rustically conceived characters and settings on the one hand and the refinement of mise-en-scène and editing technique on the other. *An Inn in Tokyo* maintains uniform styling down to the rags worn by the children, and the overgrown fields where the characters aimlessly roam are filmed in highly controlled ways, with both traveling shots and fixed compositions. An almost abstract world seems to take shape in the gratuitous attention to form, a world foreign to the free-spiritedness often associated with those living at the edges of society. In this regard, David Bordwell is very much correct when he concludes that it would be a mistake to talk about this film in comparison with the likes of De Sica's *Bicycle Thieves* (*Ladri di biciclette*, 1948) just because there are thematic resemblances.[3] What is interesting about such Ozuesque formal patterning and abstraction is the fact

---

3. Bordwell, *Ozu and the Poetics*, 262.

that the resulting absence of astonishment can at times give shape to striking details in the form of excess expressionlessness. In Ozu, when something approaches perfect control, something in excess of it is invariably set into motion.

Kihachi refers to himself as a "lumpen." His wife has left him, and he is out of work with two children to look after. While staying at a cheap lodging house located in a working-class district of Tokyo crowded with factory smokestacks, he gets to know a young woman and her daughter. The young mother, played by Yoshiko Okada, happens to pass by one afternoon while Kihachi is passing time in a field with his boys after another search for work has yielded no results, and the two strike up a conversation that stirs him to concern for her well-being. Our earnest hero decides he would like to help this woman and her daughter. Needless to say, his chivalrous spirit soon transforms to tender sentiment, something resembling what the Kihachi of *Passing Fancy* also experiences toward the young woman in that film. But no sooner does he go out and use a bit of his paltry savings to buy his sweetheart a gift than she and her daughter disappear without so much as a farewell. Reduced to drowning his sorrows, he heads to what is clearly a rather disreputable establishment and intoxicates himself as the hostess pours. The script describes the setting here as a "small tatami room in a *nomiya* [sake house]," but it is clear that this business is not one that merely serves alcohol. The hostess who attends to Kihachi with a *shamisen* at the ready seems to be a woman unaverse to sexual transactions, like the hostesses of the old *meishuya*—unlicensed brothels that fronted as purveyors of sake before the war. The two sing together and clap hands, and when Kihachi hollers for more to drink, the woman looks at him with a knowing smile before leaving the room.

Now alone and collapsed on the floor, Kihachi is pictured in a low shot framed by the legs of the table. This is followed by a brief shot of lanterns hanging from the eaves, likely inserted to indicate a short ellipsis. Next comes another shot of Kihachi, still lying on the floor but framed at a somewhat greater distance within the surrounding scenery of the room. As he props himself into a slouch to scratch his legs, the bottom half of a kimono enters the foreground and indicates with a sketch of a gesture that the woman wearing it is about to take a seat on the floor in front of him. It would be consistent with the editing technique that Ozu had perfected by this period if this shot were then followed by a frontal composition of the woman now seated, having completed the motion begun in the previous shot. But what follows here instead is a medium shot of Kihachi, staring at the woman who has just entered. For a moment, he continues to stare in silence without displaying any reaction in particular. The next shot reveals Yoshiko Okada, now kneeling in front of him, her hair disheveled. This is an unexpected encounter, but neither of the two shows any sign of surprise. Their silence is not awkward. They are not dumbfounded. What we witness here is quite simply a nakedness, an almost cruel laying bare of the faces of a man and woman reduced to what we might call the degree zero of expression. Takeshi Sakamoto proceeds to declare his disappointment in this woman evidently prepared to sell her body, and Okada breaks down in tears, explaining that her daughter fell suddenly ill and that she needed money to pay the medical expenses. But such clarifications are not especially important here. The thing that captures our attention in this scene is precisely its insistence, even to excess, on the Ozuesque absence of astonishment.

As already discussed in chapter 6 on "holding still," this uncomfortable encounter lacking any indication of surprise is portrayed in shot/reverse shot sequence. The 180-degree rule is ignored, of course, as shots of Takeshi Sakamoto and Yoshiko Okada both looking in the same slightly screen-right direction repeat in alternation. The subtle unnaturalness of this shot sequence is an effect, of course, of the prioritization of figural resemblance in the staging of the shot/reverse shot, something often thought of as unique to Ozu that, among other filmmakers of the same period, only Sacha Guitry adopted as an intentional technique. For example, at key moments in *Quadrille* (1938), a rather Lubitschian film on the level of subject matter, Guitry himself appears on screen opposite Gaby Morlay or Jacqueline Delubac, in shot/reverse shot sequences organized on the same pattern of resemblance—the same slight departure from Hollywood convention that also characterizes how Sakamoto and Okada are shown in alternation. Witnessing Guitry the dandy and Sakamoto the "lumpen" each turn the same side of his face to the camera and cast a gaze that fails to meet Gaby Morlay or Yoshiko Okada, we cannot help experiencing a feeling of excitement, an excitement having to do not so much with film history itself as with the agitating sensation that we have somehow exceeded space and time. For while in Guitry's sound film, the unnatural shot/reverse shot sequences function as part of a light prelude to a game of flirtation, in Ozu's silent film, the same kind of sequence performs the opposite function: it announces the prohibition of such games. In the world of the Ozuesque, a world defined by the absence of astonishment, these two actors reduced to the degree zero of expression are also prohibited from performing surprise. And yet, reduced to the degree zero of expression, Sakamoto and Okada somehow communicate a surprise deeper even than that of Kuniko Miyake's exaggerated discomposure in *Early Summer*. Once again, Ozu vividly demonstrates how restraint can lead to unbridled expression.

TOKYO

Anyone who looks at Ozu's films side by side will likely see how this filmmaker cynically suggests an equivalence between larceny and prostitution through repeated recourse to the theme of a child's sudden illness. The plot of *An Inn in Tokyo* is a clear example: Takeshi Sakamoto dissuades Yoshiko Okada from selling her body to obtain money for her daughter's hospital bill only to address the situation by turning to robbery himself. In the thirties' films in particular, men stealing money and women selling their bodies become interchangeable details that transcend the bounds of any individual narrative. A child's sudden illness can drive a father to theft as in *That Night's Wife* (1930), or a mother to prostitution as in *An Inn in Tokyo*. It is true that ailments like children's dysentery and acute enteritis were quite common at the time, but there is still a certain exaggeration in the way this pattern emerges in Ozu. In *Passing Fancy* the young woman Kihachi has rescued becomes troubled when she sees his son fall ill, and she announces her intention to do something to help, but Kihachi perceives what she has in mind—to earn money by pouring sake for men—and admonishes her, saying she will do no such thing. In this case, she is spared such indecency when Kihachi says he will go off to Hokkaido to earn money himself, but it is an undeniable fact that, until a certain period in the films of Ozu, numerous women do ultimately resolve to sell their bodies, and not without reason. Prostitution for women clearly corresponds to theft for men, but this can also be seen to undergo a variation of a kind in *Tokyo Chorus*, when Tokihiko Okada takes a job as a walking curry rice advertisement without informing his family. His wife Emiko Yagumo will likely have to pawn more of her good kimono to spare her husband this indignity.

Strangely, the equivalence of larceny and prostitution tends to arise as a theme in Ozu films where the word "Tokyo" appears in the title, especially in the silent period of the thirties. Vexing financial problems lie in the background of *Tokyo Chorus*, *Woman of Tokyo*, and *An Inn in Tokyo* alike, problems that mothers and fathers are compelled to confront by their respective means and that darken the connotation of "Tokyo" in Ozu. As we will see, even the postwar *Tokyo Twilight* can be understood in this context. The "Tokyo" of the celebrated *Tokyo Story* seems exceptional in the distance it maintains from these other examples, but perhaps even that film is not an exception. The children who host their aging parents on their trip to the capital city in *Tokyo Story* have themselves likely had to struggle through financial problems in a

Tokyo symbolized by darkness. Ozu's undisguised irritation at the enthusiastic critical reception *Tokyo Story* enjoyed upon its release, something he continued to grumble about even in later years, was perhaps related to the critics' insensitivity toward what is probably the connotation of "Tokyo" in this film as well: its darkness.

Among the films of the thirties, the "darkness of Tokyo" is especially profound in *Woman of Tokyo*. Yoshiko Okada is a company secretary by day, but by night she works at a disreputable bar in order to earn money for her younger brother's university tuition expenses, something she naturally keeps secret. As in *Tokyo Chorus* when Tokihiko Okada finds himself unable to tell his family that he has been fired from his job, the darkness of Tokyo we encounter here is a product of a general affliction that compels people to hide the most serious of problems even from their loved ones. When Yoshiko Okada telephones her brother Ureo Egawa and casually informs him that she will be home late again, then climbs into the luxurious car of a man waiting at the street corner, we see something in her resigned expressionlessness that resonates with the zero degree of expression she will later exhibit in *An Inn in Tokyo* when facing Takeshi Sakamoto. The image of a mother compelled to sell her body to pay for a sick child's medical treatment appears throughout the films of this period, from *An Inn in Tokyo* through the postwar *A Hen in the Wind*, but the position of men is what is particularly ambiguous here. Kihachi's eagerness to rescue women from prostitution is almost too transparent, but even he accepts that it is a certain kind of woman who tends to end up in these sorts of circumstances, and he also does not seem to exercise a great deal of self-restraint when it comes to benefiting from their assistance. The titular wife of *That Night's Wife* is a paragon of bravery and valor, stopping at nothing to protect her husband from the police after he commits a robbery. The same cannot be said of men like Ureo Egawa's university student in *Woman of Tokyo* or Shūji Sano's returned soldier in *A Hen in the Wind*. Neither is capable of accepting the idea of a sister or a wife having turned to prostitution, and neither possesses any resource but violence for dealing with the situation. We could entertain various kinds of speculations here about the hidden political intent of *Woman of Tokyo*, rendered ambiguous by censorship, or about the memory of Naoya Shiga's famous novel *A Dark Night's Passing*, which probably does hang in the background of *A Hen in the Wind*, but even taking these things into account, it remains difficult to determine just how serious a matter the theme of the equivalence of theft and prostitution really is for Ozu.

And yet, placing *Tokyo Twilight* alongside these films brings something into view, if only indistinctly. This postwar film that so clearly inherits the darkness of prewar Tokyo features Chishū Ryū as a husband without a wife, his former wife having been stolen away by an acquaintance during his absence on an overseas assignment, an absence that made him powerless to stop the transfer to another man of control over a woman who rightfully belonged to him. This means he is in a position very much like that of Shūji Sano in *A Hen in the Wind*. In a sense, Ryū's estranged wife Isuzu Yamada has committed a far more serious betrayal than Kinuyo Tanaka in *A Hen in the Wind*, who only once surrendered herself to another man. This betrayal is probably the reason for the expressionlessness Ryū displays in *Tokyo Twilight*. The fact that the same actor would also be prohibited from having a wife in many other films, as indicated in chapter 8 on "getting angry," is perhaps also not unrelated. Ryū can neither kill himself as Ureo Egawa does in *Woman of Tokyo* after learning of his older sister's secret life, nor shove a wife down the stairs like Sano does to his own in *A Hen in the Wind* when he discovers her indiscretion. He is an utterly ambiguous presence, someone compelled to use the mask of the zero degree of expression to contain the kind of sexual trauma that men in Ozu find difficult to process. The father in *Tokyo Twilight*, as a husband, is incapable of preserving the family without disguising himself behind an absence of surprise.

When the actor Chishū Ryū receives Ozu's gaze through the camera, he transforms with a smile into characters of all kinds, from a caring father in *Late Spring* to a detached grandfather in *Tokyo Story*, from a boorish older brother in *Early Summer* to a salaryman of dim prospects in *Good Morning* (1959), and from a university professor afflicted with cancer in *The Munekata Sisters* to a former warship captain who salutes on hearing the Warship March of the Imperial Japanese Navy in *An Autumn Afternoon*. If Ozu's Chishū Ryū is an uncanny presence, an actor who is at once any character and no character at all, we can perhaps say that when Kuniko Miyake recoils in fright in *Early Summer*, it is because of the way the expressionlessness of this man—her own husband—exposes a shape-shifting vacancy, a vacancy, in other words, like that of a ghost. Despite the fact that she is permitted quite an exceptional display of surprise, he is a creature for whom being surprised remains consistently prohibited.

PRANKING

Near the end of *An Autumn Afternoon*, overgrown pranksters Nobuo Nakamura and Ryūji Kita lay a carefully planned trap for Chishū Ryū and go so far as to enlist Kuniko Miyake as an accomplice, as if for the sole purpose of finally coaxing a reaction of surprise out of this expressionless actor. They are expecting him to stop by to discuss a marriage prospect for his daughter, and they have planned in advance to trick him into thinking the ship has already sailed without him. When he arrives at the Nakamura residence and is shown to the living room, his friends display a strangely unwelcoming attitude, remaining seated by the veranda and focused on a game of *go*. After a moment, Ryū broaches the topic he has come to discuss, asking his host if he will arrange a meeting for his daughter and the bachelor in question, as they have already discussed. Nakamura only half responds, leaving the question hanging as he pretends to be absorbed in his next *go* move. The talkative one this time is Kita, who proceeds to admonish Ryū for dragging his feet, announcing matter-of-factly that his daughter had competition for this bachelor, a young woman introduced by none other than himself, and that a meeting between the two took place only yesterday. Ryū is perplexed but listens intently. Hardly looking in his friend's direction, Kita confidently concludes that the matter has been settled. Nakamura nods at a beat's delay.

There are perhaps half a dozen medium close-up shots of Chishū Ryū in this exchange, seeming stunned as he looks at one friend or the other, each time venturing only a hesitant "I see" or "Is that right?" Each of these shots pictures him following the conversation in a state of nakedness, reduced to nothing else but the zero degree of expression. He does not yet comprehend the situation enough to show anger and is unable to submit so much as a word in protest against this unexpected turn of events. His face lays bare an inner vacancy. It seems that his friends have gone too far, so much so that the scene becomes almost difficult to watch, even though we realize it is just a joke. Without a Yoshiko Okada on whom to fix his gaze, as Takeshi Sakamoto does in *An Inn in Tokyo*, Ryū's eyeline is set helplessly adrift. When Kita says, "you were too slow, I'm sorry," adding a line not written in the screenplay as if to deliver the decisive blow to his disarmed and abandoned friend, Kuniko Miyake promptly appears from the next room, carrying a tray and smiling. She scolds the talkative Kita and informs Ryū that the whole thing has been an act, that his friends are lying, whereupon he at last recovers some trace of human emotion and smiles in relief. He exclaims that he is "glad they were lying," and everyone laughs. If anyone here understands just how sincere these words really are, they do not show it. This may be the last chance this widowed father will have to help his daughter find happiness. He has already let one opportunity pass through his own inaction and his insensitivity to the subtleties of feminine psychology, an opportunity to connect his daughter with someone who was close and to whom she herself was quietly drawn.

It is easy to imagine that his mischievous friends sensed a lingering reluctance to let his daughter go and probably planned their prank with the good intention of instigating decisive action, but the result is something awfully cruel. They seem to have singled out the thing he dreads most as a father, a father destined to live the degree zero of expression as a mask. On the question of whether their joke has managed to coax surprise out of Chishū Ryū, he may indeed have felt genuine surprise, but because he ultimately does not give it expression, we can say that the prank has both succeeded and failed. What is certain is that his friends have anticipated no worse from him than this, having estimated that he will never lose his temper even when deceived. Even when he mutters the words "rotten rascals," as if speaking to Kuniko Miyake at his side, his eyes betray nothing but good humor. Ryū's absence of astonishment, even when pranked, is something his mischievous friends have taken for granted from the start.

The world of the Ozuesque is predicated on the absence of astonishment, which is why the aging rascals in *An Autumn Afternoon* can take such satisfaction in playing pranks on people at every opportunity. We find another example of this kind of mischief in the aforementioned prank Nobuo Nakamura and Chishū Ryū play on restaurant hostess Toyo Takahashi, when they pretend their old friend Ryūji Kita, who has been gloating over his remarriage with a young widow, has died suddenly. Both *Equinox Flower* and *An Autumn Afternoon* contain restaurant scenes in which these men have a laugh over some similarly rather questionable jokes referencing the stout physique of their hostess, played in both instances by the same full-figured actress. Such behavior reflects a self-awareness of the cliquish nature of group laughter shared among members of an in-group, as described in the preceding chapter on "laughing." Though old enough to know better, former classmates in *late-period* Ozu indulge in thoughtless jokes that everywhere assume the absence of astonishment as a precondition—foolish games, pursued with abandon, that exceed the framework of any individual film. Do we deem this apparently male privilege innocent to the extent that it assumes the precondition of a world absent of astonishment? Are these jokes only ever permitted of men, and only ever left unpunished?

PUNISHMENT

When men in late-period Ozu behave according to the perfectly natural assumption that Chishū Ryū will remain behind the mask of the zero degree of expression, we find ourselves having to reconsider the significance of the fact that Kuniko Miyake, in the role of that actor's wife in *Early Summer*, is the only one who displays any gesture of exaggerated surprise or discomposure. It is probably not unrelated that in *An Autumn Afternoon*, Ozu's last film, it is an intervention by the same Miyake, in the role of Nobuo Nakamura's wife, that puts an end to the men's foolish pranking. The wives of these mischievous aging friends are generally quite perceptive when it comes to their husbands' sly scheming, and they are also prepared to punish their men as necessary. The role of Nakamura's wife falls to Miyake in *Late Autumn* as well. This actor has a cynical side, and when she is paired with him, as she is here, her calm smile seems far more vivid than when she is wife to Ryū, as in *Early Summer*, or to Sō Yamamura, as in *Tokyo Story*. Take, for example, the sharpness she demonstrates in the scene in *Late Autumn* where she chats ironically with Shin Saburi's wife Sadako Sawamura about the foolishness of their respective husbands and their lingering attachments to Setsuko Hara, whom the men still remember as the pretty young shopgirl they used to visit at the neighborhood pharmacy during their college days. The two women are clearly well aware even of their husbands' college exploits, and when Saburi walks into the room looking unsuspectingly comfortable in his house clothes, their knowing smiles send him quickly into retreat. We find in their behavior the same kind of unapologetic cliquishness we have encountered often in the joking of the men, but this time it is Saburi who is excluded from the in-group and sent sulking from the scene. Herein lies the Lubitschian aspect of late-period Ozu, and even if such things never lead to any obvious infidelity or adultery as in Lubitsch, they permeate the details of the films far more thoroughly than may immediately be apparent.

Like Tatsuo Saitō, who is unsuccessful at lying to his wife Kurishima Sumiko in *What Did the Lady Forget?*, Ozu's men are all incapable of fooling their spouses, and their silly jokes are no exception. Women are always the ones who know how to control the rules of the game, and not only wives. Even young, unmarried women are shrewd at manipulating the rules to conscript men into their service. Anyone who recalls what Mariko Okada does in *Late Autumn* after having sternly rebuked Shin Saburi, Nobuo Nakamura, and Ryūji Kita will understand this clearly. Saying she knows a good place to eat, she artfully convinces the three aging men to follow her to an out-of-the-way sushi shop that happens to be run by her father, then proceeds to order a lavish feast before coolly presenting Kita with the bill. True to form, the men do not become angry upon realizing that she has taken them for a ride. They may be taken aback, but they simply overlook her audacious behavior. This time, it is a young woman assuming the Ozuesque absence of astonishment as a precondition for bold action—a young woman about the same age as the men's own children. Of course, the gag of a young woman administering punishment to middle-aged men who should know better than to preoccupy themselves with foolish games is nothing exclusive to *Late Autumn*, a film uniquely blessed by the presence of Mariko Okada, whose actual father was Tokihiko Okada, star of *Tokyo Chorus*, as already discussed. And how could anyone forget the way that Fujiko Yamamoto has also marvelously tricked Shin Saburi in *Equinox Flower*?

As Ozu's first color film, *Equinox Flower* forms an undeniably striking contrast with *Tokyo Twilight*, the black-and-white film that immediately preceded it. Its light-saturated mise-en-scène stands out against the darkness of the earlier film, transforming the space of Japanese living rooms into what seem like almost abstract environments. Still, there is a kind of underlying connection that joins the two films, a connection signaled by the way Ineko Arima as the despairing daughter who ultimately commits suicide in the earlier film foreshadows the role of the daughter in the later film, who cannot budge her father Shin Saburi out of his unyielding obstinacy and ends up leaving Tokyo. *Equinox Flower* retains something reminiscent of prewar Tokyo in the bewildered expression on the face of Chishū Ryū, for example, as the father of a daughter who has left home and moved in with a boyfriend and works as a bar hostess. Shin Saburi's home and the clothing worn by his wife Kinuyo Tanaka suggest that their life is comfortable, but the way these characters are modeled conveys a strong sense that the postwar has yet to begin in Ozu. If there is anything postwar about this film made in 1958, it can probably be encapsulated in the brazen prank that an Ozu newcomer plays on a veteran of the Ozu film— namely, the ruse that Fujiko Yamamoto pulls on Shin Saburi.

Shin Saburi often stays at a Kyoto inn run by Chieko Naniwa and Fujiko Yamamoto, a mother/daughter pair who exude an atmosphere of local color specific to the Kansai region of a kind that is quite rare in Ozu. The daughter will come to Saburi seeking advice, telling him she has run off after a fight with her mother. Her mother has been trying to foist some strange man on her, a wealthy heir to a wholesale pharmaceutical business in Osaka, despite the fact that there is someone else she likes. She paints an exaggerated picture of her mother's tyranny, reciting an assortment of complaints before asking—in Kyoto dialect— if he thinks it would be alright to ignore what she says. Relaxing his habitual inflexibility, he finds himself taking her side. Contrary to what he has been telling his own daughter, he tells her that it would not be wrong for her to marry someone of her own choosing, and he even declares that there is no need for her to listen to her mother as long as she "takes responsibility for herself." Fujiko Yamamoto seizes this moment to reveal that she has been lying, that the whole thing has been a "trick." Through her little act, she has succeeded in extracting an assertion that it is alright not to listen to one's parents, and from the very Saburi who has not even made an effort to accept his own daughter's marriage plans. Having used his own logic against him and cornered him into a position from which he can hardly continue to withhold his blessing, the young woman now abandons this father and hurries cheerfully off to report the good news by telephone, leaving him to pace the room alone in irritation. Another man has been punished.

The word *lie* spoken by Fujiko Yamamoto is basically a repetition of the word *lie* as used by Kuniko Miyake at the end of *An Autumn Afternoon*. And here again, it is not merely a woman who controls the rules of the game, but a young woman. Like Mariko Okada in *Late Autumn*, she is of basically the same generation as their daughters. As elsewhere, the absence of male astonishment is also a natural precondition for the trick that Yamamoto plots and executes. And having been so admirably taken in, Shin Saburi will be reduced to wearing basically the same mask of absent expression we see on Chishū Ryū in *An Autumn Afternoon*.

If we were to understand this series of punishments administered to men by women only from the perspective of the collapse of paternal authority, for example, we would end up closing our eyes to the rich details that give shape to the films of Ozu. What takes place in these films is not merely the dissolution of families or the forfeiture of paternal privilege. We are also dealing here with a Japanese variation on the "war of the sexes" comedy and its portrayals of the pitiless battles waged between men and women. It may be that the mask of the degree zero of expression worn by Chishū Ryū conceals this aspect from view. It is also true that the films of Ozu are not shaped by the memory of Lubitsch alone. The theme of the absence of astonishment, to which Ryū is so exceptionally well suited, is clearly even anti-Lubitschian. Its otherness to Lubitsch lies precisely in the darkness of connotation surrounding Tokyo as established in the thirties. In order to really see Ozu, it is necessary to maintain both of these aspects constantly in view. But this is not as easily accomplished as encountering the word *Ozuesque* leads many to think.

CONCLUSION

Pleasure and Cruelty

THE DIFFICULTY OF SEEING

Seeing is difficult. To see Ozu is especially difficult. Not, of course, because the films of Yasujirō Ozu present difficult ideas. For the most part, audiences are capable of grasping what this filmmaker probably intended when making any given film. In fact, nothing could be more distant from the culture of the Ozuesque than misunderstanding. The difficulty of seeing Ozu begins not with misunderstanding but with the fact that everything is displayed in such vivid outline. Here, only the image as such exists, and the image hides nothing behind it. Everything is exposed on the surface of the screen, and if the shot currently in front of us does hide anything, it is only other shots not currently in front of us. The shots that make up the whole of *Tokyo Story*, a film in which there is not a single drop of rain, hide the shots that do show rain in *Floating Weeds*. The fact that all of the shots in *Early Summer* exclude stairs hides the staircase shot that does appear at the end of *An Autumn Afternoon*. The absence of any shot depicting the wedding reception in *Late Spring* hides the shots that do show the bride and groom being photographed on their wedding day at the end of *Late Autumn*.

Beyond such kinds of concealment through relationships of presence and absence, there are also shots where presence hides presence. There is intertextual concealment, as when the shot of Kinuyo Tanaka tumbling down the stairs in *A Hen in the Wind* hides the shot of Vivian Leigh tumbling down the grand staircase in *Gone with the Wind,* or when the shot of Emiko Yagumo wearing a fedora in *That Night's Wife* hides the shot of Jean Seberg wearing a fedora in Godard's *Breathless*. Relationships narrational, thematic, and otherwise such as we have carefully examined throughout this book, along with the many shots we have considered, also play against one another at games of reciprocal concealment, whether paradigmatic or syntagmatic. Suffice it to say that shots in Ozu only hide other shots, or else they simply lay themselves bare under the radiating brightness of the midsummer sun. In looking at a shot, the eye either becomes suspended in midair or else slides sideways toward other shots. It is prohibited even the illusion of being able to wander toward the background. Walls of various kinds obstruct our sight line in the most material of ways. Herein lies the cruelty of Ozu. Is there anything as difficult as seeing a film in which we only ever arrive at the shot itself, no matter how far we go?

It is clear how the eye behaves when it encounters this kind of difficulty: it erases the image. To erase the image is of course also simultaneously to abandon the function of seeing. The eye that has given up on seeing turns to playing with things Ozuesque, just as if these things were the films themselves. And when this kind of play starts to slide toward things Japanese, it strays even farther from Yasujirō Ozu. Seemingly plausible propositions about things such as Ozu and haiku, Ozu and *mono no aware,* or Ozu and *yūgen* only start to guide inquiry once the eye that has abandoned the function of seeing gradually strays even from things Ozuesque toward things Japanese, drifting ever farther from the image. To the extent that our eyes are capable of apprehending the radiating sun rays that Ozu, the auteur of broad daylight, captured on the cinematic surface, they should also be capable of sensing just how distant this imagery is from such Japanese aesthetic categories, being imagery that bears no relation to dampness or shadows. The reason there is no end of people attempting to play with things "Ozuesque" through haiku or *mono no aware* or *yūgen* is because they make a choice: they choose to integrate themselves into stories that never at any given moment actually exist on the screen, rather than to open themselves to the images exposed there as the constantly renewing present. The nineteenth-century French novelist Gustave Flaubert used the term *idées reçues*—received ideas, or clichés—in describing the rigidity of thought and sensibility to which such choices lead. In the twentieth century, Roland Barthes gave the name *mythologies* to phenomena of much the same kind.

To the extent that seeing is a cultural behavior, the look cannot be free. For one thing, just being open does not make an eye alert at every instant, and even the good intention itself of trying to see better can often end up robbing the eye of the look. It is in this sense that *seeing* a film, and *seeing* Ozu in particular, is hard. And yet, people maintain faith that seeing is always possible, a faith within which the discourse surrounding cinema moves substantially toward fictionalization— fictionalization because the meanings a shot possesses in cinema are limitlessly open, however simple the composition or however much it might resemble some actual slice of reality. In spite of this, many are satisfied to read the meanings of shots in only very limited ways. Fearing that the narrational flow will leave them behind, they take the plurality of boundlessly interweaving and unraveling meanings and reduce them to impoverished patterns, then presume a configuration that centers those patterns, pushing everything else to the periphery. If they were not able to execute this kind of instantaneous mechanical operation, they would probably be incapable of keeping up with the narrative.

This mechanical recentering, which functions to place the viewer always in a position of knowing, is nothing less than a cultural affliction impacting the look. The eye confronts the screen under conditions that are far from uncultured. What takes place under these conditions is a confusion that takes leaving things unseen for seeing—a choice, in other words, to look at the screen through thinking instead of to think about what we see. The look submits to thought and, in conforming to its rigidity, audaciously recenters the image. Needless to say, the eye is neutralized in the process.

"THE SHOT OF THE VASE"

Think, for example, of a shot frequently cited by those who talk about Ozu: the static shot of a vase in a room at an inn in Kyoto where father and daughter Chishū Ryū and Setsuko Hara spend the night near the end of *Late Spring*. What issues does this much-discussed shot raise?

Recall what has happened at this point in the plot. Setsuko Hara has acquiesced to a marriage proposal arranged by her aunt Haruko Sugimura, having nodded her consent in sullen silence as if channeling a child from one of the early salaryman films. She has now come to Kyoto with her father on what will be their last trip before her wedding. She has also been led to believe that her father intends to take a new wife. She and her father are back at the inn settling into their futons after having spent the day sightseeing with his friend Masao Mishima and his own second wife, a couple whose marriage she once called "indecent." When she next turns off the light, the unshuttered *shōji* screens in the windows fill with the glow of the moon, a dramatic transformation of mise-en-scène from which everything then proceeds. Addressing her father lying at her side, the daughter says she has come to see that there is nothing "dirty" about Mishima's second wife, who is quite refined, and that she now regrets the things she said in the past. Her father tells her not to worry, that everything is fine. But when she then starts to use the moment to broach a new topic, the sound of her father's breathing quickly intervenes, signaling that he has drifted to sleep beside her. Hara falls silent and directs her gaze at the ceiling. Then, the vase makes its appearance. What then is at issue here?

The answer to this question reveals itself already in the way this insert shot so readily becomes the "shot of the vase" despite the fact that it contains many things that are not a vase. To the left of the shot, for example, what appears to be the wooden post of an alcove is distinctly visible in the dimness, and in the background, the *shōji* screens in the window are also conspicuous, bathed in a circular glow of white moonlight.

Of course, it is clearly for the sake of convenience that this is called only the "shot of the vase." The name is ultimately just a shorthand, something *provisional*. But this provisional nomenclature is by no means idle. It instantly sets a mechanical recentering into motion, neutralizing the look. At the same time, thought makes an abrupt shift to the cultural level. This is not merely to say that thought shifts from the vase itself to whatever secondary meanings the vase might represent. The reason people are compelled to talk about the "shot of the vase" and invoke cultural symbols despite the fact that no such thing as a "shot of the vase" is possible in cinema in the first place is above all because thought mobilizes clichéd fictions even before the eye has seen anything at all. Even a shot of a vase floating in a void would not be a "shot of a vase" but a shot of a vase floating in a void, but the shot that concerns us here is rich with a good deal of information other than a void. When people insist nonetheless on calling it the "shot of the vase," or on seeing it as the "shot of the vase," it means that both thought and the look have already fallen captive to a symbolic recentering. We have thus already entered the realm of cultural constraint. Or it can at least be said that metaphor has been activated.

We will return later to the details of just what gets swept from view here. First, consider a concrete example of the kind of play in which thought engages as it continuously betrays the look.

Paul Schrader discusses the "shot of the vase" as an example of the way Ozu depicts the "disparity" between man and nature. He says it does not "resolve" disparity but "freezes it into stasis," describing it as an elegant formal achievement paradoxically capable of realizing a higher-order unity.[1] The same Paul Schrader who would soon go on to direct *American Gigolo* (1980) explains that "the vase is stasis, a form which can accept deep, contradictory emotion and transform it into an expression of something unified, permanent, transcendent."[2] Also: "In Ozu, as in Zen, stasis evokes the moods of the *furyu* [sic] and particularly *mono no aware*. Man is again one with nature, although not without sadness."[3] Schrader follows this observation with a quote from Daisetsu Suzuki about the relationship in Zen between nature and self-transcendence, making clear the extent to which thought has subjugated his look.[4]

In his translator's afterword to the Japanese edition of Schrader's book, Kikuo Yamamoto observes that many Western commentators have demonstrated a strange fixation with this "shot of the vase," and that most see it quite literally as just that: a "shot of a vase."[5] It is not our objective here to pass judgment on the contradictions of people who, in talking about "emptiness," immediately impose a mechanical recentering that excludes precisely "emptiness" itself. But the way

---

1. Schrader, *Transcendental Style in Film*, 49.
2. Schrader, 49–51. Hasumi quotes Kikuo Yamamoto's somewhat differently worded Japanese translation.
3. Schrader, 49.
4. The quote: "In this respect Nature is divine. Its 'irrationality' transcends human doubts or ambiguities, and in submitting to it, or rather accepting it, we transcend ourselves." D. T. Suzuki, "The Role of Nature in Zen Buddhism," *Zen Buddhism* (Garden City, NY: Doubleday, 1956), 253–56.
5. Schrader, *Sei naru eiga—Ozu/Buresson/Doraiyā*. No page number cited in the original.

Yamamoto describes the "differences of interpretation among Western critics versus Japanese critics," differences he summarizes with the terms "center-oriented versus periphery-oriented," does have deep connections to the theme of constrained freedom as it applies to the culturally systematized look. The problem, in other words, is that people never fully see all the diverse elements that drift into their field of view.

According to Yamamoto, Japanese viewers such as he and I have a visual field that does not stop at the vase in the foreground of the shot—which is to say the center of the composition—but extends to the background and the silhouettes of the garden plants dancing on the *shōji* screens, a play of light and shadow that evokes for us the seasonal atmosphere of late spring and the temporal feeling of a moonlit night. This assertion raises at least two issues. The first is that Western critics seem to neglect the same shadows on *shōji* that the eyes of Ozu's fellow countrymen supposedly apprehend with ease—the theme, in other words, of the systemic constraint of the look. The other is that Japanese cinematic sensitivity neither privileges nor isolates the fixed "shot of the vase" in its "stasis" but accepts it as it is, positioned within the flow of cinematic continuity—the issue, in other words, of the narrational sequencing of shots. On this point, Yamamoto highlights the music that returns with "the shot of the vase"—the same theme we have already heard accompanying some shots of mountains and pagodas representative of Kyoto—to note that it bridges to the following sequence, to shots, in other words, of Chishū Ryū not in the room at the inn but with his friend Masao Mishima at Ryōanji temple. He further notes the fact that the images here of rocks in the temple's famous Zen garden resonate with the vase. Such kinds of narrational conditions surrounding the "shot of the vase" can hardly accommodate Noël Burch's and Donald Richie's emphasis on what we could call its "vacuum of meaning" aspect. Yamamoto continues: "This vase shot is therefore not a receptacle for the feelings of viewers. It expresses a certain feeling itself." The "shot of the vase" is not related to *fūryū* refinement or to *mono no aware* (the pathos of things). Like the "haiku poem," it "expresses seasonal atmosphere and feeling" through an "elegant and organic blending of time and space (an evening in late spring and an inn in Kyoto)."

What is at issue here is a problem of interpretation that begins with questions of what a look conditioned by cultural systems does and does not see. One cultural sphere privileges the vase and stasis and unfailingly discovers in these an excess of significance, while another cultural sphere prefers to make the vase nebulous, harmonizing it with things in its surroundings. In other words, looks cultivated in different contexts simply end up playing out the same kinds of discrepancies that would probably also occur in real-life situations, except in relation to a shot from a film. This sort of thing might be of a certain degree of interest from a comparative cultural studies perspective, but it is not particularly stimulating from a cinematic point of view. Still, even as a cinematic matter it is not entirely uninteresting that commentators like Paul Schrader and Donald Richie, critics who otherwise make such conscientious efforts to investigate the meaning of signs circulating in a foreign cultural sphere, nonetheless end up decoding meaning using language quite remote from that of the context in question. What this exposes, in other words, is the common paradox in which well-intentioned efforts to understand what one does not know end up constraining freedom even further.

In real-life situations, it is true that such forms of constraint do often afford very stimulating perspectives. In the realm of thought, even serious misinterpretations can be quite productive. But in cinema, things proceed somewhat differently. This is because, in cinema, the tendency to overread often corresponds to the poverty of what one has seen. People compensate for having left things unseen by thinking and talking about shots. In other words, there is a clear paradox here, where interpretation only arrives in the domain of cultural meaning by neglecting to fully disclose the meanings of a shot.

Of course, neither a vase nor a "shot of a vase" is in itself *fūryū* or *mono no aware* or any other thing, but that is not to say that the path to becoming *fūryū* or *mono no aware* is completely blocked. It is perfectly possible that within a particular cultural context a "shot of a vase" might take on certain iconographic or symbolic meanings. This is not necessarily true of the "shot of the vase" in *Late Spring*, but it is by no means impossible that a cinematic image representing a vase might also function to symbolize something other than a vase. In the right context and with the right rhetorical framing, it is not inconceivable that a shot whose primary meaning can be "vase" might also represent a mental state or some dramatic circumstance. Depending on how it is positioned within the narrational flow of a film, or how lighting, camera angle, composition, shot length, and other such resources are deployed, a shot in cinema is clearly capable of signifying things other than what it directly depicts. Simply put, we do possess the capacity to read *through* shots, toward meanings not visually present within them, and in fact, if the possibility of such kinds of symbolic signification were withheld, the narrational flow of a film would probably never succeed at telling a story. In the abstract, at least, it is probably not entirely misguided to read *fūryū* and *mono no aware* into the "shot of the vase." But in reality, such a reading is impossible from the perspective of iconographic convention, and it is also quite a stretch to understand things this way on the level of expressive intent. This is because the vase itself in the "shot of the vase" in *Late Spring* bears no trace of any function pointing toward iconographic symbolism or rhetorical types. By contrast, there is *unmistakable* symbolic significance in the shadows cast by tree branches on the *shōji* in the background, significance in the form of the various poetic associations that the conventional seasonal image of the moonlit night does tend to conjure, at least in Japanese settings. Given its precise placement within the narrational flow, and given its aesthetic sensitivity, which surpasses that of the artificial images of shadows on moonlit *shōji* that everyone knows from

Japanese studio cinematography, this shot should indeed be capable of expressing various kinds of psychological imagery related to things like stillness or solitude. This "shot of the vase" therefore takes on a substantial amount of signifying work on its own and is impossible to describe accurately by invoking a vacuum of meaning. There is no such thing in cinema as a shot with no meaning in itself. There is always meaning, as long as a shot can be articulated visually or narratively. Whether or not a shot contains deep and hidden significance is another matter, but there is always meaning on the surface. It would probably be best to say that there are meanings in the plural, but one way or the other, meaning must unmistakably be present. Observations about meaninglessness or vacuums of meaning simply reflect problems of interpretation on the cultural level.

BACKLIGHTING AND SILHOUETTES

Does this mean that *mono no aware* should be permitted as an option among the possible symbolic meanings of the "shot of the vase" in *Late Spring?* That is up to the viewer in principle, since images do not prohibit any associative reflection. And yet, this inevitably returns us to the problem that this freedom of association is equivalent to the lack of freedom in seeing. As already described, the "shot of the vase" is composed of many elements other than the vase, including the play of moonlight and shadows on the *shōji* and the wooden post of the alcove. It is true that these things are arranged around the vase, but they are no less clearly visible or concrete as images. Still, what is important here is not what can be seen, but *how* we can see it. Before it tempts us to make associations with *mono no aware,* this composition framing the corner of a room at an inn does something else: it fills us with a sense of unease. The backlighting in this shot is something quite unusual in Ozu, so much so that it makes us question whether it should exist here at all. Is it really possible that the auteur of broad daylight, the same

Ozu whose custom it was to display everything in vivid outline and drenched in sunshine, ever evoked the forms of things in silhouette as we see here? It is true that these objects contrasting with the moonlight are not completely dark despite being backlit. But since the camera frames the glowing *shōji* from the front, the vase is mostly shrouded in shadow, dull light bathing it only at its edge as it hovers on the screen. The unusual lighting reinforces the sense of anomaly lingering from the sudden change of mise-en-scène that already took place earlier in the scene when Setsuko Hara, dressed for bed in a cotton kimono, turned out the ceiling lamp, introducing a flood of surprisingly bright moonlight, and with it the impression of a whole new composition. The vase is bathed in this anomalous light when it presents itself next.

But the lighting is not the only anomalous thing about this scene. The room at the inn is itself also anomalous as a space. It is true that, in spite of its anomalies, the scene maintains a realism in the ordinary sense of the word. It smoothly integrates an atmosphere that we easily associate with the moments before bedtime and a space that we recognize as an inn. Still, there is something quite unusual here: namely, that this father and daughter, who at home sleep on separate levels, share a bedroom at the inn. Having left their first- and second-floor sanctuaries behind, they drift to sleep in this anomalous space with their pillows arranged side by side. From a thematic perspective, this moment is exceptionally unique.

Scenes of a parent and child sleeping side by side in a hotel are also to be found in *There Was a Father* and *Late Autumn*, but in those cases the parent and child are of the same sex: a father and son in the former and a mother and daughter in the latter. It is quite rare in Ozu to find a situation in which a parent and a child of the opposite sex sleep side by side. Considering that both father and daughter have abstained from marriage to this point in the film, it even seems that Ozu may have taken on a rather indecent theme in this film, the first in which he cast Setsuko Hara in a lead role. Sex is unmistakably exposed in this scene. While

Chishū Ryū's expression can hardly be said to plant any suggestion of indulgence in licentious thoughts, the same is not true of his daughter, who clearly conveys a trembling of sexual desire. There is careful avoidance here of any patently indecent details, of course, but the moistness of the daughter's eyes as she looks up at the ceiling and speaks to her father with her head resting on her pillow communicate a clear desire to prolong this moment lying beside him in the same bedroom (fig. 26). There is no way of knowing what Ozu himself was thinking as he captured the luster of these eyes glimmering in the dimness. But when Hara announces that Masao Mishima's second wife could not be farther from the unclean image she had imagined and expresses regret for having once called their marriage "dirty," we sense a palpable desire welling up in this daughter just coming to terms with the idea of her own father's remarriage, a desire to spread her very being through the darkness of the room and to envelop him in its atmosphere. Her eyes seem to radiate love as she gazes up from her futon.

The safe approach would be to think of this as filial love, which would also be the more *Ozuesque* interpretation. And yet, after watching in close-up how her whole being flows from her eyes and expands through the room toward her father, it is hard to suppress the feeling that what we have witnessed here is sex—sex most graphically exposed—all the more so because her expression does not withhold any channeled sentiment. She expects that her father will receive this boundless emanation as love. The relationship here is unmistakably sexual. And yet, from the neighboring futon, Chishū Ryū's breathing now indicates that he has already fallen asleep. There is a shot of his head resting on the pillow, backlit and filmed in profile, and then a shot of his daughter directing her gaze back into the rafters, having sensed her father's rejection. The fact that the *shot of the vase* presents itself at just this point in the sequence should not be overlooked. As already described, the vase is lit from behind, in contrast to Setsuko Hara, whose features are distinctly visible in the glow of the moonlight. Its

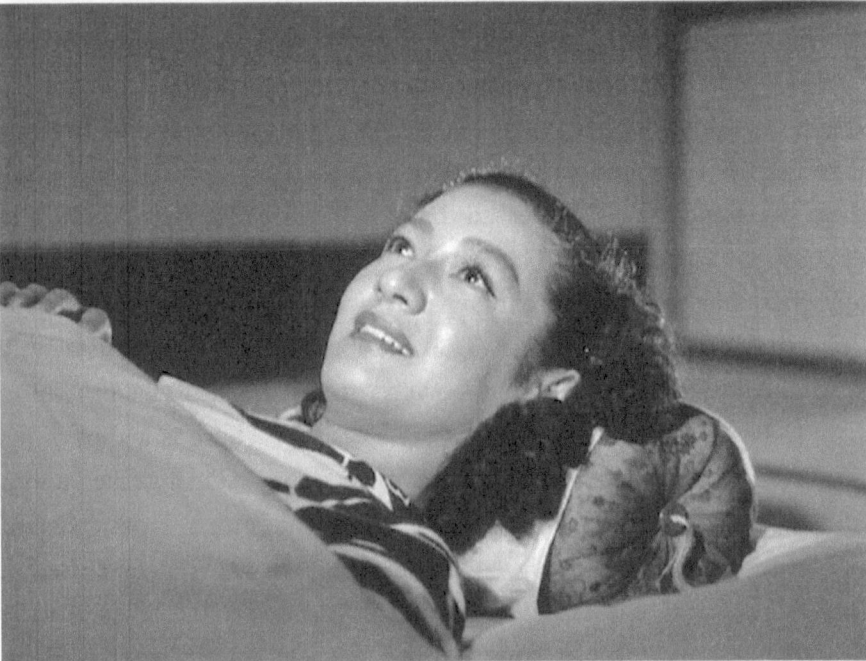

26. *Late Spring:* Bedtime on a moonlit night in Kyoto. (a) The backlit vase rhymes with the shadows on the *shōji* screens. (b) The contrast with the white glow of Setsuko Hara's face is exquisite.

silhouette is also accompanied by the sound of her father's light snoring. The exquisitely subtle technique of lighting and cinematography works to quite moving effect as it contrasts Hara's face, shimmering palely in the moonlight, with the silhouette of this inanimate object.

From the sequencing of shots, we can see the silhouette as taking on the role of emphasizing the daughter's resignation. What has blocked her tender expectations and barred her from coming any closer is not so much the sadness she feels at her father's rejection, but the cold formality of this expensive piece of decor, an object unlike anything in her own room at home and of a sort unlikely to reflect anything personal about its owner. At the same time, the fact that the "shot of the vase" is inserted twice can also be said to mark precisely the duration that elapses as sadness does begin to cloud the daughter's opened eyes. But what is more worthy of our attention is the resemblance between the sleeping father's profile and the vase, which are both pictured with backlighting, as well as the particular emphasis on the father's snoring during the shots of the vase. Like the costly decorative object in the alcove, the profile of Chishū Ryū's head poised motionlessly on a pillow beside his daughter is filmed against the bright background of the moonlit *shōji*. From this perspective, the choice to arrange the scene with him positioned on the futon closest to the window seems hardly coincidental. On the contrary, as a rhetorical matter, it can be understood as a clear necessity. The father's profile hovers, like the vase, in silhouette against the glow of the *shōji* in the background, and through this resemblance, takes on the materiality of the object in the alcove, as well as its cold formality as decor. In so doing, it resists the love radiating from the daughter and holds her expectations at bay. Various details establish the evidence for this equivalence of face and vase, including the contrast of light and dark between background and foreground, their shared motionlessness as silhouettes, and the similarity of camera angle. Ozu's talent resides in expressing things directly, in their superficiality, beyond psychology, as he does here in visually creating the conditions for a father to imitate a material object. The vase is the father himself. In fact, it even breathes, snoring softly in its alcove.

In light of all this, it should be clear just how unnatural it is to call the shot in question the "shot of the vase" and thus to isolate it from the narrational flow. The moonlight illuminating the *shōji* is also clearly significant. But its significance is not simply as an organic expression of seasonal sensibility such as described by Yamamoto. The bright moonlight on the *shōji* also encompasses the rhetorical function of hyperbole, exaggerating silhouettes produced by backlighting. The moonlit *shōji* exists as a detail that exceeds the function of representing the time and space we know as "night in late spring" or "an inn at night," a detail that gives visual expression to the situation of a father imitating a material object in order to refuse his daughter's sexual desire. The shot in question here is therefore something quite different from what Noël Burch calls the "pillow shot" after the *makurakotoba,* or "pillow word," of *waka* poetry. Despite the plurality of visual information it contains, this shot can hardly be said to perform a "decentering" function or to "suspend the diegetic flow." On the contrary, it can even be said to take on the function of actively articulating the "diegetic flow." It is a magnetic field full of signification, and from a thematic perspective, there is nothing in this shot that resembles a "semantic void" in any sense of the word.[6]

6. Burch defines pillow words as codified words in classical Japanese poetry that function as ambivalent pivots between lines of a poem. He sees a relationship between the rhetorical functions of pivot words in poetry and Ozu's "cut-away still life" transition shots, which he calls "pillow-shots." His analysis of how these shots function in Ozu is more nuanced than mere analogy with Japanese poetic convention, though he does treat the pillow-shot as existing external to the diegesis and cites its "de-centering" effect relative to the diegetic flow. Interestingly, Burch's observation that pillow-shots "lack a compositional centre" and "cannot correctly be described as merely shots of lamp-posts or of laundry hanging on the line" (162) echoes Hasumi's own polemic about nomenclature and the "shot of the vase," but Burch also goes on to describe the pillow-shot "at its purest" in the most cultural of terms: "a *satori*-like suspension of meaning," a "semantic void," a "paradigm of de-centering and meaninglessness, the filmic equivalent of the Zen-master's stick-blow answers to his disciples' earnest questions" (172). Hasumi does not provide a formal citation for his references to Burch.

But what a detour has been required just to arrive at this point! Should we really insist that it is this difficult to see a film?

THE PLEASURE OF LOOKING

It seems that people have been too content to underestimate the sexual side of Ozu, perhaps because of his efficiency of expression, which can easily be mistaken for quiet reserve. But sex is clearly a topic, and *Late Spring* can probably be said to address it in far more audacious form than even *A Hen in the Wind*.

Take, for example, the look Setsuko Hara casts at Chishū Ryū as the two pack their suitcases at the inn in Kyoto the day before their return to Tokyo, a look that seems to intercept her father's casual remark that their first stay in Kyoto in such a long time has really flown by. By this point in the film, she has accepted the idea that he will take another wife. But how can we not be flustered when she says, "marry if you want to, I just want to be by your side"? What flusters the viewer is not so much her words themselves ("please, let things stay as they are") but the way she looks into her father's eyes in speaking them. When she suddenly breaks her posture and touches the tatami floor with her left hand, her eyes moistening as she leans imploringly toward her father, it is sex that is laid bare, and with an immodesty that is almost hard to watch. The cruelty of Ozu lies in the precision of the shot sequence, which deprives viewers of the luxury of packaging such dangerous circumstances into cultural terms like "incest." The narrational flow is sent gliding by a meeting of looks as we fix with bated breath on this father awkwardly attempting to offer explanations to his daughter, this time unable to assimilate with the vase. In fact, it is probably fair to say that awkward explanation is itself the theme here, since the father's

---

See Noël Burch, *To the Distant Observer: Form and Meaning in the Japanese Cinema* (Berkeley: University of California Press, 1979; repr., Ann Arbor: University of Michigan Center for Japanese Studies, 2004), https://doi.org/10.3998/mpub.9362450.

words—about how marriage is the start of a new life, how there will be difficult times, but how in the end two people build happiness together—amount to little more than a recitation of clichés unlikely to persuade even the viewer. Psychologically speaking, these hardly seem like effective words for calming his daughter's inner distress. If they were adequate to the situation, there would have been no need for the "shot of the vase." Still, we breathe a sigh of relief at the moment when she does reluctantly nod, probably because it seems more appropriate in Ozu to believe that she has in fact been persuaded. And with this melancholic speech by a father who will soon give up his daughter even though doing so means sacrificing his own quality of life, we sense that we have somehow been carried through this scene unscathed.

But to understand what transpires between this father and daughter at the inn in Kyoto solely within the context of the father's sadness would be to adopt a framing no less abstract than the one that invokes terms like *fūryū* or *mono no aware* to summarize the "shot of the vase." After all, it is unmistakably the daughter whose sadness runs deepest here—both her emotional sadness and at the same time also her pain at being forced to suppress an unmanageable love for her father. The pain, in other words, of the death of desire. Her eyes plead for things probably beyond her conscious awareness. They are charged with a sensuality that seems almost ominous, as well as an unreasonable indignation at the clichés to which Chishū Ryū is hopelessly captive despite what are probably his good intentions—clichés like a father's sadness. Then, faced with the mechanical deflection of this father wielding the *myth* of happiness through marriage, these same eyes finally arrive at a kind of resignation. Marriage for this daughter means little more than accepting herself as a victim of cliché and resolving to play the part.

On the morning of her wedding, Setsuko Hara kneels in front of her father, dressed in bridal costume and lowering her head, both hands extended in front of her with the fingertips pressed against the tatami floor of her upstairs room. Nothing could be more moving than this moment. Looking slightly upward from under the *tsunokakushi* wedding headdress that hides the familiar sight of her forehead down to the eyebrows, she expresses her gratitude for all he has done for her over the years. With this ritualistic gesture, she seems to confess to her father that his clichés have finally won. *Late Spring* begins with women in a tearoom bowing to each other in formal salutation and progresses through an accumulation of polite bows and other gestures of greeting and farewell before arriving at this final display of gratitude by a bride parting with her father, but in spite of this progression, we find ourselves tempted to all but abandon our right to analyze the quality of emotion here. This is because, as a film, *Late Spring* meets cliché and its inevitable victory with little more than cruel ambiguity. The effect of this is difficult to articulate, but it feels as if we too become victims of cliché. Indeed, when Hara's friend Yumeji Tsukioka spontaneously hugs Chishū Ryū and kisses him on the forehead after learning that his talk of remarrying was actually just a ruse, we find ourselves at a loss as to whether his deception really merits such praise. The film remains silent about whether his daughter has faced her own marriage actually believing his lie or whether she has merely pretended to believe to sever herself from her father, bearing an even deeper burden of despair. What is clear to the viewer is only that this film—the first Ozu made with Hara—ends with her second-floor room left vacant. Little by little, a woman has been driven from her sanctuary into the outside. We have already demonstrated that this was a theme in *late-period* Ozu.

The standing mirror left behind on the vacant second floor reflects nothing, and like it, the films of Ozu also reflect nothing. Their shots merely relay the look back toward other shots. The films of Yasujirō Ozu do little more than entice us to look at other films by the same filmmaker, or else at any number of films by other filmmakers. The "shot of the vase" does not reflect *fūryū* or *mono no aware* but invites the look toward the sleeping profile of Chishū Ryū imitating a material object, much as his words do not lead thought toward what they mean but toward the structure of cliché to which the words themselves have surrendered. If things "Ozuesque" are nothing other than a privileged form of such cliché, perhaps Yasujirō Ozu himself, like Hara in *Late Spring,* was also among its victims.

In order to rescue Yasuijirō Ozu from the sway of tacit agreements known as things *Ozuesque,* we need to keep our eyes on the films. And as we slide from one shot to another, we need at all costs to avoid privileging any single one among them. The instant interpretation begins, we become powerless to prevent the annihilation of the eye. The task is to place ourselves at the focal points where one shot reflects with another shot, and there to experience our own effacement. The nothingness of *mu* is not something depicted in any film, but an experience lived in the act of looking and a pleasure—needless to say—that borders on cruelty.

Appendix: Interview with Yūharu Atsuta

SHIGUÉHIKO HASUMI: Nearly twenty years have passed since Ozu left us. It's probably been about ten years now since we started seeing a lot of revival screenings of the early-period films. In Japan, young people have been discovering the appeal of Ozu, and with films from the silent to the late period now screening abroad, people outside Japan have also begun to talk about Yasujirō Ozu's cinematic world. I would like to ask you to share your stories as Ozu's longtime cinematographer. You started working as his director of photography during the war. Ozu mostly worked at the Shōchiku Studio, but he made a handful of films at other studios and with other cinematographers: *The Munekata Sisters* at Shin Tōhō with Jōji Ohara, *Floating Weeds* at Daiei with Kazuo Miyagawa, and *The End of Summer* at Tōhō with Asakazu Nakai. At Shōchiku you were involved with almost all of the films, even before you became his director of photography, when you were working as an assistant cameraman. On the early films, Hideo Shigehara, informally known as "Mohara," was the cinematographer, and you were an assistant. . . .

YŪHARU ATSUTA: If we take things chronologically, I became a soldier in 1925.

HASUMI: Oh, that's the year you were conscripted, right?

ATSUTA: Yes. Ozu had been called up in 1924. Mohara and I were called up together in 1925. So Ozu was coming back to the Shōchiku Kamata lot (on what was then the outskirts of Tokyo) just as we were going into the military. There was a simultaneous welcome back and sending off party, and then Mohara and I left for two years of service. During our absence, Ozu was promoted to director and made *Sword of Penitence*. Mohara and I came back in I think 1927, at which point Mohara was assigned to Ozu and became his director of photography. I became Mohara's assistant and was around in that role for as long as Ozu and Mohara were a team. When Mohara later moved into sound, there were two or three films that Ozu made with other cinematographers, but after that I took over Ozu's camera.[1]

HASUMI: So you were not around at all during the making of *Sword of Penitence*?

ATSUTA: That's right. When *Sword* was made, Mohara and I had just been conscripted, so we weren't involved with that.

HASUMI: According to various sources, you've said—in the roundtable conversation transcribed in *Yasujirō Ozu: His Life and Work*, for example—that you took over the camerawork on *Brothers and Sisters of the Toda Family* halfway through the shoot. . . .

ATSUTA: That's right.

---

1. The three films were *Passing Fancy*, *A Mother Should Be Loved*, and *The Only Son*.

HASUMI: But looking at other sources . . .

ATSUTA: Sorry, it wasn't *Toda*. I shot *Toda* from the start. It was on *What Did the Lady Forget?* that I took over partway through.

HASUMI: Yes, that's what I wanted to clarify.

ATSUTA: Right, I shot the second half of *The Lady*.

HASUMI: By the way, your name is written differently in the credits for *Toda*. The second character in Yūharu is different, not the usual 雄春 but 雄治. It also appears that way in *There Was a Father*, the film you shot next. It was 雄春 in *What Did the Lady Forget?* and it starts appearing that way again in the postwar *Record of a Tenement Gentleman*. . . .

ATSUTA: Yes, that was because everyone was pronouncing my name with the Chinese instead of the Japanese reading—Yūshun instead of Yūharu—and saying it sounded like a name for a Buddhist monk. We were all born in the Meiji Period [1868–1912], you know. I used to tell everyone, I'm not a monk, it's Yū*haru*, and it's written with the same character as the *ji* in Meiji (明治).

HASUMI: Oh, so 雄治 (Yūharu) is your given name?

ATSUTA: Yes, and it's read Yū*haru*, but people get it wrong even on official documents. I say Yūharu and they write 雄春. So I just ended up going by 雄春. I think it's written like that in my family registry too.

HASUMI: Most of the filmographies I've seen only include 雄春. It's only recently that I first saw 雄治 included, on something put out by the National Film Center.

ATSUTA: The studio had a say in this. Under the old system, directors of photography . . . I mean, there were some real big shot directors. During the Kamata years, people regarded as master directors had as many as four assistant directors assigned to them. Other directors only had two. Cameramen, the ones who were assigned to the big directors, also had as many as four assistants. We didn't have those two extra regular crew members. The Ozu unit at the time consisted of Ozu and an assistant director whose name was . . . what was it? Negishi. Then Mohara as cameraman, and Kuribayashi who was just above me in seniority. Shooting together was the best. We worked together continuously, as a unit.

HASUMI: Shōchiku traditionally had a classing system for directors and actors and various other roles, right? Ranked groups, like first tier, second tier?

ATSUTA: Yes, yes, that's right.

HASUMI: So at first Ozu was in the second tier?

ATSUTA: You could say that. With respect to the big directors at the time, first there was Hōtei Nomura, then (Kiyohiko) Ushihara, (Yoshinobu) Ikeda, (Yasujirō) Shimazu. They were the big ones. Then there were the mid-level directors who debuted a little later, like (Tsutomu) Shigemune, (Jirō) Yoshino, (Torajirō) Saitō, (Tokuji) Ozawa. And then the Ozu unit was in the third tier. (Heinosuke) Gosho was in the same cohort with Ozu. Mikio Naruse came a little later, then Shirō Toyoda, Shigeyoshi Suzuki. That's as I recall. Then there were what you might call factions, even back then.

HASUMI: I'm sure [*laughs*].

ATSUTA: That's how it goes, isn't it? Even cameras—the cameramen assigned to the big shot director units all had dedicated camera equipment. We didn't have dedicated cameras, so we had to go around to other units and borrow theirs. Even the Ozu unit had to do that for a time.

Those of us who became cameramen at that time were what we called *"Mei/Daisei,"* people born in the Meiji and Taishō years [before 1927]. People born in Meiji in particular [1912 and earlier] were brought up in a relatively conservative educational environment. For example, if you were assigned to a cameraman as an assistant and worked with him over the years, he would acknowledge your service and say, "let's make you a cameraman." You would get your independence when the time came.

HASUMI: It was an apprentice system.

ATSUTA: Yes, an apprentice system [*laughs*]. But it depended on the cameraman. I was the first one assigned to Mohara. There were people junior to me who were assigned to other people and became cameramen in their own right before me. That was how things worked at the time. I used to joke and say, "it takes peach and chestnut trees three years to flower, persimmon trees eight years, Yūharu Atsuta fifteen years." It was fifteen years from the time that I started as an assistant cameraman to the time that I became a director of photography. In order to become a cameraman in your own right . . . there was an association of technicians. You had to be approved by the association, and then there would be a notice of promotion from the company saying, "we're making you a cameraman." A notice indicating the new salary saying, "you are appointed to so and so for this amount." Cameramen who came up through the studios at the time—Shōchiku, Nikkatsu, then Tōhō came later—were held in relatively high esteem. The people who worked for independent productions or in news films didn't have it quite so good.

I became a cameraman midway through *What Did the Lady Forget?* and then worked alongside Ozu continuously through the postwar years. He was really very strict about the picture.[2] As you know, he started out in cinematography himself, so he was accustomed to thinking about camera position. He transferred to the directing division later. Ozu and Mohara had started at Kamata a little before me and were friends from that time. They

---

2. Hasumi glosses *picture* as "composition."

had nicknames for each other: Otchan, Motchan. There was an area in the Koyasu neighborhood of Yokohama that was kind of like a little geisha district, and Ozu used to go there with Tora Saitō and various other rambunctious young guys and have a good time. He and Mohara got to know each other that way and ended up becoming a team and working together. Mohara also developed a feel for giving Ozu what he wanted. The low camera position was something that came from Ozu. He wanted low camera positions and disliked high-angle shots. High-angle shots were too easy. Almost every run-of-the-mill filmmaker used them, whether amateur or professional. Ozu really was not a fan. I got to know his preferences for camera position and composition while working in his unit, and of course observed these things even when Mohara was still the one behind the camera. Ozu would say, "that's no good, it should be like this and this." I got a feel for lots of these kinds of things. I also had the sense that Ozu would have liked to do his own camerawork.

HASUMI: *The Only Son* was Ozu's first talkie. The sound process on that film was the so-called "Mohara-style" system developed by Mohara, his cinematographer. Ozu continued making silent films until it was ready for use, keeping a promise to Mohara, but Shōchiku ended up adopting the Dobashi process instead, so Ozu also switched to that system from his next film *What Did the Lady Forget?*. This was the point at which you gained your independence as a cameraman?

ATSUTA: Mohara moved into sound recording with *The Only Son*. I still was not able to take over the camera at that point, so Shōjirō Sugimoto was assigned to the film. Sugimoto was a little different from Mohara. His attitude was, I'm the cameraman and I'm going to shoot things as I see fit. Well, things may have appeared to go well, but this did not sit right with Ozu. We filmed *The

Only Son at the old Kamata lot with a lot of night shoots, which was difficult. Kamata wasn't equipped for talkies. We would start shooting after the last train of the night because of the noise, but then the newspaper train would come through at 1:00 a.m. and we would have to stop and wait. Then it was hard work until the first passenger train of the morning. We moved to the newer Shōchiku facilities at Ōfuna for Ozu's second talkie *What Did the Lady Forget?*. Mohara went back behind the camera for that one, but partway through he was called up for the reserves, or maybe his mother passed away. Anyway, he asked me to substitute for him. Once I had taken over, he said, just do the second half. You can finish this one. So I ended up seeing *What Did the Lady Forget?* through on my own. After that Mohara went independent and worked with what was then the Shinkō Kinema company, and I became Ozu's cameraman.

HASUMI: Mohara was married to Chōko Iida, who played the role of the mother in *The Only Son*. When did he pass away?

ATSUTA: After the war. He went independent and did sound for Shinkō Kinema at their facilities in Ōizumi (Tokyo).

HASUMI: Which is now the Tōei production lot.

ATSUTA: Right. I don't know the whole trajectory, but he started his own company called Mohara Labs where he was doing both film processing and sound. He was still running a related business after the war when he died.

HASUMI: I'd like to ask you a somewhat unusual question. From the time that you became Ozu's cinematographer, did you ever shoot any rain scenes?

ATSUTA: Hmm, let me see. I don't think so now that you mention it. There was the rain scene in *Floating Weeds*.

HASUMI: The postwar version was shot at Daiei, so the cinematographer wasn't you but (Kazuo) Miyagawa.

ATSUTA: Right. I remember that in the earlier 1934 version, *A Story of Floating Weeds* [shot by Mohara], we had the lead actor (Takeshi) Sakamoto carry an umbrella to evoke the feeling of rain.

HASUMI: In *Floating Weeds*, there's a face-off in the rain between Machiko Kyō and Ganjirō [Nakamura], but I suspect that as someone who worked at Shōchiku continuously throughout your career you probably never shot a rain scene like that yourself. One reason I've wanted to meet you is to ask you just this question [*laughs*].

ATSUTA: You're right. There were never any rain scenes for as long as I was a cameraman.

HASUMI: Why do you think that was? The sets for the interiors of houses do usually feature umbrellas as props.

ATSUTA: That's true. Those umbrellas . . .

HASUMI: They're often hanging on the wall.

ATSUTA: This was something related to the set design as a whole. Hanging objects around the rooms was basically a way to create a humble atmosphere. Ozu was like that, unpretentious for the most part. I myself am also of the masses, if anything. Before the war, people in upper-class households tended to think it was low class to hang things around the room. It was looked down on. So hanging things around became really effective for creating the domestic setting, a sense of unpretentious simplicity. We did more scenes of working-class life in the earlier years. After the war, things changed and there were fewer of these. Anyway, that was the idea for hanging things around.

HASUMI: I see.

ATSUTA: One more thing: as you probably know, when I was still working alongside Mohara we would switch between 50 mm and 75 mm lenses, even from one shot to the next, but after I became a cameraman, it was all two-inch lenses . . . 50 mm. I would say to Ozu, "this is a little tight, I can't get everything in the frame, how about trying a 40 mm?" And he would say, "I hate the 40 mm, it makes it hard to maintain balance in the composition."

HASUMI: Because 40 mm is a wider lens?

ATSUTA: Yes, and that's true. A shortcoming of using wide lenses is that it's easy to lose the sense of perspective due to lens distortion. For example, if you're shooting with a 40 mm and have someone approach the camera, you end up with a scene where they're small in the long shot but transform suddenly into something big as they come close. Ozu often placed beer bottles or rice bowls on tables in the foreground of shots. If we used a wide lens for those compositions, the balance between the foreground objects and the characters in the scene behind them would be thrown off. That's why Ozu didn't like wide lenses, and I tried to avoid them as much as possible. We really only rarely used a 40 mm lens. We also mostly didn't use three-inch [75 mm] lenses either. Not to be humble, but I was fine just being the Ozu unit "camera attendant"—the "camera-*ban*," not the "cameraman." I often joked about this. I would just tell Ozu, "I know the drill." When I was still an assistant, there were times when I would just set something up, and if it was not what Ozu had in mind, he would come and say, "doesn't that seem wrong?" That helped me learn what he liked. When Mohara and I were working together with him, he would just say, "put it here," and that was that. I never asked Miyagawa or Nakai about what it was like for them to work with Ozu when he shot films at their studios, but I did hear that Ohara was quite defiant.

HASUMI: Is that right? Ohara who shot *The Munekata Sisters* at Shin Tōhō?

ATSUTA: Yes. Ohara, who was senior to me, once said to me, "hey, you shouldn't have to crouch so much with that Ozu 'low position.' You should shoot more level with the actors. Don't you think it's wrong to shoot so low?" I told him, "I'm just the camera attendant, the camera-*ban*." That was fine with me; I wasn't being humble. Ozu's compositions came with that position, what Ozu wanted to show and do, and my job was to put the camera there, in that position and get the shot, to show what Ozu wanted to show and do it the way he wanted. But there were places where things would be a little off along the edges of the frame, for example. Especially with the low shots, lines in the background could appear to curve as an effect of optical aberration. When this came up, I would talk to Ozu about how to fix it. With those low shots, it could be difficult to catch distortion just by looking through the viewfinder. It's hard to explain. I just got a feel for it. I was the only one. I would look through the lens and say, "it's distorting a little there." Then I would fine-tune to get a straight line, and we'd still have a slight curve. But there was always an angle. I would say, "the angle is a little too low here and this is happening with the background, so I'm going to fix it," and Ozu would say, "okay." Ozu would decide the framing and I would make it work. There were a lot of shots where I compensated for things. Lighting was crucial. I did all of that myself.

I wonder how it is for cinematographers now. Today it seems like lighting is all done by lighting people. But cinematographers also have to be able to think about how scene changes affect lighting design. It's difficult to recreate natural lighting, so there's a satisfaction in bringing your own lighting ideas close to something that feels natural. I designed the lighting this way for all kinds of scenes: realistic ones and stylized ones, or if we were shooting on location, scenes where I just had to capture something realistic in bright conditions. Ozu trusted me on this. But when it came to the composition, he took charge of everything.

HASUMI: There's a scene in *Early Summer* where the lighting on Chieko Higashiyama's face is a little out of the ordinary. Her daughter Setsuko Hara has decided to get married without consulting her family. Her parents are taken aback and go up to their room on the second floor. I recall that when Higashiyama kneels on her futon and worries aloud about her daughter, part of her face is obscured by a fairly heavy shadow.

ATSUTA: For Ozu, when I wanted to shoot something low key, for example, I would say, "this is a dark scene, so I think I'll shoot low key, alright?" And Ozu would say, "that doesn't quite work, let's do high key on her face." So I would make adjustments accordingly. Or he would say, "this isn't going to cut well," and I would adjust, even when it seemed a little unnatural. I probably made a mistake in this case.

HASUMI: Looking at that shot today, the shadow seems quite effective. I remember being struck by it, thinking that it was unusual to see shadows on a face in an Ozu film.

ATSUTA: I would leave a little shadow sometimes if it wasn't covering the whole face, if it was just on the side and it seemed unnatural not to have any shadow at all. One more thing Ozu told me was not to get too fancy. "You can try elaborate techniques down the road, but for now, this is Shōchiku and we're shooting bright. That's safest." Personally, I liked low-key lighting.

My biggest regret is *Tokyo Story*. We lost the original negative in a lab fire. What exists today is only a positive dupe that has been used to strike prints. The lab over-exposed the dupe and it's pretty flat and rough in places. When we shot *Tokyo Story*, we thought it would probably be our last black-and-white picture and I really poured my heart and soul into the work. I wanted to evoke the summer heat, for example. When we started out, I asked Ozu how many months were supposed to elapse over the course of the story. He told me, "It takes place from spring to summer." I asked if it was okay not to dwell on the change of seasons, and he said, "that's fine." That was it. When shooting for summer, you overexpose exteriors and underexpose interiors. That conveys a sense of heat. But doing this makes it hard to see the actors' faces in interior scenes. This was something we were aware of. Ozu gave his approval. There's a scene in the doctor's house where four people are talking, and there's a long shot showing all of their faces. The lab forced the exposure when they printed it, and it looks pretty rough as a result.

HASUMI: I'm interested to hear that you asked about the seasons during which *Tokyo Story* takes place. The postwar films often take place from spring to summer or fall, right?

ATSUTA: Yes.

HASUMI: Of course, Tokyo has a rainy season in the summer, but you wouldn't know that from the films [*laughs*].

ATSUTA: That's right. After the war, Ozu came back from Singapore and said, let's do something interesting. First we made *Record of a Tenement Gentleman,* and he was very pleased with that. After that it was *A Hen in the Wind*. Ryōsuke Saitō, who wrote the script with Ozu, came to me and said, "this one's a little strange, quite dark." When I read it, I saw what he meant and wondered why we were doing it. Ultimately it wasn't a success. Then we did *Late Spring*. From *Late Spring* onward the scripts were written with a seasonal concept, and we would do a lot of location scouting in the summers. There are probably a lot of summer scenes because we were location scouting a lot during the summer. The seasonal imagery was more varied in the silent period.

HASUMI: Ozu still wasn't a first-tier director at the time, right? He must have been going out and making films on a tight schedule, shooting in the winter, even in snow, for New Year holiday releases.

ATSUTA: Yes, it snowed when we were shooting on location for *A Mother Should Be Loved*.

HASUMI: We can see that in the scene where the two boys walk to school. There's a parked car, and it's snowing.

ATSUTA: That was on Reinanzaka Street in Akasaka, next to the US Embassy.

HASUMI: So the snow was a coincidence?

ATSUTA: Yes, well, it snowed so we made it a snow scene.

HASUMI: For a Japanese film director, Ozu really didn't use rain or snow much, did he? Though *Tokyo Twilight* does take place in the winter, and we see snow falling outside through the window in that film. . . .

ATSUTA: Rain can be hard to photograph. In the past, rain effects were also a little cheap.

HASUMI: The watering can? [*Laughs.*]

ATSUTA: Ozu hated cheap effects.

HASUMI: That's why when it rains in *Floating Weeds* it really rains?

ATSUTA: Right, a downpour. These days they do artificial rain pretty convincingly. But even so, rain is hard to shoot. It's difficult to modulate depth of field. Then angles, point of view, compositional balance all present challenges. It's hard to get a steady image. I would probably use backlight for rain, lighting from the back at reduced brightness. You have to be careful about not letting the foreground get too dark. But if you don't do this, movement doesn't stand out.

HASUMI: When filmmakers outside of Japan talk about Ozu, they tend to dwell on all sorts of things that *aren't* there in the films.

There's no this, no that. No camera movement, hardly any crane shots. But I've hardly ever heard anyone mention the lack of rain. I think about this though, and I think there are various reasons for it. In the beginning, Ozu had to shoot year-round in all the seasons. Weather even intrudes as an element of chance, like the snow we already mentioned. But Ozu had a hit with *There Was a Father*. That film really drew crowds and made him a first-tier director, and from that point on he had an easier schedule. He would basically write scripts from spring to summer, go location hunting in the summer, and then shoot in good weather from summer to fall.

ATSUTA: Yes, that's how it was.

HASUMI: In other words, once he became a first-tier director, it seems like there was no more room for rain [*laughs*].

ATSUTA: That's probably right. Also . . . how to put this? He hated things that looked cheap. Shōchiku was a pretty miserly place, from the early days. Even with rain, you couldn't get a good effect without spending some money. He would say, if they're not spending, there's no point in doing it. He would give up on it.

HASUMI: He shot that dramatic downpour in *Floating Weeds* at Daiei. Do you think he tried to do things a little differently when working at different studios?

ATSUTA: Probably so. Then there's *The Munekata Sisters,* which he shot at Shin Tōhō, and which from our perspective really didn't have much of Ozu in it, none of the Ozu touch. We had the impression he was holding back there.

HASUMI: It also seems like that story material was a little out of the ordinary.

ATSUTA: Anyway, the crew on the Ozu unit were treated pretty well in the lower-level roles. After I rose to the top I would often get yelled at, but my assistants, for example, would be spared even if they made mistakes. I was the one who would take the heat: "You're undisciplined. Get it together!"

Going back to what we were saying about rain as something missing from Ozu: if he was going to do it, he was going to do it right. Where money was on the line, it was fine if the result was good, but if not, there was no point. This was a concern, and there were times when he would just decide against doing things. Those kinds of things wouldn't even make it into the script. Recreating rainfall on the set also took time. Ozu preferred to focus on the performances. Time is precious, you know.

HASUMI: Yes, well, I was wondering if I hadn't missed something myself and thought I would ask if you if you'd ever filmed a rain scene with Ozu, but it seems the answer is no after all.

ATSUTA: You're right. If I did shoot something like that, it would have been relatively early on. I don't think I did.

HASUMI: The fact that there's no rain is actually quite interesting. There are the technical costs, but I wonder if Ozu also didn't want rain for narrative reasons. If he just preferred clear, hot weather over humidity and gloom.

ATSUTA: One more thing. It can be difficult to keep subjects in focus in the rain. The focus tends to be a little off and the picture loses clarity. Action in particular doesn't come out very well in the rain with low shots.

HASUMI: I see, so this has something to do with Ozu's low camera position?

ATSUTA: I feel like it must be related.

HASUMI: People also say that there are hardly any high-angle shots in Ozu, but there's one in *Early Spring*, for example, looking down from the office building in Marunouchi at people arriving from Tokyo Station. Then there's the moment in *Early Summer* when Shūji Sano says to Setsuko Hara, "Tokyo's not so bad, have a look," and the next shot shows the street outside from above.

ATSUTA: With a high-angle shot, the camera points down, but here, for example, we wanted to shoot without tilting too much, so we went up to the second and third and fourth floors of the building one by one and looked through the camera trying to find a position from which we could keep it as close to level as possible. Ozu decided the third floor was best, so we put the camera there. Shooting on location made it challenging to find the right place for the camera. Anyway, those shots might look like high-angle shots, but they're not. The lens isn't pointing down.

HASUMI: I see.

ATSUTA: In instances like this I might ask if we didn't need some foreground, and he would say, "okay, let's change the position." Ozu would often talk casually with us about these things. He would say, "I don't like looking down on people. High-angle shots look down on people. It's best to keep the camera level." When I was still an assistant, Ozu said to me: "Someday foreigners will understand my pictures. I'm not kidding. I make pictures on the inside of everyday life in Japan. So even 'hairy Westerners' (*ketō*) will be able to look at them and understand that this is what life was like in Japan. Even if everyone says that if foreigners saw my pictures they would ignore them."

HASUMI: They've finally understood them now, as Ozu predicted.

ATSUTA: Yes, looking back now, I find this amazing.

HASUMI: In the opening scene of *Dragnet Girl* there's a high-angle shot that's so dramatic you can't even see the horizon.

ATSUTA: Yes, we did some of that during the silent period.

HASUMI: There are high-angle shots and pans. What about crane shots? I've heard *Early Summer* was the only time you used them?

ATSUTA: There, Ozu couldn't watch the composition through the viewfinder the way he always wanted to, even when there was camera movement. A crane takes several people to operate, and there's no space for the director to get in and look. You could do any number of takes, and things would still be out of balance. Camera movement tended not to go very well. We spent three days on those crane shots before we got them to where they were okay. He was not happy about that.

HASUMI: You're talking about the scene in the dunes in *Early Summer*?

ATSUTA: Yes, with Setsuko Hara and Kuniko Miyake.

HASUMI: The crane shot there seems to move into the scene a little and rise upward.

ATSUTA: Yes, that was the only time we used a crane, on *Early Summer*. We had to put down reinforcements so the crane wouldn't shift in the sand. The camera moves straight inward and rises slowly. But even with the crane, it wasn't what you would call a high-angle shot.

Even in the silent period we didn't use cranes. Cranes came into use more in the postwar years. We didn't have that kind of equipment before. The studio didn't have an appreciation for the technical aspects of cinematography for the most part, so we were always relatively behind on advances in technology. That changed quickly after the war.

HASUMI: But with crane shooting, I think of Kenji Mizoguchi, at least.

ATSUTA: Oh yes, you're right.

HASUMI: In Mizoguchi, the crane moves in really very elaborate ways, and the shooting angle with it. I wonder what Ozu thought of this. Did he ever say anything about it?

ATSUTA: No, I don't think so. I neglected to ask him, even though he did a public exchange with Mizoguchi about acting. When it came to other people's films, he tended only to talk to me about what he thought were the good parts. I mostly didn't hear him say things like, this was bad, or this was clumsy. It didn't matter who the director was. He didn't bad-mouth other people's films.

HASUMI: Changing the topic, I'd like to ask about when you were all in Singapore at the end of the war. The idea that Ozu mostly spent this time playing tennis and watching American movies has become a kind of legend for some of us [*laughs*].

ATSUTA: It's true.

HASUMI: I've heard that he even watched Orson Welles's *Citizen Kane* during this time. Did you watch it with him?

ATSUTA: I did, and that's another interesting story. The Ozu unit had gone over there to shoot a picture that was to be called *Harukanari fubo no kuni* (*The Faraway Country of My Parents*). Before that, Shōchiku hadn't been making many war pictures, and the military took notice. Tōhō had made *The War at Sea from Hawai'i to Malaya* (*Hawai Marē oki kaisen*, 1942), for example. Film distribution was basically controlled by the military at the time. Film projects would come in. It was a regulated system, and Shōchiku was not performing well. So we were told to focus a little more on military films. (Keisuke) Kinoshita made *Army* (*Rikugun*, 1944). (Kōzaburō) Yoshimura made *Legend of the Tank Commander Nishizumi* (*Nishizumi Senshachō-den*, 1940). Yasushi Sasaki made several in between those. This helped Shōchiku's image a little, and at that point the studio asked Ozu to make a war documentary on orders from the military. The film was *Faraway Country*. So he was put on military contract and sent off to scout locations.

HASUMI: Did he actually intend to make the film?

ATSUTA: He did. And then, well, the reason he was granted some accommodations by the military is because there were some Ozu fans among the commissioned officers in the news division. So things went smoothly from there. It was decided that (Shūji) Sano and (Chishū) Ryū would be part of the film, and because they were all men there was no problem sending them on location. It was a unit. There was discussion in advance about the script, and then Ozu went ahead to Singapore with Ryōsuke Saitō and Kōsaku Akiyama, who was the assistant director and producer. They went ahead and I departed about ten days after them. Once there, we became attached to the news division of the Southern Command Headquarters. But as we were preparing the film, the war situation was worsening. We were told to put the documentary on hold and make another film in the meantime, about Chandra Bose's independent Indian National Army (INA) forces.

HASUMI: This was something you learned after you had arrived?

ATSUTA: Yes. It was decided at a meeting of the heads of the Hikari Kikan, which was a military Special Services Organization [Tokumu Kikan] charged with Indian affairs. They told us to make the film, and then the head of the news division met with Ozu and Saitō and Chandra Bose and had discussions about producing a propaganda film on the INA. A script was to be written quickly. The project was given the working title *Derī e, Derī e* [To Delhi, to Delhi].

HASUMI: [*Laughs.*]

ATSUTA: Anyway, the war situation, the situation on the Burma side, grew progressively worse to the point that a film started to seem out of the question. Also, I had only brought a camera for silent shooting when I came ahead to Singapore. I didn't have any crew. I got some young people together on site and shot some scenes of military exercises at INA barracks and of soldier combat drills, but the actual soldiers were growing anxious. Things were going badly on the front. We decided to call off the film and cancel the dispatch of the crew who were standing by back in Tokyo. But telegrams were not being delivered right away at the time. Military telegrams were delivered immediately, but a private message from a civilian like me would get opened and read along the way and arrive delayed. The crew were dispatched to Singapore before my telegram arrived.

HASUMI: Oh!

ATSUTA: When we received the news that the secondary Ozu unit crew had been sent from Tokyo, I was really at a loss. With the war situation as it was, their ship might have been attacked at sea. Ozu was really worried and called me in. I was quite frightened at that moment. His eyes were all red and he really let me have it. "It's so dangerous for the rest of the crew to be coming here with the fighting everywhere. Didn't I call off the film? Why are they coming?" I told him I didn't want to make excuses, but I had sent a telegram telling them not to come.

HASUMI: And the telegram arrived with a delay.

ATSUTA: Yes. The crew did then arrive safely in Singapore, having risked their lives. They were in the last convoy. Once they had come all that way, it seemed wrong to tell them to just play around. So we temporarily started shooting again, using British POWs as extras. We shot peaceful scenes, like scenery of the urban patrol, officers swimming in a pool, rest time. But shortly after we finished this, the war conditions became even worse, and we were no longer able to film at all. Then a local emergency draft was announced. Ozu, Saitō, Akiyama, and I were all secondary, but the rest of the Ozu unit crew got draft orders and were enlisted in the Southern Command. They were all killed. And then the war ended.

HASUMI: On the films you watched in Singapore, were they confiscated American films, or did you watch them in a regular movie theater?

ATSUTA: Oh yes, I changed the subject. They were enemy films that came in. And the guy who impounded them would melt them down to make paint for airplanes or something.

HASUMI: Oh!

ATSUTA: The flying corps would come to do pickups.

HASUMI: And melt down the films for war.

ATSUTA: Yes. And I told the guy they didn't have to use the films for paint. Fortunately, there was a film section in the news division that we could use as a screening room. It was in the Cathay Building, and I was in charge of it!

HASUMI: Well!

ATSUTA: [*Laughs.*] The only problem was that patrols in the news division would come around while we were watching films. They would say, "what are you doing?" And we would say, "we're inspecting the projector," or something along those lines. That was how we were able to watch them. There was a lot in there, in confiscation—*Citizen Kane, Fantasia, Dumbo, Gone with the Wind*. There were even film books. Magazines. Ozu loved those. He would read through them and make lists of films he wanted to screen. When it rained, he would ask if we had this or that film and say to bring everything out. Finally, he came and said, "show me *Gone with the Wind*." We did that one in secret. There were projectionists who didn't want to do that one, because it was long. We didn't show that during the day. People came at night. It was also easier to keep it to one or two hours, so we ended up skipping some reels.

HASUMI: Oh! [*Laughs.*]

ATSUTA: The first thing we skipped was the opening music since it was in the first reel.

HASUMI: Were you running the screenings, or was there a projectionist?

ATSUTA: There was a local operator. Just a facility overseer. He wanted to show us an anti-Japanese propaganda film. It was quite something. I wondered when such a thing was put together. There was an insert shot of the emperor. Anti-Japanese films were really quite something.

HASUMI: You've often talked about how you were really impressed by Orson Welles. Was Welles already known in Japan by this point? His name?

ATSUTA: Yes, he was known. People were talking about *Citizen Kane*, but it hadn't come to Japan yet. Ozu wanted to see it firsthand and we happened to have the opportunity at this point in time. Also because Gregg Toland was the cameraman.

HASUMI: Known for pan-focus.

ATSUTA: Yes, so I was already quite looking forward to this one. We had to go to the news division in the mornings for roll call, but after that I would go to the screening room, since I was already there, or else go for walks in town. That's how I spent my days. Mostly watching movies. But Ozu did more movie watching. *Citizen Kane* . . . what were some others?

HASUMI: Wyler?

ATSUTA: We had Wyler too. There was *The Letter* (1940). Ozu really liked that one and watched it more than once. He would talk about how he liked the last scene. Then King Vidor. What was it? *The Grapes of Wrath* (1940)?

HASUMI: *The Grapes of Wrath* was Ford.

ATSUTA: Right. John Ford. Anyway, I didn't know English very well, but the one I understood the most was *Waterloo Bridge*

(1940). A local had told us that there was a film that was really popular in Singapore and Java. When we asked what it was . . .

HASUMI: *Waterloo Bridge?* [*Laughs.*]

ATSUTA: *Waterloo Bridge.* I said, let's screen it. What I really liked about that one was (Joseph) Ruttenberg's camerawork. It was an Eastman Kodak [Ektachrome] print, and the image was very good. I was really impressed by the scene where they put out all the candles shot by shot. The half-tones there were wonderful.

HASUMI: The camerawork in the underground air-raid shelter was great, in the darkness.

ATSUTA: Yes, that was great. I rewatched it recently on television. It moves back and forth quite a bit. But anyone can follow it.

HASUMI: Even if you don't understand English, it's easy to understand that these are flashbacks, right?

ATSUTA: Yes.

HASUMI: Going back to Ozu, there aren't a lot of flashbacks in his films, are there? The films tend to progress forward in time, from the beginning straight to the end. But there are also temporal leaps in the middle.

ATSUTA: Yes, that's right.

HASUMI: I still don't know how those leaps don't seem unnatural. In *Early Summer,* for example, there's a son who didn't return from the war. Chieko Higashiyama had two sons, but it's actually only Chishū Ryū who's alive. She keeps hoping the other son will return. Her husband says she listens to *Missing Persons Hour* every day on the radio. At this moment, she turns her head and looks off to the side. Ichirō Sugai, her husband, is also looking in this direction. Then, the next shot . . .

ATSUTA: Isn't it of a barley field?

HASUMI: No. It's May, and the next shot shows *koinobori* carp streamers swaying in the breeze.

ATSUTA: Oh, that's right.

HASUMI: It's hard to know from watching this whether those carp streamers are something the husband and wife are looking at. Is this what they're looking at, or have we jumped forward in time to a different day? I don't know.

ATSUTA: I think this has to do with the fact that Ozu mostly didn't use fade ins and fade outs, so when you suddenly get an image like that, it seems subjective. So thinking of this as whether they were or weren't looking at it, I think, yes, the carp streamers show the passage of time but are at the same time also on some level an expression of the couple's recollection of their lost son.

HASUMI: The passage of time, right? Not what they are looking at.

ATSUTA: With the passage of time, it can be a real problem if you lose the sense of it. On this point, Ozu's editor (Yoshiyasu) Hamamura was very strict in editing sequences of scenery, sequences that expressed the passing of time. He would use the storyboard and count the feet of film down to the frame. One shot equaled basically seven feet of film. Sometimes he would add or cut a little, I think usually no more than about four or five frames. But as you know, even one second can be long, like in commercials that may be only fifteen seconds total.

For example, Ozu didn't like filming scenery, of Atami, say, and then superimposing a title saying, "Atami." He thought that was silly. So how are you supposed to show that you're in Atami? It's more difficult, but Ozu would shoot just one isolated part to represent the scenery of Atami.

HASUMI: Right, not the whole landscape.

ATSUTA: This kind of approach gave us what is pictorially unique about Ozu. As you know, he didn't like camera movement or pans. With a pan, the image flows by and you lose the composition.

Other directors do things like cut from pans to close-ups as a way of disrupting balance in the tempo for effect. When I would shoot films with other directors, if we had a scene with someone sitting and then standing up, they would tell me to tilt up and follow the motion. The motion might actually be calm, but to follow it with the camera, you have to tilt fast. The camera has to tilt fast. It's the camera that moves fast. And then you ruin the tempo of the performance. So pans can be very difficult. I find them hard. Even when I was working with other units, I mostly didn't use them when I didn't have to. When there was camera movement with Ozu, we had to keep the frame steady. He was strict about not wanting a lot of shifting up and down or side to side, which meant a lot of hard work. When I was still an assistant, having to do a dolly shot in or out could bring me to tears. We had to match the number of steps. Everything would seem fine, but then we would do the take over and over again. Moving the camera inward went fairly well, but pulling back out was a problem. We weren't able to put down tracks. The camera was supposed to move in a straight line, but of course it wasn't going to be perfect.

HASUMI: There's a famous story about Ozu telling you to practice with a baby carriage?

ATSUTA: Yes, he said that to me. "Hey, I'll buy you a baby carriage." As a result, I became good at pushing babies. I could put my own grandchild to sleep with the baby carriage [*laughs*]. I told all this to Ozu. "It's thanks to you that I know how to push babies." We all had a laugh.

HASUMI: The last shot of *Early Summer* is a tracking shot in Yamato. We see a mountain behind the village. The camera moves slowly across the scenery. Was this camera movement in a straight line, or is there a bit of a curve?

ATSUTA: That was a lateral shot, but we were in the barley fields and had to follow the row, so the movement was in a straight line but at a bit of an angle.

HASUMI: That makes sense.

ATSUTA: That's why things on the left side of the screen look a little small and things on the right side get bigger.

HASUMI: Because we're approaching at an angle?

ATSUTA: Right. The field was at an angle. If you kept going, there was a farmhouse with an impressive roof. We were moving the camera toward the farmhouse.

HASUMI: The individual ears of barley are in focus. It's impressive. The effort you put into the shot shows.

ATSUTA: We spent a whole day on that. It turned out that there was a flaw in the negative at a key point. Hamamura cut and repaired it expertly, but when we looked at the rushes, Ozu said, "Hama, from what I can tell, there's a strange cut in the middle of the shot. It skips. What's going on?" Hamamura explained that there was a flaw on one frame that he had cut out. This was a really small detail. We all said to him, the actors and everyone, "it's okay if it's not perfect." We were always told, "it's okay if it's not perfect, just bring your passion to everything, give it your all." Even if an actor was not so great, no one said so. Even people who were not so great could work hard, and because they worked hard, people would say, "oh, they're really good!" The ones we gave up on were the ones who were half-hearted and not serious. We were always told: "There's no good or bad in work. If you're enthusiastic, your enthusiasm will come through—radiant energy. If you have that, you're good."

When something wasn't going so well, I would look through the viewfinder. If there was an actor who was having a hard time, for example. We might be rehearsing the same shot over and over again and get to a point where it was one time too many. I got a sense for what Ozu needed here. He would say, "Ready?" And when we were at that point, I would say, "Just a minute, I have to fix the lighting." So then it would be, "Oh, it's the cameraman's fault that we have to do it again." I always felt I had to work with an understanding of how the director was feeling. Working this way made rehearsals as peaceful as the shoots themselves. People would say that coming onto the Ozu unit set was like walking into a wake, it was so calm. But that wasn't really the case. The issue is that other units were loud. In other units, if something wasn't going well in rehearsal, they would make all kinds of noise.

HASUMI: Shouting?

ATSUTA: All around. "What's that about? Stop that, now!" Or, "That's even worse than before!" We were never allowed to say such things to crew in the Ozu unit. With us, it was always as if we were actually shooting, even during rehearsal. "Lights, camera, action!"

HASUMI: This is a completely different topic, but earlier we talked about how you didn't film rain scenes. With a few exceptions, you also didn't film stairs, right?

ATSUTA: Hmm, stairs. Are you thinking of *A Hen in the Wind*?

HASUMI: There's *A Hen in the Wind*, and then in Ozu's last film *An Autumn Afternoon* there's a very prominent staircase at the end.

ATSUTA: *An Autumn Afternoon*?

HASUMI: Yes, in the scene with the father after his daughter has left her room on the second floor.

ATSUTA: You're right, there's a staircase there.

HASUMI: Elsewhere we see people who look like they're about to climb stairs, but we don't see the stairs themselves. Did those staircases actually exist on the sets? For example, in *Early Summer* there's the elderly couple who live on the second floor. We see them from the hallway as they're about to climb the stairs, but the stairs aren't pictured at all. Were there stairs on the set in the places where we don't see them?

ATSUTA: Yes, those sets did have stairs. We measured the time it took to go up and down and would use that to determine where to cut. Then, upstairs, we would make some use of the empty scene.

HASUMI: Right, before the character enters.

ATSUTA: I didn't see this much with other directors. I think this was probably something unique to Ozu.

HASUMI: Yes, it feels like the time it should take to climb the stairs. I don't know if it's actually how long it took, but there's a certain interval when watching a film. With respect to the second-floor shots that start with empty scenery, how many frames was the interval in general?

ATSUTA: Around eight to ten frames. In any case, different actors had different ways of walking, regardless of how Ozu rehearsed them. The architectural style of hallways and stairs could also reflect the relative wealth or class of a household. Ozu liked to use hallways and stairs as a means of bringing out the atmosphere of everyday, ordinary homes. As for me, I was not very good at shooting Western-style rooms.

HASUMI: Is that why Ohara stepped in on *The Munekata Sisters*, where the architecture is a little Western-influenced?

ATSUTA: That's right.

HASUMI: In *A Hen in the Wind*, where Kinuyo Tanaka gets shoved down the stairs, you filmed that from both above and below, high angle and low angle. Did you feel like what you were doing with that scene was different from how you usually approached scenes with Ozu?

ATSUTA: Yes, we covered that from above.

HASUMI: Right.

ATSUTA: We shot that with a female acrobat from the Asakusa theater district.

HASUMI: Is that right?

ATSUTA: Yes, and we joked about the scene in *Gone with the Wind* where Vivian Leigh falls down the stairs, about whether that was a stunt double. We had seen that in Singapore.

HASUMI: Were there other times you used a stunt double, apart from the scene on the stairs?

ATSUTA: No, I don't think so.

HASUMI: What about other stand-ins? Did you ever use them in the Ozu unit?

ATSUTA: For stand-ins we usually used the assistant director or the camera assistants. For example, if we had someone who was right around the size of Jun Usami, we would have him sit to decide on the framing and adjust the lighting on his face before bringing in the actors to rehearse the shot. It was hot in the summer, so we would cut the lights. We made the actors rehearse multiple times, so we would set up a fan to the side. We were always considerate. There were no actors who came to the Ozu unit and complained about their treatment. The characters were also mostly written with something particular about the actor in mind.

For example, when I was still an assistant, we shot *A Story of Floating Weeds*. There's the scene with the people dressed up in a horse costume. An actor named Yamada was doing the hind legs but just wasn't making it work. So I said, "What's the problem, you can't even do a horse walk?" At which point Ozu said, "Okay, Atsuta, let's see you do it." [*Laughs.*] What could I say? I became the horse's hind legs. Then I got teased: "One, two, one, two!" I finally pulled it off. Then there was the first scene of the same film where the train pulls into the station (Kioroshi Station in Chiba) at night. There's a shot where a platform worker receives the track signal ring from the train conductor as the train passes through the station. The actual platform worker didn't want to take part in the film, so I stood in. But the location shot had to connect with what we did on the set. I was told that the way I walked didn't match [*laughs*]. We had some takes that didn't work. Anyway, behind the scenes people often ended up appearing in the films. Shizuo Yamanouchi is in top management now, but on *Late Autumn* he ended up playing the middle school teacher in the school photograph scene.

HASUMI: Oh, the scene of the school trip to the lake?

ATSUTA: Yes. Ozu said, "You be the schoolteacher." And to me he said, "Atsuta, I'm sorry, but you carry the banner advertising the inn." So I ended up in that film too, carrying a banner [*laughs*]. After finishing a location shoot, most directors would quickly disappear, but never Ozu. Even after everyone, including the crew, had gone home, he would still be there helping take care of the electric setup or something like that. When we were on location, the location manager would recruit extras on the street or wherever he could find them, extras for helping with clean-up. Everyone pitched in at the end of a location shoot. We all cleaned up. I think this meticulousness ultimately comes through in the films themselves.

Ozu got along with Mizoguchi, and when Ozu went to Kyoto, even a heavyweight like Mizoguchi went to meet him at the station. Ozu was taking Masuko to Kyoto . . . Masuko Nakai, who would later marry Keiji Sada. When they got off the train, he said, "What a nice welcome, Mizo! This here, let's keep it between us." "Huh?" "Look, Mizo. . . ." "Who's this woman?" "Oh, her? She's my future you-know-what." "Oh!" From there, the rumor spread that Ozu had come around with a girlfriend [*laughs*].

HASUMI: Ozu often teased Mizoguchi, didn't he?

ATSUTA: The two of them teased each other. Ozu would often mimic Mizoguchi [*laughs*].

HASUMI: I've heard, for example, that Ozu purposely held a baseball game when Mizoguchi came to visit, saying, "Mizoguchi doesn't understand this kind of thing." [*Laughs*.]

ATSUTA: That's right. We were on location somewhere, for *Early Summer*. The whole crew was playing baseball. Kazuo Miyagawa [Mizoguchi's cinematographer] was on a baseball team in Kyoto. There was the Kansai team and the Ōfuna Studio team, and we thought we should play each other, so we did for a day. Mizoguchi showed up with (Yoshikata) Yoda and stood watching in the stands. Mizoguchi said to me, "Atsuta, this is how Ozu spends his time? Playing baseball?" [*Laughs*.] "Well, you're about to find out." I teased him and he laughed. "Can he run?" But Ozu really could hit the ball.

HASUMI: I've also heard that Ozu played tennis all the time while he was in Singapore?

ATSUTA: There was an officer in Singapore, maybe his name was Hidaka. I think he became an executive at Nissan after the war. Ozu played tennis with him. Then at night, after all that exercise, Ozu would come back and read. He really seemed like some kind of god. Normally people would go out and have fun at night, but Ozu was different.

HASUMI: The writers Chōtarō Kawasaki and Rintarō Takeda wrote stories that talk about Ozu and a geisha in the red-light district of Odawara. The geisha seems like someone who might have appeared in Ozu's films?

ATSUTA: That's an interesting story [*laughs*]. Takeda first got to know Ozu in Singapore.

HASUMI: Is that right?

ATSUTA: Kenkichi Hara [an assistant director for Ozu] seems to be the one who passed the story to Takeda. But Ozu and this woman weren't all that close. The story was embellished. Before the war, Ozu was living at his house in Takanawa with his mother and younger brother Nobuzō and commuting to Ōfuna. I was commuting from near Asakusa, and Ozu told me to come meet him along the way on the days when we weren't shooting. We had a regular meeting time to catch what we called the "Imperial Train" [*omeshi ressha*]. The Imperial Train was an Odawara-bound train that left from Shinagawa at 1:07 and was basically empty. We could sleep on the way to Ōfuna. One day, I went to meet Ozu and he said, "get on," and when I got on he was drawing a picture on a kimono sash and there was a woman sitting next to him. I thought she was somehow related to him and greeted her formally with a bow, to which he replied, "Why are you greeting my lover that way?" But she already had another patron.

At that time, playing around in Odawara meant gathering at a place called the Chigasakikan. That was the headquarters. Ryōsuke Saitō and some other screenwriters lived there. Tadao Ikeda, Tsuji, they all lived there. So everyone else would gather there at Ryōsuke Saitō's. They'd get fired up and go to Odawara to play around. Everyone was young. All sorts of things happened. When it came to Ozu and that woman, they had similar personalities. They were both playful and teasing. I thought they had chemistry [*laughs*].

Ozu was a very fastidious person. He would be formal toward women, even in the bar. Take Setsuko Hara, for example. Everyone called her "Sacchan." She was in the German-Japanese production *The Daughter of the Samurai* (*Atarashiki tsuchi* / *Die Tochter des Samurai*, a.k.a. *The New Earth*, 1937). Everyone was young then, and when we saw that film at the theater, we all said, "What a great actress!" Ozu agreed and said, "Well, she has good energy, it might be good to use her in a film." That was around 1937.

HASUMI: So if he spotted her in 1937 or 1938, that means it took more than ten years before he was able to cast her in *Late Spring*. In the late thirties, Mitsuko Yoshikawa was in a lot of his films.

ATSUTA: Yes, at the time we weren't able to use stars. Yoshikawa was in training at Kamata, and we cast her a lot. I always said that the thing with Setsuko Hara was that she let everyone imagine things about her. Ozu was actually a pretty shy man. He could be quite timid, despite his large frame. Especially toward actresses. When he would meet new actresses before a shoot, he would look down while greeting them and his cheeks would turn a little red. There's a scene in *Tokyo Story* where Setsuko Hara massages Chieko Higashiyama's shoulders. With a real massage you'd have your shirt off and you'd really get your shoulders worked. I said, "Wouldn't it be good for you to massage Sacchan a bit?" Ozu turned bright red and said, "Don't get carried away." Then I said to Ozu, "It's okay, you're a handsome guy!" I started to arrange the two of them. I touched her shoulder and said to Ozu, "Your position is a little off, can you turn a bit more toward Hara?" "What do you mean, handsome?" [*Laughs.*] "Live a little!" I tried to create an opportunity, but he was shy. "You're the one who touched her first!" We would joke like this sometimes. It was very friendly.

HASUMI: It's often said that eyelines in Ozu's films don't match.

ATSUTA: That's right, people often say that.

HASUMI: Did Ozu tell actors to look directly into the lens, or just a little off?

ATSUTA: A little.

HASUMI: A little off?

ATSUTA: People used to get uncomfortable if you said to look straight ahead, straight into the lens. There were times when Ozu himself also wanted to avoid that kind of thing.

HASUMI: Out of a kind of superstition?

ATSUTA: That was probably part of it. But in general, actors are supposed to look a little off. Of course, where eyelines fall can differ a lot depending on the actor. The recent television show *Ironside,* for example, really does a lot with the drama of eyes. In Ozu's case, the placement of the camera was determined by calculation of distance and of the relative positioning of the actors. This precision could create the illusion that actors were looking into the lens.

HASUMI: Exactly. Ozu's shot/reverse shot sequences sometimes give that impression when there's cutting back and forth between people looking at each other.

ATSUTA: An assistant director once tried to correct this, saying, "Look a little more to the side," and Ozu said, "No, I like it this way." Ordinarily in a shot/reverse shot sequence, you make the eyelines match by having the actor in each shot face the camera in a different direction, one to the right and the other to the left. But there were times when we ended up with both actors looking in the same direction, a little to the right, and we would have to cut the sequence together that way. Maybe because Ozu changed his mind while shooting. Then he'd say, "Which way were they looking in the last shots?" And I would say, "Straight ahead, sir!" [*Laughs.*] The narrowness of the range we used for eyelines could create these situations. Narrow is probably a good word for it.

There was also the issue of composition and visual balance. Say that two people are playing tennis. Ordinarily you would place the camera to one side of the action and cut back and forth between the players from that position. Both of the players are facing each other, so in this position the camera would film a little from one player's right side and a little from the other's left side. But if both players are holding their rackets in their right hands, the racquet of the player filmed from the left is going to be farther from the camera and will look a little smaller on screen. Ozu would change the camera position back and forth, shooting both players from their right sides in order to preserve the visual balance between the rackets. Ozu was interested in balance, but this meant that eyelines would start to feel like they didn't match. Keeping balance between shots was itself difficult. Think of the sequences with beer bottles. If you have a shot with a beer bottle in it, and then in the next shot you have the same beer bottle but with the camera positioned closer, the bottle will look bigger on screen, and you'll lose the sense of balance. So we would get a big beer bottle and a small beer bottle and use the smaller one for closer shots to keep its size constant on screen.

HASUMI: Did you have other techniques like this? Maintaining visual balance by switching between large and small beer bottles?

ATSUTA: For filming men and women, yes. If you film a man and a woman in medium close-up and cut back and forth between them, the size of their heads will often look different on screen. If we filmed the man's face from three feet away, we would get closer for the shot of the woman to maintain visual balance. Two and a half feet.

HASUMI: I see. And where on the face would you set the focal point?

ATSUTA: On the eyes. It's easier to set focus on some faces than on others. It was hard with flat faces. People with defined features were easier. Setsuko Hara and Kuniko Miyake were very easy to film. Shūji Sano was another story. But there was another difficulty with well-defined features. Even if it was easy to set the focus, we'd end up with shadows on the eyes. We used what we called a catch light for this, a small spotlight with a narrow opening that we pointed straight at the eyes.

HASUMI: But that kind of lighting means the actor has to hold still, right?

ATSUTA: Yes, I think that is an effect. In the Atami sequence in *Tokyo Story* where Chishū Ryū says, "The sea is so quiet," ordinarily you would expect him to look at the person he's talking to. Chieko Higashiyama responds "yes," but here he just looks straight ahead, not at her. We couldn't really have him turn his head. Her response is just a simple agreement. Usually, people say things like that matter-of-factly, but in Ozu they draw out the syllables, put breath into it, and bring out the feeling. There's probably some aspect of illusion here too.

HASUMI: Interesting that you say "illusion." You don't find a lot of dialogue in Ozu that bridges between shots and connects them.

ATSUTA: Ozu was pretty unique on this. He always cuts after the same simple expressions in series, probably to make the last syllable clear. I never really asked Ozu about this kind of line elocution.

HASUMI: In Ozu, there's usually one shot per line of dialogue. If someone says, "hmm," then there's a cut to the next shot. On rare occasions there's also dialogue that bridges a cut.

ATSUTA: Is that right?

HASUMI: I think in *Early Summer* this happens with Kuniko Miyake.

ATSUTA: When she nods?

HASUMI: Yes, she's talking and nodding, and there's a cut to Chishū Ryū while she's still talking.

ATSUTA: You can have something like this: a character says something and then you have a close-up of another person following what was said by the one who is now off screen. The one who was listening might respond, "yes, that's right," and then the first person says, "right," with a cut right at the start of the word. This cutting connects them and makes it seem like they are facing each other. But you'll have pauses in between the lines that can be shortened or lengthened.

On the topic of conversation scenes, some people talk about Ozu's eyelines using photos from the set to establish where the camera must have been positioned, but what they say is not always accurate. In the scene at the inn in *There Was a Father*, for example, Chishū Ryū and Shūji Sano appear to be facing each other across a low table when the camera is at a distance, but they're actually not seated across from one another. They're on a diagonal.

HASUMI: The same is true in the earlier scene at the inn when Sano's character is still a child.

ATSUTA: Right. When you get the cut-in shots of each character in medium close-up, it looks like they're both facing the same direction, not looking at each other. They're both facing screen-left. People have looked at the stills from the set and called this a shooting mistake, but that's not accurate. The characters are not actually eating face to face but are sitting at a diagonal to each other.

HASUMI: On the subject of sets, the rooms of inns and houses in Ozu's films often open onto interior courtyards or gardens. They're studio sets, of course, and lit from above. But there's always a wall or another house on the far side, right?

ATSUTA: Right. Apartments or free-standing houses or inns. I think that was to evoke a sense of the surrounding environment, the closeness of things.

HASUMI: In *There Was a Father,* the father and his son go on a trip together. In *Late Autumn* it's a mother and daughter who travel together, but in both films, there is a scene in basically the same kind of inn where you can see other rooms across from their room on the far side of a courtyard. When you shot this scene in *Late Autumn,* were you consciously thinking of the earlier film?

ATSUTA: Yes, we had that in mind. Then there was the question of what you might call predilection. For example, Ozu really liked the color red. There's a lot of red in the later films. I used to joke, "Red is for geniuses and madmen." A similar kind of predilection applied to the inns in these two films, at Isogo and Ikaho Hot Springs. With Tokyo, it was either apartments or cluttered houses. When we shot *Late Spring,* there was a wooded area in front of the set, so even from the second floor the sky wasn't visible in the background. Anyway, I think this was the feeling of these places, that these structures were built with the purpose of evoking this feeling in viewers who would look at them later. The sense of closeness was part of that. Usually what's standing behind the scenery in films is just set construction, but in the Ozu unit, sets were really well built. With Ozu, the design and layout always took a long time, and Ozu would revise until the result was completely what he wanted.

HASUMI: We don't find many shots in Ozu taken from outside looking in through windows, do we?

ATSUTA: No.

HASUMI: There's a shot in *Early Summer* where the camera moves along the outside wall of the university hospital building where Chishū Ryū works and comes to a stop at something like an instrument enclosure in the yard. At that point Ryū is visible through the window working in his lab.

ATSUTA: There were instances like this in the silent films too.

HASUMI: Oh yes. In the silent period there was *A Mother Should Be Loved* and the hotel in the Honmoku area.

ATSUTA: Right.

HASUMI: In the later films we don't see these kinds of windows.

ATSUTA: You're right, there aren't many shots taken through windows.

HASUMI: There is the shot in *Late Autumn* where we see a view of the Holy Resurrection Cathedral, and next a shot of Hiroshi Nihon'yanagi and Setsuko Hara looking out the window of the café. Did you shoot any footage of the exterior of the café?

ATSUTA: Nothing of the exterior. That café doesn't exist anymore, the one you could see the cathedral from. Anyway, it just didn't work. I went back to the café, but there were people all around. There was no good shot. Ozu never used those kinds of supplemental insert shots anyway. He would arrange everything himself.

HASUMI: So there was no second unit?

ATSUTA: No. There were two times when we had a second unit, but we didn't use anything they shot. Only when I was still an assistant did we use a second-unit long take. I was sent off to shoot it.

HASUMI: That was for *Where Now Are the Dreams of Youth?*

ATSUTA: That's right. That was the only thing I was tasked with shooting. Ozu oversaw the rest.

HASUMI: That means that you were in a pretty unique position within the Japanese film industry, as a cameraman working without a second unit. Even Kurosawa has recently been using second unit coverage. While we're talking about the silent films, how about the streetcar in *Tokyo Chorus*? Was that the real thing?

ATSUTA: Oh, that streetcar. There was a streetcar sidetrack in Akasaka Mitsuke where we rented one. We took it to Shinbashi and back for filming. But the exterior shots are in Yokohama. The streetscape was better in Yokohama. We put the camera on a truck and filmed Tokihiko Okada walking down the street and made it look like the exterior and interior shots went together.

HASUMI: You also filmed in Yokohama for *That Night's Wife*?

ATSUTA: Yes, we chose a location where a lot of Indian immigrants were living—for its narrow streets—alongside where the Mitsukoshi Building is now. Speaking of trucks, there was the scene in *Late Spring* where Jun Usami and Setsuko Hara ride bikes. We shot that with a low-bed truck. We attached the bikes to the truck, and then cut the engine and had the assistants push the truck, slowly so it wouldn't rock.

HASUMI: Oh, that explains the gliding sensation of that scene. Takashi Kawamata must have been one of the assistants pushing the truck. . . .

ATSUTA: But shooting on location is a pain. Today there's more traffic, and we wouldn't be able to shoot on that road the way we did. That kind of thing won't go over in the middle of Tokyo anymore. During the silent years, we even shot on the central street in Ginza with a hearse.

HASUMI: For *The Sorrow of the Beautiful Woman*?

ATSUTA: Right. We had the rear door of the hearse open, and Tokihiko Okada sat there looking toward the camera and throwing flowers. In central Ginza. Mohara was filming from a car driving behind, from Owarichō toward Kyōbashi. I was crouching in the hearse behind Okada. Hearses smell. But Ozu said that riding in a hearse would give you a long life [*laughs*].

HASUMI: As someone who shot Ozu's films over all those years, did you anticipate that young people would start going back and watching the films the way they seem to be doing now?

ATSUTA: I did worry about whether people would continue to watch them.

HASUMI: These days the screenings always fill up, whether at the National Film Center or in local movie theaters.

ATSUTA: This is really very wonderful to hear. It feels like a luxury. Ozu often joked that I shouldn't be his apprentice. If we're dogs, he would say, you should at least be a dog in a wealthy house. Then I would say, "So I'll act as though I had ten thousand yen"—one hundred yen in those days—"and stroll around Ginza," and he would say, "Yes, that's the spirit, that's natural." Or I'd say, "I may not have any fine sake, but I'll drink as if it cost one hundred yen," and he'd say, "Yes, people who don't take that attitude won't drink at all." "There's grief and there's joy." He said a lot of things like that.

In his later years, Ozu had a really playful spirit. He liked to joke around. How to put this? People need a sense of place. You always have to keep creating that. He would say, "Atsuta, if I ever have to stop making pictures, you and I will fry pork. You'll be the delivery man." "Stick with me," was the attitude. Then it was, "Atsuta, don't get fixated on luxuries." "Why?" "You were too impressed with the socks they were wearing in that picture." He paid attention to these little things. I often heard others complain that he was always putting luxury in front of the camera. But doesn't all this reflect the soft side of that kind of sentiment? I don't drink, but Ozu did, of course. His favorite thing was to drink and talk. That comes out in his art, don't you think? "There's part of me that doesn't like classicism," he would say. "I couldn't do what I do without the lowly melodrama.

That's why I say a tofu maker is a tofu maker." That was something he liked to repeat. That's what the Ozu brand might have looked like under somewhat different circumstances. Ozu Tofu, registered trademark. But the question is about the old and the new. I'm really moved by this new interest in Ozu. I already mentioned this, but Ozu used to say, "It's not unreasonable to think that people wouldn't understand my pictures if they were shown overseas. But I do think people would understand them. We Japanese sit on the floor. People will understand the general character, what this position is about."

HASUMI: This is actually what has happened. I've had numerous occasions to observe the reaction to screenings of Ozu films abroad. Even young men cry in the films, even hippie types with long hair and wild beards. Audiences understand.

ATSUTA: There's the theme of maternal love that comes up in the films. That's particularly Japanese. . . .

HASUMI: I think that comes across. It has universal aspects.

ATSUTA: At any rate, maybe it's best that Japan lost. That's why young people now are looking at the films. There are fewer parents with those kinds of feelings today. People talk about those born in the Meiji and Taishō Periods. I was born in Meiji. I'm going to be seventy-seven.

HASUMI: You're in very good health!

ATSUTA: How has it been for people born in the Taishō Period (1912–1926), I wonder. In the film world, it seems like there are a lot of half-hearted people among the Taishō babies, relatively speaking.

HASUMI: I wonder. Are there any people from the generations after yours, among recent Japanese filmmakers, who you find interesting? Any films you like?

ATSUTA: For me, at this point, I'm not really watching much. It's hard for me to say, "This person is good, this one bad." It would just be subjective.

HASUMI: Anything you felt glad that you watched?

ATSUTA: I'm more impressed with foreign films. I'm old-fashioned, so I'm not very into sci-fi, for example. Even on television, it's pictures by the old directors that I end up watching. John Ford, for example, or Wyler. I've been retired from active practice for a while now and am quite behind on what people are watching these days. I have a grandchild in junior high school who I sometimes ask about what's popular at the moment. Sometimes there are dramas I want to watch on television, but I end up feeling like the people behind them aren't very serious. They fall flat. Then there's the dubbing of foreign films. The voice actors tend to be a bit odd and that makes it hard to get into the film. So I do this . . .

HASUMI: Turn down the sound?

ATSUTA: Yes, I turn down the sound, but then I fall asleep in front of the TV. I do wonder who the interesting young filmmakers are these days.

June 8, 1981/February 14, 1983

This interview by Shiguéhiko Hasumi expands a conversation originally published as Yūharu Atsuta, "Ozu Yasujirō, aruiwa fuzai no ame," *Mononkuru* 1, no. 4 (February 1981): 109–15.

Index

PERSONS CITED

Abe, Masahiko, xii
Akiyama, Kōsaku, 317–318
Aoki, Tomihiro (Hōhi), 175
Aoyama, Shinji, xxiii
Aratama, Michiyo, 138, 223–224, 231, 246
Arima, Ineko, 80, 83, 96, 157, 195, 200–203, 209, 217–218, 224–225, 229, 231, 275
Asanuma, Keiji, xxv
Atsumi, Kiyoshi, 90n3
Atsuta, Yūharu, 7, 46, 141n16, 192, 193, 299–341
Awashima, Chikage, 86, 120, 134–135, 143, 158, 209, 216, 218, 224, 230–231

Bancroft, George, 69
Barthes, Roland, xi, xxiii, xxx, 280
Beery, Wallace, 72
Belmondo, Jean-Paul, 70
Berkeley, Busby, 113
Bogart, Humphrey, 79
Bordwell, David, xxv, xxix, xxxii, 20–21, 240, 250, 250n3, 251, 254, 263
Bose, Chandra, 317
Bresson, Robert, 112–113
Burch, Noël, xxii, 284, 292, 292n6
Buttons, Red, 254

Clair, René, 113
Cook, Ryan, xxx–xxxi, xxxiii

Deleuze, Gilles, xi
Delubac, Jacqueline, 266
Derrida, Jacques, xiv, xxx
De Sica, Vittorio, 263
Dreyer, Carl Theodor, 112–113

Egawa, Urio, 131, 226, 268–269

Fellini, Federico, 112–113, 118
Flaubert, Gustave, xi–xii, xvii, 24, 24n16, 280
Ford, John, xxvi, 39, 205, 320, 341
Foucault, Michel, xiv, xxiii
Fujino, Hideo, 174
Fujiwara, Chris, xvi–xvii, xxxii–xxxiii

Godard, Jean-Luc, 70, 79, 279
Gonda, Yasunosuke, xxiv
Gosho, Heinosuke, 302
Griffith, David Wark, 121
Guitry, Sacha, 265–266

Hamaguchi, Ryūsuke, x
Hamamura, Yoshiyasu, 154, 322, 324
Hara, Kenkichi, 330
Hara, Setsuko, xix, 23, 29*fig.*, 33–35, 48–50, 49*fig.*, 57, 77, 79, 81, 83, 85–86, 90–93, 96, 100*fig.*, 105, 120, 132, 134–135, 138–139*fig.*, 141–143, 142*fig.*, 146, 148, 156–159, 163–165, 167–168, 171–172*fig.*, 177, 179, 179*fig.*, 181, 189–190, 196, 198, 200–201, 203–204, 209, 214–215, 220, 227, 236–238, 243, 245–247, 251–252, 255, 258–261, 273, 281–282, 288–296, 290*fig.*, 309, 314–315, 330, 331, 334, 337–338
Hatano, Tetsurō, xxv
Hawks, Howard, 18, 79, 129, 254
Higashiyama, Chieko, 35, 56, 77, 145–147*fig.*, 155*fig.*, 160, 167–168, 171–172*fig.*, 176–177, 182, 186–190, 220, 241, 309, 321, 331, 334
Himori, Shin'ichi, 46–47
Hitchcock, Alfred, 103
Huston, Walter, 69

Iida, Chōko, 46, 175, 305
Iijima, Tadashi, xxiv

Ikebe, Ryō, 113, 119–120, 160, 202, 216
Ikeda, Tadao, 330
Ikeda, Yoshinobu, 302
Inoue, Yukiko, 7
Ishihara, Shintarō, 122–123
Iwasaki, Akira, xxiv
Iwashita, Shima, 73, 83, 85, 90, 179, 208–209, 211, 213–218, 214*fig.*, 223–225, 231–232, 243

Karina, Anna, 79
Katō, Daisuke, 261
Katsuragi, Fumiko, 97, 174
Kawaguchi, Hiroshi, 140
Kawamata, Takashi, 338
Kawasaki, Chōtarō, 329
Kawasaki, Hiroko, 70
Keaton, Buster, 14
Kido, Shirō, 250n3
Kinoshita, Chika, xvii
Kinoshita, Keisuke, 316
Kishi, Keiko, 120, 157, 202, 216
Kishida, Kyōko, 73, 178, 210
Kita, Ryūji, 23, 29*fig.*, 87–89, 221, 228, 230, 235, 237, 243, 262, 270–272, 274
Kitagawa, Fuyuhiko, xxiv
Kitano, Takeshi, xxxi
Kobayashi, Keiju, 223
Kogure, Michiyo, 241
Kuga, Yoshiko, 80
Kuribayashi, Minoru, 302
Kurosawa, Akira, 183–184, 205–206, 337
Kurosawa, Kiyoshi, xxiii
Kyō, Machiko, 158, 165, 193, 195, 306

Lang, Fritz, 18, 113, 199
Leigh, Vivian, 44, 279, 327

Lubitsch, Ernst, 266, 274, 276–277
The Lumière Brothers, 125

Manda, Kunitoshi, xxiii
Martin du Gard, Roger, 257
The Marx Brothers, 93
Matsuda, Masao, xxiv, xxv
Matsumoto, Toshio, xxiv
McCarey, Leo, 195
Mikami, Shin'ichirō, 215
Milne, Tom, 184
Mishima, Masao, 221, 261, 281–282, 284, 289
Mitsui, Kōji (Hideo), 65, 200–201
Miyagawa, Kazuo, 193, 299, 305, 307, 329
Miyaguchi, Seiji, 163–164, 199
Miyake, Kuniko, 24, 33, 48–49*fig.*, 57, 101, 132, 172*fig.*, 219, 221–222, 243, 247, 257–262, 259*fig.*, 266, 270–273, 276, 315, 334
Mizoguchi, Kenji, 183–184, 205–206, 315, 328–329
Mizukubo, Sumiko, 65, 200–201
Morlay, Gaby, 266

Nagae, Michitarō, xxiv
Nakai, Asakazu, 299, 307
Nakai, Masuko, 328
Nakamura, Ganjirō, 55, 57–59, 61, 71, 138, 140, 140n15, 148, 157, 165, 189, 193, 195, 211, 220, 223, 241, 245–246, 252–254, 306
Nakamura, Nobuo, 23, 29*fig.*, 57–59, 61, 87–89, 92, 94, 165, 204, 210–211, 221–223, 225, 230, 235, 237, 239, 243–244, 262, 270–274
Naniwa, Chieko, 80, 140, 241, 253, 275
Naruse, Mikio, 242, 302
Negishi, Hamao, 302

Nihon'yanagi, Hiroshi, 34, 48–50, 49*fig.*, 120, 159, 337
Noda, Kōgo, 95, 201
Nomura, Hōtei, 302

Obinata, Den, 201–202
Ohara, Jōji, 299, 307–308, 326
Okada, Mariko, 105, 161–162*fig.*, 227–231, 274
Okada, Susumu, xxv
Okada, Tokihiko, 25, 28–30, 66–67, 69–71, 127, 229, 252, 267–268, 274, 276, 338
Okada, Yoshiko, 225, 263–266, 268, 271
Okajima, Hisashi, 131
Oka, Jōji, 64–65
Ōsaka, Shirō, 56, 191–192
Osaki, Midori, xxiv
Ōshima, Nagisa, 98
Ozawa, Tokuji, 302

Renoir, Jean, 2, 18, 39, 205
Resnais, Alain, 142
Richie, Donald, xxv, 9, 13–18, 109–110, 113, 122–123, 151, 164, 182, 184, 284–285
Ruttenberg, Joseph, 321
Ryū, Chishū, 25–27, 33, 35, 48, 56, 71, 73, 76, 79, 80, 84, 87–89, 92–94, 104–105, 136, 142, 146, 155*fig.*-156, 160–161, 163–168, 172–173, 172*fig.*, 178–179, 181, 184, 188–190, 195, 198, 203–204, 210, 212–213, 215, 218–223, 225, 241, 243–244, 258–262, 259*fig.*, 269–273, 275–276, 281, 284, 289, 291–295, 317, 321, 334–337

Saburi, Shin, 29*fig.*, 33, 59, 61, 80, 87, 98, 141, 165, 173, 210, 213, 220–223, 226, 228–230, 235, 237–239*fig.*, 273–276
Sada, Keiji, 25, 105, 109–110*fig.*, 113, 177, 328

Said, Edward, xxii
Saitō, Ryōsuke, 310, 317–318, 330
Saitō, Tatsuo, 14, 25, 27, 29–30, 38, 45, 50, 60–61, 129, 131, 133, 165, 226, 249, 251, 274
Saitō, Torajirō, 302, 304
Sakamoto, Takeshi, 71–73, 125, 211, 211n1, 249, 251, 254, 263, 265–266, 268, 271, 306
Sano, Shūji, 19, 25, 41, 43, 102, 136–137, 141, 226, 268–269, 314, 317, 334–335
Sasaki, Yasushi, 316
Satō, Tadao, xxiii, 9, 41–42, 44, 166–167
Sawamura, Sadako, 273
Schrader, Paul, xxv, 15–19, 110, 113, 184, 283, 285
Seberg, Jean, 70, 279
Shiga, Naoya, 44, 269
Shigehara, Hideo (Mohara), 7, 46, 300, 302–307, 338
Shigemune, Tsutomu, 302
Shimazu, Yasujirō, 302
Shin, Kinzō, 203
Sugai, Ichirō, 24, 35, 77, 145, 147*fig.*, 160, 171–172*fig.*, 176–177, 182, 321
Sugimoto, Shōjirō, 46, 304
Sugimura, Haruko, 34–35, 56, 140, 145, 185, 191, 193, 195, 212, 281
Suo, Masayuki, xxiii
Suzuki, Daisetsu, 283, 283n4
Suzuki, Shigeyoshi, 302

Takada, Minoru, 70
Takahashi, Toyo, 87–88, 94, 237, 272
Takamine, Hideko, 101, 209, 247
Takamine, Mieko, 97, 101, 173, 209
Takarada, Akira, 109
Takasugi, Sanae, 101
Takeda, Rintarō, 329–330

Tanaka, Kinuyo, 4, 19, 43, 45, 50, 59–61, 64–67, 69–70, 80, 96, 102, 129, 135, 144, 187, 196, 222–226, 231, 247, 269, 275, 279, 326
Taura, Masami, 200, 225
Thompson, Kristin, 20–21
Toland, Gregg, 320
Tōno, Eijirō, 27, 195, 210, 212, 242
Tosaka, Jun, xxiv
Toyoda, Shirō, 302
Truffaut, François, 153–154, 157
Tsuda, Haruhiko, 139*fig.*
Tsukasa, Yōko, 23, 29*fig.*, 58, 83, 86, 96, 109–110*fig.*, 113, 132, 137–139*fig.*, 142*fig.*, 148, 161–162*fig.*, 177–179*fig.*, 209–210, 214, 227–229, 236, 238, 245–247, 251–252, 255
Tsukioka, Yumeji, 91, 105, 230, 295
Tsuruta, Kōji, 109
Tsushima, Keiko, 109

Usami, Jun, 327, 338
Ushihara, Kiyohiko, 302

Venuti, Lawrence, xviii
Vidor, King, 72, 320

Walsh, Raoul, 65, 72, 95
Watts, Alan, 184n3
Welles, Orson, 123, 316, 320
Wyler, William, 320, 341

Yagumo, Emiko, 4, 67–70, 68*figs.*, 267
Yamada, Isuzu, 165, 196, 203, 217, 269
Yamada, Kazuo, xxiv
Yamada, Yōji, 90
Yamamoto, Fujiko, 80, 274–276
Yamamoto, Kikuo, 283–284, 292

Yamamura, Sō, 56, 191, 194, 203, 222, 241, 273
Yamane, Sadao, xxv
Yamanouchi, Shizuo, 328
Yanagi, Eijirō, 210
Yoda, Yoshikata, 329
Yomota, Inuhiko, xxxii, 175,
Yoshida, Kijū, xxii, 260
Yoshikawa, Mitsuko, 226, 331
Yoshimura, Kōzaburō, 316
Yoshino, Jirō, 302
Yūki, Ichirō, 129

FILMS CITED

American Gigolo, 283
An Autumn Afternoon (*Sanma no aji*), xxviii, 6, 22, 26–27, 33, 73, 78, 83, 88, 91, 94–95, 100*fig.*, 104, 106*fig.*, 130, 142–143*fig.*, 178–180, 183, 185, 194, 199, 208, 210–214*fig.*, 216–219, 221, 223, 231, 239, 242–244, 261–262, 270, 272–273, 276, 279, 325
Apart from You (*Kimi to wakarete*), 242
Army (*Rikugun*), 316

Bicycle Thieves (*Ladri di biciclette*), 263
The Big Sleep, 79
The Bowery, 72
Breathless (*À bout de souffle*), 70, 279
Brothers and Sisters of the Toda Family (*Toda-ke no kyōdai*), 97–98, 101, 137, 173–176, 209, 224, 226, 229–300

The Ceremony (*Gishiki*), 98
The Champ, 72
Citizen Kane, 123, 316, 319, 320
Colorado Territory, 95

Daughter of the Samurai (*Atarashiki tsuchi / Die Tochter des Samurai*, a.k.a *The New Earth*), 331
Days of Youth (*Gakusei romansu Wakaki hi*), 6, 14, 61, 125–131, 133, 135, 165, 199, 202, 204
Dragnet Girl (*Hijōsen no onna*), 4, 17–18, 64–67, 69–70, 127, 200, 314
Duck Soup, 195
Dumbo, 319

Early Spring (*Sōshun*), 79, 111, 113, 117, 119, 124, 127, 144, 157, 160, 172*fig.*, 200, 202, 209, 216, 218, 231, 313
Early Summer (*Bakushū*), 22n14, 24–25, 33–34, 40, 48–50, 49*fig.*, 77, 79, 81, 86, 98, 112*fig.*, 118, 120, 132–135, 143–147*fig.*, 158–159, 163–166, 171–174, 172*fig.*, 176–178, 182–183, 185, 186, 194, 209, 211, 219, 230, 241, 247, 257, 259*fig.*, 260–262, 266, 270, 273, 279, 309, 313–315, 321, 323, 325, 329, 334, 336
The End of Summer (*Kohayagawa-ke no aki*), 55, 57, 59, 71, 79, 81, 83, 86, 96, 109, 118, 130, 132, 138, 142, 142*fig.*, 160, 174, 189, 191, 209, 211, 220, 223, 224, 231, 241, 244–247, 251–252, 299
Equinox Flower (*Higanbana*), 59, 79–80, 83, 87, 96, 165, 177, 183, 209–210, 213, 219–225, 231, 243, 272, 274–275

Fantasia, 319
The Faraway Country of my Parents (*Haruka nari fubo no kuni*), 316
Fighting Friends (*Wasei kenka tomodachi*), 241
The Flavor of Green Tea over Rice (*Ochazuke no aji*), 22, 33, 79, 109, 210, 241

Floating Weeds (Ukigusa), xxxi, 57, 63, 103, 130, 140, 148, 158, 162, 165, 168–170fig., 182, 185, 193–199, 201, 205, 211, 219, 227, 278, 299, 305–306, 311–312

Gone with the Wind, 44, 279, 319, 327
Good Morning (Ohayō), 39–40, 43, 79, 143, 184, 219, 226, 270
The Grapes of Wrath, 320

Hatari!, 254
A Hen in the Wind (Kaze no naka no mendori), xxix, 19, 41–44, 47, 62, 78, 97, 102, 173, 187–188, 196–197, 199, 205, 226, 268–269, 279, 293, 310, 325–326
High Sierra, 95

The Idiot (Hakuchi), 184
I Flunked, But . . . (Rakuda wa shita keredo), 44, 47–48, 50, 60–62, 125–129, 131, 135, 144
I Graduated, But . . . (Daigaku wa deta keredo), 62, 194
An Inn in Tokyo (Tokyo no yado), 80, 194, 211n1, 263, 266–268, 271
An Innocent Maid (Hakoiri musume), 263
Ironside, 332
I Was Born, But . . . (Umarete wa mita keredo), 36–39, 41, 43, 66, 80, 131, 133, 195, 225–226, 249–250, 250n3, 340

Kagamijishi (a.k.a Kikugorō no Kagamijishi and The Lion Dance), 263

The Lady and the Beard (Shukujo to hige), 66–67, 70, 166, 252
Last Year at Marienbad (L'année dernière à Marienbad), 142

Late Autumn (Akibiyori), 23, 25, 29fig., 53, 57, 59, 78, 95, 97, 109–111, 110fig., 117–118, 127, 136–142, 139figs., 148, 159, 161–162fig., 175, 177–180, 179fig., 189, 191–192, 201, 209–211, 214, 221–222, 227, 229, 231, 234–239fig., 242, 244–247, 273–274, 276, 279, 288, 328, 336–337
Late Spring (Banshun), xix, xxi, 3, 6, 18, 35, 42, 57, 71, 76–79, 81, 83, 91, 94–97, 100fig., 105, 136–137, 142, 163–166, 175, 178–179, 183, 201, 209, 212–214, 218–221, 230, 237, 243, 260–261, 270, 279, 281–296, 290figs., 310, 331, 336, 338
Legend of the Tank Commander (Nishizumi Senshachō-den), 316
The Letter, 320

Made in U.S.A, 79
Metropolis, 113
Le Million, 113
A Mother Should Be Loved (Haha o kowazuya), 81, 174, 199, 201–203, 219–220, 311, 337
The Munekata Sisters (Munekata kyōdai), 101, 194, 203, 209, 219, 247, 270, 299, 307, 312, 326

Notorious, 103
À nous la liberté, 113
La nuit du carrefour, 18

The Only Son (Hitori musuko), 6, 26–28fig., 46, 62, 81, 131, 175, 219, 263, 300n1, 304–305

Passing Fancy (Dekigokoro), 70–73, 80, 131, 211n1, 219, 263–264, 267, 300n1

Quadrille, 266

Radishes and Carrots (Daikon to ninjin), 22
Record of a Tenement Gentleman (Nagaya shinshiroku), 78, 175–176, 301, 310
Rio Bravo, 79
The Rules of the Game (Les règles du jeu), 2

Scarface, 18
The Sorrow of the Beautiful Woman (Bijin aishū), 7, 194, 199, 338
Sound of the Mountain (Yama no oto), 242
Spring Comes from the Ladies (Haru wa gofujin kara), 62
A Story of Floating Weeds (Ukigusa monogatari), 57, 63, 71, 81, 131–132, 162, 165, 194, 201, 211n1, 219, 227, 263, 306, 327
Stray Dog (Nora inu), 184
Suspicion, 103
Sword of Penitence (Zange no yaiba), 6, 14, 263, 300

That Night's Wife (Sono yo no tsuma), 4, 64–65, 67–70, 68figs., 76, 267–268, 279, 338
There Was a Father (Chichi ariki), 26, 79, 81, 95, 131–132, 136–137, 139fig., 161, 165, 172–173, 175, 218–219, 288, 301, 312, 335–336
To Delhi, to Delhi (Derī e, Derī e), 317
Tokyo Chorus (Tokyo gasshō), 25–28, 62, 66, 71, 80, 127, 133, 165–166, 252, 267–268, 274, 338

Tokyo Story (Tokyo monogatari), xxi, xxxiii, 56, 79, 81, 97–98, 132, 142, 146, 155figs., 160, 165–169, 174, 177, 181–182, 184–189, 187fig., 192, 195, 199, 204, 215, 219, 220, 222, 224, 241, 243, 267–268, 270, 273, 278, 309–310, 331, 334
Tokyo Twilight (Tokyo boshoku), 157, 165, 195–196, 198–205, 210, 213, 216–220, 225, 229, 231, 267, 269, 274, 311

Until the Day We Meet Again (Mata au hi made), 63

Walk Cheerfully (Hogaraka ni ayume), 64–65, 70, 76, 127–128, 166, 219
The War at Sea from Hawai'i to Malaya (Hawai Marē oki kaisen), 316
Waterloo Bridge, 320–321
What Did the Lady Forget (Shukujo wa nani o wasureta ka), 7, 251–252, 274, 301, 303–305
Where Now Are the Dreams of Youth? (Seishun no yume ima izuko), 61, 63, 125–126, 131, 165, 174, 337
Woman of Tokyo (Tokyo no onna), 225–226, 267–269
Workers Leaving the Factory (La sortie des usines de Montplaisir), 125

You Only Live Once, 18
The Young Beast (Wakai kemono), 123

About the Author

BORN IN TOKYO IN 1936, Shiguéhiko Hasumi is a film critic, literary critic, and scholar of French literature. He was the twenty-sixth president of the University of Tokyo, where he is professor emeritus. He earned his doctorate at the University of Paris in 1965 with a dissertation on Gustave Flaubert's *Madame Bovary*. He has received numerous awards, including the Yomiuri Bungaku Award for *Han-Nihongoron* [*Anti-Nihongoron*, 1977], the Geijutsu Senshō Ministry of Education, Science, Sports and Culture Award for *Bon'yō na geijutsuka no shōzō: Makushimu Dyu Kan-ron* [*Portrait of a Mediocre Artist: On Maxime Du Camp*, 1988], and the Ordre des Arts et des Lettres Commandeur, awarded by the French Ministry of Culture (1999). He has also authored novels, including *Hakushaku fujin* [*The Countess*, 2016], winner of the Mishima Yukio Award. His other important works (all untranslated) include *Sōseki Natsume-ron* [*On Natsume Sōseki*, 1978], *Fūkō, Dorūzu, Derida* [*Foucault, Deleuze, Derrida*, 1978], *Hyōsō hihyō sengen* [*Surface Criticism Manifesto*, 1979], *Eiga no shinwagaku* [*Film Mythologies*, 1979], *Eizō no shigaku* [*Image Poetics*, 1979], *Ōe Kenzaburō-ron* [*On Kenzaburō Ōe*, 1980], *Monogatari* hihan josetsu [*An Introduction to Narrative Criticism*, 1985], *Teikoku no inbō* [*Imperial Intrigues*, 1991], *Hariuddo eiga-shi kōgi: Kageri no rekishi no tame ni* [*Lectures on Hollywood Film History: In Pursuit of a History of Darkness*, 1993], *Aka no yūwaku: Fikushon-ron josetsu* [*The Seduction of Red: An Introduction to the Theory of Fiction*, 2007], *Godāru, Manē, Fūkō: Shikō to kansei o meguru danpenteki na kōsatsu* [*Godard, Manet, Foucault: Fragmentary Reflections on Thought and Sensitivity*, 2008], *Bovarī fujin-ron* [*On Madame Bovary*, 2014], *Shotto to wa nani ka* [*What Is a Shot?*, 2022], and *Jon Fōdo-ron* [*On John Ford*, 2022]. He was instrumental in introducing Japanese readers to major French writers, from Alain Robbe-Grillet and Claude Simon to Roland Barthes, Michel Foucault, Gilles Deleuze, and Jacques Derrida. The first English translation of his critical dialogue with Foucault, conducted in Paris and Tokyo in 1978, appears in *The Japan Lectures: A Transnational Critical Encounter* (Routledge, 2024). He mentored many prominent Japanese filmmakers, including Kiyoshi Kurosawa, Shinji Aoyama, Masayuki Suo, Kunitoshi Manda, Akihiko Shiota, Hideo Nakata, and Shō Miyake. Through his work in film criticism, he also developed intimate and productive relationships with international filmmakers, including Jean-Luc Godard, François Truffaut, Manoel de Oliveira, Theo Angelopoulos, Daniel Schmid, Wim Wenders, Hou Hsiao-hsien, Edward Yang, Pedro Costa, Leos Carax, and Ryūsuke Hamaguchi. Hasumi was first inspired to write film criticism by his indignance at the lack of recognition for such American filmmakers of the 1950s as Nicholas Ray, Don Siegel, Robert Aldrich, and Richard Fleischer. He awaits the day when John Ford and Raoul Walsh are properly recognized in the United States as the greatest of filmmakers. He lives in Tokyo with his wife, Chantal.

About the Translator and Contributor

RYAN COOK is a film scholar, translator, and librarian. He completed a PhD in Japanese film history at Yale University and has taught at Yale, Harvard, and Emory University.

AARON GEROW is A. Whitney Griswold Professor of East Asian Languages and Literatures, and of Film and Media Studies, at Yale University. He is the author of *Visions of Japanese Modernity: Articulations of Cinema, Nation, and Spectatorship, 1895–1925*.

Founded in 1893,
UNIVERSITY OF CALIFORNIA PRESS
publishes bold, progressive books and journals
on topics in the arts, humanities, social sciences,
and natural sciences—with a focus on social
justice issues—that inspire thought and action
among readers worldwide.

The UC PRESS FOUNDATION
raises funds to uphold the press's vital role
as an independent, nonprofit publisher, and
receives philanthropic support from a wide
range of individuals and institutions—and from
committed readers like you. To learn more, visit
ucpress.edu/supportus.